The
MONTEREY BAY,
BIG SUR & GOLD COAST
WINE COUNTRY
Book
A Complete Guide

Don Fukuda

The
MONTEREY BAY,
BIG SUR & GOLD COAST
WINE COUNTRY
Book
A Complete Guide

A Revision of The Central Coast of California Book

BUZ BEZORE & CHRISTINA WATERS
with Karen Reardanz & Mary Spicuzza

Berkshire House Publishers
Lee, Massachusetts

On the cover and frontispiece
Front cover: *California Highway 1 along the Big Sur Coast,* photo © Justine Hill
Frontispiece: *Forested slopes and meadows, typical of the Central Coast, dominate the bluffs overlooking the ocean beyond,* photo © Don Fukuda.
Back cover: *Anemone,* photo © Jay Ireland & Georgienne E. Bradley; *Hearst Castle, San Simeon,* photo © Justine Hill; *A leisurely ride on Monterey Bay,* photo © Eugene Johnson

The Monterey Bay, Big Sur & Gold Coast Wine Country Book: A Complete Guide
Copyright © 1994, 1998 by Berkshire House Publishers
Cover and interior photographs © 1998 by credited photographers

Library of Congress Cataloging-in-Publication Data
Bezore, Buz.
    The Monterey Bay, Big Sur & Gold Coast wine country book : a complete guide / Buz Bezore & Christina Waters with Karen Reardanz & Mary Spicuzza.
        p.   cm. — (The great destinations series, ISSN 1056-7968)
    Rev. ed. of: The Central Coast of California book / Christina Waters & Buz Bezore, c1994.
    Includes bibliographical references and indexes.
    ISBN 0-936399-99-6
    1. Pacific Coast (Calif.)—Guidebooks. I. Waters, Christina, 1946- . II. Waters, Christina, 1946- Central Coast of California book. III. Title. IV. Series.
F868.P33B49   1998
917.94'70453—dc21   98-22303
                                                 CIP

ISBN 0-936399-99-6
ISSN 1056-7968 (series)

Editor: Constance Lee Oxley. Managing Editor: Philip Rich. Text design and layout: Dianne Pinkowitz. Original design for Great Destinations™ series: Janice Lindstom. Cover design: Jane McWhorter. Maps: Matt Paul/Yankee Doodles.

Berkshire House books are available at substantial discounts for bulk purchases by corporations and other organizations' promotions and premiums. Special personalized editions can also be produced in large quantities. For more information, contact:

Berkshire House Publishers
480 Pleasant St., Ste. 5; Lee, Massachusetts 01238
800-321-8526
E-mail: info@berkshirehouse.com
Web: www.berkshirehouse.com

Manufactured in the United States of America

First printing 1998
10 9 8 7 6 5 4 3 2 1

No complimentary meals or lodgings were accepted by the author and reviewers in gathering information for this work.

The <u>GREAT DESTINATIONS</u>™ Series

The Great Destinations™ series features regions in the United States rich in natural beauty and culture. Each Great Destinations™ guidebook reviews an extensive selection of lodgings, restaurants, cultural events, historic sites, shops, and recreational opportunities, and outlines the region's natural and social history. Written by resident authors, the guides are a resource for visitor and resident alike. The books feature maps, photographs, directions to and around the region, lists of helpful telephone numbers and addresses, and indexes.

To our friends and loved ones
in the great meerkat village:
We are nothing alone
and everything together.

Contents

CHAPTER ONE
Of Blue & Golden Dreams
HISTORY
1

CHAPTER TWO
The Freeway & The Right Way
TRANSPORTATION
29

CHAPTER THREE
The Eden at World's End
SANTA CRUZ
37

CHAPTER FOUR
Head of the Class
MONTEREY, CARMEL & BIG SUR
109

CHAPTER FIVE
Gold Coasting
SAN LUIS OBISPO & THE SANTA YNEZ VALLEY
179

CHAPTER SIX
Grape Expectations
WINERIES
227

CHAPTER SEVEN
Nuts & Bolts
INFORMATION

Acknowledgments

We were lucky enough to be able to draw on a wealth of expert regional informants whose suggestions, insights and generous contributions allowed us to present readers with a comprehensive taste of the splendid and varied Central Coast.

As they have always done in past projects that we've shared, award-winning photographers Robert Scheer, Kim Reierson, Rick Browne and Shmuel Thaler infuse these pages with the atmospheric images of the Central Coast landscape and sense of place. Additional thanks go to lens people Stan Cacitti, Jay Swanson, Paul Schraub, Don Fukuda and Dan Coyro.

Everywhere we traveled throughout the length of this stretch of California, we met experts on history, local color, restaurants, recreation, attractions and wines who were generous with their accumulated wisdom.

Providing insightful feedback every step of the way was our seasoned global traveling companion Rosemary Bryan. Rita Bottoms, head of the University of California, Santa Cruz' Special Collections, was always forthcoming with background lore on the region's historic flock of artists, writers and trendsetting dreamers. The careful reading by historian Ross Eric Gibson lent expert credibility to the research-intensive, Chapter One, History.

Seasoned wine and food writers Joe Tarantino and Jeanne Howard (Monterey and Carmel) and Christopher Weir (San Luis Obispo and the Santa Ynez Valley) contributed the lion's share of the writing of the dining and wine sections for those two areas of the Central Coast. And nods of appreciation to Traci Hukill and Tai Moses who added polish and perfection to the writing on some pages and to Christa Palmer, Sarah Quelland, Heather Zimmerman and Sarah Reinhardt who provided supplemental field work and play.

Our hardworking and talented researchers and fact checkers — Karen Reardanz and Mary Spicuzza — also contributed their graceful writings to too many sections of the book to specify. Just let it be said that they wrote as much of this new edition as we did and made sure that we didn't embarrass ourselves in print.

Throughout the writing of this book, we were inspired by the accomplishments of a great interweaving of cultures — the Chumash and Ohlone, the Spanish and Yankee immigrants and the twentieth-century settlers — all of whom at one time or another called the Central Coast home, and all of whom make us who live here today what we are.

Introduction

In the twenty years that we have worked and lived on the Central Coast, we've never taken for granted the sheer beauty of the place that we call home. How clever of our great-great grandparents to have settled in what amounts to one of the natural treasures of the country. We've been fortunate to have our professional lives segue smoothly with our personal interests. In creating countless, weekend getaway pieces for a variety of regional publications, we've combed the area, enjoying unforgettable accommodations, sampling cuisine that continues to set trends and soaking up ambiance that attracts visitors from all over the world.

From our house, we can walk to the beach in under three minutes and can thread through coastal bluffs and ancient oak groves by the simple act of driving to work. The walk from the parking lot to the office affords astonishing views of the shimmering Monterey Bay in the distance through a frame of towering redwoods. It would be impossible to take all of this for granted. Besides, we firmly believe in being tourists in our own hometown. When the surf's up, we're there gawking at the hypnotic waves right along with visitors from New York, Italy and Australia. Fine fall weather sends us out beachcombing or wine tasting at some of our favorite microwineries.

Not a day goes by that we aren't firmly impressed by the fact that we happen to live in a place that other people covet as a destination. That's another reason why vacations often find us exploring some new nook or cranny of the Central Coast instead of getting on a plane to somewhere else. We already live in one of the most desirable parts of the world. And while we're convinced that it will take a lifetime to explore it all and to savor it's richness, we've already begun tasting the best of this region. Frankly, we don't mind sharing it one bit. After all, we can hardly blame visitors smart enough to make our slice of paradise their next vacation spot.

Buz Bezore and Christina Waters
Santa Cruz, California

THE WAY THIS BOOK WORKS

This book is divided into seven chapters. There are three geographically based chapters covering the following regions: the Santa Cruz coast; Monterey Bay, Carmel and Big Sur; and San Luis Obispo and the Santa Ynez Valley. Each has its own introduction, orienting the reader to the unique personality of the region. The remaining four chapters, History, Transportation, Wineries and Information are thematic and concern all three regions.

Travelers driving along the Central Coast can turn to the regional chapter that they're interested in and can look over where they may want to stay, dine, shop or simply enjoy whatever activity that would enrich their visit in towns coming up on their trip.

Some entries include specific information (telephone numbers, addresses, hours, etc.), which is organized for quick and easy reference in blocks in the left-hand column. All information was rechecked as close to publication as possible, but since these details can change unexpectedly, it's a good idea to call ahead.

PRICES

Within each regional chapter, lodging prices are noted in information blocks and are based on a per-room, double occupancy during the summer months. Off-season rates are invariably less expensive.

Price Codes

Dining

Inexpensive	Up to $10
Moderate	$10 to $25
Expensive	$25 to $40
Very Expensive	$40 or more

Credit Cards are abbreviated as follows:

AE — American Express	DC — Diner's Club
CB — Carte Blanche	MC — MasterCard
D — Discover	V — Visa

The
MONTEREY BAY,
BIG SUR & GOLD COAST
WINE COUNTRY
Book
A Complete Guide

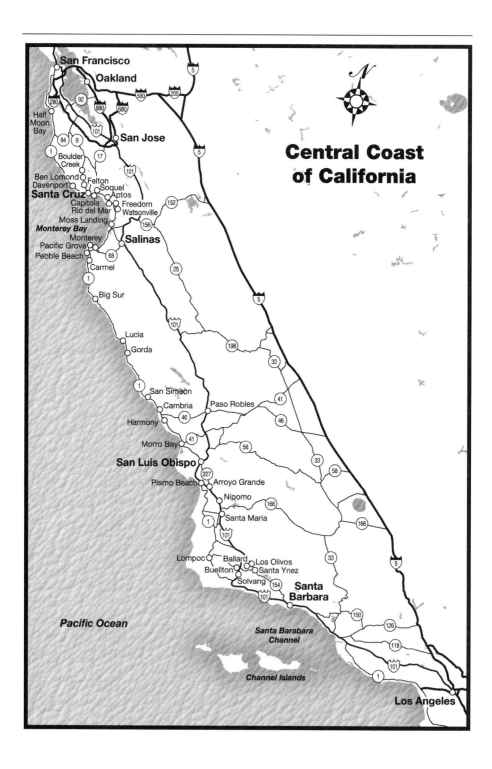

Central Coast of California

CHAPTER ONE
Of Blue & Golden Dreams
HISTORY

Running the length of California, the coastal mountain range forced its way through Golden State soil over 100 million years ago when two great continental landmasses collided, a contentious meeting that marked the birth of the infamous San Andreas Fault. The slow-grinding dance of the Pacific and North American tectonic plates pushed

Shmuel Thaler

Typical of the northern portion of the Central Coast are large rock outcroppings that protect white sand beaches.

the northern ranges up to a height of 5,000 feet and moved the edge of the land 100 miles westward. Once upon a time — a mere 150 million years ago — the coast of California called eastern Nevada home.

Erosion of strata from millions of years ago carved the labyrinthine tide pools of the northern Santa Cruz and Monterey coastlines, and the action of wind on sand has produced acres of softly shifting sand dunes along the southern stretches of San Luis Obispo. The combined effect of glaciers formed during the last ice age and the resulting lowering sea level — a process reversed as the glaciers melted — gently flooded channels carved into the land, forming estuaries of wetlands throughout the region.

NATURAL HISTORY

Natural harbors and sheltered coves teeming with marine wildlife dominate a coastline still young in geological terms, while offshore, the ocean conspires with a strong high pressure system to create the Central Coast's distinctive Mediterranean climate. Winter days tend to be wet and mild, and summers remain blissfully tolerable thanks to the daily blanket of fog. The fog nurtures lush ferns and lofty redwoods that starve in drier, warmer climes. In response to the climate, highly specialized ecological niches — tide pools, estuaries, chaparral, oak woods, redwood forests — flourish today in all of their rich diversity.

Majestic redwood stands stretch from the summits of the coast ranges to the ocean shore along the full length of the Central Coast.

Shmuel Thaler

The northern Central Coast is a showcase for forests of towering redwoods, the *sequoia sempervirens* first noted by early Spanish explorers. Reaching heights of up to 325 feet and living to a great age — some 2,000-year-old specimens have been identified — the evergreens attracted ax-wielding hordes of nineteenth-century loggers.

The heart of the Central Coast preserves its ranch land sprawl of chaparral grasslands dotted by enormous Spanish oaks, a zone above and beyond the fog line where wild lilac and manzanita bloom in the summer heat. These same hills and neighboring agricultural fields in very early spring, however, assault the eye with acres of chartreuse wild mustard, a plant once prized by industrious Chinese immigrants who pressed it into a multipurpose oil. The state flower, the brilliant orange California poppy, grows abundantly along every roadside, often in the company of broad swaths of purple lupine.

In the dappled woodland sunlight of 1,000-foot elevations, solid oaks coexist with the graceful madrone, whose thin red bark peels off in tightly rolled curls to expose flesh-colored limbs. In the heat of the afternoon, the heady scent of bay fills the upper canopy, while low to the ground grows the pungent yerba buena — the "good herb" prized by Native Americans and latter-day tea drinkers alike. Western gray squirrels, raccoons, opossums and skunks share the harvests of acorns and native berries with woodpeckers, while overhead soaring hawks survey the entire scene.

While the grizzly bear disappeared from California early this century, mountain lions, wild boar and black bear still roam protected niches of the coastal mountains. With little to disturb their solitude, gray fox, mule deer and coyotes flourish in the brushlands of steep coastal canyons. Winter ushers in the annual

Whole Lotta Shakin' Goin' On

The formidable San Andreas Fault runs halfway up the California coast, from the Gulf of California in the south to just off San Francisco's shore in the north. This capricious terror has been responsible for earthshaking mischief ranging from the nerve-wracking to the deadly during the last century. The shiftings and bucklings of neighboring continental plates that produce this volatile, seismic activity have been responsible for the 1906 earthquake, which hurled the cultural outpost of San Francisco into international headlines, as well as the 7.1 (on the Richter Scale) Loma Prieta quake that rearranged private and public fortunes, as well as buildings and bridges, along the northern stretches of the Central Coast in 1989.

While countless adjacent fault lines create seismic disturbances, none have acted with more dramatic impact than the San Andreas, a sensitive gash where the earth's crustal plates drift and snag uneasily, the Pacific side sidling northward past the larger North American plate at the rate of two inches per year. When the stress of this momentous and largely invisible encounter builds up sufficiently, the effect creates ruptures, many as mild as ocean tides. Some, however, create temblors of unforgettable impact.

These fault line upsurges invariably wrench landscapes apart, not to mention gas lines and water mains, and prove especially devastating to areas lying upon sandy soils, where a liquefaction effect magnifies the violence of the shift. When a major quake occurs, ensuing shock waves ("aftershocks" to anyone still standing) often serve as deadly collaborators, exponentially enlarging the initial damage.

The miracle is that the Central Coast has preserved as much of its original architectural heritage as it has. Unfortunately, many of its oldest settlements, including almost all of the earliest mission complexes, retain only pieces of their original structure, with the rest painstakingly recreated in the lulls following episodes of seismic destruction. Shaken, but not stirred, Central Coast residents periodically rebuild, invariably accepting earthquakes as a small price to pay for living in what many consider the most beautiful spot on earth.

migration of millions of monarch butterflies, who drape their favorite coastal groves of eucalyptus trees with a living fabric of fluorescent yellow wings.

Winter also announces the yearly return of gray and humpback whales, an event that brings legions of nature lovers within easy viewing distance of some of the planet's largest mammals. The barnacle-encrusted cetaceans join sea lions, dolphins, salmon, shellfish and bonito in the region's teeming marine sanctuaries.

Vast expanses of sandy beach invariably give way all along the coast to spectacular tide pools and jagged cliffs carved over the millennia by wind and wave. The rocky outcroppings of Año Nuevo and Point Lobos provide safe harbor for the delicate ecology of tide pools and their resident hermit crabs, anemones, starfish and sand dollars. Majestic underwater kelp forests stretch tendrils up onto the rocks and sand, while unusual seaweeds make tide pooling an exotic adventure.

Where the Central Coast's many small rivers meander to the sea, wetland

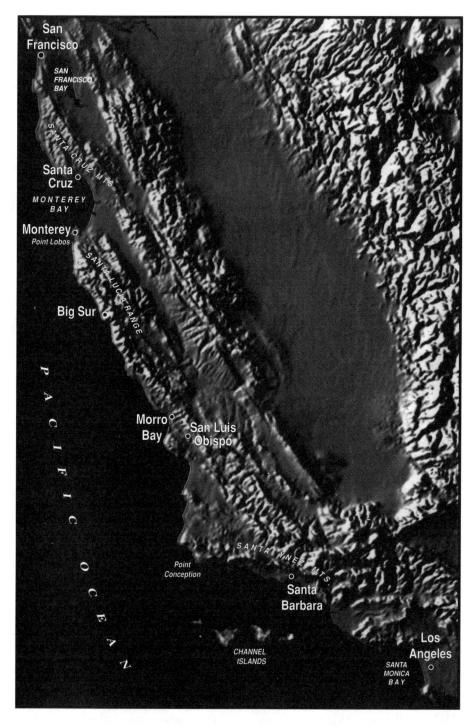

TOPOGRAPHY OF THE CENTRAL COAST

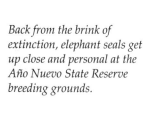

Back from the brink of extinction, elephant seals get up close and personal at the Año Nuevo State Reserve breeding grounds.

Shmuel Thaler

estuaries provide ecologically sensitive habitats for a plethora of diverse sea life, including oysters, shrimp and crabs, all of which feed on the nutrient-rich blend of salt- and fresh water. These shellfish, in turn, attract amazing throngs of harbor seals, sea otters and scores of fish and bird species. At Elkhorn Slough, where the Salinas River meets Monterey Bay at Moss Landing, bird-watchers often think that they've reached the promised land. Here tens of thousands of shearwater gulls, white egrets, blue herons and migratory ducks and geese gather, feed and nest. Needless to say, the fishing here is excellent.

Thanks to a chain of rigorously maintained state parks and beaches, the Central Coast tempts nature-loving visitors with ample opportunities for wilderness camping, beachcombing and wildlife observing in accessible, protected environmental preserves.

SOCIAL HISTORY

PARADISE LOST: THE NATIVE CALIFORNIANS

At the time Hernando Cortez began his new-world expeditions in the sixteenth century, the Central Coast was home to several hundreds of thousands of Native Americans, the largest tribes being the Ohlone in the north and the Chumash in the south. These nomadic hunter/gatherer peoples had arrived in the region at least 2,000 to 3,000 years earlier. The temperate climate, ample fresh water and abundance of edible plants, wild game and marine life allowed these peaceful native Californians to exist in easy harmony with their environment. But their uncomplicated, Edenic social structure, as well as their lack of agriculture, made them no match for the Europeans who invaded their lands in the seventeenth century.

From San Francisco Bay south to San Luis Obispo, the Ohlone dwelled in temporary villages of dome-shaped, tule-thatched huts invariably clustered close to springs and rivers along the coast. From the sea, the Ohlone gathered abalone and oysters, whose shells piled up over the years into giant middens, some of which persist to this day. From the forests, which they managed through controlled burning techniques, they gleaned the berries and pine nuts that formed staples of their diet. Blanching acorns to remove toxins, they ground them into an all-purpose meal that provided a year-round supply of starch. The region's huge herds of buffalo, together with quail, deer, elk and bear, augmented their simple, yet diverse, diet.

South of San Luis Obispo, the Chumash had evolved a more complex culture, one involving active trade links with the tribes of the Channel Islands. Here also the sea provided a wealth of fresh produce — bonito and sardines caught by net, salmon speared by stick, even the occasional whale taken by harpoon. These native peoples, who so skillfully employed the natural elements of their environment, were in turn to provide the raw material for an abrupt religious and territorial conquest that transformed the face of the western frontier forever.

MEN WITH A MISSION: THE SPANISH CONQUEST

Thanks to overblown reports of potential riches and the discovery of fabulous natural harbors in the area by explorer Juan Rodriguez Cabrillo, Spain laid claim to the entire coast of California in 1542. Once claimed, the land remained largely unexplored for the next fifty years, during which Spanish galleons laden with trade sailed near the Central Coast on lucrative voyages between colonies in Mexico and Manila.

The need for a convenient port on the California coast prompted new exploration in Alta (upper) California. The search was on for a spot that could be used by Spain's ships to lay over and restock much-needed supplies halfway through the arduous intercontinental trading voyages. Basque mariner Sebastian Vizcaino set out on such a venture in 1602 and discovered Monterey Bay in the process. Naming it after the Viceroy of Mexico, Vizcaino described Monterey in such wildly exaggerated terms that it took several encounters before those who followed could recognize it.

When King Charles III took the Spanish throne in 1759, he was determined to pump more muscle into Spanish new-world enterprises (both economic and religious) and ordered an expansion of the mission system already present in Baja (lower) California. Taking up the quest was the Spanish governor of Baja California, Gaspar de Portola. In 1769, he led the "Sacred Expedition" to Alta California, accompanied by the *padre presidente* of the Franciscan missionary effort, the indefatigable Padre Junipero Serra.

When the mountains of gold that they pursued evaporated to fantasy, the

A painting of the original Mission La Exaltación de La Santa Cruz.

Covello & Covello

colonial powers of New Spain envisioned a reborn El Dorado in the form of land and potential Christian souls in the people that lived upon it. Joining forces, the military and the Franciscan clergy set out together to found missions and spread the word of Christ, to cultivate the fertile land and to erect military forts, *presidios,* which headquartered the soldiers accompanying the monks and served to protect the newly won territory. Their successes inspired hopeful civilian colonists from Mexico, who followed and built pueblo settlements in the shadows of the missions.

Bringing with them herds of cattle, which would form the backbone of thriving beef, leather and tallow (for soap and candles) industries for over a century, Serra and Portola began their conversion of territory and native peoples in San Diego in 1769. With Serra remaining in San Diego to found the first Californian mission, Portola continued overland (the first European to do so) through San Luis Obispo and Monterey, whose bay, of course, he failed to recognize, turning around within sight of San Francisco Bay. On a second trip a year later, Portola finally extracted the reality of the Monterey Bay from Vizcaino's hyperbole and developed the presidio there.

The padres and soldiers brought with them agriculture, orchards, vineyards, irrigation techniques, the waterwheel, horses, cattle and written language. They also brought about the demise of many societies, wiping entire peoples from existence. In the pages of the missions' past, the shape of the present Central Coast was indelibly written.

THE RANCHO & BIRTH OF THE BEAR REPUBLIC

Once Mexico successfully won its independence from Spain in 1821, vast holdings once belonging to the Catholic Church were divided into generous land grants. These were deeded to the loyal Californio citizens or sold at rock-bottom prices to the highest, and most adventurous, bidder. The name of the game was ranching. Family fortunes were made and sustained by herds of cattle whose hides were tanned by another booming local industry and sent by ship to destinations around the world. Some of the *ranchos* subsequently became the core of the Central Coast's richest territory, surviving today as huge ranches, private farms, golf courses and state-owned natural parklands.

With the Spanish monopoly on trading irrevocably broken, new American entrepreneurs came to seek their fortunes. Many ended up staying and marrying into Californio families. From England and New England, Virginia and France, Canada and Kentucky, the middle part of the nineteenth century saw an influx of whalers, tanners, dairy farmers, merchants, fur traders and loggers — all redefining the term "Yankee ingenuity" as they tangled with the unlimited possibilities of an almost virgin coast.

Even as dissatisfaction with Mexican rule intensified in the 1830s, American settlers were busy building gristmills, tanneries and dairies. In the 1840s, John C. Fremont — pathfinder, military engineer and future United States senator — explored Central California on a mission from the United States government, whose alertness to the far west was rapidly increasing. With the help of Fremont's men and aided by the underground efforts of wealthy Yankee merchants like Monterey's Thomas Larkin, a peaceful coup occurred in 1846 at the Sonoma headquarters of Mexican General Mariano Vallejo. There, a makeshift flag bearing the emblem of the territory's mighty grizzly bear proclaimed the end of the Mexican era.

The Bear Republic (itself an unofficial and very short-lived affair) marked the swan song of the die-hard *Californios* and gave way to statehood. Anticipating this event, delegates from all over the state convened in Monterey in 1849 for a constitutional convention. In 1850, the sun officially set on Old California one day and rose again the next on the new State of California.

GOLDEN OPPORTUNITIES: THE RUSH WAS ON

The discovery of gold near Sacramento in 1848 ushered in a rush of Americans, Europeans and Chinese eager to get rich quick in the gold fields of the Sierra Nevada foothills. Raising the temperature of migration, gold fever helped trigger a tidal wave of adventurers to the Central Coast, where a wealth of virgin timber spewed forth an avalanche of sawmills, wharves and logging settlements, expanded further still by an overnight shipping industry. Sawmills sprang up on every bluff, and ships laden with lumber sailed up and down the coast, a coast increasingly dotted with schools, churches, courthouses, Victorian cottages and mansions. Though the mines and streams quickly ceased to "pan out" — the expression itself is another legacy of the forty-niners — the youthful new population of Americans stayed on to become the business and political leaders of the late nineteenth and early twentieth centuries.

The story of the Central Coast's accelerating fishing industry is also a saga of cultural competition. Chinese immigrants, who came to mine gold and build the growing network of railroads after statehood, stayed to establish the first fishing industry in a succession of highly lucrative villages hugging the coast.

Quong Chong was a leading Chinese merchant (and proud father) in turn-of-the-century Santa Cruz.

Special Collections, UCSC

Well over 100,000 Chinese had taken up residence in the state, including large settlements in Santa Cruz, Watsonville and Monterey by the mid-1870s. By 1890, following an unfortunate period of vigilante activity against the industrious Asian immigrants, who were willing to work for well below the going wages, the Chinese domination of the maritime wealth was eclipsed by Italians, Portuguese and Japanese.

CAPTAINS OF INDUSTRY & THE PURSUIT OF PLEASURE

A mericans of European ancestry soon put the stamp of Victorian architecture on the growing towns along the coast. Prosperity was being fed by a plethora of industries, and fortunes boomed in the new communications networks — shipping and the railroad. Once the Golden Spike was laid in Utah in 1869, linking railroads across the continent, settlers rushed to the West from all over the country. Writers like Charles Nordhoff wrote such glowing accounts of the natural wonders of the Golden State in popular books and magazines that, overnight, California was literally put on the map. The great resorts of the coast thronged with Victorians enamored of salt air vacations, eager to loosen their corsets with a bit of sea bathing.

Travel up and down the Central Coast was an arduous undertaking in the years following California's statehood. Impossible or nonexistent roadways and the rugged terrain of the coastal mountains kept townships relatively iso-

The Central Coast fishing industry was established in the mid-nineteenth century by the Chinese, but by 1910, the Santa Cruz Wharf was the domain of Italian immigrant fishermen.

Covello & Covello

lated, and most travel involved lengthy sea journeys. In 1861, a stagecoach line began carrying mail and passengers three times a week from Los Angeles to San Francisco with a stop in San Luis Obispo. Once the system had been "refined," the journey, including four relays of horses, could be made in just under four days. Each year new towns were added to the stage lines, which were met in 1873 by the Southern Pacific Railroad as far south as Salinas. It took twenty more years for the relative safety and comfort of rail travel to extend down the Central Coast as far as San Luis Obispo.

In 1906, entrepreneur Fred Swanton concocted a fabulous Brighton-style resort casino, dance palace and amusement park at the water's edge in Santa Cruz. A major attraction for legions of tourists from its opening day, the Boardwalk thrives today as the last example of its kind on the California Coast. The turn of the century saw the germination of efforts to preserve the region's breathtaking natural resources with the first coastal parklands — Big Basin Redwoods in Santa Cruz — purchased with the help of the Sempervirens Club in 1902.

OUT OF THE DUST, INTO THE FUTURE

The rise of the glitzy Hollywood movie, which painted California as a land of romantic opportunity, coupled with the crushing grip of the Depression, lured yet another wave of eager immigrants to the temperate climes of the Central Coast during the 1930s. They came from America's drought-stricken dust bowl to add their energy and urgency to the creative melting pot of the Golden State. They were the Okies, Arkies and other heartland refugees who fled foreclosed farms to pick the lettuce, work the sardine canneries of John Steinbeck's *Cannery Row* and fuel the gritty drama of his *Grapes of Wrath*. By 1935, almost one fifth of California's population was on the dole. But unlike the harsh Midwest, the climate here was mild, and if a body was going to go hungry, paradise was a good place to do it.

Those who came and stayed during the lean times were rewarded by full employment during World War II, which brought military bases and the aero-

In 1906, the legendary Fred Swanton built his pleasure dome in Santa Cruz to attract San Franciscans with leisure time and open wallets.

Covello & Covello

nautics industry to eager workers. The opening of the University of California, Santa Barbara just after the war piqued the fortunes of that community, as did the coming of the University of California, Santa Cruz to that tiny resort in the mid-1960s.

The postwar period witnessed an increase of private building and public ownership along the Central Coast. Enormous military bases built for coastal defense scooped up prime beachfront real estate. These installations lured defense industries to the region and sculpted the growth of entire towns full of families and businesses dependent upon the military presence. A state park system that was to become a showcase for the rest of the nation burgeoned to protect huge expanses of native flora and fauna.

ARTISTS, DREAMERS & THE AGE OF AQUARIUS

In the years between the two World Wars, the scenery and seclusion of the Central Coast acted with the force of a siren song on literary bohemians, freethinkers and metaphysical cults. Isadora Duncan, John Steinbeck, Henry Miller, Robinson Jeffers, Jack London, Emil White and Mark Twain all immortalized the liberated lifestyles and meditative splendor of the region's secluded canyons, natural springs and coffeehouses.

Big Sur was the Beat Generation's vacation hideaway. When quintessential bad boy Jack Kerouac went *On the Road,* he did it along the coast roads linking San Francisco with Big Sur, where he stopped for a breather in the mountain cabin owned by poet Lawrence Ferlinghetti and penned the book that spawned a generation of rebels without a cause. At Carmel, photographers Ansel Adams and Edward Weston captured the haunting marriage of earth, sky and sea, creating indelible black and white images that still define California coastal magic a full fifty years later. The bewitching landscape and maverick heritage that attracted Robert Louis Stevenson and Richard Henry Dana a century before continued to exert their pull.

Hidden and out of the way, the rugged coast formed a logical sanctuary for those marching to a different drummer. Theosophists led by the Russian expatriate Madame Blavatsky, Zen Buddhists and naturalists came, stayed, set up salons and meditative retreats and preached the good life far from the status quo of staid and traditional America.

During the 1960s, consciousnesses expanded up and down the western seaboard, and the Central Coast became a nursery for the emerging human potential movement. As the counterculture entered the New Age, the Central Coast led the way with its consciousness-raising centers at Esalen, Tassajara and Big Sur. The hippies' experimentation with mind-altering drugs gradually gave way to attitude adjustments of nonchemical varieties. After being found, the "inner child" needed to be fed — organically. The leading edge of the natural foods and organic gardening movement emerged here, and doing one's own thing was further institutionalized when the University of California opened its innovative campus in Santa Cruz.

Before they cut their hair and moved on (though quite a few never did), the hippies had infused every inch of the Central Coast with their attitude of tolerance. It was a logical fit, since people had been "doing their own thing" in the relative inaccessibility of the rugged coastal mountains since the beginning.

The hills and canyons of the Central Coast were, and still are, alive with the truly laid-back and self-sufficient, all seeking an alternative approach to life in Eden. Up and down the coast, the footprints in the sand remain more likely to be made by Birkenstocks or thong sandals than anything resembling a leather oxford.

THE NEW COAST GUARDIANS

With consciousness-raising, inevitably came political correctness, and by the 1970s, the Central Coast boasted what appeared to be an entire population of environmental activists. Beaches, increasingly snapped up by the state for management and protection, were kept clean with a vengeance. Litterers became outcasts, and recycling was an unwritten law.

With the rise of offshore oil drilling along the southern reaches of the Central Coast, environmental protection legislation aggressively signaled concern for the region's natural treasures. The state formed the Coastal Commission in 1976 to serve as a watchdog of unchecked development and to maintain and to protect the unique biosystems of the coastline. National wildlife sanctuaries were designated to protect rare wildlife habitats along the coast and in the sea, the latest and largest being the Monterey Bay National Marine Sanctuary.

In the short 150 years since the twilight of Junipero Serra's missions, the Central Coast has managed to nurture the past, while protecting its privileged resources for the future.

Seclusion & Retreat

The Central Coast of California is as famous for its free-spirited way of thinking as it is for its picturesque locations, and visitors flock to the area not only for the sensual, but also for the spiritual as well. For the civilization weary, there's a host of retreats and spiritual centers for those needing to sit back, relax and begin the search for inner peace. **St. Clare's Retreat House** (408/423-8093; 2381 Laurel Glen Rd., Soquel, CA 95073) is a completely silent mountain retreat founded in 1950 by two Franciscan sisters. Now the sprawling commune attracts up to ninety guests each weekend for silent contemplation and specific concerns, such as alcoholism. St. Clare's is run by Catholics, but the staff is quick to point out that not all guests are Catholic. The postcard view of the mountain-perched **Mount Madonna Center** (408/847-0406; 445 Summit Rd., Watsonville, CA 95076) adds to the charm of this facility that offers private, individual and group retreat facilities along with weekend and weeklong seminars, such as "A Retreat for Lawyers," "The Energetics of Relationships" and "The Perils and Promises of the Spiritual Path." The center also appeals to the body as well as the mind with hiking trails, volleyball, tennis, a spa and massage therapists. The mineral springs and idyllic oak grove setting of the Buddhist-oriented **Tassajara Zen Mountain Center** (Tassajara Springs Rd., Carmel Valley, CA 93924) are a prime spot for meditation or to participate in workshops like "Introduction to Zen" or "Zen/Yoga." The redwood or Japanese-style cabins, including a private bath and three meals a day, cost around $100 a weekend. For reservations, write to the **Zen Center** (415/431-3771; 300 Page St., San Francisco, CA 94102). In addition to providing a laid-back cutting edge to the West Coast's human potential movement, the sybaritic sanctuary **Esalen Institute** (reservations: 408/667-3005; general information: 408/667-3000; Big Sur, CA 93920) became famous in the conscious-raising 1960s. Now the "center for experimental education" allows visitors to take courses designed to heal and expand, while settling into the hot springs bath. Lodgings are much sought after — the best route is to sign up for one of Esalen's workshops. On the site of a former stagecoach and railroad depot, rustic **Sycamore Mineral Springs Resort** (800/234-5831; 805/595-7302; 1215 Avila Beach Dr., Avila Beach, CA 93424), with its own swimming pool and California cuisine restaurant, caters to those seeking spiritual rejuvenation without the help of meditation, religion or workshops. Sycamore Springs offers massage therapy, hot tubs and outdoor pepper- and sulphur-scented, 110-degree mineral waters to ease visitors into the world of relaxation.

JOURNEY DOWN THE COAST

A drive down the Central Coast is a drive through California's historic past, through layers of distinctive landscapes shaped as much by generations of explorers, ranchers and pioneers as by wind and wave. Three hundred miles of spectacular seascapes, forests and rambling ranch lands, this region can be best, and most intimately, savored by skirting the ocean along Coastal

Highway 1. The following section is a brief tour of these coastal pleasures, with more information about what to see and where to stay detailed in later chapters.

HALF MOON BAY

Nestled squarely on the Central Coast's legendary Highway 1, this hamlet is known to locals as the halfway point between San Francisco and Santa Cruz. An arts-and-crafts emporium called "Spanishtown" pays tribute to the town's nickname circa 1840 when Baja Californian immigrants claimed this slice of the coast for their own. When Prohibition dried up the nation's official alcohol reserves, Half Moon Bay's many secluded coves did a brisk business harboring eager rum smugglers, who supplied San Francisco with spirits enough to wait out the dry years.

Soothed by prevailing fogs, the hemispherical bay still nurtures the rich fisheries and moist growing season that attracted its Portuguese, Spanish and Italian settlers in the nineteenth century. From here, fleets plumb the coastal waters for salmon, anchovies and herring, while surrounding fields boast countless Christmas tree farms and pumpkins. Artichokes, berries and Brussels sprouts share the roomy hillsides with cattle and sheep, while greenhouses supplying cut flowers to the entire state line the highway leading south.

PESCADERO

Ghosts of Californio ranchers and Japanese fishing pioneers haunt this tiny, one-street town, whose name means "the fisherman" in Spanish. A gateway to redwood campgrounds, prime surf and the convoluted stretches of Pescadero State Beach, the town is populated by houses, barns and authentic general stores straight out of the frontier West. The top destination is Duarte's Tavern, with a saloon heavily populated with real cowboys, migrant workers and colorful raconteurs.

An idyllic, 210-acre expanse of wildlife sanctuary faces Pescadero Beach across Highway 1. On one side of the road waves plunge against miles of wide tide pools, while on the other side elegant egrets, mallards, blue herons and brilliantly colored wood ducks pose and sail blissfully on lagoons threaded by giant cattails. This is a favorite secret playground for northern California's hip, young community and has been since the 1960s.

AÑO NUEVO & POINTS SOUTH

In January, when the velvety grasses of the Central Coast's "false spring" add a certain elegance to the rough-hewn land, this stretch of the coast offers irresistible driving pleasure. Propelled by storms out at sea, the ocean churns itself into enormous lathers of surf and crashing waves, presenting postcard interpretations of heaving wintry seas. The winter months are also famous along the coast for whale watching and, for those who join the guided tours at Año Nuevo State Reserve, elephant seal mating rituals.

Redwood forests — many protected as part of Big Basin and Butano State Parks — crown the coastal highlands, which momentarily fan out into verdant rivers of artichokes or Brussels sprouts before plunging into the sea. It's perhaps this unique blend of redwood crests, deep canyons crosshatched with small pockets of cultivation and high, wild limestone bluffs that defines this stretch of coast.

Two state beaches merit special attention. Just north of Davenport, the stately lagoon of Scott Creek sparkles like something out of an Arthurian legend. Ghostly pampas grass rims the steep ridges behind, and Canadian geese, coots and mallards float noisily on pools fringed with cattails and tule. Across the road, soft, sandy beaches curve out of sight around jutting, limestone sentinels of the continental United States.

Down the road a piece, Waddell Creek finally spills out into the Pacific after tumbling down from its source high in Big Basin Park. Hang gliders and windsurfers have laid claim to this windy spot, and on most days spectators can watch their jewel-colored sails dipping in and out of the waves like playful birds. Nearby, waterfowl stake out their plots in saltwater marshes and freshwater lagoons. This is a magic location for year-round beachcombing (look for gnarled driftwood and sea-smoothed rocks).

Cruciform from Another Plant

Stretching from Half Moon Bay down through Monterey county, mighty portions of the Central Coast lie cultivated with miles of Brussels sprouts, which flourish in the lengthy growing season and cool summer fog of this moist seaside climate. Like an exotic and primitive cabbage, the Brussels sprout is, indeed, a cruciform and a distant relative of the mustard family. Almost extraterrestrial in appearance, the stalks are studded with miniature cabbage heads, gray-green knobs growing the entire two-foot length. Harvested when the little heads are still tiny and tender, Brussels sprouts provide luxurious eating, simply steamed and bathed in butter and vinegar.

Grower Steve Bontadelli proudly holds a stalk of Brussels sprouts, an important Central Coast crop.

DAVENPORT

The tiny village of Davenport was, since shortly after the turn of the century, a company town built, owned and operated by and for the Santa Cruz Portland Cement Company. Everything and everyone in the town was white from cement dust — houses, cars, people and gardens. All of that was cleaned up in the 1960s, but if you squint, your imagination can do the rest. There are still signs of the past in some of the original, identical houses — one of which, the Bath House, turned saloon, then sporting house, is now part of the New Davenport Bed and Breakfast establishment.

On the bluffs across the street from the bustling Cash Store — a lodging, restaurant, community core and global arts and crafts emporium — the whale watching is as good as it gets. From here, whalers from all over the world came in the mid-nineteenth century to fill their ships with precious oil and line their pockets with gold. One of those adventurous souls was Rhode Island's John Davenport, who came in 1850 and ended up running not only a major whaling operation, but also a lumber wharf. (In those days, you were nobody unless you had your own wharf.)

Today, the town that Davenport settled is still distinguished by two primary landmarks — the spouts of gigantic gray whales as they migrate south and the tall stacks of the cement plant, visible for miles. Davenport is charm itself, easily circumnavigated on foot in under a half an hour, a tour that rewards visitors with glimpses into world-class glassblowing, boatbuilding and knife-making studios.

SANTA CRUZ

Long one of the state's most appealing and popular seaside resorts, the town of Santa Cruz supports an eclectic population of artists, writers, computer mavericks, winemakers, restaurateurs and rabble-rousers. Originally settled by the Franciscan fathers who established the Mission La Exaltación de la Santa Cruz in 1791, the town initially flourished thanks to the nearby large Branciforte Pueblo, the center of town life in Spanish days, then by Mexican land grant ranchos that followed the pueblo's breakup and, finally, by American entrepreneurs attracted by the matchless setting of mountains descending into the hemispherical Monterey Bay.

While the original mission was twice destroyed by an earthquake and exists today as a one-third scale replica, the past persists in the city's tree-lined streets of impeccably maintained Victorian mansions and classic examples of Craftsman bungalows.

Devastated by the 1989 earthquake (centered a mere eight miles away), downtown Santa Cruz lost many of its historic commercial buildings. The rebuilding effort is nearly completed, and a restoration of the nineteenth-century St. George Hotel and the erection of a nearby cinema complex now forms the cultural heart of the town.

For well over 100 years, the expansive main beach of Santa Cruz has hosted throngs of visitors, many flocking to the massive amusement park of the Santa Cruz Beach Boardwalk. The Victorian ballroom of the Cocoanut Grove regularly features big name Latin American and rock groups. In addition to a colorful assortment of death-defying rides, the Boardwalk is graced with the Giant Dipper (the oldest wooden roller coaster in the country) and an enchanting 1879 carousel bedecked with hand-carved painted horses.

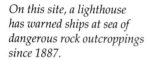

On this site, a lighthouse has warned ships at sea of dangerous rock outcroppings since 1887.

Buz Bezore

Lined with stately summer homes and the graceful shade of Monterey pines and cypress, West Cliff Drive curves along the coast, linking the end of the Santa Cruz Municipal Wharf with the wild cliffs of Natural Bridges State Park a few miles northward. In the middle, just at the point where the sheltered Monterey Bay gives way again to the turbulent Pacific Ocean proper, is Lighthouse Point. Today's tiny beacon, replacing the badly undermined original in 1967, still warns fishing fleets at dawn and houses the state's first surfing museum.

Following the uphill curve of High Street past historic Mission Plaza, visitors arrive at the former ranch of lime and cattle potentate Henry Cowell. This splendid 2,000-acre site, whose sweeping fields are alive with deer and coyote and framed by thick stands of redwoods, is now the home of the youngest campus of the University of California. The original limestone quarry and many of Cowell's lime kilns, barns and ranch buildings are still scattered scenically throughout the campus. The sweeping view of the entire Monterey Bay from this academic vantage point is worth the drive.

CAPITOLA & SOQUEL

Once the intersection of Victorian-era commerce and well-worn stage lines, these sister cities face each other across diminutive Soquel Creek, which empties peacefully into a broad, sheltered beach at Capitola. Today, Capitola-by-the-Sea (named in a failed bid to be the state's first capital) attracts sunbathers to its sheltered children's beach and shoppers to its fine galleries, crafts shops and boutiques. Both the beach and the shopping area adjoin the airy esplanade, where trendy watering holes jostle with seafood restaurants for patrons.

Soquel Creek empties into the Monterey Bay at the lively beach community of Capitola.

Shmuel Thaler

Across the creek and Highway 1 lies sleepy Soquel, founded by Yankee merchants, settled by ambitious loggers and peopled by generations of cattle ranchers and horse trainers. Country roads wind away from the ocean and up into the Santa Cruz Mountains through endless pastures, small organic farms and thriving microwineries. This is also begonia country, where vast fields and nurseries breed the large, luscious blooms sold to dealers and florists around the world.

APTOS & RIO DEL MAR

Sugar beet king Claus Spreckels made such a fortune in the fields near Aptos Creek that the imprint of his private polo grounds can still be seen lying just outside the entrance to 10,000 pristine acres of redwood lands that form the Forest of Nisene Marks. Made infamous in recent years as the epicenter of the Loma Prieta earthquake of 1989, this otherwise undisturbed forest offers endless hiking and horseback trails extending far into the interior of the coast ranges. The slender stretch of Highway 1 occupied by Aptos Village offers some of the most picturesque dining in the Central Coast.

At the coast, Aptos yields to the seaside community of Rio Del Mar, an attractive amalgam of beach homes abutting a short esplanade and miles of wide beachfront that includes spacious camping, barbecuing and seaside roaming possibilities. In the middle of Seacliff State Beach (a short stroll away) sits the wreck of a vintage World War I cement ship. Accessible by a slender pier, the boat is a popular surf-fishing attraction. In addition to camping, hiking and fishing opportunities, the primarily residential areas of Rio Del Mar and Seacliff offer secluded sunning, surfing and for the young and hardy, swimming conditions in water that remains just a few degrees too cool for most adults without wet suits. Further south, the state beaches of Manresa and Sunset offer broad expanses of sand, fine swimming, excellent surfing and unhurried beachcombing.

MOSS LANDING

Marking the midway point of the Monterey Bay, where the Salinas River bisects the low-lying artichoke fields between Santa Cruz and Monterey, Moss Landing lies just south of the sensational bird-watching mother lode of Elkhorn Slough. The slough's 2,500 acres of salt marsh and tidal flats not only provide sanctuary for tens of thousands of waterfowl, but also teem with plankton rich enough to nurse oyster and shrimp farms supplying Central Coast restaurants.

In 1864, this scene bustled with activity. Established as a whaling station by Captain Charles Moss, a busy harbor soon serviced schooners loaded with produce from the Salinas Valley and whaling ships from around the world. Today, Moss Landing is essentially a faded postcard of a fishing village — a collection of piers, docks and duck-filled lagoons without a town in sight. Curiously enough, what Moss Landing does have is scores of vintage antique stores lining the one road that twists through its ramshackle collection of docks.

The drive inland from Moss Landing wanders through a gray-green sea of artichokes that extends as far as the eye can see. In the middle of it all lies Castroville, a heartland ranching and agricultural settlement with one foot in the last century. Comprised of a single street and fortified by produce stands, tiny Castroville proudly lays claim to the title of Artichoke Capitol of the World. None dare argue.

MONTEREY

Fifty years after Columbus sailed to the New World, Spanish explorers began bumping into Monterey, first Cabrillo in 1542, Vizcaino in 1602 and in 1769, military commander Portola. Father Serra joined Portola in Monterey in 1770, and the duo founded the second mission and presidio in the Alta California conquest. The mission, originally built in what is today downtown

Global Matters

Shmuel Thaler

Cooled by coastal fog, Castroville (near Moss Landing) is the Artichoke Capital of the World.

The artichoke, a Mediterranean native and member of the thistle family, was widely cultivated by Italian immigrants attracted by the climatic and scenic resemblance of the Central Coast to their European homeland. Thriving along the Central Coast — most especially in Monterey and Santa Cruz counties — artichoke fields, in some places, spill down to the very edge of bluffs overlooking the ocean. The distinctive sea green plant grows in round "islands" of feathery leaves, crowned by the fat globe that is the edible prize. The ultimate finger food, steamed artichoke leaves are simply pulled off, dipped in a lemon-butter mixture or dragged through garlic-infused mayonnaise and with the teeth, scraped clean of the tender meat. Nestled in the thistled interior lies the succulent heart, favored by Californians and prepared in myriad ways. Roadside produce stands offer artichokes fresh from the fields and, like all roadside produce stands, these are hard to resist.

Monterey, was moved in 1771 to the more fertile fields and abundant fresh water of Carmel, a few miles to the south.

Monterey is an impeccably maintained fabric of historic old sections, waterfront wharves and piers, Cannery Row tourism and well-groomed conference hotels and seaside lodgings, all ringed by the teeming natural kingdom of the Monterey Bay. Fisherman's Wharf — originally built in 1846 and once bursting with international whaling traffic — offers a galaxy of seafood dining and souvenir shopping as well as fine sportfishing amid the nets, boats and paraphernalia of today's busy tuna, bonito and salmon industries. This is a prime vantage point for observing the antics of sea otters and for watching the fat harbor seals sun themselves.

Starting at the wharf, Monterey's historic district of plazas, streets and calles is best experienced on foot. A walking tour of this "Path of History" takes visitors through the corridors of the eighteenth and nineteenth centuries.

Poised at the tip of the bay as it begins to yield to the open waters of the Pacific Ocean, the first fort of the Spanish empire in California, the Monterey Presidio, still maintains a military watch over the harbor. From its commanding position, the old bastion marks the beginning of Cannery Row, in its prime a cheek-by-jowl amalgam of sardine canneries and processing plants, colorfully chronicled in the 1940s by the pen of John Steinbeck. Today, the canneries offer their atmospherically ruined foundations to the seagulls and kelp beds.

At many points around the Monterey Bay, the area's fabled golf links skirt both the sea and sun-splashed shoreline.

Dan Coyro

Many former canneries now house galleries, gift shops, wine-tasting rooms and fine restaurants.

The centerpiece of this seafront revival is the spectacular Monterey Bay Aquarium, where visitors come from all over the world to wonder at innovative natural habitat exhibits — some several stories high and literally carved out of the rock and underwater sanctuaries of the bay itself. Giant kelp forests teem with otters, octopi and tiger sharks, and baby rays and starfish are available on a one-on-one level at the Aquarium's Touch Tide Pool.

PACIFIC GROVE

Founded in the 1870s as a seaside retreat for the Methodist Church, this quiet gem adjoining the northern edge of Monterey proper boasts incomparable Victorian homes turned into inviting, often luxurious, bed and breakfast accommodations. Long a popular conference site, Pacific Grove houses the landmark Asilomar Meeting Center, designed by Julia Morgan, whose architectual abilities also shaped the Hearst Castle at San Simeon.

At Asilomar State Park, sand dunes give way to a wildly dramatic expanse of prime tide pools reaching tentatively into surf crashing wildly on the rocks of Point Pinos — alleged to be the first Central Coast location spied by Cabrillo. The spot still boasts a tiny searchlight of the Point Pinos Lighthouse, which has steered ships away from the treacherous rocks since 1856 (it is open for tours). Local abalone divers continue to search the waters off the point for the prized sea delicacy, whose huge, iridescent shells formed great mounds, marking Native American habitation.

Each November, Pacific Grove captures its fair share of the limelight when the orange and black magic of hundreds of thousands of monarch butterflies fill the trees of the town's main avenue with a glory of quivering color.

PEBBLE BEACH & 17 MILE DRIVE

Landed gentry flocked to this region of incomparable cliffs, churning surf and occasional movie crews. Winding between Pacific Grove and Carmel is an extraordinary stretch of road affording fabulous ocean vistas and glimpses of the lifestyles of the rich and famous. Here some of California's founding families laid down their own versions of great European country homes, most designed by the leading architects of the early twentieth century.

The 5,000-acre Del Monte Forest is a sanctuary for the rare Monterey cypress, including that most photographed of Central Coast trees, the Lone Cypress. Thick groves of the trees gave shelter to the landing party headed by Portola during his 1769 exploration of Alta California. The waters along this circuitous drive have been the graveyard of countless cargo ships, dashed to bits on the razor-edged rocks during the past two centuries.

At each turn of this popular drive, some new yet strangely familiar estate pops into view through the Monterey pines and stone gatehouses. Hitchcock's *Rebecca* was among the many Golden Age of Hollywood films set in these monuments to conspicuous, if tasteful, consumption.

In addition to truly spectacular coastal vistas, this area is a testament to lavish country club living. For the $10 toll to drive 17 Mile Drive, visitors can take a gander at the action on some of the world's most famous golf courses, such as legendary Pebble Beach and Spyglass Hill.

CARMEL

Carefully nurtured artistic ambiance and romantic windswept cypresses define the borders of Carmel, one of the gems of early Spanish mission architecture. Here photographer Ansel Adams flourished, Clint Eastwood became mayor and eating isn't allowed on the streets. Neon signs and telephone poles also are banned. Preserving its quaintness with a vengeance has paid off for this diminutive village, a slice of almost English country refinement perched on the edge of the continent. Tidy and almost impossibly tasteful in its collection of landscaped cottages, elegant lodgings and upscale restaurants, Carmel still exerts its undeniable, if conservative, appeal.

History has left its mark most vividly in the nearby Mission San Carlos Borromeo del Rio Carmelo established in 1771 by Father Junipero Serra. With its barrel-vaulted ceiling, Moorish tower and authentically replicated kitchen, sleeping quarters and refectory, the mission well rewards visitors seeking a taste of Spanish occupation in the New World.

Bohemian painters, writers, photographers and bon vivants flocked here at the turn of the century, drawn by the magnanimous deal of land barons James Devendorf and Frank H. Powers: dirt cheap land to anyone actively engaged in the fine arts. The offer, plus fragrant pine forests at the edge of a serene beach, attracted the likes of Upton Sinclair, Jack London, George Sterling and Edward Weston, as well as hundreds of their best friends, hangers-on and lesser-known colleagues. Robinson Jeffers found the peaceful inspiration that he sought in the amazing Tor House and Hawk Tower, built in 1914 completely of rounded, native stone — an intrepid landmark not to be missed by visitors.

Each year the Monterey Jazz Festival spills sparkling into Carmel's streets, and the brilliant brass and contrapuntal melodies of the baroque masters fill the town each year during the Carmel Bach Festival. And everybody (tourist and local alike) stops for a cocktail at Clint Eastwood's Hog's Breath Inn.

CARMEL VALLEY

Across from the Carmel Mission, Carmel Valley Road threads its way along the tiny Rio Carmel, climbing into the hills through lands once graced by enormous land grant ranchos. Much of Carmel Valley continues to be owned by the very wealthy and has been immaculately groomed into an elegant patchwork of golf courses, country clubs and plush resorts. Thriving remnants of the early rancho period dot this Spanish oak-drenched slice of the coast ranges, perhaps the purest taste of the *Californio* essence still to be found. Orchards of pear, apricot and walnut line the verdant valley floor, which rises abruptly into picturesque slopes studded with grazing herds of cattle. Up in chaparral country, Carmel Valley offers prime side road exploration through steep canyons and onto ridges that offer stunning views of the ocean below.

BIG SUR COAST

Most signs of human habitation disappear abruptly just south of Carmel. For the next ninety miles, the majestic coastal splendor of Big Sur reigns supreme. With few permanent residents and no towns to speak of, this pristine coastline still boasts unspoiled, breathtaking grandeur. Here Highway 1 earns its reputation as the most beautiful, if vertiginous, highway in the country. That the road exists at all — carved out of sheer cliffs dropping straight into the swirling tide below — is a miracle. Spectacular bridges defy gravity to span deep canyons and gorges — the best and most photographed of which is Bixby Creek Bridge, with a central span of over 300 feet. This is definitely a must visit.

From Bixby Creek, two noteworthy side roads, Palo Colorado and the Old Coast Road, take inquiring drivers deep into the interior of the coast mountains, through fern canyons and up to windswept hilltops, affording stunning views of the entire Monterey Bay.

The Ventana Wilderness joins with the Los Padres National Forest at Big Sur, offering close to two million acres of pristine hiking and riding trails and

*Big Sur's spectacularly
rugged seascape has lured
travelers to the Central Coast
for generations.*

Shmuel Thaler

awe-inspiring forests, beaches and hilltops. Immediately south of the "town" of Big Sur lie the beautiful beaches, caves and cliffs of Pfeiffer Beach. After a day of beachcombing and hiking, locals trickle in for a sunset cocktail at the legendary Nepenthe, a restaurant/arts complex situated almost 1,000 feet above the sea. A hangout since 1949 for local culturati, Nepenthe has since been joined by other fashionable resort neighbors, including Ventana Inn just across the road.

On each side of the highway continuing southward, state parks, beaches and forests extend as far as the eye can see, working their way to the very end of Monterey county. Julia Pfeiffer Burns State Park haunts the coast starting ten miles south of Nepenthe, its border encircling waterfalls, creek trails and dizzying ridges. After a dip in the public-access hot springs and the tubs at the New Age think tank of the nearby Esalen Institute, visitors might continue southward to partake of the prime, meandering possibilities of Sand Dollar Beach and Jade Cove.

Throughout the southern Big Sur area, rugged side roads — many overlaying old ranch trails — lead from the coast through redwoods and chaparral, retracing the steps of early pioneers. One of the loveliest of these, Nacimiento Road, begins south of Lucia and ascends 3,000 feet through oak groves and brush-covered ridges. It ends in the isolated setting of Junipero Serra's third mission, the authentically restored Mission San Antonio de Padua, founded in 1771.

Nowhere else on the Central Coast is so much unspoiled coastal wilderness available to the public as Big Sur Coast. There are convenient pull-outs and vista points available almost every mile of the way, and most travelers find themselves using them frequently. If ever one stretch of road demanded a camera and binoculars, the Big Sur stretch of Highway 1 is it.

SAN SIMEON

A s Monterey county gives way to San Luis Obispo county, the steep and agitated profile of Big Sur relaxes, gradually rambling downhill toward the border of superb beach country. The Central Coast's Mediterranean climate blooms as you head further south, the days jumping up in temperature a few degrees, the evenings staying balmier longer.

The most graphic reminder of old-world influence, though, is that fantastical version of the Spanish Renaissance — William Randolph Hearst's, La Cuesta Encantada (The Enchanted Hill). Hearst inherited hundreds of thousands of acres of San Simeon land grant from his indomitable mother Phoebe and senator father George.

Between 1919 and 1947, the newspaper magnate unleashed his massive fortune and passion for architectural overstatement on the superb hillside setting framed by the Santa Lucia Range. With architect Julia Morgan to temper his pipe dreams, Hearst proceeded to construct a tile, marble, wood and gilt complex of thirty-seven bedrooms, fabulous indoor swimming pools, fountains, endless gardens and even a zoo. Richly satirized in Orson Welles' *Citizen Kane,* San Simeon is a kingdom unto itself and must be seen to be believed.

CAMBRIA

S outh of San Simeon, Highway 1 slides through gentle beach country to the artists' colony of Cambria, which also serves as the lodging center for visitors to the Hearst Castle a few miles up the road. Settled in the 1860s by Welsh miners attracted by news of copper and quicksilver prospects, Cambria's lumber industry, dairy farming and superb swimming beaches have maintained the community's popularity up to the present.

All along this section of coastline, great stands of blue-green eucalyptus dominate the hillsides and saturate the air with a heady, mentholated perfume. Imported from Australia in the last century under the misguided notion that they would provide fast-growing timber for construction, the eucalyptus has long since gone native, in some places choking out the original flora. Though their lumber proved unsturdy, these distinctive trees crop up along the entire Central Coast as ranch land windbreaks and as the region's signature ocean backdrop.

Golden hills, like these near Cambria, parallel the sea throughout the southern portion of the Central Coast.

Visnius

MORRO BAY

Crowned by a formidable volcanic peak, the extensive beaches of this popular playground are home to abundant shellfish and spectacular processions of windswept dunes. A busy fishing port, the bay is one of the major waterfowl habitats in the country. Before that, this twelve-mile stretch of coast, extending from Morro Strand State Beach down to Montaña de Oro State Park, was a prized harbor and hub of the shipping industry. By 1879, coastal steamers regularly put in at its sheltering bay. Protected by a slender sandspit of high dunes, the bay is chockablock with waterfront development, pleasure and commercial fishing boat docks and every possible amenity catering to the visitors who stream to this outdoor sports magnet.

In every sense, the pinnacle of this portion of the San Luis Obispo coast is dramatic Morro Rock, highest of a dozen volcanic plugs still visible in the area along Highway 1. At almost 600 feet, the miniature Gibraltar commands the entrance to the bay and was formed by the same volcanic eruptions that produced the intricate stratifications of Montaña de Oro State Park's tide pools. Hikers and beachcombers are free to explore the base of the rock, but its upper cliffs and crags — a sanctuary protecting the nests of peregrine falcons — are off limits to humans. Exposed at low tide, the vast mudflats around this monolith provide a smorgasbord of tiny crustacean snacks for 250 species of shorebird. Outstanding variety and quantity of wildlife combine with the recreational possibilities of dunes and surf to make this area a hit with vacationing Californians. Fine camping opportunities abound at Morro Bay State Park, the site of protected heron rookeries high in eucalyptus groves where the stately birds nest for half the year beginning in January.

The Pismo Clam

The prized Pismo clam finds a devoted following in Morro Bay vacationers. An entire culture devoted to clamming in the sand at low tide emphasizes proper digging technique and proper clam fork usage and engages in lively debate over the virtues of steaming vs. grilling the harvested shellfish. Wily veterans will gladly give advice upon any aspect of clamming if approached, but all that you really need to know is that the obliging Pismo clam spends most of its time burrowing less than six inches into the sand. Licenses for clamming are required and are available at every roadside attraction. Areas of state beaches, where clamming is off limits, are all clearly marked.

SAN LUIS OBISPO

An eclectic blend of frontier ranching, intensive agriculture, Spanish mission memories and Victorian vernacular, this often overlooked community nestles against the Santa Lucia Mountains ten miles from the ocean. San Luis Obispo is another coastal town that owes its existence to the industrious Father Serra, who established his fifth outpost of Christian civilization here among the Chumash people in 1772. One of the richest missions in the California chain, Mission San Luis Obispo boasted thousands of head of cattle, huge wheat harvests and eight sheep farms on and around its fertile fields. Twenty-five years later, Serra's successor established the chain's sixteenth mission, Mission San Miguel Arcángel, to the northeast. The two Franciscan compounds are nicely preserved examples of the world of the fathers and their ranching abilities, an expertise continued today in the best tradition of hell-for-leather land grant cattlemen.

Almost 100 years ago, the state of California established a technical college in the rambling ranch lands once cultivated by Spanish settlers. Nowadays, San Luis Obispo maintains its lively pulse thanks to the presence of California State Polytechnic College (affectionately known as Cal Poly) and the posthippie baby boomers, who have settled in and maintained the area's considerable appeal. San Luis also enjoys its share of well-preserved adobes and historical buildings. Clustered together in the heart of the tiny downtown are the mission and its grassy plaza, the two-story Sauer-Adams Adobe, the region's first Episcopal church built in 1867, and the circa 1874 Ah Louis Store — a reminder of the strong Chinese presence during the railroad-building period.

SOUTHERN BEACH TOWNS & DUNES

Tiny secluded coves and bluffs covered with Day-Glo-hued ice plant and coreopsis merge southward into small communities at Avila Beach, Pismo Beach and Grover Beach. Several piers providing top fishing vantage points extend out into the curve of San Luis Obispo Bay. At Avila Beach — one of the prettiest beaches imaginable in what seems like an endless procession of the prettiest beaches imaginable — the sybaritic pleasures of mineral springs bathing can be added to your list of required play.

One giant, fifteen-mile-long recreation area, the town, beaches and sand dunes of Pismo (named for the mighty clam), seem to exist only for life in the great outdoors. Beach rentals and mobile homes cluster together to form the heart of the town of Pismo Beach, an appropriately ramshackle assortment of lodgings and conveniences saved from the mundane by an outstanding stretch of sand dunes.

Increasingly, the peace over the dunes, comprising the Nipomo Dunes Preserve south of Pismo Beach, is shattered by the raucous sounds of dune buggies, those unlovable all-terrain vehicles with huge tires that usually turn up just over the next sand dune, where you least expect or want them.

THE SANTA YNEZ VALLEY

Turning right abruptly at Point Conception, the Central Coast heads into the Santa Ynez Mountains at the town of Lompoc, a sprawling land grant rancho whose latter-day growing fields produce more flower seed than anywhere else in the world. During the summer and autumn, when the brilliantly patterned fields blaze with near-neon color, it's easy to believe that this town produces almost half of the United States' annual flower crop.

Continuing on, Hans Christian Andersen would feel right at home in Solvang, a little taste of Denmark located ten miles from the coast in the prime dairy country of the Santa Ynez Valley. Settled by Danes attracted to pasturelands that mimicked the Old Country, Solvang defined itself with the establishment of Atterdag College in 1911. This began the perpetuation of Danish folk customs, architecture and language that make the town a small, commercial Scandinavian theme park. Though it boasts its own restored Spanish mission and museum — Mission Santa Inés, founded in 1804 as the nineteenth in the Franciscan chain — Solvang draws the lion's share of its visitors with the allure of half-timbered shops, picturesque old-world windmills, thatched roofs and cobblestone streets.

Solvang is also the gateway to several dozen wineries tucked into the transverse hillsides and valleys of the Santa Ynez Mountains. Here the temperate climate produced by sea breezes and coastal fog conspires to yield distinctive handmade wines rapidly attracting the attention of international connoisseurs.

CHAPTER TWO
The Freeway & The Right Way
TRANSPORTATION

Since this region cries out to be seen up close, most visitors spend some time touring the Pacific Coast Highway before settling into their destinations. Not surprisingly, Highway 1 is the ultimate visual thoroughfare, claiming some of the most enjoyable stretches of blacktop anywhere, and the coastal mountains are laced with connecting scenic highways, many following the routes of original stagecoach circuits.

Shmuel Thaler

Chaparral-covered mountains run along the entire Central Coast.

Highway 1 is easily connected to California's primary north/south freeway system and its two main arteries: Highway 101, which follows the El Camino Real — the eighteenth-century "King's Highway" laid down by Franciscan fathers and their military protectors, and Interstate 5. Train buffs can soak up most of the Pacific coastline's spectacular scenery by taking Amtrak to major Central Coast destinations.

Scoring a perfect ten on the boring meter, Interstate 5 is far and away the fastest way to get up and down the length of the state. It's also the main route used by truckers, recreational vehicles and lead-foot commuters. Straight, fast and unencumbered by scenic vistas, this highway is considered dangerous by many locals who've fallen asleep at the wheel during long, monotonous journeys.

Running much closer to the coast, Highway 101 adds a few curves to slow down the traffic and throws in ample scenery, as well as opportunities for food and lodging along the way. Highway 101 fuses with Coast Highway 1 for the short jaunt between San Luis Obispo and Pismo State Beach and again for a longer coastal stretch between Goleta and Oxnard, just south of Santa Barbara.

For those who come to feast their eyes on the incomparable scenery of the

Central Coast, there is only one road. However tortuous the turns, steep the cliffs or slow the traffic during summer weekends, Highway 1 is the most beautiful road in the world. It certainly reigns supreme in California. Often it's a snug fit just to find room enough for two cars to pass each other safely in narrow corridors tunneled out of solid rock. This isn't the route for those in a hurry, but it is the royal road of coastal panoramas.

GETTING TO THE CENTRAL COAST

BY CAR

Unless you're entering the state from due north or due south, all roads to the Central Coast lead west. Out-of-state visitors immediately will encounter the major topographical features of this 1,000-mile-long edge of the United States — the formidable Sierra Nevada Mountains, the broad, flat Central Valley (known as San Juaquin in the north, Imperial in the south) and the slender but persistent uplift of the Coast Ranges. One way or another, all major Interstate highways entering California to the coast will take you over these natural landmarks.

Entering the state from Arizona, motorists manage to miss the high Sierra passes by following Interstate 10 through the Mojave Desert to Los Angeles and by hooking up there with the Coast Highway for all points north. Travelers from Las Vegas will find Interstate 15 the fastest route to the middle-of-nowhere crossroads of Barstow. From that dusty way station, Highway 58 heads through the tail end of the Sierras over the 4,000-foot Tehachapi Summit to connect with Interstate 5.

Visitors driving to the coast from northern Nevada and Idaho will find Interstate 80 a fabulous passage through the Sierras. It travels through the infamous Donner Pass (7,227 feet) before dropping to Sacramento and the San Francisco Bay Area. All of these east-west highways are fast, multilane, state-of-the-art thoroughfares. All hook up with the mighty Interstate 5, the widest and fastest, if the plainest, of them all. For all of its shortcomings, Interstate 5, which begins at the Canadian border and blazes all the way down to Mexico, provides driving convenience in a straight north/west shot through the center of California. From here, visitors can negotiate the coastal pass of their choice to arrive at seaside destinations from Half Moon Bay all the way down to Santa Barbara.

FROM SAN FRANCISCO

It is tempting to approach Santa Cruz and parts south from San Francisco via the corkscrew turns and sweeping vistas of Highway 1. But that would be the furthest thing possible from a shortcut. A better idea — one utilized morning and evening by Central Coast commuters — is to take Highway 280 south from San Francisco (always referred to as "The City" by locals) and then cut across the coast ranges via Highway 92, connecting with Highway 1 at Half Moon Bay. A more circuitous route, but one rife with primeval redwood glens and fern canyons, is La Honda Road, which exits Highway 280 farther south and connects eventually with the Coast Highway at Pescadero.

FROM SAN JOSE

Many roads — some over scenic mountain passes, all of them extremely rural — lead from San Jose and the broad Santa Clara Valley south of San Francisco into various portions of Monterey county. One pastoral stretch of Highway 101 skips through Morgan Hill and Gilroy, before cutting across cultivated acres of artichokes, strawberries and lettuce at Highway 156 to join the ocean at Moss Landing.

From San Jose, Highway 17 (a daredevil's dream that offers twenty-three miles of nonstop twists and turns) traverses the Santa Cruz Mountains to connect with Highway 1 at Santa Cruz, affording fine views of Loma Prieta Mountain, which lent its name to the 1989 earthquake, and the Monterey Bay. The quickest way into the heart of California's nineteenth-century ranching country is Highway 101, which leads south 100 miles from San Francisco to King City and beyond. By turning west on rustic Nacimiento Road, adventurous drivers can literally tack the ridges and canyons of the Santa Lucia Mountains, winding through classic cattle country and groves of superb Spanish oaks all the way to the southern Big Sur coast. Though slow, challenging going, this gorgeous back road is well worth the extra time.

FROM LOS ANGELES

The place where freeways were born, Los Angeles is a driver's dream, or worst nightmare, depending on your mood and blood sugar level. It is possible, however, to locate the threads through this labyrinth and to get to the coast. One obvious route is to head toward the ocean until you find Highway 1 at Santa Monica and then to work your way up to the Central Coast. Another possibility is to take the queen of gridlock, Highway 405, until it bumps into Highway 101 northwest of the metropolitan area; Highway 101 connects with Highway 1 at Ventura. Then you're on your way to the good stuff on the Central Coast.

Bad Road Conditions Hot Line

Travelers can call **CalTrans Information Network** (800/427-7623) for recorded details of adverse highway conditions, updated as they change. Don't call for anything else, no humans are around.

CENTRAL COAST ACCESS

Miles and approximate driving times
from the following cities to Santa Cruz:

City	Miles	Hours
Albuquerque	1,090	22:00
Big Sur	75	1:30
Denver	1,380	28:00
Fresno	210	4:15
Half Moon Bay	60	1:15
Las Vegas	580	12:00
Los Angeles	385	8:00
Monterey	45	1:00
Phoenix	770	15:15
Portland	750	14:15
Reno	315	6:30
Sacramento	175	3:45
Salt Lake City	835	16:45
San Diego	500	10:15
San Francisco	80	1:45
San Jose	35	0:45
San Luis Obispo	180	4:00
Seattle	915	17:30

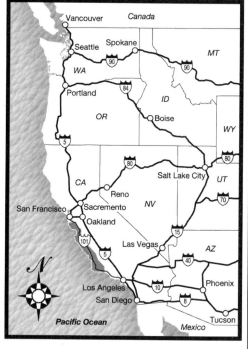

Miles and approximate driving times
from the following cities to Monterey:

City	Miles	Hours
Albuquerque	1,045	21:00
Big Sur	105	2:15
Denver	1,425	29:00
Fresno	165	3:15
Half Moon Bay	100	2:00
Las Vegas	530	11:00
Los Angeles	340	7:00
Phoenix	725	14:15
Portland	795	15:15
Reno	360	7:30
Sacramento	220	4:30
Salt Lake City	880	17:45
San Diego	455	9:15
San Francisco	125	2:45
San Jose	80	1:45
San Luis Obispo	135	3:00
Santa Cruz	45	1:00
Seattle	960	18:30

CENTRAL COAST ACCESS

Miles and approximate driving times
from the following cities to San Luis Obispo:

City	Miles	Hours
Albuquerque	1,010	20:00
Big Sur	105	2:30
Denver	1,185	23:00
Fresno	120	2:30
Half Moon Bay	240	5:00
Las Vegas	425	8:30
Los Angeles	200	4:00
Monterey	135	3:15
Phoenix	590	11:15
Portland	930	18:15
Reno	495	10:30
Sacramento	360	7:45
Salt Lake City	1,020	20:45
San Diego	320	6:15
San Francisco	260	5:45
San Jose	215	5:00
Santa Cruz	180	4:15
Seattle	1,095	21:30

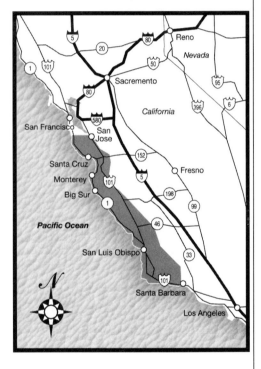

Miles and approximate driving
times from the following cities to
Santa Ynez:

City	Miles	Hours
Albuquerque	872	16:50
Big Sur	172	3:50
Denver	1,122	21:50
Fresno	212	4:20
Half Moon Bay	307	6:20
Las Vegas	352	6:50
Los Angeles	57	1:20
Monterey	212	4:35
Phoenix	442	8:35
Portland	1,002	19:35
Reno	562	11:50
Sacramento	467	9:20
Salt Lake City	782	15:20
San Diego	82	1:35
San Francisco	332	7:05
San Jose	282	6:20
Santa Cruz	252	5:35
Seattle	1,162	23:05

BY BUS

Any out-of-state or interstate bus traveler headed for the Central Coast must pass through either of two major hubs, Los Angeles or San Francisco, and connect to buses headed for their destinations. Here are the surest, fastest and most scenic options available.

Greyhound's 614 departs San Francisco three times daily for Santa Cruz (mid-1993 prices were $10.55 one way/$19.10 round-trip) and Monterey ($14/$27.50), stopping at San Francisco Airport en route. From Monterey on the coast, buses veer inland to Salinas, another major hub. The 618 leaves San Francisco five times daily on its inland Los Angeles run, reaching San Luis Obispo ($25.50/$50.50) on the coast at midjourney.

From Los Angeles, Greyhound schedules ten buses daily on its San Francisco 618 route that stops at San Luis Obispo ($21.50/$42.50) before heading inland.

Call Greyhound's San Francisco depot (415/495-1575) or Los Angeles station (213/629-8400) for exact departure and arrival times.

Peerless Stages travels between San Jose Airport and Santa Cruz four times daily ($4.30/$8.20). Call Santa Cruz Peerless (831/423-0769) for exact departure and arrival times.

BY PLANE

Although most travelers will make their way to the Central Coast by car, a good portion will arrive via plane. Listed below are the state's major international airports and the regional fields that have connecting express flights to the primary hubs, as well as the airlines that serve the hubs. You might also call your local FAA flight service station for up-to-the-hour weather information regarding your destination.

Los Angeles International Airport (310/646-5252) All major airlines fly into LAX.

Monterey Peninsula Airport (831/648-7000) American Eagle, Skywest, United, United Express, USAir.

Oakland International Airport (510/577-4000) Alaska, American, America West, Delta, Mexicana, Morris Air, Northwest, Southwest, TWA, United.

San Francisco International Airport (415/876-2100) All major airlines fly into SFO.

San Jose International Airport (831/277-5366) Alaska, American, America West, Continental, Delta, Mexicana, Northwest, Skywest, Southwest, TWA, United, United Express.

San Luis Obispo County Airport (805/781-5205) American Eagle; Skywest, United Express.

Santa Barbara Municipal Airport (805/967-7111) American, Skywest, United, United Express, USAir Express.

BY RAIL

A mtrak's (800/USA-RAIL) Oakland to Los Angeles **Coast Starlight** makes a daily run up and down the California coast with stops in Monterey and San Luis Obispo. For the ultimate in armchair travel, the train can't be beat. The scenery that travelers can enjoy from the Starlight's windows, however, is priceless: crashing surf, smooth beaches, wetlands and sloughs, as well as rugged mountain peaks and canyons, glide by while you relax. The track hugs the edge of the land most of the way between Monterey county and the Santa Ynez Valley, offering glimpses of hard-to-get-to pristine coastal stretches. Between Monterey and the Santa Ynez Valley, the train threads its way through artichoke fields and lagoons and provides eye-popping vistas of Morro Rock and its neighboring volcanic peaks as it starts down the San Luis Obispo side of Cuesta Pass. Travelers stopping in the city of San Luis Obispo can connect at the station by bus for tours of the stately Hearst Castle. Continuing south, the train follows the inside curve of the sand dunes, stretching between Pismo Beach and the Santa Ynez Valley.

GETTING AROUND THE CENTRAL COAST

BY CAR

H ighway 1 is the majestic lifeline caressing the Central Coast and connecting all points surveyed in this book. Stretching the length of California, it links the major cities of San Diego, Los Angeles and San Francisco and feeds into the freeways of the interior via scenic mountain back roads.

Automobile Club Hot Lines

Members can call these 24-hour emergency telephone numbers for immediate road service and assistance: **AAA-California State Automobile Association** (800/400-4222); **National Automobile Club** (800/622-2130).

BY RENTAL CAR

A lthough car culture originated elsewhere, it hit its stride in California. Gifted with pliant, scenic highways, the Central Coast offers plenty of wheels-to-rent options, some corporate, some decidedly independent. Here are listings of the top reliable agencies in the region.

Avis Rent-A-Car (800/831-2847).
Budget Rent-A-Car (800/527-0700).
Dollar Rent-A-Car (800/800-4000).
Enterprise Rent-A-Car (800/325-8007).
Hertz Rent-A-Car (800/654-3131).
National Car Rental (800/227-7368).
Sears Rent-A-Car (800/527-0700).
Thrifty Car Rental (800/367-2277).
USA Rent-A-Car (800/325-8007).
U-Save Auto Rental (800/394-1862).

CHAPTER THREE
The Eden at World's End ·
SANTA CRUZ

Bob Hill

Time flies when you're having fun in Santa Cruz, long recognized as the playground of the Central Coast.

Crisscrossed by the infamous San Andreas Fault, Santa Cruz has enjoyed its occasional date with destiny since the mid-1700s when Spanish conquistadors and padres marched up from Mexico to see what riches New Spain might hold. Redwood forests that had stood since the pre-Christian era, splendid seashores teeming with marine life and tide pools and a climate straight from the Mediterranean greeted the newcomers.

Between the establishment of a mission and a military garrison, the tiny community of Holy Cross (Santa Cruz) was off to a rousing start, even before Yankee captains of industry arrived in the early 1800s to take advantage of the natural riches — and, naturally, to get rich themselves. Those who might have passed through the area on their way to the Gold Rush, ended up staying to romance the incomparable scenery. Once the Golden Spike was driven in Utah in 1869, linking railroads across the continent, settlers rushed to Santa Cruz county from all over the country.

Glowing magazine accounts touted the glories of taking the saltwater and — thanks to entrepreneur Fred Swanton — a fabulous Brighton-style resort casino, dance palace and amusement park sprang up at the water's edge near the turn of the century.

Even today, Santa Cruzans are justly famed for, and proud of, their recreational opportunities. Surfing rules along the superb coastline, where world-class surfers come to test the heaving winter waves or to cruise the long, slow summer swells. It was at Steamer Lane, just north of the Santa Cruz Municipal Wharf that two Hawaiian princes caught a few waves in the late 1880s and began a craze for this potentially dangerous sport. Surfing still attracts youthful adventurers from far and near — sometimes from as near as the University of California, Santa Cruz, which established its ninth campus here thirty years ago.

Like all university towns, Santa Cruz prides itself on more than its fair share of diversity. Multiculturism plays itself out in a continuous world beat of music, fashion and food, while the UCSC campus inflects the sophisticated accents and tastes of the small community, and the famed Cabrillo Music Festival and Shakespeare/Santa Cruz conclave draws globe-trotting culturati to the area every summer.

The redwood communities up in the mountains, overlooking the magnificent Monterey Bay, have long attracted artists, writers, composers and movie stars. Alfred Hitchcock summered here, Spencer Tracy played polo on the hillside below the present-day university and composer Lou Harrison works his musical magic from a studio south of town. Glassblowers, ceramists, filmmakers and computer animators all have found out that they can enjoy creative freedom — yet still have access to a far-flung market — from this little spot of Eden.

Today the seaside blooms during the summer and fall with holiday travelers anxious to unwind on the series of clean, white beaches and to try out their sense of adventure on the oldest wooden roller coaster in the world. The proximity to Silicon Valley has made the area a bedroom community and recreational outlet for new millionaires. Yet, it's the quiet cliffs that gather into gold at sunset, the primeval silence of the magnificent old redwoods and the small-time camaraderie that casts the most enduring spell.

Santa Cruz is infused by a laid-back sense of play. Nothing is taken too seriously with weather this good. It's an idyllic setting for sipping one of the many fine locally made wines — the Santa Cruz Mountains appellation creates a variety of award-winning Chardonnays, Merlots and Zinfandels — while sampling some of the fresh seafood caught from the bay — the local halibut and salmon have no peer.

Bussed by morning fog in the summer, as well as some serious rains in the winter, Santa Cruz bathes its visitors and residents alike in that famous Mediterranean sunshine seven months of the year.

The only caveat about this Central Coast community just seventy miles

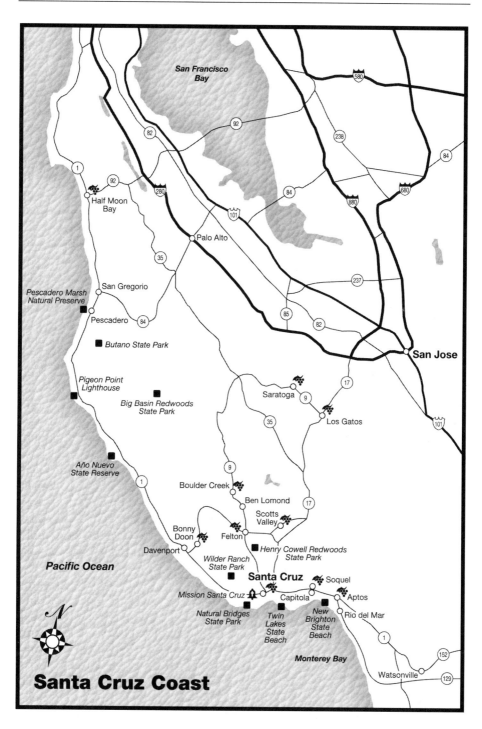

Santa Cruz Coast

south of San Francisco — it's very, very difficult to leave. Just ask any local. Chances are that they are among the huge transplant community who just passed through town . . . and never left.

LODGING

No visit to this seaside playground would be complete without an overnight near the beach, where accommodations present panoramic views of the blue Pacific and the sensation of waves ushering you into the soundest night's sleep. Along the shore and in the redwood forests are many carefully appointed B&Bs that also offer an eclectic blend of architectural styles.

Credit Cards

AE – American Express
CB – Carte Blanche
D – Discover Card

DC – Diner's Club
MC – MasterCard
V – Visa

SANTA CRUZ COAST

Half Moon Bay

CYPRESS INN ON MIRAMAR BEACH
Innkeepers: Suzie Lankes & Dan Floyd.
800/83-BEACH; 650/726-6002; 650/712-0380 Fax; lodging@cypressinn.com E-mail; www.cypressinn.com Web site.
407 Mirada Rd., Half Moon Bay, CA 94019.
Price: $165-$275, includes breakfast.
Credit Cards: AE, D, MC, V.
Children: No.
Smoking: No.
Handicap Access: Yes.

Romantic, relaxing and nestled on the sprawling sands of the Pacific Ocean shore, this converted beach house located two miles up the coast from downtown Half Moon Bay offers plush comfort and attentive service in a beautiful setting. Eight rooms in the main building and four elaborate suites in the newly constructed back beach house are all decorated in a warm Southwestern motif with muted colors, wicker furniture and native art. All rooms boast fireplaces, private patios and quite possibly the world's most decadent feather beds, and a few rooms come complete with in-room Jacuzzis. The innkeepers keep a roaring fire going and offer a constant flow of coffees, teas and hot chocolate in the main room throughout the day. A spread of wine, sparkling cider and hors d'oeuvres appear at sunset and indulgent homemade desserts and coffee at night. A full breakfast can be taken in the dining area or in your room, where you can savor the sight, smell and sound of the rolling ocean while you dine.

The innkeepers are more than happy to recommend sight-seeing excursions and to make restaurant reservations.

HARBOR HOUSE
Innkeeper: Chris
  Mickelson.
650/728-1572; 650/728-
  8271 Fax; www.harbor
  housebandb.com Web
  site.
346 Princeton Ave., Half
  Moon Bay, CA 94019.
Price: $125-$250.
Credit Cards: MC, V.
Children: No.
Smoking: No.
Handicap Access: One
  room.

Harbor House is located on the northern end of Pillar Point with a beautiful on-the-water view of the harbor and Half Moon Bay. Though only a little over a year old and architecturally modern on the exterior, all six rooms are simplistically elegant in decor. The comfortable, spacious and secluded rooms boast both quiet and privacy. The only sounds that one hears are the lapping of calm waves, the seabirds' calls and the intermittent foghorn in the distance. Each of the rooms has a queen-sized bed with down comforter, private bathroom, a gas fireplace for foggy northern California evenings, TV, coffeemaker, pastries in the morning and an assortment of fruit and juices. A stroll from the B&B's door leads you through a sleepy fishing community, dramatic coastal hills and nearby beaches.

Stan Cacitti

Half Moon Bay's popular Mill Rose Inn is graced by abundant gardens and secluded patios.

MILL ROSE INN
Innkeepers: Eve & Terry
  Baldwin.

Sheer indulgence in a vibrant garden setting is the motif of this wonderful retreat, which features

800/829-7673; 650/726-8750; 650/726-3031 Fax; millroseinn@email.msn. com E-mail; www.millrose inn.com Web site. 615 Mill St., Half Moon Bay, CA 94019.
Price: $165-$275, includes breakfast.
Credit Cards: AE, D, MC, V.
Children: Over 12 only.
Smoking: Outside only.
Handicap Access: Limited.

four rooms and two suites with TV/VCR, well-stocked refrigerators and amenities like liqueurs, fruit basket, coffeemaker and hair dryer. Five of the rooms boast fireplaces, and all are decorated with Victorian and Arts and Crafts antiques, as well as down comforters and brass beds. All rooms have private entrances, and the front garden pays colorful tribute to the horticultural expertise of the innkeepers, who've filled this blooming sanctuary with hundreds of varieties of fragrant roses, poppies, irises, delphiniums and lilies. A back garden showcases yet more flowers, an inviting brick patio and a gazebo outfitted with a whirlpool spa. A Champagne breakfast can be brought to your room, or you can indulge in multicourse morning offerings, including hot chocolate, fresh fruit drinks, soufflés and hot dishes. Wine and light appetizers are provided at sundown. The historic village of Half Moon Bay, in which the inn is set, offers fine dining and shopping possibilities, plus splendid coastal scenery and beaches a short drive away.

OLD THYME INN
Innkeepers: George & Marcia Dempsey.
650/726-1616; 650/726-6394 Fax; oldthyme@coast side.net E-mail; www. oldthymeinn.com Web site.
779 Main St., Half Moon Bay, CA 94019.
Price: $115-$170, includes breakfast.
Credit Cards: AE, MC, V.
Children: Allowed with limits.
Smoking: No.
Handicap Access: No.

The innkeepers at this restored 1899 Queen Anne Victorian have infused their California village establishment with old-world hospitality and a sweet-scented garden, whose eighty varieties of herbs invariably end up perfuming teas and freshly made dishes at the inn's full complimentary breakfast. All seven rooms are decorated and wallpapered in turn-of-the-century style and offer private baths. Three rooms have fireplaces, and three boast whirlpool tubs big enough for two. One detached suite ($165 weekdays, $220 weekends) has its own private garden entrance and is equipped for a romantic stay with fireplace, oversized whirlpool tub, TV/VCR and plush four-poster canopy bed. Evening Champagne, wine and sherry are all the more relaxing taken in front of the main room's blazing fireplace. The innkeepers are happy to provide local sight-seeing tips and restaurant recommendations.

San Gregorio

RANCHO SAN GREGORIO
Innkeepers: Bud & Lee Raynor.

A secluded California Mission-style coastal retreat, the inn is set on fifteen acres of rolling ranch land affording fine views of the surrounding redwood forests and lush farmlands just a few

650/747-0810; 650/747-0184 Fax; rsgleebud@aol.com E-mail; www.cruznet.com/`prankstr/rancho/home.html Web site.
Rte. 1, Box 54, 5086 San Gregorio Rd., San Gregorio, CA 94074.
Price: $80-$135, includes breakfast.
Credit Cards: AE, D, MC, V.
Children: Yes.
Smoking: Outside only.
Handicap Access: No.

miles from San Gregorio Beach. The graceful home is adorned with terra-cotta tile floors and an antique-laden courtyard. Each of the five guest rooms is distinctively decorated and has its own bathroom accommodations and private porch. Three rooms provide the charm of wood-burning stoves. In addition to old-fashioned country games like badminton, horseshoes and croquet, as well as a creekside picnic area, the Rancho offers a fine full country breakfast highlighted by home-baked breads, muffins and fresh fruit specialties. This is a charming, well-kept secret hideaway offering easy access to the dramatic cliffs, beaches and coastal mountain scenery between Half Moon Bay and Santa Cruz.

Pescadero

OLD SAW MILL LODGE
Innkeepers: Tom & Annie Hines.
800/596-6455; 650/879-0111.
700 Ranch Rd. W., Pescadero, CA 94060.
Price: $100-$200, includes full breakfast.
Credit Cards: MC, V.
Children: Allowed with limits.
Smoking: Outside only.
Handicap Access: Yes.

Nestled in the northernmost mountain range of the Santa Cruz Mountains and high on top of a ridge above the town, this retreat sports ocean and canyon views. Named for its location next to a sawmill, which was operational until the mid-1900s, the inn's rooms are named after logging crew members. Each comfortable room is decorated in rich jewel tones, appealing to those less than enamored with frilly lace and pastels. Do laps in the pool, hike the many surrounding trails or unwind in the spa or next to the massive rock fireplace. The inn serves a hearty breakfast prepared by its own professional chef. Sandy beaches, the Año Nuevo State Elephant Seal Reserve and many county and state parks surrounding Old Saw Mill Lodge make for tempting daytime excursions, but make sure to get back in time for the inn's beautiful sunset vantage point.

Davenport

NEW DAVENPORT BED & BREAKFAST INN
Innkeepers: Bruce & Marcia McDougal.
831/425-1818; 831/426-4122; 831/423-1160 Fax; inn@swanton.com

At the heart of this picturesque village, a former whaling port just north of Santa Cruz, is the eclectic new Davenport Cash Store, a tile-floored, high-ceilinged restaurant, plus a fine international and local arts emporium that also offers fine B&B facilities. The twelve rooms with private baths

E-mail; www.swanton.
    com/BnB Web site.
Box J, 31 Davenport Ave.,
    Davenport, CA 95017.
Price: $75-$105, includes
    breakfast and two
    complimentary drinks
    from the full bar.
Credit Cards: MC, V.
Children: Allowed in
    family rooms.
Smoking: Outside only.
Handicap Access: Yes.

occupy two distinctive locations, one a charming, former turn-of-the-century bathhouse attractively appointed with antiques, the other offering bracing ocean vistas on the floor above the Cash Store. The upstairs rooms have been decorated with ethnic treasures gathered from the global travels of artist/owners Bruce and Marcia McDougal, and the wraparound porch provides prime viewing of the migrating gray whales who cruise just offshore from Jan.-May. A bountiful Continental breakfast features delectable pastries from the Cash Store's bakery. The downstairs restaurant's sensuous breakfasts are the stuff of local legend. Cove beaches beckon just across Hwy. 1.

Santa Cruz

The Babbling Brook B&B Inn in Santa Cruz is noted for its spectacular grounds and plush accommodations.

Buz Bezore

**BABBLING BROOK BED
    & BREAKFAST INN**
Innkeepers: Suzie Lankes &
    Dan Floyd.
800/866-1131; 831/427-
    2437; 831/427-2457 Fax;
    lodging@bablingbrookinn
    .com E-mail; www.
    babblingbrookinn.com
    Web site.
1025 Laurel St., Santa Cruz,
    CA 95060.
Price: $145-$195, includes
    breakfast.

A great getaway boasting a central location snuggled in between residential and downtown Santa Cruz, the Babbling Brook is charm itself. Innkeepers Suzie Lankes and Dan Floyd have made each of the fourteen temptingly decorated rooms a secluded oasis. The guest rooms are clustered around a central, multilevel cedar building whose stone foundation dates from the late eighteenth century when the property was a gristmill. The soft sounds of the creek that flows through the property's lovely gardens serenade

Credit Cards: AE, D, DC, MC, V.
Children: Allowed with limits.
Smoking: Outside only.
Handicap Access: Yes.

each room, and the Honeymoon Suite's private deck even overlooks a waterfall. All rooms, with many offering private decks, have fireplaces, private baths, telephones and TVs and are decorated in a French country theme. The new Artist's Retreat at the highest point of the inn provides a full view of the garden and brook, plus a large deck and recessed hot tub. An elegant full breakfast is served in the charming living room, and a blazing, sitting room fireplace forms the centerpiece of afternoon wine tastings. The gardens and the white gazebo are a favorite wedding site.

Buz Bezore

The view from the Casablanca Inn overlooks Santa Cruz's main beach, pier and nearby Boardwalk.

CASABLANCA INN
Innkeepers: Glyn & Ray Luttrell.
831/423-1570;
831/423-0235 Fax.
Beach & Main Sts., Santa Cruz, CA 95060.
Price: $78-$195, no breakfast included.
Credit Cards: AE, DC, MC, V.
Children: Yes.
Smoking: Yes.
Handicap Access: Limited.

This red tile-roofed, former seaside retreat of a San Francisco judge (circa 1920) has long been one of Santa Cruz's most distinctive landmarks. Located just across the street from the Santa Cruz's popular main beach, the colorful boardwalk and the Cocoanut Grove Ballroom, the Casablanca offers bountiful ocean views and the soothing sounds of the waves to lull guests to sleep. Over the years, innkeepers Glyn and Ray Luttrell have combed antiques emporia for the attractive, unpretentious furnishings of each distinctive room. Some rooms retain the original bathroom tile work and fixtures, and spacious Room 22 sports a fireplace, four-poster bed and private terrace overlooking seacoast sites. The Luttrells purchased the rest of Judge Cerf's estate in 1997, giving the inn six more suites in the original ballroom, carriage house and servants' quarters. Essentially a small hotel ringed with a satellite of attractive motel units, the multilevel, Mediterranean-style main building hangs on the hillside just above its own Casablanca Restaurant, long regarded as one of the best in town, where contemporary seafood specialties and California cuisine are freshly prepared with an eye to innovative seasonings and elegant presentation. The restaurant's astonishing wine list — the most extensive in the area — regularly wins *Wine Spectator* awards for comprehensiveness, and it's a great place to sample locally made vintages. The dining room is utterly romantic, offering unparalleled views of the waterfront and a justifiably popular Sunday brunch.

The Cliff Crest sits in Victorian splendor high atop Beach Hill in Santa Cruz.

Buz Bezore

CLIFF CREST BED & BREAKFAST INN
Innkeepers: Bruce & Sharon Taylor.
800/427-2609; 831/427-2609; 831/427-2710 Fax; innkpr@cliffcrestinn.com E-mail; www.cliffcrest inn.com Web site.
407 Cliff St., Santa Cruz, CA 95060.
Price: $95-$175, includes breakfast.
Credit Cards: AE, D, DC, MC, V.
Children: No.
Smoking: No.
Handicap Access: No.

The beautiful interiors of this lovely Queen Anne Victoriana — historic landmark home built by California's Lieutenant Governor William Jeter in 1890 — immediately cast a spell on visitors. Period details like Oriental rugs and antique furniture blend with the small mansion's abundant stained and beveled glass and intricate built-in woodwork. Only two blocks from Santa Cruz's main beach, each of the inn's five rooms offers a private bath, and two rooms sport fireplaces. The charming Pineapple Room is named for its queen-sized four-poster bed, whose bedposts feature an artfully carved pineapple design. The spacious Empire Room offers eighteenth-century ambiance with twelve-foot ceilings, king-sized canopy bed, double armoire and a soothing view of the garden through lace-covered windows. Most guests are further charmed by the lush estate gardens, created by John McLaren, the man who designed San Francisco's Golden Gate Park. At sunset, regional wines and cheeses are offered in the antique-filled parlor. Breakfast in the garden solarium involves multiple courses that can include fresh juices and fruits, muffins, coffee cake, egg dishes, quiche, French toast, pancakes and sausage.

The Darling House on West Cliff Drive in Santa Cruz was designed by celebrated architect William Weeks.

Buz Bezore

DARLING HOUSE
Innkeepers: Darrell & Karen Darling.
800/458-1958; 831/458-1958; www.infopoint. com/sc/lodging/darling / Web site.
314 W. Cliff Dr., Santa Cruz, CA 95060.
Price: $95-$225, includes breakfast.
Credit Cards: AE, D, MC, V.
Children: Yes.
Smoking: Cottage only.
Handicap Access: Limited.

The beveled-glass windows and red-tiled roofs of this distinguished Mission Revival mansion overlook a spectacular view of the Santa Cruz coast, municipal wharf and Monterey Bay beyond. Built as a private home in 1910 by revered California architect William Weeks, this gorgeous home — graced with hardwood interior, Tiffany lamps and tile-decorated fireplace — is situated at the foot of Santa Cruz's scenic W. Cliff Dr. Each of its eight rooms (two with private baths) has been attractively appointed with period antiques by innkeepers Darrell and Karen Darling, who preside over hearty Continental breakfasts each morning in the ornate dining and sitting rooms. Sherry is served in the late afternoons, and savvy guests quickly learn that the expansive, ocean-view verandah is the top spot to take in the sights of sailboats and surfers dotting the sunsets. Each overnight room is appealing, but especially noteworthy is the large second-floor chamber overlooking the ocean, offering its own fireplace and a resident telescope for viewing the abundant marine life of the Monterey Bay. One of the shared bathrooms boasts an enormous, claw-foot, vintage "bordello" tub, great for extended soaking for two. A small cottage nestling in the mansion's back gardens sleeps four, and an outdoor hot tub spa offers a pampering soak after a day on the beach.

INN AT LAGUNA CREEK
Innkeepers: Jim & Gay Holley.
800/730-5398; 831/425-0692; 831/426-9331 Fax; www.infopoint.com/sc/lodgings/laguna-creek Web site.
2727 Smith Grade, Santa Cruz, CA 95060.
Price: $95–$210, includes breakfast.
Credit Cards: AE, D, MC, V.
Children: Two people per room.
Smoking: No.
Handicap Access: No.

Designed as a family residence back in the mid-1970s, this B&B is a perfect getaway. Secluded, private and nestled deep in a redwood forest, the Inn at Laguna Creek has only two guest rooms. Large and comfy — one decorated in a country motif, the other in a rosy English pattern — each room is complete with queen-sized bed, down comforters, private bath and deck. The extensive book and video library makes the inn a home away from home. The idyllic nature setting is only a skip away from wine tasting, hiking and beachcombing, or you can just soak in the sun and the solitude on one of the inn's redwood decks. The pampering continues with a full country breakfast and round-the-clock teas, cookies and fresh fruit. The rooms also are available as a two-room suite.

Capitola

INN AT DEPOT HILL
Innkeepers: Suzie Lankes & Dan Floyd.
800/572-2632; 831/462-3376; 831/462-3697 Fax; lodging@innatdepothill.com E-mail; www.innatdepothill.com Web site.
P.O. Box 1934, 250 Monterey Ave., Capitola, CA 95010.
Price: $190-$275, includes breakfast.
Credit Cards: AE, D, MC, V.
Children: No.
Smoking: Outside only.
Handicap Access: Yes.

Crowning a knoll within a few minutes' stroll of the sparkling beach and downtown Capitola Village, this stalwart 1901 railway station has been lavishly transformed into a spiffy B&B. In keeping with the architectural features of this former depot, the elegant appointments showcase an Orient Express-style theme. Each room bears the name of a glamorous destination and appropriately sophisticated appointments by a San Francisco interior decorator. The rooms are shamelessly sybaritic, like the sophisticated Paris Suite, whose black-and-white marble bathroom features a spacious two-person shower and French doors leading to the outdoor garden. The sky blue Delft Room offers a sumptuous feather bed draped in linen and lace, plus a sitting room and Jacuzzi tub for two in its private garden. The Railroad Baron's Room — ablaze with deep red velvet upholstery, damask wall treatment and a dramatic domed ceiling — recreates the feel of a Victorian Pullman coach and provides its own enormous soaking tub under a skylight that opens to the stars. In sunny weather, breakfast is taken on an outdoor brick patio whose sheltering shrubbery walls and musical fountain create the illusion of being in a Mediterranean villa, rather than two blocks from one of the area's most popular playgrounds. At the end of the day, guests are treated to a selection of fine wines and hors d'oeuvres laid out on a marble sideboard in the beautiful public rooms, which are filled with antique furniture, a vintage baby grand piano and a wall of well-stocked bookshelves running to the very top of the sixteen-foot ceilings. A luscious dessert is served each evening with coffee. The skillful innkeepers and staff minister to your every need, and all twelve suites come with telephones, private baths, fireplaces, fresh flowers, TVs, VCRs, stereo systems, fax/modem connections, bathrobes and hair dryers. Off-street parking — always scarce in this bustling beach town — is included in the price of your room.

Aptos

BAYVIEW HOTEL BED & BREAKFAST INN
Innkeepers: Suzie Lankes & Dan Floyd.
800/422-9843; 831/688-8654; 831/688-5128 Fax; lodging@bayviewhotel. com E-mail; www.bay viewhotel.com Web site.
8041 Soquel Dr., Aptos, CA 95003.
Price: $90–$150, includes breakfast.
Credit Cards: AE, MC, V.
Children: Allowed with limits.
Smoking: Outside only.
Handicap Access: No.

Built as lodging in 1878 during the Santa Cruz Mountains logging boom, this three-story, eleven-room Victorian has been attractively renovated with lovely antiques and simple period furnishings that blend beautifully with its old-fashioned ten-foot ceilings. The stairway to seven second-floor guest rooms, all with private baths, including one two-room suite, ascends from a cozy guest parlor with fireplace. Four new rooms on the third floor are spacious and lavishly decorated, and two rooms boast fireplaces and two-person spa tubs. The Bayview is located near the bevy of small antique stores, shops and restaurants of tiny Aptos Village, just across Hwy. 1 from fine beaches. The natural splendor of the redwood Forest of Nisene Marks, with miles of hiking and equestrian trails, lies literally just outside the front door.

THE INN AT MANRESA BEACH
Innkeepers: Brian Denny & Susan Van Horn.
888/523-2244; 831/728-1000; 831/728-8294 Fax; the inn@indevelop ment.com E-mail; www. indevelop ment. com Web site.
1258 San Andreas Rd., Aptos, CA 95003.
Price: $110–$249.
Credit Cards: AE, D, MC, V.
Children: Yes.

This beautiful old mansion stands proudly among the rolling hills near Manresa Beach. The historic Thurwachter house, the first home built in Pajaro Valley back in 1867, was a favorite of famous photographer Ansel Adams. Now converted to an inn, it features nine spacious rooms, all with private baths, TVs, VCRs and fireplaces. Special treats like massage therapy and baby-sitting also are offered, and some rooms feature the added comfort of luxurious spa tubs. For those wishing to get active, this historic inn has croquet, two restored clay tennis courts and volleyball courts on its grounds. The mansion is located min-

Smoking: Outside only.
Handicap Access: Yes.

MANGELS HOUSE
Innkeepers: Jacqueline &
  Ron Fisher.
800/320-7401; 831/688-
  7982; www.innaccess.
  com/mangels Web site.
P.O. Box 301, 570 Aptos
  Creek Rd., Aptos, CA
  95003.
Price: $115-$150, includes
  breakfast.
Credit Cards: AE, MC, V.
Children: Over 12 only.
Smoking: Outside only.
Handicap Access: No.

utes from Nisene Marks State Park and its 10,000 acres of lush hikers' paradise.

Brothers-in-law (and California sugar kings) Claus Mangels and Claus Spreckles built this Italianate mansion in the 1880s as a summer home for their families. Today, English-born innkeeper Jackie Fisher and husband Ron have maintained the Victorian ambiance while equipping their six rooms with private baths and antique appointments (one has its own fireplace). The inn's four acres border the 10,000-acre redwood sanctuary of the Forest of Nisene Marks, an irresistible spot for leisurely walks or all-day hikes. Afternoon tea and sherry are available at all times in the spacious sitting room, which is highlighted by a fireplace and a grand piano. In the morning, a bountiful homemade breakfast complete with fresh fruit, an egg specialty, scones and pastries properly begins the day. Lovely English gardens exude pastoral seclusion, yet the inn is situated a few minutes' drive to many expansive beaches.

DINING

The educated palates of Santa Cruz's university residents and world-traveled artists have long demanded and consumed an astonishing variety of exotic cuisine in what otherwise appears to be a rustic resort community. Dining is as much an attraction as the fabled beaches and redwoods, so don't travel far without sampling the food at the following distinctive restaurants. Locally made goat cheeses, free-range poultry, seasonal game, roasted peppers and garden-fresh herbs highlight the culinary style now accepted at dining capitals the world over. But regional restaurants also showcase popular contemporary Italian menus, authentic Mexican recipes and the omnipresent influence of Asia, so much so that wild mushrooms, black beans, lemongrass, ginger and cilantro have become standards of the repertoire.

Dining Price Code

The price range below includes the cost of a single dinner that includes an appetizer, entrée, dessert and coffee. Cocktails, wine, beer, tax or gratuities are not included. *Note:* Smoking is not allowed in any restaurant or eatery in the state of California.

Inexpensive	Up to $10
Moderate	$10–$25
Expensive	$25–$40
Very Expensive	$40 or more

Credit Cards

AE – American Express	DC – Diner's Club
CB – Carte Blanche	MC – MasterCard
D – Discover Card	V – Visa

SANTA CRUZ COAST

Half Moon Bay

MEZZA LUNA
650/712-9223.
3048 Cabrillo Hwy., Half Moon Bay, CA 94019.
Open: Mon.–Sat., L 11:30 a.m.–3:00 p.m.; D 5:00 p.m.–10:30 p.m.
Price: Moderate.
Cuisine: Italian.
Serving: L, D.
Reservations: Recommended.
Credit Cards: MC, V.
Handicap Access: Yes.

A comfortable, raucous trattoria, Mezza Luna is a little slice of Italy located up the coast from downtown Half Moon Bay. Bustling, boisterous and complete with charming Italian waiters who've perfected the art of gracious service, it's an obvious local favorite. It offers an extensive array of fresh pastas, seafood and chicken and a wine list featuring both California wines and Italian varietals. The bruschetta is a classic, with slices of tomatoes and basil leaves smothering the crusty bread. The seafood linguine — a stewy combination of enormous mussels, clams, prawns and linguine — is a seafood lover's treat. Finish with a strong espresso and biscotti dipped in dark or white chocolate.

PASTA MOON
650/726-5125.
315 Main St., Half Moon Bay, CA 94019.
Open: Daily.
Price: Moderate.
Cuisine: California/ Mediterranean.
Serving: L, D.
Reservations: Recommended.
Credit Cards: AE, DC, MC, V.
Handicap Access: Yes.

Innovative and made-before-your-eyes pasta dishes are the signature of this smart, cafe-style eatery located at the end of Half Moon Bay's tiny, Main St. Service is accommodating and knowledgeable, and the tiny tables are located close enough together to allow plenty of menu comparisons with fellow diners, trattoria style. Creative salads involve intriguing herb blends and baby lettuces. Even the Caesar salad is first-rate. But the homemade sauces and sausages, ripe tomatoes and ethereal pastas that make up the main creations are truly stunning. An entrée cioppino, packed with shellfish, could feed three hungry adults. A selective wine list — long on bright, young Italians and vintage Californians — complements the sassy cuisine, and the art-lined ambiance is vibrant. Terrific value for the money.

SUSHI MAIN STREET
650/726-6336.
315 Main St., Half Moon
   Bay, CA 94019
Open: Mon.–Sat., L 11:30
   a.m.–2:30 p.m.; daily, D
   5:00 p.m.–9:00 p.m.
Price: Moderate.
Cuisine: Sushi.
Serving: L, D.
Reservations: For four or
   more.
Credit Cards: MC, V.
Handicap Access: Yes.

An elegantly ornate Japanese restaurant, Sushi Main Street pays as much attention to the details of its decor as it does to its food. With dark, gilded walls, comfortable tables and a low-sprawling sushi bar, this small restaurant presents an extensive roster of sushi and tempura. Creative rolls, such as the Hot Tuna Roll with tempura tuna, spicy sauce, avocado and daikon sprouts, and the sashimi and nigiri are expertly prepared. The menu also offers a delicious selection of soups like the warm seafood nabeyaki (scallops, mussels, shrimp, clams, snapper, mushrooms and udon). The staff is knowledgeable and accommodating.

Pescadero

The Duarte family has run its Pescadero restaurant on San Mateo's coast for over fifty years.

Robert Scheer

DUARTE'S TAVERN
650/879-0464.
202 Stage Rd., Pescadero,
   CA 94060.
Open: Daily.
Price: Inexpensive.
Cuisine: Classic Central
   Coast.
Serving: B, L, D.

A local legend for over fifty years, this dark wood roadhouse (and its classically Hollywood-Western bar) is very popular with locals who can't get enough of the flavorful house cuisine. There's an outstanding abalone sandwich and a bevy of intensely flavored soups highlighted by the legendary artichoke soup made from the ubiquitous agricultural staple that flourishes along this stretch

Reservations: Recommended for weekend lunch and dinner.
Credit Cards: AE, MC, V.
Handicap Access: Yes.

of coast. If you eat at the counter, you can watch cooks preparing your order of simple luxuries like fresh crab sandwiches, flavor-running steaks and some of the finest omelettes in the land. Among the major listing of fresh berry pies, the locally grown olallieberry (a variety of blackberry) version is absolutely unforgettable. A regional treasure.

Santa Cruz

CASABLANCA RESTAURANT
831/426-9063.
101 Main St., Santa Cruz, CA 95060.
Open: Daily.
Price: Expensive.
Cuisine: Continental.
Serving: D, Sun. Br.
Reservations: Recommended.
Credit Cards: AE, DC, MC, V.
Handicap Access: Limited.

Romantic is the word for this fine dining room set in a 1920s Mediterranean estate-turned-inn perched on the hillside over the main Santa Cruz beach and wharf. Lots of gleaming brass, candle-light and enormous picture windows frame a capti-vating view of the water, all the prettier at night. Enhanced by an award-winning list of over 400 wines, Casablanca has creative fun with contempo-rary California cuisine. Superior fresh seafoods, filet mignon, rack of lamb and grilled duck are standards. An appetizer of roasted ancho chile stuffed with cheese and served with a red bell pep-per sauce is wonderful. The house salad of baby butterhead lettuce and Dijon vinaigrette is a stand-out, and all of the fresh fish ideas work brilliantly, especially a linguine with prawns, sea scallops and clams in lemon thyme and fresh tomato cream. Elegant desserts feature seasonal berries and creamy pastries. The Sunday Brunch, for reasons of the beachfront view and the superlative egg specialties served with lots of Champagne, is justly popular.

CLOUD'S
831/429-2000.
110 Church St., Santa Cruz, CA 95060.
Open: Daily.
Price: Moderate.
Cuisine: American/ California.
Serving: L, D.
Reservations: Recommended.
Credit Cards: D, DC, MC, V.
Handicap Access: Yes.

Call it the linchpin of the "new" downtown Santa Cruz or call it the culmination of Lou Caviglia's latest dining vision, but make no mis-take — Cloud's Downtown is one hoppin' joint! A magnet to veteran downtown habitués who order up martinis and Scotch on the rocks like there's no tomorrow, Cloud's sleek copper-topped bar, black spiral chandeliers and colorful abstract canvases provide a distinctively modern backdrop to homey, American culinary classics. You'll find real men and women ordering pot roast and garlic mashed potatoes, rotisserie turkey swathed in fresh and tangy cranberry relish and juicy baby back ribs. Cloud's also boasts an impressive wine list as well as a generously stocked bar and indulges any libational whim with the greatest of ease.

Frank Barbieri

The Crow's Nest is a required dining adventure for visitors to Santa Cruz's scenic Yacht Harbor.

CROW'S NEST
831/476-4560.
2218 E. Cliff Dr., Santa
    Cruz, CA 95060.
Open: Daily.
Price: Moderate.
Cuisine: American/
    Seafood.
Serving: L, D.
Reservations:
    Recommended.
Credit Cards: AE, D, DC,
    MC, V.
Handicap Access: Yes.

The Crow's Nest and its incomparable Yacht Harbor location never fail to deliver a textbook beachfront experience. Many devotees of this handsome, split-level establishment situated right on the beach make tracks upstairs to the extremely popular bar, where attractive singles and live music on weekends heat up the recreational possibilities. There's also an oyster bar in the upper level and some outdoor seating. Downstairs and out on the glass-enwrapped decks, a menu of seafood standards is served along with the area's most comprehensive and inviting salad bar. The fresh grilled fish is fine, especially the teriyaki salmon, as are the fat sirloin steak sandwiches at lunch and aged filet mignon at night.

EL PALOMAR
831/425-7575.
1336 Pacific Ave., Santa
    Cruz, CA 95060.
Open: Daily.
Price: Inexpensive to
    Moderate.
Cuisine: Mexican.
Serving: L, D, Sun. Br.

This wildly popular dining room that has it all — inventive and invitingly priced Mexican cuisine, world-class margaritas and the charismatic setting of an historic 1930s Spanish Revival hotel, whose lofty ceilings encompass the nonstop activity. While fine cocktails are served under the light and airy skylighting of the adjoining lounge, the

Reservations: Not required, accepted Sun.–Thurs. for large parties.
Credit Cards: AE, D, MC, V.
Handicap Access: Yes.

main dining room best showcases the exciting food. The warm, fresh corn tortillas are the real thing and wrap perfectly around tender cooked pork and shredded chicken in outstanding lunch tacos. For less than ten dollars, you can fill up on crisp puffy *sopes,* filled with chicken, vegetables, shredded cabbage and sour cream, or work through something grander in the form of fresh garlic-grilled prawns bathed in cilantro-laced, fiery hot guajilla chile sauce. Late brunches of voluptuous refried beans topped with a fried egg are without peer, and the house *pozole* — a rich pork-and-hominy soup topped with lime, cabbage and cilantro — will cure the worst cold (or hangover). Housed in the tallest building in downtown Santa Cruz, El Palomar is hard to miss and impossible to beat.

HOLLINS HOUSE
831/459-9177.
20 Clubhouse Rd., Santa Cruz, CA 95060.
Open: Wed.–Sat., 5:30 p.m.–9:30 p.m.; Sun. Br., 10:00 a.m.–1:30 p.m.
Price: Moderate to Expensive.
Cuisine: New American.
Serving: D, Sun. Br.
Reservations: Recommended.
Credit Cards: MC, V.
Handicap Access: Yes.

The sweeping vista of the Monterey Bay creeps right up to the front porch of golf matriarch Marian Hollins' graceful home, which now houses a club and restaurant bearing her name. If you're expecting *haute bourgeoisie* fare like prime rib and sparkling rosé, you'd better brace yourself. Those who visit Hollins House — a short drive from downtown Santa Cruz but a sybaritic million miles away in atmospheric isolation — will find Canadian smoked goose quesadillas, seared ahi tuna, Jamaican prawns and plenty of portabello mushrooms on the menu, matched by a sensitive listing of top California wines emphasizing top local premiums. The vintage 1930s California-French dining room, with its high ceilings, candlelight and view-capturing windows, suggests formality, but the youthful staff and enlightened menu exude relaxed hospitality.

MOBO SUSHI
831/425-1700.
105 S. River St., Santa Cruz, CA 95060.
Open: Daily.
Price: Moderate.
Cuisine: Japanese/Sushi Bar.
Serving: L (except Sat., Sun.), D.
Reservations: Accepted but not recommended.
Credit Cards: MC, V.
Handicap Access: Yes.

A vibrant scene, intriguing taped musical selections and imaginative fresh sushi creations make this a hit with fans of one of Japan's most enduring exports. While the very young, skilled staff keeps the orders flowing, all the classic tekkamakis, nigiris and anari sushis find tasteful expression, as do variations that could only have been created on the Central Coast. For example, the Rock & Roll is filled with freshwater eel and avocado, while Sushi Rage combines avocado, garlic and macadamia nuts as well as buttery yellowtail hamachi and sticky rice. The

Presto Maki Roll is a local favorite, packed with pungent fresh basil and hamachi tuna. Tiny daikon sprouts and a crisp mountain yam adorn many jewellike creations, but the emphasis here is on adventurous dining rather than slavish traditionalism — nothing too precocious and everything fresh, fresh, fresh.

O'MEI RESTAURANT
831/425-8458.
2316 Mission St., Santa Cruz, CA 95060.
Open: Daily.
Price: Moderate.
Cuisine: Contemporary Asian.
Serving: L, except weekends, D.
Reservations: Recommended but not required.
Credit Cards: AE, MC, V.
Handicap Access: Yes.

The Pacific Rim culinary genius of Roger Grigsby has made the sleek, serene dining rooms of O'Mei one of the area's most popular and consistently excellent restaurants since its opening over fifteen years ago. Regular trips to the Far East recharge Grigsby's inventive menu palette, translated through contemporary California emphasis on light, fresh presentation. The results are disarming. Tiny dishes of intriguing appetizers are brought around to each table, and diners can choose from baby ears of pickled corn, chile-infused carrots or vinegary straw mushrooms — whatever moves the kitchen that evening. The seasonally transmuting menu is always tantalizing, and appetizer standouts invariably involve the sumptuous red oil dumplings and fabulous slender green beans tossed with fermented shrimp. Vegetables like the yu xiang eggplant, vibrant with the haunting perfume of Szechuan peppercorns or asparagus in garlicky black bean sauce are meals unto themselves. More complex, but equally accessible, are special creations like mala corn chicken, black pepper shrimp or crispy Taiwan-style rock cod. Desserts are naturally inventive, and the wines by-the-glass listing provides access to the finest from area microwineries. A favorite with visiting celebrities, politicos, artists and the U.C., Santa Cruz power structure.

OSWALD
831/423-7427.
1547 Pacific Ave., Santa Cruz, CA 95060.
Open: Nightly from 5:30 p.m.
Price: Moderate to Expensive.
Cuisine: California.
Serving: D.
Reservations: Recommended.
Credit Cards: AE, D, MC, V.
Handicap Access: Yes, except rest room.

A smart, urban bistro with few pretensions, Oswald was developed under the guidance of culinary genius Charlie Deal. Now under the command of chef Damani Thomas, the menu explores seasonal ingredients served with generous eye appeal and a sense of culinary style. An extensive wine list, bold on local and California wines, offers choice accompaniment for pan-roasted yellowtail with black chanterelles, portabellos and sweet potatoes or rack of lamb paired with scalloped potatoes inflected with butternut squash. Desserts are original and decadent, like a seasonal trio of sorbets flavored with blood oranges, mandarin oranges and Meyer lemon. Try the cinnamon bread pudding.

Pearl Alley Bistro wine expert Mark Curtis and chef Marc Westburg offer one of the Central Coast's best wine lists and many of the region's most inventive dishes.

Robert Scheer

PEARL ALLEY BISTRO & WINE BAR
831/429-8070.
110 Pearl Alley bet. Pacific Ave. & Cedar St., Santa Cruz, CA 95060.
Open: Daily.
Price: Moderate to Expensive.
Cuisine: Global Bistro.
Serving: L, D, Sun Br.
Reservations: Recommended.
Credit Cards: AE, D, DC, MC, V.
Handicap Access: No.

Before culinary *wunderkind* Marc Westburg opened this accessibly chichi bistro on the site of a longtime favorite wine bar, he'd cooked all over the world and done a stint as Trader Vic's personal chef. The multicultural flavor, texture and seasoning ideas gleaned from this extensive experience power some of the most innovative dishes on the Central Coast. The small dining room, whose hardwood floors accentuate the convivial hubbub, offers a constantly changing menu long on small dishes. The fiery Pacific Rim haunts dishes like an exquisite fresh kimchee salmon served with the house pickled cabbage and toasted *nori*, while more European are signature dishes like tournedos of lamb in a rose geranium jelly glaze. All have developed cult followings. Dreamy pastas are accented with whatever the chef's found in the day's marketplace, and look for risottos with unusual ingredients like burdock root. Special menus featuring the cuisine of different parts of the globe headline for a week each month, so adventuresome gourmands can eat everything from kangaroo to antelope when their timing is right. The long wood bar attracts solo diners as well as connoisseurs of Pearl Alley's lengthy listing of outstanding Central Coast and French vintages, most available by the glass.

REAL THAI KITCHEN
831/427-2559.
1632 Seabright Ave., Santa
    Cruz, CA 95060.
Open: Daily.
Price: Inexpensive.
Cuisine: Thai.
Serving: L, D.
Reservations:
    Recommended for
    weekend dinner.
Credit Cards: AE, MC, V.
Handicap Access: Yes.

Fans of the brilliant flavor complexities of Thai cuisine have made this small, colorfully decorated restaurant their second home. Using the freshest local produce and seafoods as a primary base, chef Prasit Saranyaphiphat expertly applies the traditional seasonings of chiles, garlic, basil, lemongrass and lime to a wide range of authentic dishes. The creamy pad Thai stir-fried rice noodles beautifully support a flotilla of shrimp, chicken, egg, tofu and ground peanuts. Southern Thai curries, richly layered with sweet basil, fiery chiles and satiny coconut milk, are unforgettable, especially those involving roasted duck or fresh seafoods. Many people come simply for sensuous appetizers like the fine spicy shrimp soup filled with mushrooms, lemongrass and coconut milk or the chicken larb (minced poultry, toasted rice powder, lime, chiles, basil, cilantro and shredded lettuce), which puts to shame any other chicken salad that you could contemplate. Don't miss the barbecued pork ribs paired with an icy Singha beer. Vivacious hostess/partner Ellen Saranyaphiphat is a gem.

RISTORANTE AVANTI
831/427-0135.
1711 Mission St., Santa
    Cruz, CA 95060.
Open: Daily.
Price: Moderate.
Cuisine: Italian.
Serving: B, L, D, Sat.–Sun.
    Br.
Reservations: A good idea.
Credit Cards: AE, MC, V.
Handicap Access: Yes.

A small trattoria that's very popular with the nearby U.C., Santa Cruz community, Ristorante Avanti makes patrons feel at home with its warm service and unfussy ambiance. Many lunch patrons like to dine at the long wine bar counter, where a good selection of Italian and locally made vintages are available by the glass. Excellent bruschettas, roasted garlic with crostini and grilled eggplant and roast peppers get diners warmed up for generous entrées like rib eye steak, assorted wild mushroom dishes, garlicky linguine with clam sauce, sprightly flavored three-cheese ravioli and fresh fish specials. All of the vegetables are organically produced. Don't miss the creamy polenta and chicken cacciatore — fantasy dishes seemingly from the hands of an Italian grandmother. The prices are quite reasonable, and the camaraderie is irresistible.

ROSA'S ROTICERIA
831/479-3536.
493 B Lake Ave., Santa
    Cruz, CA 95060.
Open: Daily.
Price: Inexpensive.
Cuisine: Mexican/
    Seafood/Rotisserie.
Serving: L, D.

Outrageously flavorful, top-quality rotisserie and slow-simmered combinations stress the Mexican heritage and the spice of Creole attitude that characterizes Rosa's sassy take on dining. You can watch your meal being expertly prepared in the exhibition kitchen, an asset that adds to Rosa's laid-back attitude. It may be best known for its tender, moist rotisserie meats, but the seaside restaurant

*Lee Rhau and David
Gutierrez have made their
Rosa's Rosticeria at the Santa
Cruz Yacht Harbor the most
deliciously festive seafood
stop in town.*

Robert Scheer

Reservations: No.
Credit Cards: No.
Handicap Access: Yes.

also has a wonderful way with seafood, to which it devotes creative, world-beat attention. Burritos bulging with scallops, asparagus, pea pods and potatoes and blackened yellowtail accompanied by Oaxaqueña flavors like raisin- and cinnamon-spiced mole make up the order of the day. Vivacious, kicky and very affordable.

**SEA CLOUD
RESTAURANT &
SOCIAL CLUB**
831/458-9393.
650 Municipal Wharf, Santa
  Cruz, CA 95060.
Open: Daily.
Price: Moderate to
  Expensive.
Cuisine: California/
  Seafood.
Serving: L (except
  weekends), D.
Reservations:
  Recommended.
Credit Cards: AE, D, DC,
  MC, V.
Handicap Access: Yes.

No visit to the Santa Cruz Wharf is complete without a stop at the beautiful Sea Cloud. The contemporary nautical theme is enhanced by glorious burnished woodwork, and the friendly bar serves superior cocktails and fine local wines. Afternoon drinks here are a religion, offering clear views of the waves and surfing activity at Lighthouse Point. From one of the main dining rooms, the panoramic view is filled by the main beach, colorful boardwalk attractions and the Santa Cruz Mountains beyond. Masterminded with California culinary expertise, the menu has its charms, long on fresh seafoods with touches of Southwestern and Pacific Rim inspiration. Tiny muyagi oysters on the half shell and excellent clam chowder start things off, with innovative shellfish pasta creations and a sumptuous filet mignon proving consistent hits.

The warm confit of duck salad is an intensely flavored pleasure of baby lettuces, rich tender duck and fresh local goat cheese bathed in a warm balsamic vinaigrette. The heart of romaine salad with Gorgonzola and balsamic vinaigrette is splendid, as are the freshly made desserts, especially the hazelnut mousse. Service is flawless, and views of marine life, ubiquitous gulls and pelicans, seals and the occasional dolphin and whale fuel the waterfront ambiance.

Jean-Pierre Iuliano and Luca Lorenzina deliver old-world joy and comfort at their Star Bene Italian eatery in Santa Cruz.

Robert Scheer

STAR BENE
831/479-4307.
2-1245 E. Cliff Dr., Santa
  Cruz, CA 95060.
Open: Daily.
Price: Moderate.
Cuisine: Italian.
Serving: L Tues.–Sat, D.
Reservations:
  Recommended
  Thurs.–Sun.
Credit Cards: AE, MC, V.
Handicap Access: Yes.

At Star Bene, Italian is not only spoken and eaten, it fills the air with unhurried ambiance. Charmingly decorated with sparkling white linens and a sheltered courtyard for al fresco dining in the warmer months, Star Bene provides a shimmering glimpse of the Mediterranean right on the Central Coast. The menu doesn't attempt to reinvent. Instead it enhances delicate salads, antipasti, pastas and some meat and fish dishes simply and elegantly. A classic appetizer like prosciutto and melon becomes an elegant experience — mezzaluna wedges of sweet cantaloupe are finessed with cured Parma ham and a trio of kalamata olives. Cornish game hens and fresh fish are perfect choices for meat lovers, but Star Bene's girello vegetariano — three elegant pinwheels of handmade vegetable-layered pasta splashed with bright red and béchamel cream sauces, then flecked with parsley — could easily be the ultimate luxury vegetarian dish.

SUKEROKU
831/426-6660.
1701 Mission St., Santa
  Cruz, CA 95060.
Open: Tues.–Sun.
Price: Moderate.
Cuisine: Japanese.

Since the late 1970s, this tiny Japanese restaurant and even tinier sushi bar have satisfied the cravings for soy, sake and sushi on the part of neighbors and university regulars in this westside Santa Cruz community. Blonde wood tables and the occasional travel poster make up the spare

Serving: L Tues.–Fri., D.
Reservations: No.
Credit Cards: MC, V.
Handicap Access: Yes.

decor, but the real star here is the wonderful food. Exceptional bowls of fat udon noodles filled with shiitakes, prawns and vegetables are available at dinner, while lunches involve consummate teriyaki salmon and pork or feather-light tempura. The sushi is first-rate, served up with friendly flair, as is the occasional outburst of song by legendary chef/owner Isao Hamashi. A local treasure.

VASILI'S
831/458-9808.
1501 Mission St., Santa
    Cruz, CA 95060.
Open: Tues.–Sun.
Price: Moderate.
Cuisine: Greek.
Serving: L, D.
Reservations: A good idea.
Credit Cards: No.
Handicap Access: No.

If you're looking for an energetic backdrop to international dining, this place is nothing less than a gift from the Greek gods. Owner and chef Vasili Karagiannopoulos has a bountiful exuberance for food, and it's always evident in his simple taverna. The warm hearth is lined with photos, pottery and faux frescos of Zorbaesque dancers and is always packed with jubilant regulars digging into platters full of fragrant country-style pork *shishkebabs,* piles of delicately sautéed calamari and Greek salad, mounds of chopped tomatoes, Bermuda onions, cucumbers, peppers and feta liberally adorned with capers. No visit to a Greek restaurant would be complete without a few swills of pine-scented retsina or some sweet, hearty rice pudding. Saturday nights are particularly jovial, as Vasili and his crew do traditional dances to rowdy live music. The top-drawer staff is knowledgeable and friendly.

Capitola/Soquel

MASAYUKI
831/476-7284.
427 Capitola Ave., Capitola,
    CA 95010.
Open: Daily, except Tues.
Price: Moderate.
Cuisine: Japanese.
Serving: D.
Reservations: No.
Credit Cards: MC, V.
Handicap Access: Yes.

There's nothing incongruous about a sushi bar tucked into a tiny beach bungalow cottage, as expertly proven by the finesse of Masayuki's, long ranked by those in the know as the top of the local sushi food chain. Here the edible exquisiteness of master Masa is perpetuated in the very freshest ingredients, flawless service and a playful attitude that welcomes newcomers while catering to the neighborhood regulars. Crimson lengths of maguro and albacore tuna lie poised by an emerald bouquet of fresh shiso leaves. From the open kitchen behind the main sushi station, pungent aromas of tempura and broiled specialties heightened the atmosphere. Masayuki's menu is rife with all of the traditional favorites — gyoza, teriyaki, tempura, soba — as well as the classical canon of nigiri, sushi rolls and sashimi. Sushi doesn't get much better than this.

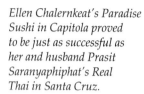

Ellen Chalernkeat's Paradise Sushi in Capitola proved to be just as successful as her and husband Prasit Saranyaphiphat's Real Thai in Santa Cruz.

Robert Scheer

PARADISE SUSHI
831/464-3328.
200 Monterey Ave.,
   Capitola, CA 95010.
Open: Daily.
Price: Moderate.
Cuisine: Japanese.
Serving: L, D.
Reservations: No.
Credit Cards: AE, MC, V.
Handicap Access: Yes.

A sushi palace that treats its clientele to an ocean view of Pacific Rim possibilities, Paradise Sushi sits high above the Capitola Village, encircled in curved picture windows that allow a stunning view. Glowing with a forest of paper lanterns and divided by deep green cloth banners, the sleek sushi bar and alcove rooms make for a handsome Japanese dining experience. Owner/chef Prasit Saranyaphiphat, who also owns Real Thai with his wife Ellen, creates both classic and experimental sushi, catering to traditionalist and West Coast tastes. It's sushi with an edge — tempura soft-shell crab rolled with tobiko and cilantro or a spicy salmon, avocado, cilantro and nopalitos cactus combination. Pair it with sake or a Sapporo draft, and this lunch or dinner could be paradise found.

SHADOWBROOK
831/475-1511.
1750 Wharf Rd., Capitola,
   CA 95010.
Open: Daily.
Price: Moderate to
   Expensive.
Cuisine: American.
Serving: D, Sun. Br.
Reservations:
   Recommended.
Credit Cards: AE, D, DC,
   MC, V.
Handicap Access: Yes.

Proof that even long-standing restaurant legends can earn their reputations, the Shadowbrook is not only *de rigueur* for out-of-town visitors and special occasions, it's on the cognoscentis' shortlist of consistently fine dining experiences. This rustically elegant sprawl of multilevel stone and wood-beamed dining rooms turns out expert California cuisine served by an unerring waitstaff. From the full bar upstairs, guests wander down past the central stone fireplace to a favorite private booth or round oak table overlooking Soquel Creek below. Fresh seafoods are a specialty, but many swear by the stellar prime rib served with horseradish-laced sour cream. Sunday brunches out on the patio involve inventive seafood Benedict, a grilled chicken on penne pasta and a marvelous Italian-style roast beef sandwich piled high with sweet red peppers and Fontina cheese. Ride the charming funicular down from street level to the restaurant below, and then stroll back through waterfalls and lush gardens. It's all shamelessly romantic.

THEO'S
831/462-3657.
3101 N. Main St., Soquel,
   CA 95073.
Open: Tues.–Sat.
Price: Moderate.
Cuisine: New American.
Serving: D.
Reservations:
   Recommended.
Credit Cards: AE, V.
Handicap Access: Yes.

Prime New American cuisine is one reason to visit Theo's, but the restaurant's organic gardens are equally wonderful. Touring these splendid, green flowery mazes takes the quality of the Theo's dining experience to the next level. The menu teams American classics like roast duck on a creamy rich confit with nouvelle offerings, such as a barely seared, sashimi-grade Japanese yellowtail resting in a bed of "cucumber" noodles, and all are always orchestrated beautifully, flecked with herbs and seductively matched with edible flowers. The wine list is extensive, and the desserts, like a blood orange tart enhanced by a layer of crème anglaise, sinfully satisfy. An aesthetic dining experience.

Aptos/Rio Del Mar

BITTERSWEET BISTRO
831/662-9799.
787 Rio Del Mar Blvd., Rio
   Del Mar, CA 95003.
Open: Tues.–Sun.
Price: Moderate.
Cuisine: California
   Continental.
Serving: D, Bistro 3:00
   p.m.–6:00 p.m.
Reservations:
   Recommended for
   weekends.
Credit Cards: AE, MC, V.
Handicap Access: Yes.

This inviting bistro proved to be an instant success, mostly because it's fueled by the skill of chef Thomas Vinolus and partner Elizabeth Clark. Banquette and booth seating provide a cozy arena for people watching, but the low-priced menu of utterly fresh, expertly prepared California bistro fare is the top draw. Starters involve succulent grilled shrimp or salmon over wilted baby greens with sides of perfect garlic/sage-infused white beans. Main courses include classic rib eye steaks grilled with a shallot Merlot sauce, sand dabs and roasted chicken — all served with exceptional vegetables, highlighted by the house signature scalloped potatoes. The chef, trained in intricate pastries, creates a lemon-raspberry napoleon of crisp phyllo pastry layered with creamy lemon custard and tart raspberry coulis. The crème brûlée is outstanding.

CAFE SPARROW
831/688-6238.
8042 Soquel Dr., Aptos, CA
   95003.

Updated Continental classics find a lovely home in this small, prettily decorated cafe. Very popular with residents of the village and beach

Open: Daily.
Price: Moderate to
  Expensive.
Cuisine: Bistro.
Serving: B Sat., L, D, Sun.
  Br.
Reservations:
  Recommended for
  dinner.
Credit Cards: MC, V.
Handicap Access: Yes.

communities surrounding Aptos, Cafe Sparrow turns gourmet sandwiches and vibrant salads into memorable experiences. The dinner entrées are an eclectic assortment of Continental variations and include an excellent peppered Angus filet mignon, rich New Zealand venison in a brandied cherry demi-glacé, as well as bistro fare like grilled chicken and breaded oysters with a lemon-caper crème. The pretty desserts and an award-winning wine list heighten the luster of this charming eatery.

Chef Jack Chyle and his wife Renee have turned Aptos' charming Chez Renee into one of the most highly honored restaurants on the Central Coast.

Robert Scheer

CHEZ RENEE
831/688-5566.
9051 Soquel Dr., Aptos, CA
  95003.
Open: Tues.–Sat.
Price: Moderate to
  Expensive.
Cuisine: French/Italian.
Serving: L Wed.–Fri., D
  Tues.–Sat.
Reservations:
  Recommended.
Credit Cards: MC, V.
Handicap Access: Yes.

A very pretty restaurant, superbly run by California Culinary Academy-trained owners Jack and Renee Chyle, Chez Renee has been showered with awards in its illustrious career. Considered by many among the very top dining spots of the Monterey Bay area, the ambiance is personally orchestrated by the vivacious Renee, who also creates some of the exquisite desserts. The soft peach-toned dining room has a stone fireplace, lit in cool months for the ultimate in romantic atmosphere. Though the restaurant boasts an award-winning wine list, especially strong in French and California vintages, including many from the Santa Cruz Mountains, the food is the whole brilliant point. Jack Chyle is a sorcerer with duck, which he finesses with fresh, seasonal fruit and berry sauces and splashes with an imaginative palette of wines or liqueurs. The house-smoked salmon is an exquisite opener, as are the pristine Pacific Northwest oysters on the half shell and ripe figs with prosciutto. The pastas, veal and seafoods are all amazing, and beef eaters swear by the filet mignon served with a port wine sauce. The freshly made desserts, especially the warm soufflés and the ethereal cheesecake, are the stuff of lifelong memories. A serious selection of single malt Scotches and premium vodkas is available at the tiny adjoining bar.

MANUEL'S
831/688-4848.
261 Center St., Aptos, CA
  95003.
Open: Daily.
Price: Inexpensive.
Cuisine: Mexican.
Serving: L, D.
Reservations:
  Recommended for
  dinner.
Credit Cards: MC, V.
Handicap Access: Limited.

Talented artist Manuel Santana would be a local legend even if he and his wife Alicia hadn't founded this vivacious Mexican restaurant overlooking Seacliff State Beach. But they did, and for over twenty-five years the rich and humble have given thanks over bottles of ice-cold Corona, tangy margaritas and plates of rich refried beans. Always crowded and alive with a convivial crowd of regulars who all seem to have grown up with each other, Manuel's feels like a culinary fiesta, with artwork on the dark wood walls and plenty of south-of-the-border tile work accenting the decor. Menu highlights include the soothing chile rellenos, fruity enchiladas tropicales and snapper smothered in chile and sour cream sauce. The guacamole and hot sauce are addictive, as are the house salads topped with guacamole, tomato slices, garbanzo beans and a very vinegary vinaigrette. Innovation isn't the point — Mexican comfort food with lively ambiance is.

FOOD PURVEYORS

BAKERIES

Aldo's (831/476-3470; 4628 Soquel Dr., Soquel) Featured here are fragrant, rustic, fresh-baked breads and pastries, including the mighty Italian raisin fugasa.
The Buttery (831/458-3020; 702 Soquel Ave., Santa Cruz) The Buttery bakes great breads, but the sumptuously frosted cakes and elegant cookies are even better. Don't miss the zucchini muffins and pecan sandies.
Emily's Good Things to Eat (831/429-9866; 1129 Mission St., Santa Cruz) Emily's cooks up such aromatic attractions as pumpkin muffins and round, fragrant sourdough bread, plus brews some of the strongest coffee this side of Colombia.
The Farm (831/684-0266; 6790 Soquel Dr., Aptos) A Soquel baking institution, The Farm is the place to settle in for a cappuccino, tarts or a vast selection of homemade breads. Cozy, atmospheric and satisfying.

HMB Bakery (650/726-4841; 514 Main St., Half Moon Bay) HMB is a traditional bakery with a wide assortment of cakes, cookies, pastries and its famously rich and sticky Hot Cross Buns.

Kelly's French Pastry (831/423-9059; 1547 Pacific Ave., Santa Cruz; 831/662-2911; 7486 Soquel Dr., Aptos) Authentic French breads, cakes and pastries, killer pear tarts and *pain d'amande* has put this institution on the map.

Moonside Bakery (650/726-9070; 604 Main St., Half Moon Bay) Pastries, cookies, fresh-baked bread, plus breakfasts make this downtown bakery a perfect stop for a quick fix or a languorous morning.

COFFEEHOUSES

Caffe Pergolesi (831/426-1775; 418 Cedar St., Santa Cruz) The Perg attracts young and aggressively avant-garde students and artists who congregate to swill industrial-strength coffee and wait to be discovered.

Georgiana's (831/427-9900; 1520 Pacific Ave., Santa Cruz) A caffeine-infused meeting spot housed in the front of Bookshop Santa Cruz, Georgiana's is wildly popular with outdoor cafe types.

Half Moon Bay Coffee Company (650/726-1994; 315 Main St., Half Moon Bay) Upscale and full-service, this coffeehouse offers a full range of fresh coffee, espresso drinks and unique teas, as well as soup, sandwiches and desserts.

Jahva House (831/459-9876; 120 Union St., Santa Cruz) A 1960s-style, neohippie hangout, featuring weathered couches, big leafy plants and terrific caffe latté, it is a destination hangout for locals.

Java Junction (831/423-5282; 519 Seabright Ave., Santa Cruz) This seaside caffeine haven is beachy in ambiance with its sunny patio, and it fixes up all kinds of coffee drinks, smoothies and goodies like bagels, muffins and gooey, sinful cinnamon rolls.

La Di Da (650/726-1663; 507 Purissima at Kelly Ave., Half Moon Bay) The self-proclaimed "coolest cafe on the coast" serves up special coffee drinks, whimsical desserts, sandwiches and art, plus the tastiest fruit-flavored water on the coast.

M Coffee (650/726-6241; 522 Main St., Half Moon Bay) Cozy and cute, M comes complete with round, paisley-print tables, pastries, delicious lattés and sandwiches.

Mr. Toots (831/475-3679; 221 Esplanade, Capitola) A lovely coffeehouse that offers an ocean view and upper room, dark-wood ambiance, Toots has a long-standing following and wonderful mochas.

FARMERS' MARKETS

The weekly tradition of cruising the freshest locally grown produce, displayed in colorful booths by the growers, has become a fixture of Central

Coast life. Farmers' Market day is a chance to meet the growers and to select their freshly harvested, certified organic fruits, nuts, vegetables and honey, plus fresh-caught seafood, eggs, honey, cheeses and flowers in an open-air market setting.

Aptos Certified Farmers' Market (831/479-5005; 6500 Soquel Dr., Cabrillo College lower parking lot, Aptos; Sat. 8:00 a.m.–12:00 noon) Aptos Market is considered the granddaddy of the area's open-air organic produce emporia, vending everything from fertile brown eggs to purple potatoes.

Downtown Farmers' Market of Santa Cruz (831/429-8433; Pacific Ave. bet. Cathcart & Lincoln, Santa Cruz; Wed. 2:00 p.m.–7:00 p.m.) This market bounces with friendly, festive, folksy atmosphere, laced with live music and street entertainment.

UCSC Farm & Garden Project (831/459-4140; U.C., Santa Cruz, Bay Ave. & Empire Grade Rd., Santa Cruz; Tues., Fri. 12:00 noon–5:00 p.m.) This group sells produce and flowers (remarkable for their diversity, freshness and often downright unusualness) grown on the campus' experimental agroecology lands in a funky, roadside setting.

ICE CREAM

Double Rainbow (831/423-3231; 1123 Pacific Ave., Santa Cruz) This youth-run ice-cream parlor satisfies the sweet craving with its decadent assortment of ice-cream flavors, plus milk shakes and sundaes, and it also offers soups, salads, sandwiches and gooey pastries.

Marianne's (831/458-1447; 1020 Ocean St., Santa Cruz) A landmark for decades, opulent with sinful creaminess like vanilla bean milk shakes, this parlor serves sugar cones filled with California 17, a killer version of Rocky Road.

Polar Bear Ice Cream (831/425-5188; 1224 Soquel Ave., Santa Cruz) Polar Bear is known for fine espressos and delectable ice creams, including good berries and a superior pumpkin flavor.

Saturn Cafe (831/429-8505; 1230 Mission St., Santa Cruz) For twenty years, this transformed Pizza Hut has remained a destination for cool dessert lovers of all ages. Everyone should experience this funky restaurant's infamous Chocolate Madness at least once in life.

MICROBREWERIES

In the 1980s, the repeal of a prohibition against selling and making beers on the same location prompted an explosion of microbreweries all over the Central Coast, where freshly made and boldly flavored handmade brews are on tap at on-site pubs. These beers bear absolutely no relation to those alleged brews advertised on TV. Tours are usually available, and in many cases, glass walls allow a full view of the "exhibition brewing."

Santa Cruz Brewing Company/Front Street Pub (831/429-8838; 516 Front St., Santa Cruz) This brewery offers fine house lager, amber, porter and seasonal items like barley wine and wheat beer on tap (or by the bottle at area markets) at a lively brewpub that's always packed with thirsty bodies.

Allison Smith is recognized as the personable Princess of the Patio at eastside Santa Cruz's award-winning Seabright Brewery.

George Sakkestad

Seabright Brewery (831/426-2739; 519 Seabright Ave. #107, Santa Cruz) Seabright features outdoor patio seating to enjoy Pelican pale, Seabright Amber, Ace's Ale and Oatmeal Stout, all made on the sleek contemporary premises and all award winners.

CULTURE

ARCHITECTURE

In the carefully groomed residential streets surrounding downtown Santa Cruz, rows of pastel-hued cottages and mansions preserve the aura of the nineteenth-century boom in this seaside mecca. City fathers filled Walnut Street with the curved archways, steep gables and ornate turrets marking the high point of Stick, Gothic Revival and Queen Anne style, all of which flourish today surrounded by historic landscaping and vintage trees. Wealthy land and cattle barons filled the town's Beach Hill district with majestic Victorian mansions, while the Oceanview Avenue district overlooking the city is literally lined with fine, ornate Queen Anne beauties.

The ubiquitous architect William Weeks was just hitting his stride in the 1920s, peppering the entire state with memorable schools, libraries, courthouses, hotels and public buildings. The colorful tiles, Mission Revival poly-chromed ceilings and curved roofline of Santa Cruz' Palomar Hotel carry on his legacy. A half mile away, on West Cliff Drive overlooking the Santa Cruz Boardwalk, one of Weeks' rare private homes still boasts its arched terrace, red tile roof and copper flashing details as the exquisite Darling House bed and breakfast inn.

CINEMA

Nickelodeon (831/426-7500; 210 Lincoln St., Santa Cruz) This four-screen complex specializes in the best current art films from the U.S. and abroad. A favorite with area culturati and the university crowd who relish the good popcorn (freshly made with real butter) and fresh fruit juices.

Rio Theatre (831/423-2000; 1205 Soquel Ave., Santa Cruz) A large vintage movie palace with plush seats, tiled rest rooms and an upstairs "crying room" for very young filmgoers. Usually screens mainstream blockbusters.

Santa Cruz Cinema 9 Theatres (831/460-2599; 1405 Pacific Ave., Santa Cruz) This latest addition to the local cinema scene features a wide selection of mainstream movies, especially big budget blockbusters. The large nine-plex, complete with neon lights and a huge snack bar that offers espresso drinks, creates a high-tech feel very different from most local theaters.

Skyview Drive-In Theatre (831/475-3405; 2260 Soquel Dr., Santa Cruz) Skyview remains the area's sole reminder of the glory days of the drive-in. The theatre offers a choice of two films, often thrillers, to be enjoyed the old-school way.

GARDENS

Half Moon Bay Nursery (650/726-5392; 11691 San Mateo Rd., Half Moon Bay) An eye-popping panorama of colorful perennials fills the greenhouses of this florists' nirvana. Open daily, 9:00 a.m.–5:00 p.m.

University of California, Santa Cruz Arboretum (831/427-2998; off Empire Grade Rd., Santa Cruz) Experimental and showpiece gardens, both empha-sizing indigenous plants, are on display along the arboretum's many trails. Amidst the groves of various eucalyptus trees, the collections of plants from Australia and South Africa are considered among the best in the world. The displays include ten genera of redwood trees, a California garden and a Mediterranean garden. Open for self-guided tours daily, 9:00 a.m.–5:00 p.m. The Jean & Bill Lane Library is open Wed.–Sun., 1:00 p.m.–4:00 p.m.

University of California, Santa Cruz Farm and Garden Project (831/459-4140; off Coolidge Dr., Santa Cruz) A working farm/agroecology project nestled at the foot of the hilltop campus, this twenty-five-acre meadow filled with vegetable and flower beds, orchards and row crops was founded by French-intensive master gardener Alan Chadwick, whose students have continued to experiment with organics in these fertile fields. The project provides a vivid opportunity to observe one of the hotbeds of ecologically correct Central Coast growing techniques. Open daily, dawn to dusk for self-guided tours. Docent tours are offered 12:00 noon, Thurs. and 2:00 p.m., Sun.

HISTORIC PLACES

**EVERGREEN
HISTORICAL
CEMETERY**
831/429-1964.
Evergreen & Coral Sts.,
    Santa Cruz, CA 95060.
Open: Daily, dawn to dusk;
    docent-led tours,
    summer 10:00 a.m. Sat.
Admission: Free, donations
    appreciated.

One of the oldest Protestant cemeteries in the state, in 1850, this verdant hillside became a final resting place for area settlers, from judges to courtesans. Beneath the weathered and tottering headstones lie Civil War veterans, Freemasons and civic fathers, plus a few civic mothers sprinkled among the boys. An entire section devoted to the graves of Chinese immigrants marks the burial site of those who came to build the region's railroads, bridges and roads.

*The New England-style
James Johnston House has
stood watch over the Half
Moon Bay coastline since
the middle of the nineteenth
century.*

Stan Cacitti

**JAMES JOHNSTON
HOUSE AND
WILLIAM JOHNSTON
HOUSE**
No telephone.
Higgins Purissima Rd.,
    Half Moon Bay, CA
    94019.
Open: Daily, dawn to dusk.
Admission: Donations.

The only remaining example of the New England saltbox-style dwelling on the northern Central Coast, the two-story, white clapboard house built in 1853 by one of the original forty-niners, Ohio-born James Johnston, remains one of this area's most important and earliest structures. Built in the 1860s, the neighboring home of William Johnston still shows off its wooden peg construction and original shutters and corner boards. The lovely country road itself curves for almost ten miles through old Santa Cruz Mountains farms, pastures and meadows before rejoining Hwy. 1.

MISSION LA EXALTACIÓN DE LA SANTA CRUZ
831/426-5686.
126 High St. at Emmet St., Santa Cruz, CA 95060.
Open: Tues.–Sat., 10:00 a.m.–4:00 p.m.; Sun., 10:00 a.m.–2:00 p.m.
Admission: Free.

Founded in 1791, Mission la Exaltación de la Santa Cruz was the twelfth California mission. With a seemingly unlimited and willing population of Native Americans, rich grazing lands and proximity to ocean trade, this setting promised to be one of the richest in the Franciscan empire. But all turned sour when the civilian Pueblo of Branciforte sprang up across the river, populated by a rough crew of former convicts, pirates and opportunists, hard men who lured the Ohlone converts away with the temptations of drink, gambling and avarice. After falling into disrepair during the early nineteenth century, the original mission was leveled by an earthquake in 1857. Today, the mission site is occupied by a Catholic church built in 1889. Across the street, a one-third scale replica of the mission and its domed tower houses a chapel and the mission's original paintings and statues.

PURISSIMA TOWN SITE
No telephone.
Verde Rd., Half Moon Bay, CA 94019.
Open: Daily, dawn to dusk.
Admission: Free.

One of the earliest American settlements in Half Moon Bay, this ghost town was a lively stagecoach stop and mercantile center in the 1870s. Today, its rustic cemetery and remodeled schoolhouse still exude the spell of yesteryear.

ROARING CAMP AND BIG TREES NARROW GAUGE RAILROAD
831/335-4400.
Graham Hill Rd. off Mount Hermon Rd., Felton, CA 95018.
Open: Daily, Jun. 8–Sept. 7, 11:00 a.m.–3:00 p.m.; Sept.–May, Sat.–Sun., 12:00 noon–3:00 p.m.
Admission: Round-trip train rides $15 adults/$11 children 3–12/free under 3.

Ensconced near the stately, old-growth redwoods of Henry Cowell State Park, this colorfully recreated, steam railroad depot town continues to delight visitors with its Old West flavor and scenic, narrow-gauge train rides. Shops, concessions and sawmill recreations all bustle with attendants clad in vintage 1870s attire. Two-hour rides, involving round-trip odysseys through the primal redwood forests of the Santa Cruz Mountains, begin here twice a day. Up steep grades and down through the logging country of days past, the railway follows original tracks descending from Roaring Camp to the sunny oceanfront activity of the Santa Cruz Beach and Boardwalk.

SANTA CRUZ MUNICIPAL WHARF
831/429-3628.
W. Cliff Dr. & Front St., Santa Cruz, CA 95060.
Open: Daily, dawn–2:00 a.m.

The incessant bellowing of the resident colony of harbor seals who lounge among the wharf's huge pilings welcomes visitors to this shop and restaurant-lined fishing pier. Offering terrific wraparound views of the surfing action at Steamer Lane and the turn-of-the-century boardwalk casino

Admission: Free (except parking).

and arcade, the wharf buzzes with open-air fish markets and gift and sporting boutiques, as well as bay excursion crafts for hire. Constructed in 1914, this fishing and pleasure pier extends out into Monterey Bay near where four earlier versions were built, the first one in 1853 to fill sailing ships with the produce of the fertile Santa Cruz Mountains countryside. Today, the casual pace begins at dawn for local anglers and winds down with sunset cocktails for locals and visitors alike.

WILDER RANCH STATE PARK
831/426-0505.
Coast Rd. off Hwy. l, Santa Cruz, CA 95060.
Open: Daily, 8:00 a.m.–dusk; visitor's center and dairy, Fri.–Sun., 10:00 a.m.–4:00 p.m.
Admission: $6 per vehicle parking fee.

This graceful relic of the dairy barons of the 1880s occupies a special place in the hearts of area residents. Stretching over 5,000 acres of the most sumptuous and varied terrain on the Central Coast, the ranch — a former dairy ranch turned cattle ranch turned state park — sprawls from its seaside tide pools and plover sanctuary all the way up to redwood groves crowning a 2,000-foot mountaintop. Along the way, the spread encompasses magnificent meadows, ponds, springs and myriad wildlife habitats, including blue heron rookeries and fox and coyote dens.

At the foot of the property is the beautifully maintained Victorian compound of the Wilder dairy ranch. All of the buildings, including the long barn that housed the state's first cream separator, the antique stable, the workshop with original water-driven machinery, the bunkhouse and the owners' large, period-furnished, Victorian manor house, are open to the public. Nearby stand the worn remains of the original adobe, the house in which Russian Jose Bolcoff married Spanish land grant heiress Maria Castro back when the ranch was part of the 10,000-acre Rancho Refugio.

The full exhilaration of this land is best enjoyed by strapping on some sturdy shoes and by filling a day pack with food, water, a camera and binoculars before heading up along the ranch's many hiking, biking and equestrian trails. It's a trip back into the solitude and open grandeur of the Old West.

HISTORIC WALKING TOURS

Half Moon Bay/Pescadero Historic Walking Tours A self-guided tour brochure of some of the vintage nineteenth-century dwellings built by fishing and ranching settlers is available from the local Chamber of Commerce (650/726-5202; 225 S. Cabrillo, Hwy. 1, Half Moon Bay, CA 94019). Highlights include **Spanishtown** landmarks of the nineteenth-century Spanish and Portuguese settlement, the Half Moon Bay community **Methodist Church** (built in 1872), 1853 **Johnston House** (one of the finest examples extant of the New England saltbox style) and the 1820 **Pilarcitos Catholic Cemetery.**

Santa Cruz Mission Plaza Walking Tour In addition to boasting an historic Mission adobe, the plaza surrounding the **Santa Cruz Mission State Historic Park** (831/425-5849; 144 School St. at Adobe St., Santa Cruz, CA 95060) enjoys the distinction of being the first area populated by the earliest influx of American settlers. Built in 1822 to house native inhabitants who worked at Mission Santa Cruz, the adobe house is the only authentically restored Native American residence in the California Mission chain. The seven rooms are set up to show how the occupants lived over the years and are open Thurs.–Sun., 10:00 a.m.–4:00 p.m. (tours Sun., 12:00 noon). Impressive early homes are still to be seen on a self-guided walking tour of the area, including Santa Cruz's oldest house, the 1850 **Francisco Alzina** home (107 Sylvar St.), an intricate Stick-style villa (207 Mission St.) built in 1883 and a splendid Gothic home with classical railings and gable (127 Green St.) built in 1867.

KIDS' STUFF

Shmuel Thaler

The dolphin tank at Long Marine Lab in Santa Cruz keeps inquisitive kids on their learning toes.

Long Marine Lab (831/459-4308; end of Delaware Ave., Santa Cruz) Docents lead tours through the public aquarium and touch tanks, where visitors can get up close and personal with hermit crabs, sea anemones and more. They also teach about the marine environment of the Monterey Bay. $2/$1 (seniors and students)/free children under 12. Open Tues.–Sun., 1:00 p.m.–4:00 p.m.

Mystery Spot (831/423-8897; 465 Mystery Spot Rd., Santa Cruz) A wacky local landmark where trees grow at weird angles and buildings defy the laws of physics. People seem to change size and balls roll uphill. Is it due to the mysterious force of some buried meteor, or is it simply an optical illusion? Whatever it is, this wooded 150-foot plot offers lots of gee-whiz, brain-tickling fun. $5/$2 children 5–11. Open daily, 9:00 a.m.–5:00 p.m. (summertime until dusk).

Pacific Edge (831/454-9254; 104 Bronson St. #12, Santa Cruz) For the kid in everyone, Pacific Edge offers a chance to experience the thrill of rock climbing in an indoor, safe environment. Learn the skills of safe climbing or perfect your technique. Special kids classes available, as are day passes. $12/$6 (children under 11). Open daily, Mon. 5:00 p.m.–10 p.m.; Tues., Thurs., 9:00 a.m.–10:00 p.m.; Wed., Fri., 11:00 a.m.–10:00 p.m.; Sat., Sun., 10:00 a.m.–7:00 p.m.

Since 1907, the Santa Cruz Beach Boardwalk has greeted generations of vacationers who flock to Santa Cruz' wide main beach intent on fun in the sun.

Santa Cruz Beach Boardwalk (831/423-5590; 400 Beach St., Santa Cruz) More than twenty exciting rides, including an old-fashioned wooden roller coaster, the Giant Dipper, make this heaven for youngsters. Rides at either end of the boardwalk, including a mellow Ferris wheel, bumper cars, "underground" train excursions and a colorful vintage 1911 carousel, will please the very young. Wilder rides, including the state-of-the-art, stomach-churning, mild-melting Typhoon will test the endurance of teenagers and impress even the most jaded thrill seeker. Neptune's Kingdom, an indoor pirate-theme amusement center with a video arcade, historical displays, snack bars and a two-story miniature golf course is perfect for the entire family.

MUSEUMS

CAL MUSEUM GALLERY
92 WEST
650/726-6335.

A nonprofit, cooperative gallery, this "artists' gallery" treats all of its artwork as museum

The Light Fantastic

Necessity and technology conspired in the erection of these brilliant beacons clinging to the rockiest edges of the Central California coast during the nineteenth century. Armed with the high candlepower of the French Fresnel lens, which ingeniously utilized over 1,000 pieces of cut glass to magnify its light, the slender lighthouses and their stalwart attendants kept faith with mariners until the coming of automation and the computer. Always a charming sight, a few of these curved towers continue to shed light along the Central Coast. The **Pigeon Point Lighthouse,** located just south of Half Moon Bay, was built in 1872 on a murderous outcropping of rocks and contains a Fresnel lens that was first used on Cape Hatteras during the Civil War. It still manages to pierce the often pea-soup fog that clings to the North Central Coast and now functions as both a Coast Guard outpost and a hostel run by American Youth Hostels.

A youth hostel is lodged inside the 1872 Pigeon Point Lighthouse, the second tallest lighthouse on the California coast.

Shmuel Thaler

520 Kelly Ave., Half Moon Bay, CA 94019.
Open: Thurs.–Mon., 12:00 noon–5:00 p.m.
Admission: Free.

MARY PORTER SESNON GALLERY
831/459-3606.
Porter College, U.C., Santa Cruz, Santa Cruz, CA 95060.
Open: Tues.–Sun., 12:00 noon–5:00 p.m.
Admission: Free.

quality and exhibits it as such. Shows are installed every five weeks and showcase the best in traditionalist, regional and incisive art from Half Moon Bay and Bay Area artists.

Innovative schedule of exhibitions in two small galleries highlight contemporary California, Native American and Latin American artists. Cutting-edge installations in a friendly setting.

**MUSEUM OF ART AND
HISTORY**
831/429-1964.
705 Front St., Santa Cruz,
CA 95060.
Open: Tues.–Sun., 12:00
noon–5:00 p.m.; Fri.,
12:00 noon–7:00 p.m.
Admission: $3/adults; free
students, children; free,
first Fri. each month.

One of the cornerstones of post-earthquake-of-1989 Santa Cruz, this joint cultural venture of the Art Museum of Santa Cruz County and the Santa Cruz County Historical Trust offers revolving exhibitions highlighting regional history and contemporary artists. A permanent installation, packed with heirloom clothing, tools, trunks and telegraphs on the second floor of the main building, accesses the entire history of human habitation in the area, from the Ohlone people through the frontier logging boom to the boardwalk fantasy world. The museum presents talks, tours and films on art and history-related themes and features a rental gallery of work by area artists.

**SANTA CRUZ ART
LEAGUE**
831/426-5787.
526 Broadway Ave., Santa
Cruz, CA 95060.
Open: Wed.–Sat., 11:00
a.m.–5:00 p.m.; Sun.,
12:00 noon–4:00 p.m.
Admission: Donations.

A showcase for revolving exhibitions of top California and Monterey Bay artists, including invitational and juried collections.

**SANTA CRUZ CITY
MUSEUM OF
NATURAL HISTORY**
831/429-3773.
1305 E. Cliff Dr., Santa
Cruz, CA 95060.
Open: Tues.–Sun., 10:00
a.m.–5:00 p.m.
Admission: Donations.

Housed in a graceful seaside mansion overlooking the Monterey Bay, the museum offers visitors an eyeful in the way of exhibits detailing the natural and cultural history of the northern Central Coast area. Ohlone artifacts share space with illustrated specimens of local flora and fauna and fossil remains. Docent-led museum tours, field trips, classes and workshops are available, as well as year-round classes for youngsters on natural history topics. Not to be missed are April's wildflower show and January's Fungus Fair.

**SANTA CRUZ SURFING
MUSEUM**
831/429-3429.
Mark Abbott Mem.
Lighthouse, W. Cliff Dr.,
Santa Cruz, CA 95060.
Open: Wed.–Mon., 12:00
noon–4:00 p.m.
Admission: Free.

Billing itself as the only surfing museum in the world, this eclectic collection of vintage longboards, videos, photographs and memorabilia, including the first wet suit, tracks the history of surfing in Santa Cruz. The tiny collection is housed inside the Mark Abbott Memorial Lighthouse, perched above the world-class surf activity of Steamer Lane, features a sweeping view of the

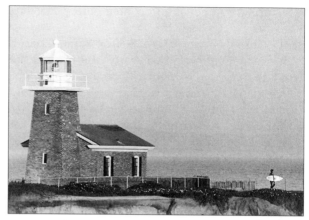

Overlooking some of the best surfing in the world, Lighthouse Point's diminutive beacon now marks the home of the Santa Cruz Surfing Museum.

Shmuel Thaler

Santa Cruz Beach and Boardwalk. On this spot in the late 1900s, Hawaiian princes first brought the ancient Polynesian sport to the New World.

MUSIC

Cabrillo Music Festival (831/426-6966; tickets 831/429-3444; Santa Cruz Civic Auditorium, Santa Cruz) For over a quarter of a century, this internationally acclaimed two-week summer festival (usually held during the first weeks of Aug.) of new, adventurous and avant-garde music takes the Santa Cruz cultural community by storm. Guest artists have included John Cage, Phillip Collins, Lou Harrison, Phillip Glass and Keith Jarret. The season's highlight is the closing day of performances in and around the Mission San Juan Bautista.

New Music Works (831/427-2225; U.C., Santa Cruz, Santa Cruz) The music ensemble, comprised of professional musicians and composers, showcases the best in contemporary classical music during its winter-summer season. Conductor Phillip Collins takes the group through myriad chamber music and musical theatre pieces, including its annual *Night of the Living Composers,* and culminates with the whimsical *Avant Garden Party* in the summer.

Santa Cruz Baroque Festival (831/457-9693; First Congregational Church and U.C., Santa Cruz, Santa Cruz) Top baroque interpreters and virtuosos of harpsichord, forte piano and vocal repertoire from around the San Francisco and Monterey Bay areas perform in this stellar series of early masters concerts. Bach, Vivaldi, Mozart, Scarlotti and their colleagues are brilliantly represented by solo, chamber and baroque specialists during its winter-spring season.

Santa Cruz Chamber Players (831/425-3149; U.C., Santa Cruz, Santa Cruz) A group of local musicians with an appreciation of unusual chamber music, featuring traditional and contemporary masterpieces, during its fall-spring season.

Santa Cruz Chorale (831/427-8023; Santa Cruz) A fifty-member community chorus that performs two yearly concerts and special performances throughout the year. The highlight of the chorale's season is the much-adored "Messiah Sing-Along," held at the beautiful Holy Cross Church every Dec.

Santa Cruz County Symphony (831/462-0553; Santa Cruz Civic Auditorium, Santa Cruz) A dynamic series of classical and contemporary orchestral masterworks performed by resident symphony and guest virtuosos in the acoustically renovated, Art Deco civic landmark during a fall-spring season.

Bach Dancing & Dynamite Society

Jazz nut and self-proclaimed beach bum Pete Douglas has run this homey, nonprofit music emporium on Miramar Beach for over thirty years. Sixteen to $20 will get you great music (often from touring headliners or up-and-coming Young Turks between gigs in San Francisco and Los Angeles) and incomparable ocean views. For a few dollars more, you can partake of a buffet. Attention: bring your own wine. Classical music on most Sat., 8:00 p.m.; jazz on Sun., 4:30 p.m. A mailer of coming attractions is available upon request (650/726-4143; P.O. Box 302, El Granada, CA 94108).

NIGHTLIFE

The Avenue (831/426-3434; 711 Pacific Ave., Santa Cruz) The recent renovations include nicely appointed private booths, a wood floor and a tasteful back patio sporting an outdoor bar. It's a place where urban professionals in their early thirties would feel quite comfortable — though it's more akin to a working-class rumpus room. As the plethora of video games and tight shirts would suggest, young college kids looking for love still fill the place on a Friday night.

Blue Lagoon (831/423-7117; 923 Pacific Ave, Santa Cruz) The Blue Lagoon remains the best place in town to get down to techno and disco music. Its full bar offers an amazing selection of libations, and a celebration of any sort isn't the same without one of the bar's famous Flaming Dr. Peppers. Expect a diverse crowd, from the leather-clad to those in velour hip-huggers. Don't be shocked if there's a line out the door — more and more people have come to know and love Santa Cruz's oldest gay bar.

Catalyst (831/423-1336; 1011 Pacific Ave., Santa Cruz) One of the coast's top venues, the friendly dance hall, affectionately nicknamed the "Cat" by locals, offers a billiards room, three bars, a great sound system and a massive dance floor. Every form of rock and world-fusion music is booked, including area artists and some of the biggest names in the biz like

Emmylou Harris, Pearl Jam and Neil Young. The Catalyst serves food daily, has three full bars, multiple pool tables and a tropical, vine-ensconced atrium where smaller acts sometimes play.

Cocoanut Grove Ballroom (831/423-2053; 400 Beach St., at the Boardwalk, Santa Cruz) A little bit of cultural history thrives in this boardwalk institution. Built back in the 1940s, the elegant ballroom has seen its share of big names, magical nights and frolicking patrons. Glenn Miller, Tito Puente, David Crosby and James Brown are just some of the acts who've done their magic on the retro bandstand.

Crow's Nest (831/476-4560; 218 E. Cliff Dr., Santa Cruz Yacht Harbor) Like a grand old galleon, this venerable drinking (and eating) establishment keeps sailing right along, only stopping to pick up devoted new passengers. It's a one-size-fits-all spot, though definitely not a gen-X place. The Nest caters to the yachting — or wanna-be yachting — crowd. Good drinks, seasoned atmosphere and plenty of people upon which to feast your eyes.

Front Street Pub (831/429-8838; 516 Front St., Santa Cruz) For over a decade, downtown's Santa Cruz Brewing Company has been brewing and bottling its own creations. The Thursday "Happy Evening" prices can't be beat, and the garlic fries have quite a kick — just don't order them if you're in a hurry. The Brewery is user-friendly, with large wooden booths, a backroom full of pool tables and pinball games, a patio and frequent entertainment by local bands. The Lighthouse Amber and F.G.S. are definite winners. Don't expect cocktails, though, it's beer and wine only.

Ideal Bar and Grill (831/423-5271; 106 Beach St., Santa Cruz) Best known as a restaurant, Ideal also has a bar located right at the mouth of the Santa Cruz Wharf. Settled seductively along the sand, Ideal's interior is as light and breezy as the beach air — viney greenery winds its way around the nooks and crannies, and surfboards and surfer pix adorn the walls. There's a square bar chock-full of all of the libations that one could hope for and a small, live music stage. Almost every night, smooth jazz, rock and pop accompany the drinking and dining.

Kuumbwa Jazz Center (831/427-2227; 320-2 Cedar St., Santa Cruz) A Santa Cruz institution for over twenty years, Kuumbwa attracts some of the top names in folk and both classic and experimental jazz, A nonprofit club propelled mostly by the success of big name, sellout shows, donations and grants, it offers an outlet for both local performers and those of worldwide acclaim. Fridays tend to see area artists playing world-beat, trance and acid jazz, while the Monday Night Concert Series boasts the *crème de la crème* of the jazz world. Nestled in between downtown SC's Bagelry and Poet & Patriot, it's an intimate venue that attracts appreciative, knowledgeable audiences. Wine, beer and tasty grub are served in the back.

Mobo Sushi (831/425-1700; 105 S. River St., Santa Cruz) Mobo Sushi uniquely blends traditional and unconventional flavors and serves them up with live entertainment every Thurs., Fri. and Sat. nights. A complete bar on one side, a sushi bar on the other, Mobo offers sake, beer, wine and all of the fixings to wash down The Flying Tiger, Landshark, Mad Dog or any other Japanese fare that the friendly sushi chefs roll up.

Moe's Alley (831/479-1854; 1535 Commercial Way, Santa Cruz) Moe's has all of the makings of a classic roadhouse joint. Smoky, dimly lit and appealing to all walks of life, from aging hippies, old-time bluesmen and cowpokes to college kids, hipsters and singles. It's a clean, comfortable spot to enjoy live music any night of the week. Local bands, plus blues' powerhouses like Joe Louis Walker, Charlie Musselwhite and Duke Robillard, play the best in funky covers and original material.

99 Bottles of Beer (831/459-9999; 110 Walnut Ave., Santa Cruz) The perfect bar for those who love their suds, 99 Bottles has a warm, brick-and-hardwood interior that just begs patrons to settle in for the long haul. As the name implies, there's a huge selection of the frothy stuff, from local microbrews to foreign beers — drink 'em all (not at one sitting, of course) and you'll find your name on the wall of fame. Features an upstairs gaming room and a ton of pub food to complement all that beer.

Palookaville (831/454-0600; 1133 Pacific Ave., Santa Cruz) An intimate venue, though it can pack in a whopping 600 clubgoers, Palookaville plays host to live music many nights of the week. Sporting an excellent sound system and a formidable lineup of musicians — Maceo Parker, Herbie Hancock, Frank Black — this downtown venue allows showgoers to cut a rug on its expansive dance floor. For those not inclined to groove, there's an upstairs balcony and plenty of tables arranged for the best views from a seated position. Pizza, sandwiches and desserts, as well as beer and wine, are served.

Poet & Patriot Irish Pub (831/426-8620; 320 Cedar St., Santa Cruz) When Celtic musicians aren't fiddling and drumming in the front room, the Poet overflows with university types tossing back pints and talking about their goatees and the revolution — in that order. The other room is dedicated to darts, which gets a little serious at times, and the bar stools belong to old hippies and card-carrying Irishmen. Dark, low-ceilinged, smoky-aired and sticky-tabled, this is a bar that feels like an old friend with interesting opinions. Word to the curious: reading the walls is good "edutainment."

Red Room (831/426-2994; The Santa Cruz Hotel, 1003 Cedar St., Santa Cruz) Easily the loudest, most irritating, most forgiving place to get a drink in town. The multiple pierced, the almost retired, the grunged, the lifted, the alternatively gendered, the manic — they all come here, sooner or later, and form an immediate pod of evening camaraderie. After 9:00 p.m., laughter at this bar becomes a collective bonding ritual. Even the socially deficient leave with new best friends. A rite of passage. A way of life.

Seabright Brewery (831/426-2739; 519 Seabright Ave., Santa Cruz) One of the most popular spots on the eastside, the brewery boasts beers brewed on-site, a menu of appetizers, burgers and salads and one of the finest outdoor patios for sun-soaked afternoons and heater-warmed nights. Tuesday marks the famed "Neighborhood Night" — those from outside the burg are also welcomed with open arms — for a night of discount pitchers from 3:00 p.m. until closing. Seabright ushers in the weekend with live music every Fri. evening.

Severino's (831/688-8987; 7500 Old Dominion Crt., Aptos) The Seacliff Inn's very own restaurant, bar and dance spot, Severino's is a spot for well-heeled, cultured adults looking to let loose for a night. Don those spiffy clothes, be on your best behavior (at least until you've downed a few martinis) and soak in the sights. There's live jazz and pop standards on the weekends, an outdoor patio and a trickling waterfall. It's a comfortable, attentive nightspot.

THEATER

Actors' Theatre (831/425-7529; 1001 Center St., Santa Cruz) Dramatic and musical performances, plus a series of readings of new plays are offered by this lively, local, year-round production company in a small theater venue.

Santa Cruz Bay City Opera (831/IC–OPERA; Cabrillo College Main Theater, Aptos) The opera company elaborately stages full productions of classic operas like *Carmen* and *The Barber of Seville*. All productions are sung nontraditionally in English, but feature full sets and original costumes and have a chorus and a chamber orchestra.

Santa Cruz Bay Lyric Opera (831/475-3518; Capitola Theater, 120 Monterey Ave., Capitola) A recent addition to Santa Cruz's stage world, the Bay Lyric Opera performs some of the world's classic operas like Puccini's *La Boheme.* Fully staged productions complete with a twenty-six-piece orchestra, the Bay Lyric company holds its productions in the vintage Capitola Theater.

Santa Cruz Dance Gallery (831/457-1448; 418 Front St., Santa Cruz) The Dance Gallery is one of Santa Cruz's local hot spots for innovative, up-and-coming dance talent. It doubles as a dance studio and performance gallery, offering classes in everything from traditional dance to drum-inspired tribal dances, and plays host to shows by local dance luminaries and young, experimental talent.

Shakespeare Santa Cruz (831/459-2121; Performing Arts Complex, U.C., Santa Cruz, Santa Cruz) A vivacious professional theater company of top American and British actors hosts innovative and critically acclaimed productions of Shakespeare and related contemporary dramatic works. The three-play summer festival holds forth in repertory performances on the large Performing Arts Theater stage, as well as in the outdoor redwood glen.

Tandy Beal & Company/New Pickle Circus (831/429-1324) Santa Cruz is the home base of the nationally acclaimed troupe, an innovative touring ensemble that performs its engaging blend of soaring contemporary choreography and witty multimedia work several times each year in Santa Cruz and Monterey, as well as in major big city venues.

Dancer/choreographer Tandy Beal leads her Central Coast-based modern dance company on annual international tours.

Mark Wagner

This Side of the Hill Players (650/726-0998; 650/726-9208; 1167 Main St., Half Moon Bay) The local theater company stages three full productions a year, including original and classic plays like *The Great Toy Conspiracy* and *The Fantasticks.*

UC Santa Cruz Presents (831/459-2826; U.C., Santa Cruz, Santa Cruz) The campus' arts and lecture series books top multicultural troupes from around the world and innovative dance faculty choreographers to dance on the university's Performing Arts Theatre stage.

SEASONAL EVENTS

January

Fungus Fair (831/429-3773; Santa Cruz).
Heritage Day Festival (650/726-2418; Half Moon Bay).

February

Boardwalk's Clam Chowder Cook-Off (831/429-3477; Santa Cruz).
Cultural Council's Hearts for the Arts (831/688-5399; Santa Cruz).
Natural Bridges Monarch Butterfly Migration Festival (831/423-4609; Santa Cruz).

March

Great Chowder Chase Running Race (831/429-3477; Santa Cruz).
Kayak Surf Festival (800/499-3648; Santa Cruz).

Each January, Santa Cruz area mycologists gather to trade notes, sample wild mushrooms and don silly costumes at the Fungus Fair.

Shmuel Thaler

April

Big Basin & Castle Basin State Parks Trail Days (831/968-7065; Santa Cruz).
Classic Golf Tournament (831/429-3477; Santa Cruz).
Masters' Cup Open Disc Golf Tournament (831/423-7214; Santa Cruz).
Rhododendron Show (831/475-3024; Santa Cruz).
Spring Wildflower Show (831/429-3773; Santa Cruz).

May

Bluegrass Art & Wine Festival (831/335-4441; Felton).
Blues Festival (831/479-9814; Aptos).
Boulder Creek Art & Wine Festival (831/338-7099; Boulder Creek).
Celebrate Santa Cruz (831/429-8433; Santa Cruz).
Chamarita Festival (650/726-2729; Half Moon Bay).
Cinco de Mayo Celebration (831/429-3504; Santa Cruz).
Flower Festival (650/726-3194; Half Moon Bay).
Great Salsa Taste-Off (831/429-3477; Santa Cruz).
Heritage Day Festival (650/726-2418; Half Moon Bay).
Longboard Invitational (831/425-8943; Santa Cruz).
Strawberry Festival (831/724-3954; Watsonville).
Vintners' Festival (831/479-9463; Santa Cruz county).

June

Japanese Cultural Fair (831/475-2115; Santa Cruz).
Vintners' Festival (831/458-5030; Santa Cruz).
Woodies on the Wharf (831/429-3477; Santa Cruz).

July

Fat Fry (831/476-5024; Aptos).
Firecracker 10K Race (831/429-3477; Santa Cruz).
Fourth of July Celebration (831/429-3477; Santa Cruz).
Old-Fashioned Fourth of July (650/728-3313; Half Moon Bay).
Wharf to Wharf Race (831/475-2196; Santa Cruz).
World's Shortest Fourth of July Parade (831/688-2428; Aptos).

August

Arts & Fun Festival (650/879-0848; Pescadero).
Cabrillo Art & Wine Festival (831/426-6966; Santa Cruz).
Calamari Festival (831/427-3554; Santa Cruz).
Civil War Re-enactment (650/726-4162; Half Moon Bay).
County Fair (650/574-3247; San Mateo).
Dickens Universe (831/459-2103; U.C., Santa Cruz).
Jose Cuervo Pro Beach Volleyball Tour (800-793-TOUR; Santa Cruz).
Roughwater Swim (831/429-3477; Santa Cruz).

September

Begonia Festival (831/476-3566; Capitola).
Capitola Art and Wine Festival (831/475-5179; Capitola).
County Fair (831/688-3384; Santa Cruz).
Greek Festival (831/429-6500; Santa Cruz).
Harbor Days (650/726-5727; Pillar Point).
Labor Day Ultimate Frisbee Invitational (831/459-2531; Santa Cruz).
Open Horseshoe Tournament (831/429-3477; Santa Cruz).

October

Apple Butter Festival (831/722-1056; Watsonville).
Arts & Crafts Festival (831/438-6038; Aptos).
Fireworks Spectacular (831/429-3477; Santa Cruz).
Hallcrest Vineyards Harvest Fair (831/335-4441; Felton).
Italian Heritage Festival (831/423-5590; Santa Cruz).
Mission Parade and Fiesta (831/429-3663; Santa Cruz).
Open Studios Tour (831/688-5399; Santa Cruz).
Pumpkin and Art Festival (650/726-9652; Half Moon Bay).
Sentinel Triathlon (831/423-4242; Santa Cruz).

November

Christmas Crafts and Gifts Festival (831/423-5590; Santa Cruz).
Women's Surfing Contest (831/475-6522; Capitola).

December

Christmas Bird Count (831/427-2288; Davenport).
First Night Santa Cruz (831/425-7277; Santa Cruz).
Harbor Lighting (650/726-4723; Pillar Point).
Lighted Boat Parade (831/425-0690; Santa Cruz).
Music for the Feast of Christmas (831/429-3477; Santa Cruz).

RECREATION

Obsessed with the outdoors and drawn to the sea, Santa Cruzans relish reinventing ways to play in the open air. No stretch of scenic road is without its walkers, runners and cyclists. Rain or shine, beaches bloom with tide pooling and volleyball enthusiasts. Beyond the edge of the land, the ocean simmers with surfers, swimmers and sailors. Parasailers, windsurfers and hang gliders tempt the fates at myriad chance-taking sites. Fishing enthusiasts find reverie and fuel for tall tales in wave, pond and stream. Camping along the coast and in its forests and valleys is *de rigueur* for all. Whatever the recreational itch, Santa Cruz has the exact pastime to scratch it.

BEACHES

Bean Hollow State Beach (Hwy. 1 north of Bean Hollow Rd., Santa Cruz) A
little gem of curved beach and lagoon offers a view of pounding waves and

The sheltered sands of Capitola City Beach offer a haven for beach lovers and sand castle builders of all ages.

Shmuel Thaler

dangerous surf. Parking, rest rooms and picnic tables are available. No entrance fee.

Bonny Doon Beach (Hwy. 1 at Bonny Doon Rd., south of Davenport) Hidden from view, this stretch is a cult favorite with surfers throughout the northern Central Coast. No facilities, no entrance fee.

Capitola City Beach (Esplanade & Monterey Sts., Capitola) Restaurants, shops and galleries line the esplanade framing this popular swimming, sunbathing and people-watching area. A safe play area for children is formed by the curve of Soquel Creek as it meets the sea, and nonstop volleyball is practically a religion. Parking is almost impossible, so take the shuttle located at the Hwy. 1 & Park Ave. exit. No entrance fee.

Corcoran Lagoon Beach (E. Cliff Dr. at 21st Ave., Santa Cruz) Frequented by the local beach community, this undeveloped cove is accessible by stairs at 20th Ave. and offers some fine tide pools, as well as sand. No entrance fee.

A sheltered shore and gentle waves have made Cowell Beach in Santa Cruz popular with ocean swimmers and beginning surfers.

Paul Schraub

Cowell Beach (W. Cliff Dr. & Bay St., Santa Cruz) Stairways lead down to this prime day-use location at the top of Santa Cruz's main beach, featuring volleyball during the summer and year-round surfing at Steamer Lane, one of the legendary sites on the Pacific Ocean. A paved walkway leads to rest rooms, and wheelchair access to the shore is provided during the summer season. Parking and lifeguard on duty during the crowded summer season. No entrance fee.

Davenport Beach (Hwy. 1 at Davenport) Undeveloped and sheltered, this beach roams along cliffs and bluffs. Parking only on highway shoulders and in the town of Davenport. No entrance fee.

Dunes Beach (off Young Ave., Half Moon Bay) A dirt road provides access to this prime setting for horseback riding on the beach. Horse rentals are nearby just off Hwy. 1. Ample parking. No entrance fee.

El Granada Beach (bet. E. Breakwater & Mirada Rd., Half Moon Bay) A seawall keeps this sheltered, sandy stretch particularly peaceful. Come prepared for cool, foggy conditions. Parking and rest rooms are available. No entrance fee.

Francis Beach (at Kelly Ave., Half Moon Bay) One of the fishing village's main beach areas, this spot offers fifty campsites and RV slots, with picnic tables on bluffs overlooking the beach. Rest rooms and beach alike are wheelchair accessible. Fees for camping and day use.

Hooper Beach (Capitola Wharf, Capitola) Peacefully out of the way from Capitola's main beach, this secluded stretch is perfect for undisturbed wave watching and picnicking. Parking is available but usually a challenge. No entrance fee.

Laguna Creek Beach (Hwy. 1 at Laguna Creek) Another of this stretch of the coast's many hidden, cliff-hewn cove beaches. Undeveloped to the delight of privacy-conscious sun worshippers. No entrance fee.

Lighthouse Field State Beach (W. Cliff Dr. & Pelton Ave., Santa Cruz) Just north of Lighthouse Point, this broad stretch of beach offers fine swimming and is accessible by walkways down to the sand. The basic theme here is "endless summer," with plenty of impromptu musical and drumming sessions, frolicking dogs and kids. Across the street is an undeveloped park of wildflowers and trees crisscrossed by walking and biking paths and studded with picnic tables. This is a favorite local spot for early morning and sunset walking rituals, cycling, in-line skating and front-row viewing of the surfing just off Lighthouse Point. Parking is available. No entrance fee.

Manresa State Beach (Hwy. 1 to San Andreas Rd. exit, La Selva) A treasure in this stretch of the coast, Manresa is accessible via stairway and paths from the main parking lot and by Sand Dollar Dr. walkway. Lovely for strolling and wading with the abundant shorebirds. Swimmers beware: Manresa possesses formidable rip currents. Rest rooms and sixty-three campsites for tent camping are available. Entrance fee.

Martin's Beach (Hwy. 1, 6 miles south of Half Moon Bay) Prime surf fishing, especially for smelt, is the top attraction of this privately developed cove beach. Rest rooms and picnic tables are available. Toll road with entrance fee.

Natural Bridges State Beach (2531 W. Cliff Dr. off Hwy. 1 (Mission St.), Santa Cruz) At the northern edge of Santa Cruz proper, rugged cliffs and sandstone rock formations sculpted by wind and wave create an enchanting setting. Unfortunately, the graceful arches that gave the beach its name have succumbed to the elements. Features over fifty acres of cypress and eucalyptus groves, to which the brilliant orange monarch butterflies migrate each year. On weekends from Oct.–Feb., guided tours of the Butterfly Natural

Preserve are available. Natural Bridges is famous for tide pools filled with pink-tentacled anemones, black turban snails, prehistoric-looking mossy chiton and purple sea urchins. Sandy beaches adjoin picnic sites, and much of the lovely property is wheelchair accessible. Rest rooms and ample parking are available. No entrance fee.

New Brighton State Beach (Hwy. 1 Park Ave. exit, 4 miles south of Santa Cruz) Pristinely sheltered, these sixty-eight sandy acres are crowned by bluffs of fragrant eucalyptus and offer myriad trails through beachfront forests and beach access by stairway. A good waterfowl viewing area, the long sandy beach offers rest rooms that are wheelchair accessible, 115 campsites, showers and bicycle camping sites. Fire pits along the beach make this a popular location for al fresco cookery. A splendid view of the Monterey coastline, just across the bay, makes this a favorite with vacationers and daytrippers alike. Entrance fee.

Opal Cliffs-Key Beach (E. Cliff Dr. south of 41st Ave., Santa Cruz) Some of the top surfers in the country haunt this charming pocket beach, accessible via walkway through private property. Undeveloped, it offers minimal parking. No entrance fee.

Palm Beach (Hwy. 1 to Hwy. 129 exit then to Beach Rd., Watsonville) Encompassing a driftwood mother lode at the mouth of the Pajaro River, this is a lovely getaway beach boasting wheelchair-accessible rest rooms, a picnic area and a fitness trail. Day-use fee.

Panther Beach (Hwy. 1, 1 mile north of Bonny Doon Rd., near Davenport) Accessible only by a trail through artichoke fields, this secluded setting remains undeveloped and heavily frequented by die-hard surfers and boozing teens from the Santa Clara Valley. Fistfights and car break-ins compete with the crashing waves for visitors' attention.

Pebble Beach (Hwy. 1 bet. Hill Rd. & Artichoke Rd., 1.5 miles south of Pescadero Rd., Pescadero) Pebbles worn round and smooth by the waves are the specialty here, including varieties of agate. Tiny but inviting, there is a self-guided nature trail leading south to Bean Hollow State Beach. Rest rooms and picnic tables are available. No entrance fee.

Pescadero State Beach (Hwy. 1 at Pescadero Rd., Pescadero) This mile-long beach offers an irresistible diversity of terrain, from soft dunes to highly explorable tide pools. Just across the Coast Highway from the sights and sounds of the wildlife preserve of Pescadero Marsh and offering lots of rest room facilities and picnic sites, this is a top all-day destination. Plenty of parking and hiking trails. No entrance fee.

Pleasure Point Beach (E. Cliff Dr. & 41st Ave., Santa Cruz) A number of rocky trails lead to this surfing, swimming and clamming spot. The bluffs above the beach offer spectacular views of Monterey Bay, and several tide pools invite exploration. No entrance fee.

Pomponio State Beach (Hwy. 1, 3 miles north of Pescadero Rd., Pescadero) A luscious stretch of beach offers prime driftwood-gathering possibilities, thanks to the confluence of a scenic creek. Many facilities, including rest rooms, picnic tables, cooking grills and ample parking are available. Day-use fee.

Red, White & Blue Beach (Hwy. 1 at Scaroni Rd., 5.5 miles north of Santa Cruz) A red, white and blue mailbox marks the spot south of Davenport for fans of clothing-optional sunbathing. Long a private beach, this naturists' mecca offers picnic tables but frowns on cameras and dogs. Day-use and camping fee.

Rio Del Mar Beach (south end of Seacliff State Beach, take Seacliff exit off Hwy. 1, Rio Del Mar) An esplanade well stocked with convenience stores and a fine seafood restaurant and bar fronts this wide expanse of sand that offers lots of privacy and long stretches of strolling during the week. On the weekends, the secret is poorly kept. Gentle waves make it attractive for bodysurfing during the late summer and early fall. A bike path/walking trail connects with nearby Seacliff State Beach. Rest rooms and ample parking are available. No entrance fee.

San Gregorio Beach (Hwy. 1 & San Gregorio Rd., San Gregorio) At the intersection of an old stagecoach road, this idyllic cove setting is framed by encircling coastal hills and rolling farmlands. The spot marks one of the campsites of Portola's 1769 Spanish expedition to the San Francisco Bay. Watch out for rip currents. Rest rooms and picnic tables supply all-day comfort. Day-use entrance fee.

Santa Cruz Beach and Boardwalk (Beach St. near Front St., Santa Cruz) The Boardwalk with its vendors, games and rides is the last remaining oceanfront amusement park in California. On a hot day, the adjoining Santa Cruz and Cowell beaches are where the action is — whether it's surfing, sunbathing, swimming, volleyball or strolling on the pier. Ample pay parking. No entrance fee.

Scott Creek Beach (Hwy. 1 north of Davenport Landing, Davenport) The broad expanse of sand offers plenty of room for sunbathers and beachcombers. An intertidal reef and numerous tide pools teem with marine life. Rest rooms and parking are available. No entrance fee.

Seabright Beach (E. Cliff Dr. & Seabright Ave., Santa Cruz) Known to locals as Castle Beach, this wide, sandy shoreline abuts the wonderful Santa Cruz Museum of Natural History. Good water sport spot. Limited parking. No entrance fee.

Seacliff State Beach (Seacliff exit off Hwy. 1., Rio Del Mar) You'll find a natural history center, covered picnic areas and twenty-six RV sites along this long, sandy, eighty-five-acre beach, which stretches below picturesque bluffs. The swimming is good, and fishing is allowed from a pier where the concrete-hulled freighter *Palo Alto* (a user-friendly curiosity left over from World War I) is docked. Showers are available. Entrance fee.

Sunset State Beach (San Andreas Rd. off Hwy. 1, Watsonville) Diverse flora and fauna, huge sand dunes and a pine-forested, ninety-tent site and RV campground distinguish this long expanse of beach. Located in a rural area just south of Manresa State Beach, its seven miles of sandy shoreline are great for beachcombing, picnicking, fishing and clamming. Showers are available. Entrance fee.

Twin Lakes State Beach (7th Ave. at E. Cliff Dr., Santa Cruz) Warm, wide and sheltered, this inviting expanse of sand curves around the mouth of a lagoon abundantly populated with ducks, geese and native waterfowl. Popular with lovers, sunbathers, families and fishing buffs who patrol the nearby harbor jetty. An irresistible stretch of powdery white sand, the beach offers lots of windsurfing and volleyball action, plus the eye appeal of boats weaving in and out of the yacht harbor. Rest rooms are available. Parking is on roadway shoulders (a bit dicey during the summer). No entrance fee.

Venice Beach (Venice Blvd., Half Moon Bay) Adjoins Dunes Beach by way of a dirt road. Offers luxurious sand, perfect for horseback riding and all-day beachcombing. No entrance fee.

Waddell Creek Beach (Hwy. 1, 1 mile south of San Mateo/Santa Cruz co. line) Adored by those who live here, this is the quintessential northern Central Coast beach. At the southwest tip of Big Basin State Park, this beautiful setting offers prime beachcombing and leisurely walks. Hang gliders love to soar overhead, and the surf beyond is invariably flecked with the multicolored sails of windsurfers. Coastal access is available via plenty of well-marked paths, as well as trails worn over the years by legions of die-hard surfers. Use trails through private property with discretion, since many of the local farmers are not amused by trespassers, however innocent or athletic. But if you feel the need to take your shoes off and gambol in the ebb tide with someone you love, this is the place. On the romantic scale of one to ten, Waddell Creek is a twelve. Rest rooms and parking are available. No entrance fee.

BICYCLING

BICYCLE RENTALS

Bicycle Center (831/426-8687; 131 Center St., Santa Cruz).
Bicyclery (650/726-6000; 415 Main St., Half Moon Bay).
Dutchman Bicycles (831/476-9555; 3961 Portola Dr., Santa Cruz).
Family Cycling Center (831/475-3883; 950 41st Ave., Santa Cruz).
Mission Street Cyclery (831/426-7299; 1211 Mission St., Santa Cruz).
Pacific Avenue Cycles (831/423-1314; 709 Pacific Ave., Santa Cruz).

TOP RIDES

Bonny Doon to San Lorenzo Valley Bonny Doon Rd. invites the lover of winding mountain roads to pedal through some classic redwood country. After a fairly serious climb, the road turns into Empire Grade, which follows

On a clear day, the hills of Monterey across the bay are visible to bicyclists enjoying the bluffs above Santa Cruz.

Shmuel Thaler

a rocky ridge north through a level road dotted with old orchards, farmhouses and vineyards. Descending Empire Grade into the small town of Felton and Hwy. 9, the cyclist encounters forests filled with moss-covered bay trees, madrones and redwoods that all but blot out the sun and form a long, green cathedral corridor.

East Cliff Drive A pleasant route that runs along both sides of E. Cliff Dr. offers a spectacular view of Monterey Bay.

Natural Bridges State Park Bike paths traverse this fifty-four-acre forest and beach area.

New Brighton State Beach Cycle through this sixty-eight-acre beach located four miles south of Santa Cruz.

San Lorenzo River Bikepath Bike paths run along both sides of the San Lorenzo River levee from Front St. to Santa Cruz Beach.

UC Santa Cruz Campus This scenic campus is crisscrossed with bike paths and affords cyclists a spectacular view of Monterey Bay.

West Cliff Drive A popular, flat ride from Natural Bridges State Park to the boardwalk that meanders along the coast past surfers, beachcombers and joggers and through fields of wildflowers and native grasses.

BIRD-WATCHING

Pescadero Marsh Natural Preserve (Hwy. 1 north of Pescadero Rd., 15 miles south of Half Moon Bay) Over 160 species of birds regularly visit and breed in this beautiful, undeveloped sanctuary, the largest coastal marshlands between Marin and Elkhorn Slough. Magnificent blue herons and egrets are among the most charismatic. The finest bird-watching seasons are late fall and early spring when the waters teem with loons and grebes, visually stunning additions to the resident community of egrets, herons, kites, hawks, mallards and cinnamon teal. Bird-watching is allowed along Pescadero Rd. and on marked interpretive trails off Hwy. 1, but tread lightly since this is a sensitive area.

Scott Creek (Hwy. 1 north of Davenport) An idyllic vision of tule-lined wetlands is gracefully encircled by the sandy beach on one side and the canyons and redwood-topped slopes of the Santa Cruz Mountains on the other. Wood ducks, cinnamon teals, mallards and coots keep company with grebes, herons and egrets in this languid oasis, especially beautiful in the early morning when mists rise from the surface of the deep green water.

Twin Lakes State Beach (E. Cliff Dr. near 7th Ave., Santa Cruz) The lagoon that spills over onto the white sandy beach originates across the slender roadway as Schwan Lagoon, a eucalyptus-ringed wildfowl refuge enjoyed via a wooded path around the park. Here pied-billed grebes and black-necked stilts glide in company with long-billed curlews and marbled godwits. Loons may be heard in the tall grasses, and a wide variety of ducks and geese are happy to be fed by those who come supplied with bags of bread.

Monarch Butterfly Migration

Great clouds of brilliant orange and black wings descend upon the Central Coast each winter as neon-hued monarch butterflies migrate south for the winter. Especially fond of wintering while packed tightly together in astonishing clusters, they literally enshroud entire groves of eucalyptus as they wait in semidormancy for the warmth of spring. Starting in October, monarchs are visible all over the coastline, but several spots are renowned for their annual populations of hundreds of thousands of these butterflies. The eucalyptus groves in the sheltered forests at **Natural Bridges State Park** (north of Santa Cruz) are prime viewing spots for this annual autumn influx of *lepidoptera*. Look, but don't touch. Docents at the park (831/423-4609) lead "butterfly walks" during the fall and winter.

Each winter huge numbers of monarch butterflies migrate south for the winter, blanketing eucalyptus groves throughout the Central Coast, especially in Santa Cruz, Pacific Grove and Morro Bay, with their neon-orange display.

Shmuel Thaler

BOATING

CANOEING & KAYAKING

Adventure Sports Unlimited (831/458-3648; Sash Mill #15, 303 Potrero St., Santa Cruz, CA 95060) Instruction, classes, rentals, sales, tours of Big Sur and Carmel.

Kayak Connection (831/479-1121; Santa Cruz Yacht Harbor, 413 Lake Ave., Santa Cruz, CA 95062) Guided tours, long and short kayak rentals, retail sales.

Venture Quest Kayaking (831/427-2267; 125 Beach St., Santa Cruz, CA 95060) Kayak rentals, sales, lessons and guided tours.

CHARTERS & CRUISES

Chardonnay Sailing Charters (831/423-1213; Santa Cruz Small Crafts Harbor, Santa Cruz, CA 95060) Three-day and sunset cruises, as well as private charters, available aboard a fifty-foot ultralight racing yacht. Ask about their wine- and beer-maker cruises as well. Trips depart from Santa Cruz Small Craft Harbor.

Earth, Sea & Sky Tours (831/688-5544; 7887 Soquel Dr., Aptos, CA 95003) Professionally guided tours. Whale-watching, fishing and diving excursions available, plus sunset, Champagne and dinner cruises.

Pacific Yachting (831/423-7245; 790 Atlantic Ave., Santa Cruz, CA 95062) Choose from 2-, 4- or 6-hour cruises.

Pleasure Point Charters (831/475-4657; E. Cliff Dr., Santa Cruz, CA 95062).

FISHING

FISHING & HUNTING REGULATIONS

California Department of Fish & Game (916-227-2244; 3211 S St., Sacramento, CA 95816) Information, licenses and tags.

CHARTERS

Huck Finn Sportfishing (650/726-7133; Pillar Point Harbor, 1016 Bancroft Ave., Half Moon Bay, CA 94019) Open-party and charter trips for salmon and rockfish aboard a sixty-foot boat. Bait, tackle and rental gear are available. Check in 5:15 a.m., depart 6:15 a.m., return 3:00 p.m.

Santa Cruz Sportfishing (831/475-6161; scfishin@cruzio.com E-mail; http://usafishing.com/Santacrz.html; P.O. Box 5235, Santa Cruz, CA 95060) Group and individual fishing trips for salmon, rock cod and albacore in both deep and shallow waters. Whale-watching tours and boat cruises are also available. Fishing equipment, licenses and bait rentals are available. Reservations recommended.

Shamrock Charters (831/476-2648; Santa Cruz Yacht Harbor, 2210 E. Cliff Dr.,

Santa Cruz, CA 95060) Open boats or private charters for salmon, rock cod and line cod fishing in season. Complete tackle shop and deli section. Licenses, bait and rod and skiff rentals are available.

Stagnaro's Fishing Trips (831/427-2334; Santa Cruz Municipal Wharf, P.O. Box 7007, Santa Cruz, CA 95060) Daily, half-day and evening trips for salmon and bottom fish, with bait provided. Fish cleaning and ice packing are available. Full-service wharf shop, bait, tackle, rentals, snacks and beer.

RENTALS, BAIT, TACKLE

Capitola Boat & Bait (831/462-2208; Capitola Wharf, 1400 Wharf Rd., Capitola) Mooring, equipment and boat rentals, bait and tackle, live bait, snacks, novelties and gifts are available. Marina open May-Sept, sunrise to sunset. Closed Dec. 25-Jan. 31.

Capitola Fishing Wharf (end of Wharf Rd., Capitola) Pier fishing. Bait and tackle shop is available.

Cement Ship (831/685-6444; 831/688-3241; State Park Dr., Aptos) The cement ship *Palo Alto* serves as a whimsical pier. Perch, halibut, flounder, sole and white croaker are caught here.

Savvy anglers have flocked to Santa Cruz county's rugged north coast for decades to catch their evening dinner.

Dan Coyro

El Granada Beach (runs along Hwy. 1 near Pillar Point Harbor, outside Half Moon Bay) Good surf fishing. The east breakwater is good for rockfishing, and surf perch, white croaker and starry flounder are most abundant.

Greyhound Rock (831/462-8333; Davenport) A favorite and beautiful, local fishing spot.

Johnson Pier (Half Moon Bay) Open twenty-four hours a day to catch rockfish and starry flounder.

Martin's Cove (private beach 6 miles south of Half Moon Bay) Small fee for surf fishing and smelt netting. Nets are available for rent.

Pomponio Beach (Hwy. 1 south of Half Moon Bay at Pomponio Creek) Surf perch, white crocker, starry flounder, and rockfish are caught here.

San Gregorio Beach (Hwy. 1 & San Gregorio Rd., San Gregorio) Surf perch, white crocker, starry flounder and rockfish abound. Rest rooms and a picnic area are available.

Santa Cruz Municipal Wharf (831/429-3628; Beach St., Santa Cruz) Bonito, croaker, flounder, halibut, ling cod and shark lead the seafood hit parade.

Santa Cruz Small Crafts Harbor (831/475-6161; Eaton St. at Lake Ave., Santa Cruz) Good fishing is available from the east jetty at the entrance. Boat rentals and supplies are available.

Sunset State Beach (831/763-7063; 201 Sunset Rd., Watsonville) Fishing and clamming. Rest rooms, picnic areas and showers are available.

Twin Lakes State Park (Portola Dr. near 7th Ave., Santa Cruz) Surf fishing is excellent. Rest rooms are available.

GOLF

Aptos Par 3 (831/688-5000; 2600 Mar Vista Dr., Aptos) Public; 9 holes, 1,044 yards, par 27, unrated.

Aptos Seascape Golf Course (831/688-3213; 610 Clubhouse Dr., Aptos) Public; 18 holes, 6,123 yards, par 72, rated 69.6. Pro shop, restaurant, banquet facility, golf lounge.

De Laveaga Golf Course (831/423-7212; 831/423-7214; Upper Park Rd. & De Laveaga Dr., Santa Cruz) Public; 18 holes, 6,010 yards, par 72, rated 70.1. Cart rental, pro shop, restaurant, bar.

Half Moon Bay Golf Links (650/726-4438; 2000 Fairway Dr., Half Moon Bay) Public; 18 holes, 7,100 yards, par 72, rated 71. Cart rental, pro shop, restaurant, bar.

Pasatiempo Golf Club (831/459-9155; 18 Clubhouse Rd., Santa Cruz) Semiprivate; 18 holes, 6,483 yards, par 72, rated 72.9. Pro shop, restaurant, bar.

HIKING

Big Basin State Park (14 miles north of Santa Cruz on Hwy. 9, extending to Hwy. 1, 30 miles north of Santa Cruz) Eighty miles of hiking trails embroider more than 18,000 acres of archetypal redwood forest stretching down to the rocky Pacific coastline. Founded in 1902, Big Basin was the first state park in the California system. Its crystal-clear streams, surging waterfalls, wildlife-rich meadows, fern canyons and towering, old-growth redwoods provide some of the finest hiking on the West Coast. Some trails are legendary. **Berry Creek Falls/Sunset** loop begins at the park headquarters and threads through cathedral stands of redwoods to the sixty-five-foot-high

---

Poison Oak Prevention

As if to even up the score in the stunning Central Coast, Mother Nature liberally populated the hills, fields and coastline with that three-leafed devil: poison oak. The oils contained in the leaves and stems of *Rhus diversiloba* are highly toxic to most people, and the allergic rash produced by contact is highly uncomfortable. The rash, with its redness, burning and excruciating itching, can last for weeks, though calamine lotion can provide some relief. The best course is to avoid *any* cross-country detours and stick to cleared areas and trails. Don't be fooled into thinking that you're safe clambering down the bluffs leading from Hwy. 1 to the shoreline below. In the rocky pockets and dense grasses right on the edge of the ocean wait some of the worst stretches of poison oak in the state. Find out what this plant looks like and memorize its shiny, three-leafed outline. It's unmistakable in the fall, when the leaves turn to a blaze of red and orange glory.

Berry Creek Falls, which cascades into a mossy pool in the heart of the forest. Experienced hikers who enjoy a variety of landscapes in a single, all-day trek will want to follow trails meandering along **Waddell Creek** and **Gazos Creek.** Leading from the park's mountain interior all the way down to the ocean at Hwy. 1, six- to eight-hour odysseys wind through stands of Douglas fir, madrone, tanbark oak, wild huckleberry, orchids, iris and western azalea. Maps for these and other tree-and-sea trails are available at the ranger's station at the park headquarters.

Butano State Park (5 miles south of Pescadero, 3 miles east of Hwy. 1) Tucked into the Santa Cruz Mountains just north of Big Basin State Park, 2,200 acres of primeval redwood canyons offer twenty miles of fine hiking trails through dramatic landscape, kept magically moist year-round thanks to coastal fogs. The redwood understory brims with sword fern, trillium, sorrel, thimbleberry and huckleberry, and it's not unusual to spot coyote, gray fox, mule deer and even the occasional bobcat. Backpackers can negotiate a pocket of first-growth redwoods on a five-mile hike to the 1,600-foot trail peak. Special guided nature walks through this natural sanctuary are offered in the summer.

Forest of Nisene Marks (Aptos Creek Rd. via Hwy. 1, Seascape exit) Ablaze with wildflowers during the spring and carpeted with velvety mosses and ferns during the lush, winter wet season, 10,000 acres of relatively undeveloped splendor showcase towering second-growth redwoods, vigorously reborn after the intensive logging of the late nineteenth century. Hiking trails lead for miles into deep canyons and up to bluffs that afford views of the ocean — the most popular of which follow Aptos Creek Canyon past the ghost town remnants of mining and logging camps. Quail, opossum and mule deer thrive here, and in the spring, the forest floor explodes with exquisite trillium, toothwort and starflowers. A monument to the revitalizing power of nature, the forest cradles the epicenter of the recent 1989 Loma

Prieta earthquake, marked by a sign on the Aptos Creek Trail. The forest offers myriad possibilities for day walks, picnics, horseback riding, bicycling and overnight camping at six rather primitive sites along West Ridge Trail.

Gazos Creek (Hwy. 1, 20 miles north of Santa Cruz) The Gazos Creek Rd. leads uphill, eventually becoming a trail that follows the creek through rugged fern canyons and meadows and ends high in the Santa Cruz Mountains at Big Basin State Park. Uphill and all-day, this hike rewards those with sturdy shoes and strong legs with fine views of the coastline and pristine, protected terrain.

New Brighton State Beach (Hwy. 1 at Park Ave. exit, Aptos) Interpretive nature trails provide prime waterfowl viewing, and sandy trails thread the beachfront, eucalyptus groves and panoramic bluffs of these sixty-eight secluded acres that front a splendid curve of the Monterey Bay. There is ample beach parking for those who want to explore the day away and 115 campsites with rest rooms for those with a longer idyll in mind. For information, call 831/475-4850.

Wilder Ranch State Park (Coast Rd. at Hwy. 1, 5 miles north of Santa Cruz) Recently purchased by the state of California, this former dairy ranch still houses authentically restored barns, stables, corrals and Victorian residential structures as part of an interpretive site celebrating ranch life on the nineteenth-century Central Coast. Hiking trails comb the park's 5,000 acres, which stretch from plover sanctuaries on the shoreline to heron rookeries, meadows and redwood bluffs at the 2,000-foot summit. Invigorating views of the ocean from the park's windswept bluffs are part of the reward for a day's walking. Open daily, 8:00 a.m. until sunset. For information about visitor center facilities, call 831/426-0505.

HORSEBACK RIDING

Big Basin Stables (831/338-8860; Hwy. 236 off Hwy. 9, Boulder Creek, CA 95006).

Redwood Riding Adventures (831/335-1334) Call for appointments, reservations or information.

Sea Horse/Friendly Acres Ranch (650/726-8550; 2159 Hwy. 1, Half Moon Bay, CA 94019).

NATURE PRESERVES & PARKS

Año Nuevo State Reserve (Hwy. 1 & New Years Creek Rd., Pescadero) Hiking trails lead along the northern bluffs, dunes and tide pools of this famous sanctuary. Gray whale sightings are legion during winter months, but the prime attraction remains the boisterous breeding ritual of the elephant seals, who gather here to mate and bear their soft, endearing young. Parking, rest rooms and a wheelchair-accessible path and viewing platform are available. Entrance fee.

Big Basin Redwoods State Park (831/338-8860; Hwy. 9 to Boulder Creek, west on Hwy. 236) Founded in 1902 as California's first state park, the vintage redwood preserve encompasses 18,000 acres of redwood and oak terrain, crisscrossed by eighty miles of hiking trails. During the summer months, rangers offer nature walks and campfire programs with lectures, slide shows and movies. An extremely popular, summer camping site since the day that it opened, the park offers a wide variety of overnight facilities, including thirty-six tent cabins with wood-burning stoves (closed in the winter), laundry facilities and showers.

Henry Cowell Redwoods State Park (831/335-4598; main entrance 1 mile south of Felton on Hwy. 9) Four thousand acres of magnificently forested redwood preserve were once the home of the Ohlone people. Today, miles of trails lead through impressive stands of oak, madrone, digger pine and chaparral terrain on sunny ridge tops. The ancient heart of this sanctuary is the stand of soaring, old-growth redwoods, easily enjoyed via the one mile Redwood Grove Nature Trail loop near the main picnic area. The oldest and most beautiful remaining on the Central Coast, this grove reduces even the jaded to genuine awe.

Año Nuevo Elephant Seal Walks

Named by the explorer Sebatian Vizcaino on January 3, 1603, this fascinating peninsula and offshore island contains tide pools filled with sea urchins, hermit crabs, anemones and other intertidal life-forms, while shell mounds left by Ohlone residents thousands of years ago still dot its rugged marsh, scrub and dunes. The Año Nuevo State Reserve protects colonies of northern elephant seals, who annually populate the sandy reaches of the reserve's more than one million acres during the winter breeding season. On guided walks, visitors may observe the enormous creatures at close hand from Dec.-Mar. Highly popular, the three-hour tour requires advance reservations (650/879-2025; Hwy. 1 & New Years Creek Rd., Pescadero).

SURFING

Capitola Jetty (Capitola village) Reef bottom, both rights and lefts; best at low tides, needs a six to eight-foot swell before it fires off, good beginner spot; lifeguards on duty during the summer.

Cowells Beach (in front of West Coast Santa Cruz Inn on W. Cliff Dr. near Santa Cruz Boardwalk) Sand bottom, very gentle rights; best at low tides, slow, easy peaks rolling onto a safe beach, perfect spot for beginners; lifeguards on duty during the summer.

Four Mile Beach (Hwy. 1, 1 mile south of Davenport) Reef break, fun rights;

intermediate to advanced spot; cars get broken into a lot; "red triangle" — great white sharks frequent area, not worth the risk to outsiders.

Hook (The) (end of 41st Ave., south of Pleasure Point, north of Capitola) Reef bottom, rights and lefts; smaller but usually faster waves than Pleasure Point, gets crowded (and angers locals), intermediate to advanced spot; exit from water dangerous at high tides (prepare to paddle half mile south to Capitola Pier).

Inside Pleasure (junc. of E. Cliff Dr. & 41st Ave.) Rocky reef bottom, all rights; good for beginners during small swell, really needs six-foot swell to work for advanced; can be gnarly (read: dangerous) during large swells, difficult to exit during high tides.

Manresa State Beach (Hwy. 1 to San Andreas Rd. exit, La Selva) Sandy beach break; best on smaller swells, large swells line up and close out, advanced; strong current during heavy surf.

Mavericks (off Pillar Point, Half Moon Bay) Known everywhere as the biggest, most treacherous waves in the world, Mavericks attracts serious surfers and daredevils. A sudden series of steep changes in depth pushes the swell up and out with explosive force, creating dangerous but exhilarating surfing conditions.

Natural Bridges Outer Reef (end of Swift St. off Hwy. 1 at northern city limits of Santa Cruz) Reef bottom, right break; needs a minus tide and big swell to work, advanced spot; nasty currents when big but a nice place for a day on the beach.

Pleasure Point (E. Cliff Dr. & 41st Ave., Santa Cruz) Reef bottom, rights and lefts; "sewer peak" has big bowls, super steep, for the advanced; 1st peak and 2nd have good longboard waves, work on any swell, intermediate to advanced.

California's Central Coast is famed for its safe, pristine and uncrowded surfing spots.

Shmuel Thaler

Scott Creek (Hwy. 1 north of Davenport Landing, Davenport) Reef bottom, beach break and a right point break; point break still rideable at fifteen to twenty feet, unpredictable, lots of kelp; "red triangle" — sharky.

Shark's Cove (Portola Dr. & 41st Ave., Santa Cruz) Reef bottom, mostly a right, left when it's small; fun, secondary waves that roll through the "hook" continue wrapping, best at low tide, larger waves line up and close out, beginner to advanced.

Steamer Lane (W. Cliff Dr. & Bay St., Santa Cruz) Reef bottom, mostly a right, left when it's big; "outsides" holds any swell, big rights that peel along the cliff line, not a beginner break, advanced; "middle peak" lines up nearly fifty yards from the cliff, holds any swell; a haven for seals and otters, kelp gets thick in some spots at low tide, high tide poses difficulties for exiting the water.

Sunset State Beach (San Andreas Rd. off Hwy. 1, Watsonville) Sand bottom, lots of peaks, lefts and rights; beginner spot when small, intermediate to advanced otherwise; can get big rips when there's a swell.

26th Avenue (off E. Cliff Dr., Santa Cruz) Reef/sand bottom, lefts and rights; underappreciated spot popular with bodysurfers, intermediate to advanced.

TENNIS

PRIVATE

Colony Club Tennis (650/726-2849; 650/726-1007; 2000 Fairway Dr., Half Moon Bay).

Imperial Courts Tennis Club (831/476-1062; 2505 Cabrillo College Dr., Aptos).

Seascape Sports Club (831/688-1993; 1505 Seascape Blvd., Aptos).

Tennis Club of Rio Del Mar (831/688-1144; 369 Sandalwood Dr., Rio Del Mar).

PUBLIC

Cabrillo College (831/479-6332; 6500 Soquel Dr., Aptos).

Derby Park (831/429-3777; Woodland Way at Natural Bridges School, Santa Cruz).

Harbor High School (831/429-3810; 300 La Fonda Ave., Santa Cruz).

Highland County Park (831/462-8333, Hwy. 9 & Glen Arbor Rd., Ben Lomond).

Jade Street Park (831/475-5935; 4400 Jade St., Capitola).

Santa Cruz High School (831/429-3960; 415 Walnut St., Santa Cruz).

Soquel High School (831/429-3909; 401 Old San Jose Rd., Soquel).

SHOPPING

The thoroughly Californian concept of shopping as entertainment remains alive and well in Santa Cruz. Shops here are not so much patronized as inhabited by gregarious locals who set up cafe colonies wherever the spirit moves them. From the area's many resident artisans come contemporary glass, jewelry, pottery and hand-sculpted furniture, sharing the modern shopping scene with top designer names in leather, silk and wool from around the world.

ANTIQUES & COLLECTIBLES

Downtown Santa Cruz Antique Fair & Collectibles (408/429-8433; Lincoln St. bet. Pacific & Cedar Sts., Santa Cruz) On the second Sun. of each month, expert collectors from the area set up shop and display a wide range of vintage goodies through the late morning and early afternoon.

Mr. Goodie's Antiques (408/427-9997; 1541 Pacific Ave., Santa Cruz) Awaiting the sharp-eyed collector are loads of wonderful stuff from bygone eras, including lavish antique and vintage costume jewelry, Depression glass and Fiesta ware, classic Hawaiian shirts and nostalgic prints.

Possibilities Unlimited (408/427-1131; 1043 Water St., Santa Cruz) A lavish expanse of old oak furniture greets the eye at this huge collective, surrounded by delightful collections of Americana, vintage prints and paintings, classic jewelry and glassware.

Shen's Gallery (408/457-4422; 1368 Pacific Ave., Santa Cruz) Perfumed by incense, this beautiful shop imports burnished Chinese furniture, jade and coral jewelry, ceramics, carvings, prints and Hsing tea pots — antiques every one.

Trader's Emporium (408/475-9201; 4940 Soquel Dr., Soquel) A popular browsing spot with local antique and collectible buffs, this gigantic old Quonset hut houses twenty-six distinct shops offering antique items of every possible description.

Wisteria Antiques (408/462-2900; 5870 Soquel Dr., Soquel) A globe-trotting buyer hauls back caches of vintage country French and European pine armoires, dining sets, rare occasional pieces and imaginative furniture. Together they stylishly populate this labyrinth of gardens and showrooms.

ARTS & CRAFTS

Annieglass (408/427-4245; 109 Cooper St., Santa Cruz; 408/426-5086; #2A 303 Potrero, Santa Cruz) Downtown's tiny boutique explodes with the bright colors of wall-to-wall unique glasswork. The studio and price-slashing outlet/showroom offers opulent designer glass tableware, serving pieces and home accessories.

Artisan's (408/423-8183; 1364 Pacific Ave., Santa Cruz) An engaging collection of the very finest in locally produced ceramics, woodwork, hand-loomed textiles, glassware, lamps, innovative toys and games and walls studded with local paintings and prints distinguish this local treasure.

Duhn Mehler Gallery (650/726-7667; 337 Mirada Rd., Half Moon Bay) Located right on the coast, this gallery features sculpture, pottery, jewelry, weavings, fine woodworkings, photography and children's books, as well as a spectacular view.

Gallery M (650/726-7167; 328 Main St., Half Moon Bay) Displays fine functional art furniture, unique sculpture, pottery, handwoven rugs and two-dimensional art handcrafted by well-known and emerging artists.

Importer extraordinaire, Barbara Horscraft of Gravago in Santa Cruz specializes in exotica from the Far and Middle East.

Paul Schraub

Gravago (408/427-2667; 111 Cooper St., Santa Cruz) Packed with fabulous finds from exotic corners of the Far and Middle East, from tapestries and antique copper and brass to Indonesian carvings and African trade bead jewelry.

Lundberg Studios (408/423-2532; 121 Old Coast Rd., Davenport) Showrooms for this internationally acclaimed art glass studio offer a world-class selection of Tiffany reproduction lamps, vases and iridescent lusterware bowls. The fabulous glassblown paperweights have found their way into the Smithsonian and Louvre gift catalogs.

New Davenport Cash Store (408/423-2532; 121 Old Coast Rd., Davenport) The finest tableware from local Santa Cruz Mountain potters shares floor-to-ceiling displays with Guatemalan hand-loomed textiles, elegant tie-dyed silks, Mexican Day of the Dead figures and antique ivory and amber, as well as stunning contemporary art jewelry.

Pacific Wave (408/458-9283; 1502 Pacific Ave., Santa Cruz) For the serious surfer or just the fashionable wanna-be, this converted bank holds a treasury of surf, skate and boogieboards, as well as quality activewear for the hip and young at heart.

Petroglyph (408/458-4278; 125 Walnut St., Santa Cruz) Creativity oozes from this brightly colored ceramics studio, the newest addition to the local arts and crafts scene. Petroglyph provides ceramics and paints, then turns customers lose with their imaginations.

Spanishtown Arts & Crafts Center (650/726-7366; 501 San Mateo Rd., Half Moon Bay) Colorful cluster of unique and high-quality regional arts and crafts in a dozen shops featuring revolving exhibits. Some shops are open during the week, all are open on the weekends.

Tenggara (408/423-1177; 1360 Pacific Ave., Santa Cruz) The art of Indonesia fills every nook and cranny of this intriguing shop, including vibrant batik designer clothing, a huge selection of distinctive wood carvings and huge quantities of jewelry to suit every taste and every credit card limit.

Walter-White Fine Arts (408/476-7001; 107 Capitola Ave., Capitola) An outstanding selection of regional art glass, as well as blown glass and silver and gold jewelry, creates a dazzling visual experience.

BOOKS

Bookshop Santa Cruz (408/423-0900; 1520 Pacific Ave., Santa Cruz) Many locals consider this sprawling, inviting store the heart of downtown Santa Cruz. Major news and magazine rack, ample seating for browsing and a lively in-house cafe make coming here an all-day event.

Bookworks (408/688-4554; 36 Rancho Del Mar Shopping Center, Aptos) A wide selection of books for all interests, with a special emphasis on young minds. Magazines and newspapers, as well as cards and gifts, an espresso bar and a small cafe round out the sprawling Aptos book cafe.

Capitola BookCafe (408/462-4415; 1475 41st Ave., Capitola) A major selection of national and international magazines highlights this well-stocked cultural mecca, graced by an in-house espresso and dessert cafe.

Gateways BookCafe (408/429-9600; 1018 Pacific Ave., Santa Cruz) Metaphysical and New Age offerings of every sort fill this engaging retreat, which also features motivational CDs and cassettes, incense, crystals and a vegetarian cafe. Very Santa Cruz.

Herland BookCafe (408/429-6636; 902 Center St., Santa Cruz) Women's bookstore in downtown Santa Cruz offers poetry readings and acoustic music some nights and also houses an espresso and vegetarian food cafe.

Literary Guillotine (408/457-1195; 204 Locust St., Santa Cruz) The rarest and best in small press and university press literature cram this tiny haunt for inquiring browsers and book lovers.

Logos (408/427-5100; 1117 Pacific Ave., Santa Cruz) Two huge floors are filled with used and rare books, including major science fiction, gothic paperback and women's sections. Used CDs, tapes and collectors' quality LPs make this place a hot, must-visit spot.

New Society Bookstore (408/423-1626; 515 Broadway, Santa Cruz) Located in the Resource Center for Nonviolence, this progressive boutique sells music, books, calendars and gifts of a politically correct persuasion. Guest speakers periodically drop by to cheer the troops. Expect sincere, homey ambiance, lively conversation and a bit of pamphleteering.

Streetlight Records (408/421-9200; 941 Pacific Ave., Santa Cruz) A good selection of both new and used record albums and CDs are available at this downtown shop. Streetlight proudly features local, underground music releases.

Zamzam (408/425-7264; 1001 Center St., Santa Cruz) Tucked in a corner of downtown's Santa Cruz Art Center, this tiny, intriguing nook is stocked with Islamic literature.

CLOTHING

Bunny's Shoes (408/423-3824; 1350 Pacific Ave., Santa Cruz) The smart, the trendy, even the avant-garde in women's footgear lie leisurely displayed in this appealing boutique for the enlightened foot fetishist.

Cat N' Canary (408/423-8696; 1100 Pacific Ave., Santa Cruz) Up-to-the-minute fashions for young men and women make this trendy shop a popular local landmark.

Cotton Tales (408/429-1956; 1201 Pacific Ave., Santa Cruz) This Santa Cruz tradition has always been a leader in providing quality, natural fiber children's clothing to the ecologically conscious community. The store also carries some baby toys and accessories and locally made quilts.

Cruz'n (408/476-2533; 127 Monterey Ave., Capitola) Geared to the young outdoorsy set, this shop features bold and sassy beachwear and resort apparel.

Hat Company (408/458-9585; 1346 Pacific Ave., Santa Cruz) Get a head of the trends at a store devoted entirely to haberdashery. This shop features every hat style imaginable, from the practical to the zany.

Hot Feet (408/476-3960; 319 Capitola Ave., Capitola) An all-encompassing shoe haven, this beachside shoe store stocks the trendy, the sensible and all of the footwear in between, plus socks, gloves and sunglasses.

Lauren's (408/462-5245; 120 San Jose Ave., Capitola) Well-chosen California sportswear and contemporary outfits, all in natural fibers, fill this tiny boutique by the beach.

Pacific Trading Company (408/476-6109; 504 Bay Ave., Capitola; 408/423-3349; 1338 Pacific Ave., Santa Cruz) Elegant, contemporary apparel, plus plenty of jewelry and accessories, have made this company popular with locals for the past decade.

Roberts (408/429-8212; 1531 Pacific Ave., Santa Cruz; 408/479-7917; 1855 41st

Ave., Capitola) Roberts is a mandatory stop for shoe lovers, both male and female. Both locations feature quality brands of casual and formal footwear, as well as leather jackets, bags and accessories. Roberts has recently expanded its selection of women's clothing.

Rue Des Anges (408/423-8466; 1533 Pacific Ave., Santa Cruz) This small boutique specializes in beautiful, delicate dresses and upscale women's clothing. It also features a selection of natural fabric casual wear and often has great sales on more elegant items.

Shandrydan (408/425-8411; 107 Walnut Ave., Santa Cruz) This spacious boutique is filled with California easy-living styles, local designer outfits and a bonanza of contemporary designer jewelry.

Yellow Bird (408/425-0542; 1129 Soquel Ave., Santa Cruz) Contemporary easy-to-wear ensembles, bold beach outfits, smashing one-of-a-kind scarves, imported and contemporary jewelry — everything with a distinctly California coastal attitude awaits the shopper at this pleasant shop.

JEWELRY

Eclectix (408/426-8305; 1139 Pacific Ave., Santa Cruz) Sensorially arresting and crammed to the rafters with exotic and antique jewelry of every description, this shop specializes in Native American and East Asian pieces that make for top-notch browsing.

Latta (408/475-1771; 120 Stockton Ave., Capitola) Contemporary variations on Art Nouveau themes distinguish the handsome, handmade jewelry created by local goldsmith Jay Latta. Set with polished and faceted gemstones, the rings are of special beauty.

Many Hands Gallery (408/429-8696; 1510 Pacific Ave., Santa Cruz) This shop features a visual feast of handcrafted gold, silver and cloisonné jewelry from top regional and California artisans, including many created in-house from antique crystal and semiprecious gemstone beads from around the world.

Thomas Mantle Designs (408/429-8234; 107 Locust St., Santa Cruz) A talented, resident goldsmith and jewelry designer creates one-of-a-kind contemporary mounted pieces in this engaging studio and showroom.

The Vault (408/426-3349; 1339 Pacific Ave., Santa Cruz) A stunning inventory of imaginative contemporary gold and silver jewelry, grouped into opulent display cases according to gemstones, make a visit to this shop feel like a stroll through a museum. In the back, a small boutique trades in exclusive silk blouses, gowns and sweaters.

SPECIALTY

Angel Moon (650/726-2133; 433 Main St., Half Moon Bay) Quintessentially Central Coast, it's a quirky, celestially oriented store filled with gifts, cards and books.

Arcangeli Grocery Company (650/879-0147; 287 Stage Rd., Pescadero) This family-style bakery and market, founded in 1929, is stocked with specialty goods like salsas, vinegars and oils, California wines, fresh-baked French breads and deli items.

Aries Arts (408/476-6655; 201 Capitola Ave., Capitola) The classic 1960s hippie shop, perfumed with incense and filled with colorful clothing, crystals and handmade jewelry.

Atlantis Fantasyworld (408/426-0158; 1020 Cedar St., Santa Cruz) This store is for the hard-core comic book and trading card aficionado. Look for collectors' items issues, plus the new and unusual for kids of all ages.

Camouflage (408/423-7613; 1329 Pacific Ave., Santa Cruz) This cozy store features a wide array of massage oils, sensual toys and books — a clean, well-lighted place to shop for lingerie and sleek women's clothing.

Cedanna Artful Living (650/726-6776; 415 Main St., Half Moon Bay) Stocked with modern furniture, art, housewares, scented candles and indulgent bath items, this eclectic store is one-stop shopping for home decoration.

Chefworks (408426-1351; 1527 Pacific Ave., Santa Cruz) A recreational chef's dream, this store is stocked to the gills with top-of-the-line pots, pans, woks, dishes, utensils and culinary accessories, plus cookbooks, olive oils, sauces and more.

Cunha's General Store (650/726-4071; 448 Main St., Half Moon Bay) The time trip starts when you enter this unique store packed with cowboy gear, dry goods and deli items. It ends when you leave, having overheard the tall tales of resident farmers and local fishermen.

Curiosa (408/423-3208; 703 Pacific Ave., Santa Cruz) An instant hit of Santa Cruz subculture, this on-the-edge shop offers body-piercing paraphernalia, leather, metal, *de rigueur* Doc Martens, banned books and an in-house piercing and tattoo parlor for that ultimate Central Coast souvenir.

Eco Goods (408/429-5758; 1130 Pacific Ave., Santa Cruz) For a little store, this downtown shop offers more ecologically correct goods than you can imagine. Eco Goods carries hemp clothing, natural fibers and environmentally friendly supplies for the entire family.

Gabriella Wine Shop (408/457-1217; 1016 Cedar St., Santa Cruz) Old-world Chiantis mingle with contemporary local wines at this quaint shop, which also features imported Mediterranean fare, fresh olives, homemade focàccia and gourmet hot lunches.

Integrand Design (408/426-4717; 1515 Pacific Ave., Santa Cruz) A local landmark for housewares, culinary accessories, contemporary furniture and luscious, imported bath items, this longtime favorite is housed inside a stately historic bank building in the heart of downtown.

Jones N' Bones (408/462-0521; 621 Capitola Ave., Capitola) An eclectic collection of specialty-flavored olive oils, vinegars, hot sauces, scone mixes and more, plus baking and cooking accessories is nestled in a charming old house with a lovely garden area in the Capitola Village.

Museum Shop (408/454-9986; 705 Front St., Santa Cruz) The Museum of Art and History's gift shop features great books of local artists, quirky knick-knacks and collector's items.

Paper Vision (408/458-1345; 1345 Pacific Ave., Santa Cruz) Books of all types are available, plus the most witty, comprehensive and mesmerizing selection of fine greetings cards in the area.

Pipeline (408/425-7473; 818 Pacific Ave., Santa Cruz) This head shop is one of the last downtown reminders of Santa Cruz's hippie heydays, the 1960s. Pipeline carries pipes and hookahs, as well as Indian and other Asian imports.

Salz Leather Store (408/423-1480; 1040 River St., Santa Cruz) Housed inside an historic, vintage 1860s tannery, this aromatic shop offers lush leather handbags, wallets and an executive line of briefcases.

Squid Row (behind Santa Cruz Art Center, just off Center & Union Sts.) A charming alley covered with blossoming plants, this one-block long street has been a traditional local center for unique arts and collectibles. It is often a site for special pottery sales featuring local artists' creations.

Tom Bihn Packs (408/423-5659; 103 Locust St., Santa Cruz) Any serious traveler should stop by this shop for its selection of backpacks, travel bags, insulated lunch sacks and other carriers for the adventurer or active types. Bihn also has a good supply of travelers' companions like passport carriers, money pouches and underclothing sacks.

Whole Lotta Peppers (408/420-0559; 111 Locust St., Santa Cruz) A perfect niche for spicy food lovers of all sorts, this downtown shop features sauces, salsas and decorations all devoted to the fiery pepper. Its chocolate-covered spicy nuts are truly one of a kind.

SPORTS

Aqua Culture Surf & Beach Shop (650/726-1155; 3032 Cabrillo Hwy. N, Half Moon Bay).

Bugaboo (408/429-6300; 1521 Pacific Ave., Santa Cruz) Boldly displayed paraphernalia for outdoor adventure — backpacking, climbing, cross-country skiing, biking and white-water rafting — top off this emporium.

Marini's at the Beach (408/423-7258; Santa Cruz Beach Boardwalk, Santa Cruz) A seriously well-stocked bastion of bathing and resort wear is peppered with Day-Glo bikinis, sensible one-piece suits of every description, men's trunks and complete lines of sandals and sunglasses.

O'Neill's Surf Shop (408/475-4151; 1115 41st Ave., Capitola) Founded by wet suit inventor Jack O'Neill, this is the Bonzai Pipeline of north Central Coast surf shops, with everything from sunglasses and baggies to surfboards.

Outdoor World, Inc. (408/423-9555; 136 River St., Santa Cruz; 408/479-1501; 1440 41st Ave., Capitola) Everything that you'll need to enjoy the great outdoors is here: sunglasses, snorkeling gear, insect repellent, racquets, balls, bathing suits, fins, goggles, canteens, compasses, shoes and shirts.

Paradise Surf Shop (408/462-3880; 3961 Portola Dr., Santa Cruz) Catering primarily to female surfers, this women-run surf shop features a choice selection of sporty clothes and swimwear, plus a fine array of surfboards.

Santa Cruz Mountaineering (408/476-2400; 940 41st Ave., Santa Cruz) Formerly MontBell, this sporting store offers everything that you'll need for an outdoor adventure. Clothing, backpacks, tents, sleeping bags and more (with a particular emphasis on camping) are offered at a discounted price. Many of the items are factory seconds and samples.

Santa Cruz Surf Shop (408/464-3233; 753 41st Ave., Santa Cruz; 811 Pacific Ave., Santa Cruz) One block from the beach and just down the road from top surfing conditions at Pleasure Point, this "locally grown" shop features a huge selection of surfboard and skateboard equipment, top brand names and locally designed Santa Cruz surfboards.

CHAPTER FOUR
Head of the Class
MONTEREY, CARMEL & BIG SUR

Cannery Row, with its destination hotels and fine restaurants, hugs the Monterey coast.

From whaling heydays past to state-of-the-art aquarium, Monterey has exerted on visitors a magnetic pull as constant as its spectacular tides. A patchwork of historic landmarks, waterfront lodgings and fishing activity, the area burst into the settler's consciousness when busy padre Junipero Serra joined Spanish explorer Portola in the founding of the mission and presidio of what was part of New Spain in the late 1700s. Surrounded by "Steinbeck country," the town of Monterey is still haunted by the ghosts of Doc Ricketts and the heroes of Cannery Row, today a pastiche of boutiques, bistros and tourist crafts galleries showcasing local artisans.

The adobes that marked the Mexican era share the limelight of careful restoration with the eighteenth- and nineteenth-century residences of sea captains and writers, such as Robert Louis Stevenson, who were attracted to the whaling and shipping milieu that enfolded Monterey. The Presidio — the first fort of the Spanish empire in California — still stands watch over the hemi-

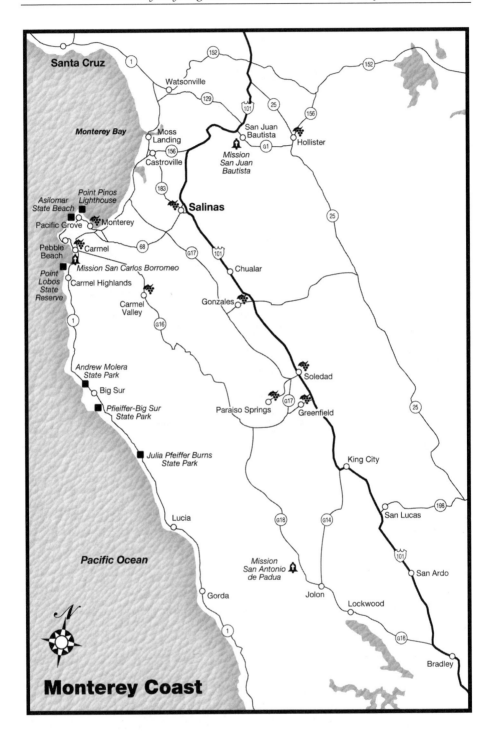

Monterey Coast

spherical Monterey Bay, though the spectacular exhibits and open-air wildlife sanctuaries of the Monterey Bay Aquarium now claim more visitors' attention. Embraced by the coast ranges to the east and the wild cliffs, rocks and tide pools that mark the crossroads of the Bay and the Pacific Ocean, Monterey continues to lure outdoor enthusiasts as well as artistic entrepreneurs.

At its geographical gateway, the tiny delta of the Salinas River, Monterey is edged by the abundant waterfowl colonies of Elkhorn Slough, visited by bird-watchers and ecologists from all over the world. The soothing coastal fogs that lend Monterey its moody ambiance also create unique habitats for rare flora, such as the Monterey cypress, and fauna, like the snowy plover and brown pelican. To its south, the town of Monterey is hugged in by the Carmel Highlands, a froth of forest and fern-laced undergrowth that announces the beginning of the challenging Big Sur coast, where the geologically youthful Coast Ranges are still lifting their way out of the ocean floor.

A pleasant architectural braid of Mediterranean terra-cotta and Iberian adobe with New England Victoriana, the texture of the entire Monterey region is permeated with the influence of the ocean. Thanks to its temperate influence, the area is embraced by a latticework of fields bearing greens — artichokes, broccoli, lettuces, strawberries — into America's markets. The town's long history as one of California's earliest settlements is balanced with its contemporary sheen as a world-class convention and conference center. Major hotel chains join scores of charming bed and breakfasts to house meetings and rendezvous of every sort. Restaurants vie with those of larger sister cities, San Francisco and Los Angeles. Dozens of local estates create handmade wines of national repute — Monterey county is increasingly the source for premium grapes in the entire state.

Tasteful, upscale, yet never far from the roots of its coastal attractions, Monterey is a vibrant emblem of the immigrant spirit that cultivated the Central Coast.

LODGING

Monterey and its coastal neighborhoods have been hosting guests since the Spanish first settled here at the end of the eighteenth century. The sheer number of high-quality, overnight possibilities testifies to the region's charisma as a destination for visitors from all over the world. The conference trade thrives in this spectacular waterfront setting, and contemporary hotel giants offer up rooms with a view and all of the amenities. Aficionados of the well-turned Victorian B&B consider Pacific Grove a treasure amounting to the mother lode. Carmel's abundance of irresistible overnight inns is as legendary as its haunting shoreline. And world-class resorts dot the coastal hills along Big Sur.

Credit Cards

AE – American Express   DC – Diner's Club
CB – Carte Blanche   MC – MasterCard
D – Discover Card   V – Visa

MONTEREY COAST

Monterey

JABBERWOCK
Innkeepers: Joan & John
  Kiliany.
888/428-7253; 831/372-
  4777; 831/655-2946 Fax.
598 Laine St., Monterey, CA
  93940.
Price: $105–$195, includes
  breakfast.
Credit Cards: MC, V.
Children: Two people (over
  age 12) per room.
Smoking: No.
Handicap Access: No.

Built in 1911 and once a convent, this post-Victorian home sits four blocks above Cannery Row and the Monterey Bay Aquarium. Charmingly homey with its *Alice in Wonderland*-ish whimsical decor, hidden gardens and waterfalls, the inn offers seven rooms decorated with beautiful antiques, plump comforters, Victorian beds with lace-trimmed sheets and fresh flowers. The Jabberwock's home-cooked breakfast may be taken in the privacy of overnight rooms or by the fireplace in the dining room. A bell rings at 5:00 p.m. each evening to announce freshly prepared hors d'oeuvres on the enclosed veranda overlooking estate gardens and Monterey Bay. Bedtime milk and heavenly chocolate chip cookies await visitors returning from their adventures. Five of the lovely rooms boast private baths, and three have fireplaces. The huge Borogrove Suite has its own cozy fireplace and a telescope for viewing shore sights. Complete with an impressive Lewis Carroll library, the Jabberwock is a hidden treasure that could inspire fairy tales of its own. A two-night stay is required on weekends.

MONTEREY PLAZA
Innkeeper: John V. Narigi.
800/631-1339 USA;
  800/334-3999 CA;
  831/646-1700;
  831/646-5937 Fax.
400 Cannery Row,
  Monterey, CA 93940.
Price: $195-$305.
Credit Cards: AE, CB, DC,
  MC, V.
Children: Yes.

Draped on pilings that extend out over the tide pools and kelp beds of Monterey Bay, this contemporary Mediterranean resort hotel enjoys a prime location just a stroll away from Cannery Row and the Monterey Bay Aquarium. Sheer elegance from its over-the-water piazza to its splendid furnishings and plush main lobby, Monterey Plaza specializes in rooms with coveted views. You can enjoy the spectacle of sea otters and seals frolicking just outside your balcony, sip an afternoon cocktail in the Schooner Bistro or take a tub in your marble bathroom before dinner in the

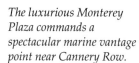

The luxurious Monterey Plaza commands a spectacular marine vantage point near Cannery Row.

Smoking: No.
Handicap Access: Yes.

SPINDRIFT INN
Innkeeper: Randy Venard.
800/841-1879; 831/646-8900; 831/646-5342 Fax.
652 Cannery Row, Monterey, CA 93940.
Price: $189–$429, includes breakfast.
Credit Cards: AE, CB, D, DC, MC, V.
Children: Yes.
Smoking: Yes.
Handicap Access: Yes.

Pacific Grove

GATEHOUSE INN
Innkeepers: Susan Kuslis & Lewis Shaefer.
800/753-1881; 831/649-8436; 831/648-8044 Fax.
225 Central Ave, Pacific Grove, CA 93950.
Price: $115–$165, includes breakfast.

hotel's Duck Club Restaurant, a showcase for grilled specialties and contemporary California cuisine.

A tastefully rebuilt vintage hotel provides a superb location right on the beach at Cannery Row, only a block away from the Monterey Bay Aquarium. Each of the forty-two guest rooms is decorated with plush canopy feather beds, imported carpeting, window seats (some with terrific waterfront views), fireplaces, TVs and refrigerators, plus marble and brass bathrooms with their own telephones and hair dryers. In-room saunas are available, and a Continental breakfast is delivered to rooms along with the morning paper. A rooftop garden patio is the perfect place for afternoon wine and cheese tastings.

L ocal lore has it that literary lion John Steinbeck regularly discussed historical trivia with the original owner of this Italianate 1884 residence. And the present-day charm of this magnificently decorated inn carries the torch high for its Victorian heyday. Much of the original decor, including lincrusta walls, has been enhanced with silk-screened, period reproduction wallpaper,

Guest rooms at Pacific Grove's Gatehouse Inn are both sunny and very comfortable.

Credit Cards: AE, D, MC, V.
Children: Limited to certain rooms.
Smoking: Outside only.
Handicap Access: Limited.

period antique furnishings and opulent themes, like one chamber that feels like a sultan's tent with mother-of-pearl inlaid headboard, Persian carpet and camel saddle chair. Each of nine double rooms comes with private bath (yes, even claw-foot tubs), and five rooms boast potbelly stoves or fireplaces. A full breakfast is served in the morning, and afternoon wine and hor d'oeuvres are part of the endless charm. The location, 100 yards from the ocean, invites strolling and access to Monterey's top sights.

GOSBY HOUSE INN
Innkeeper: Tess Arthur.
800/527-8828; 831/375-1287; 831/655-9621 Fax.
643 Lighthouse Ave.,
  Pacific Grove, CA 93950.
Price: $90–$160, includes breakfast.
Credit Cards: AE, MC, V.
Children: Yes.
Smoking: Outside only.
Handicap Access: Limited.

The distinctive front door turret and pointed cupola announce this gracious gabled inn as a showpiece Queen Anne Victorian, circa 1887. Filled stem-to-stern with distinctive finery, antiques and charming whimsy from the last century, this beautiful facility was originally built as a boardinghouse, and today offers lodgings in twenty-two rooms of varying sizes, some with fireplaces and twenty with private baths. Two rooms have kitchens, and fireplaces in twelve rooms provide coziness to match the antiques, period reproductions and plump bed linens. It's like spending a

The Queen Anne Victorian stateliness of Pacific Grove's Gosby House Inn has greeted guests since 1887.

Grant Huntington

night in the last century, with the convenience of a telephone by your carved wooden bedside. Breakfast is substantial and unpretentious, with guests helping themselves to huge breakfast rolls, muffins, scones and hot egg dishes, and then moving out to the garden for the morning meal. The parlor, straight out of a Merchant-Ivory film, is the location for afternoon sherry and savory appetizers. Bicycles are available to help maximize enjoyment of the nearby Pacific coastline and Cannery Row.

GREEN GABLES INN
Innkeeper: Jill Huesgen.
831/375-2095;
   831/375-5437 Fax.
104 Fifth St., Pacific Grove,
   CA 93950.
Price: $110–$225, includes
   breakfast, wine and hors
   d'oeuvres.
Credit Cards: AE, MC, V.
Children: In Carriage
   House rooms only.
Smoking: No.
Handicap Access: Yes.

One of oceanfront Pacific Grove's most magnetic landmarks, this multigabled Queen Anne mansion was built in 1888 by a southern California businessman for his paramour. The incredibly intricate results of the original owner's passion for bay windows, gingerbread and lavish stained-glass insets have been turned into a gracious inn, one of the prestigious Four Sisters Inns. Of the charmingly period-decorated ten rooms and one suite, several boast ocean view rooms with fireplaces, and six provide private baths, some with spa tubs. Morning brings the day's newspapers with coffee and full, family-style breakfast buffet, featuring fresh egg dishes, fruit, scones, pastries and pancakes served in the parlor. In the after-

The Green Gables Inn in Pacific Grove features turn-of-the-century atmosphere a stroll from the crashing surf.

Grant Huntington

noon, wine and appetizers are served by helpful staff members, who'll be happy to provide bicycles for touring the dramatic coastline. One of the most romantic B&B establishments on the Central Coast, in early 1998 it was named the number one B&B in North America by the Official Hotel Guide put out by U.S. travel agents.

SEVEN GABLES INN
Innkeepers: Susan, Ed, John
& Nora Flatley.
831/372-4341.
555 Ocean View Blvd.,
Pacific Grove, CA 93950.
Price: $105–$205, includes
breakfast.
Credit Cards: MC, V.
Children: Two people per
room.
Smoking: Outside only.
Handicap Access: Limited.

A stately 1886 Victorian confection of multigabled gingerbread, the grand mansion's exterior is more than matched by an inviting interior of museum-quality antiques, ornate rugs and gilded light fixtures, which houses fourteen elegant guest rooms, including several in adjoining cottages. Each comes with private bath and a stunning coastal view, and the highly desirable, second-floor Bellevue Room offers an especially sunny exposure and bay view from cozy window seats. A nineteenth-century fantasy, the inn's period theme extends to guest room appointments like antique sideboards, stained-glass windows, plush couches, huge armoires and velvet-upholstered chairs. English high tea is served in the stately dining room each afternoon, and a full breakfast greets guests in the morning. Innkeeper Susan Flatley grew up in the showy mansion and can spin great yarns about the area's history, as well as offer suggestions on visiting Monterey's many historic attractions.

Pebble Beach

**INN & LINKS AT
SPANISH BAY**
Innkeeper: Gary Davis.
800/654-9300; 831/647-
7500; 831/644-7960 Fax.
2700 17 Mile Dr., Pebble
Beach, CA 93953.
Price: $330–$2,075.
Credit Cards: AE, CB, D,
DC, MC, V.
Children: Yes.
Smoking: No.
Handicap Access: Yes.

Located on fabled 17 Mile Dr. at the edge of the brooding pines of Del Monte Forest and only a few hundred yards from the Pacific shore, this 236-acre Mediterranean-style enclave is embraced by some of the finest, championship golf terrain on the planet. Over 270 rooms and suites —— each boasting four-poster beds, marble baths, fireplaces, cable TV and most with balconies, patios and stupendous ocean views —— make this a matchless resort on arguably the most spectacular setting on the Central Coast. Guests are treated to preferred tee times at such world-class links as Pebble Beach Golf Links, Spyglass Hill Golf Course and the Tom Watson, Robert Trent Jones, Jr. and Frank Tatum-designed Links at Spanish Bay. If golf isn't your bag, there's tennis, swimming, spa-going or simply soaking up magnificent views from any of four restaurants and lounges. Complete indulgence here tends to make every guest feel like one of the rich and famous.

**THE LODGE AT PEBBLE
BEACH**
Innkeeper: David Oliver.
800/654-9300; 831/624-
3811; 831/644-7960 Fax.
1700 17 Mile Dr., Pebble
Beach, CA 93953.
Price: $370–$1,810.
Credit Cards: AE, CB, D,
DC, MC, V.
Children: Yes.
Smoking: No.
Handicap Access: Yes.

Since 1919, this elegant retreat has catered to international celebrities, sports legends and those who crave the ultimate in pampered lodgings. The view through the lobby salon's windows is straight out of the Golden Age of Hollywood, overlooking the emerald expanse of the golf course's eighteenth hole and on to the white Pacific surf swirling along the craggy shoreline. In addition to golf, there are all those luxury tennis, swimming, horseback-riding and fitness facilities. The Lodge's 161 spacious guest rooms continue the luxurious theme, with views of the ocean, fairways or vibrant gardens. In addition to fine restaurants, The Lodge boasts a dark wood Tap Room sanctuary lined with a fascinating collection of golf memorabilia.

Carmel

COBBLESTONE INN
Innkeeper: Sharon Carey.
831/625-5222; 831/625-0478
Fax.
Junipero Ave. bet. 7th & 8th
Aves., Carmel, CA 93921.

An English garden collaborates with French country overnight appointments to create a thoroughly Continental atmosphere in this well-run inn. A cobblestone courtyard leads to the main living room and lounge, where tea, sherry, wine

Price: $95–$180, includes
breakfast.
Credit Cards: AE, MC, V.
Children: Yes.
Smoking: No.
Handicap Access: No.

and appetizers are served each evening. Each of two dozen guest rooms has its own fireplace, antique decor, plump quilts, soft carpeting, private bath and TV. After a welcoming buffet breakfast of hot muffins and breads, fresh fruit, egg dishes, granola, yogurt and fresh coffee, guests can walk to Carmel Beach and to the village's many charming shops and restaurants. This fine facility is another member of the impeccable Four Sisters Inns.

Exquisite views overlooking Point Lobos and the Pacific surf are a few of the attractions of Carmel's fabled Highlands Inn.

Shmuel Thaler

HIGHLANDS INN
Innkeeper: David Fink.
800/682-4811 CA; 831/624-
3801; 831/626-1574 Fax.
P.O. Box 1700, Hwy. 1,
Carmel, CA 93921.
Price: $225–$650.
Credit Cards: AE, D, DC,
MC, V.
Children: Yes.
Smoking: Yes.
Handicap Access: Yes.

A California landmark since 1916, this world-class resort perched in the Carmel Highlands overlooking the spectacular coastline of Point Lobos exudes natural wood and stone elegance. In 1984, a $40-million renovation transformed the accommodations into cozy, contemporary retreats with fireplaces and fully equipped kitchens. The rooms are blatantly seductive, equipped with huge beds, fireplaces (stacks of firewood are strategically located all over the property) TVs, spacious dressing areas, plush terry robes, well-stocked refrigerators, coffeemakers with a variety of coffees and amazing king-sized whirlpool tubs built for two. Lavish landscaping — long on native shrubs like the elegant California wild lilac — hugs the network of walkways that lead down to the magnificent stone lodge, headquarters for a bistro overlooking the swimming pool, cocktail lounge and the sparkling Pacific's Edge restaurant with its breathtaking views of the swirling surf and tide pools below. The outstanding California cuisine here would be worth a visit alone. Literally across the street are the natural wonders of Point Lobos State Park, which you can even glimpse from your balcony through the binoculars helpfully provided in each room, but chances are that you won't be able to tear yourself away from your room, except perhaps to dine. The room service menu, a miniature of the restaurant's, is outstanding.

MISSION RANCH RESORT
Innkeeper: John Purcell.
800/538-8221; 831/624-6436; 831/626-4163 Fax.
26270 Dolores Ave.,
Carmel, CA 93921.
Price: $95–$225, includes breakfast.
Credit Cards: MC, V.
Children: Allowed with limits.
Smoking: No.
Handicap Access: Limited.

The lush ranch lands of this historic acreage near the Carmel Mission offer terrific views of meadows peacefully stocked with sheep. Guests can see the fog creeping in from the beaches of Monterey Bay and can enjoy the comfort of a recently refurbished farmhouse attractively upgraded by new owner Clint Eastwood. Yes, that Clint Eastwood. This country spread combines rustic ambiance with contemporary comfort, especially attractive to guests who like to unwind yet stay close to sights, shopping and the dining attractions of Carmel and Monterey. Overnights come with Continental breakfast and access to tennis courts and fitness facilities, with excellent hiking nearby. The property offers fine dining at its California cuisine restaurant, which includes a cozy 1930s bar and sandstone fireplace.

QUAIL LODGE RESORT AND GOLF CLUB
Innkeeper: Csaba Ajan.
800/538-9516; 831/624-1581; 831/624-3726 Fax.
8205 Valley Greens Dr.,
Carmel, CA 93921.
Price: $195–$900.
Credit Cards: AE, CB, DC, MC, V.
Children: Yes.
Smoking: Yes.
Handicap Access: Yes.

The word "luxury" takes on fresh meaning at this Mobil Five-Star resort boasting gloriously designed overnight accommodations, a destination golf course, tennis courts, swimming pools, hot tubs, fine Continental cuisine, trout fishing ponds and hiking trails that stretch 850 acres deep into the Carmel hills. It's run like a Swiss watch on a California timetable. The plush appointments and flawless service justify the price at what many consider a dream getaway. One hundred rooms and fourteen suites pamper guests in designer trappings long on exquisitely tailored furnishings, generous use of mirrors, fireplaces, plants, private decks with wooden hot tubs and tiled fireplaces. Lodgings run the gamut from lakeside lodges with balconies and terraces to cottages with wet bars and villas straight from *Architectural Digest*. Every amenity that you can think of is already in place. A short walk through extraordinary plantings that blend in with the spectacular scenery leads to The Covey, one of the finest restaurants on the Central Coast. If you're discreet, you'll spy Doris Day — a Carmel Valley resident who dines here weekly — among the dinner guests.

SANDPIPER INN
Innkeepers: Graeme &
  Irene MacKenzie.
800/633-6433 CA; 831/624-
  6433; 831/624-5964 Fax.
2408 Bay View Ave.,
  Carmel, CA 93921.
Price: $95–$195, includes
  breakfast.
Credit Cards: AE, D, MC, V.
Children: Age 12 years or
  older.
Smoking: Outside only.
Handicap Access: No.

One hundred yards from Carmel Beach, this elegant country inn occupies a 1929 prairie-style residence distinguished by spacious rooms, open-beam ceilings, wood-burning fireplaces and horizontal lines. Innkeepers Graeme and Irene MacKenzie run the attractively antique-decorated, art-filled inn with old-world warmth, generating the feeling of staying overnight at a gracious private home. Peace and quiet reigns, with the exception of the TV in the lounge. Sherry is served in the fireside lounge at 5:00 p.m. each evening, and morning brings an expanded Continental breakfast. The inn's lovely garden is filled with the rhododendrons, camellias and azaleas. There is a two-night minimum stay on weekends.

STONEHOUSE INN
Innkeepers: Terri & Kevin
  Navaille.
831/624-4569;
  831/624-8209 Fax.
P.O. Box 2517, 8th Ave.
  below Monte Verde,
  Carmel, CA 93921.
Price: $90–$189, includes
  breakfast.
Credit Cards: AE, MC, V.
Children: Age 12 years or
  older.
Smoking: Outside only.
Handicap Access: No.

Retaining the bohemian "artist's colony" flavor that attracted notable past guests like Jack London and Sinclair Lewis, this historic Carmel house (built in 1906) oozes charm in its stonework exterior, fetching gardens, old-fashioned glass front porch and white wicker furniture. Each of six overnight rooms (two with private baths) is uniquely decorated, some with four-poster beds and gabled ceilings, some with dramatic ocean views. Within easy walking distance of shopping, restaurants and beach, the inn provides a breakfast of juices, coffee, fresh fruit, pancakes, French toast and omelettes. The extraordinary, living room stone fireplace is kept blazing, and evening port and cookies may be enjoyed in the gardens or cozy interior or on the inviting porch.

Carmel Valley

CARMEL VALLEY
  RANCH RESORT
Innkeeper: Martin P.
  Nicholson.
800/422-7635; 831/625-
  9500; 831/626-2574 Fax.
1 Old Ranch Rd., Carmel
  Valley, CA 93924.
Price: $250–$650.

Once a fruit farm in the late 1800s, the lush 1,700-acre spread nestled in Carmel Valley has been upgraded to the lavish standards of a Spanish-style ranch resort. Ideal for vacationers and business travelers alike, rooms and suites are tucked into the hillsides, offering views of stately oaks, gardens and an eighteenth-hole championship golf course. Bedrooms with adjoining living rooms, decorated with antiques, woven rugs and

Credit Cards: AE, CB, D, DC, MC, V.
Children: Yes.
Smoking: Outside only.
Handicap Access: Two handicap suites.

artwork, include cathedral ceilings, wood-burning fireplaces, balconies and bleached wood walls. An exclusive resort with world-class recreation, the ranch is most widely recognized for its golf and tennis facilities. Guests can also treat themselves to a variety of spa, fitness and hiking facilities. An on-property corral adds to the authentic ranch-style experience, with horseback rides through the Santa Lucia Mountains, providing spectacular views of the property's rolling acreage. There are also two swimming pools and six whirlpool spas located throughout the resort. The main lodge, reminiscent of an old country estate, is airy and inviting with stone fireplaces and ceiling-to-floor length windows — a lovely spot to sip cocktails while watching the sunset. Also located in the main lodge, the Oaks dining room features fresh fruits and vegetables of Carmel Valley, fish caught along the coast and herbs from the resort's own garden.

STONEPINE ESTATE RESORT
Innkeeper: Daniel Barduzzi.
831/659-2245;
831/659-5160 Fax;
director@stonepinecalifornia.com E-mail;
www.stonepinecalifornia.com Web site.
150 E. Carmel Valley Rd., Carmel Valley, CA 93924.
Price: $275–$750, includes breakfast.
Credit Cards: AE, MC, V.
Children: Allowed with limits.
Smoking: No.
Handicap Access: Yes.

Imagine a French country château with Italian red tile roof set on a sophisticated 330-acre estate and equestrian center in the heart of verdant Carmel Valley. You now have a rough idea of the deeply comfortably, impossibly tasteful oasis that is Stonepine, named for a stately glen of sixty-year-old Italian pines. Designed in the 1930s for the fabulously wealthy California Crocker banking family, this pink Mediterranean villa/château has won the highest award for small hotels from the elite *Relais & Châteaux*. The tone is set by the Rolls Royce Phantom that scoops up guests arriving at the Monterey Airport. The main drawing room is ablaze with European antiques, high ceilings and elegant furnishings. Rooms and suites are sumptuously decorated in natural textiles, and all suites have private balconies or gardens, whirlpool baths, designer toiletries and TVs, plus some have fireplaces. Absolutely elegant, Stonepine shamelessly pampers and offers myriad leisure-time activities, from world-class, horseback-riding and swimming opportunities to celebrity stargazing in the splendid dining room, luminous with Baccarat and Limoges.

Big Sur

DEETJANS BIG SUR INN
Innkeeper: Andy Gagarin.

California casual pushes rusticity to the point of funk in this thoroughly Big Sur landmark,

831/667-2377.
Hwy. 1, Big Sur, CA 93920.
Price: $75–$125.
Children: Yes.
Smoking: Yes.
Handicap Access: Limited.

which specializes in weathered wood, sheltering redwoods and cozy overnight comfort. The Norwegian-style lodge — listed on the National Register of Historic Places — offers a central vantage on the spectacular natural setting. It's also just down the road from that bohemian outpost, Nepenthe, a famous watering hole housed in the former residence that Orson Welles bought for his bride, Rita Hayworth. A fine wine list accompanies delicious candlelight dining in the inn's restaurant, which also offers hearty breakfasts. The twenty overnight rooms are simple (no telephones or keys) but freshly decorated with country antiques. Some share bathrooms, some have fireplaces and new down comforters add coziness. A fire is always lit in the main lodge, where the friendly staff will help visitors find the most gorgeous beaches and the best redwood canyon hiking.

POST RANCH INN
Innkeeper: Jamie Short.
800/527-2200; 831/667-2200; 831/667-2824 Fax.
P.O. Box 219, Hwy. 1, Big Sur, CA 93920.
Price: $365–$645, includes breakfast.
Credit Cards: AE, MC, V.
Children: Discouraged.
Smoking: Outside only.
Handicap Access: Limited.

If luxury were tangible, it would feel just like the Post Ranch Inn. Set on ninety-eight acres of pristine forestland just south of Big Sur, the inn's tree houses, ocean houses and massive suites are built into the landscape so as not to disturb Mother Earth. Environmental correctness is the inn's middle name, from the strategically placed recycling bins right down to the natural, environmentally sound toiletries. When you're not reveling in the elegantly austere pleasures of the rooms' king-sized beds, expansive skylights, sunken whirlpool tubs and wood-burning fireplaces, you can hike the property's many winding trails, relax in the spa or pool, take advantage of the complimentary yoga classes and wine tastings or savor meals from the inn's four-star restaurant. The inn offers a designer breakfast of seasonal fruits, killer granola and sinfully rich, homemade pastries served either in the ocean view dining room or in your own room. Private and utterly unforgettable, the Post Ranch is worth every penny.

VENTANA INN
Innkeeper: Robert Bussinger.
800/628-6500 CA; 831/667-2331; 831/624-4812; 831/667-2419 Fax.
Hwy. 1, 28 miles south of Carmel, Big Sur, CA 93920.
Price: $180–$800, includes breakfast.

A collection of dramatic, weathered cedar lodges, clinging to the ancient oak groves and overlooking the wild Big Sur coastline, form one of the most charismatic retreats on any resort horizon. Spreading across a summit ridge 1,000 feet above the coast, the Ventana Inn complex, including a landmark restaurant (from where many trace the origins of California cuisine), two swimming pools, a general store and fabulous, tiled sunken spas, is

Robert E. Bussinger

Relaxing at Big Sur's Ventana Inn can be as simple as taking a hot tub on private decks adjoining guest rooms.

Credit Cards: AE, CB, D, DC, MC, V.
Children: Allowed with limits.
Smoking: Yes
Handicap Access: Yes.

one of the ultimate Central Coast resorts. The guest rooms (many with raised fireplaces and hot tubs sunk into private decks) are lavishly decorated with natural wood and tile work, including huge shower, bathing and dressing room areas. Still, the feeling is distinctly rustic, harmonizing effortlessly with the mountain terrain that brings grazing deer to your door and ravens soaring through the nearby sheltering forests. Each room, suite and secluded cottage boasts a TV/VCR and a refrigerator. The suite of central spas offers hot swirling water, deep enough to swim in and private enough for honeymooners. Breakfast, taken before the main lodge's roaring stone fireplace, features fresh juices, fruit, home-baked coffee cakes and breads and pots of excellent coffee. Walk through the woods or ride a golf cart shuttle to the trend-setting restaurant, from whose enormous decks sunset takes on new meaning.

DINING

Fed by year-round harvests and the delicious influence of Pacific Rim neighbors, California cuisine has a vivacious reputation the world over. Food historians like to trace the origins of this bold, light culinary style to the Central Coast. After all, it was at Ventana Inn in Big Sur that California cuisine artist Jeremiah Tower roasted his first red bell pepper and launched the evolving trend toward mesquite grilling. It's no surprise that in this stretch of the Central Coast, seafood is king, especially the silken flesh of the Monterey spot prawn, farm-raised abalone and wild Monterey Bay King salmon. Italian cuisine, a legacy from the pioneering fishing families, is another great specialty.

Dining Price Code

The price range below indicates the cost of a single dinner that includes an appetizer, entrée, dessert and coffee. Cocktails, wine, beer, tax or gratuities are not included. *Note:* Smoking is not allowed in any restaurant or eatery in the state of California.

Inexpensive	Up to $10
Moderate	$10–$25
Expensive	$25–$40
Very Expensive	$40 or more

Credit Cards

AE — American Express	DC – Diner's Club
CB — Carte Blanche	MC – MasterCard
D — Discover Card	V – Visa

MONTEREY COAST

Moss Landing

Phil DiGirolamo's Phil's Fish House & Eatery in Moss Landing features fresh seafood pastas and locally caught salmon and Monterey Bay spot prawns to take home.

Robert Scheer

PHIL'S FISH HOUSE & EATERY
831/633-2152.
7640 Sandholdt Rd., Moss Landing, CA 95039.
Open: Daily.
Price: Inexpensive.

King of a domain of fish and seafood so fresh that they practically flirt, legions of addicts trek, ice chests in hand, to Phil's Fish House to savor Phil DiGirolamo's fresh seafood pastas and to take home locally caught salmon, halibut and snapper. In a white-tablecloth joint, grilled yellow-

Cuisine: Seafood.
Serving: L, D.
Reservations: No.
Credit Cards: AE, D, MC, V.
Handicap Access: Yes.

tail and garlicky pastas loaded with Monterey Bay spot prawns would cost $30. At Phil's, where the forks are plastic and the plates are paper, the dish is $10 and superb. Phil also loves sand dabs, his personal favorite fish. Phil always has the fattest salmon, the freshest flounder and often rare items, such as luvar. What Phil really deals in is hospitality. "I love people — ya gotta love people. We're a fish market," he admits, "but above all we're telling people how to eat fish, how to enjoy the best. The bay is alive." If the broad-shouldered Sicilian can't sell you a fish, you must be a vegetarian. The enormous tanks, coolers and central table — piled high with everything from baby octopus and slithery calamari to whole salmon and cod, slabs of opa, mahimahi and mountains of scallops — make an arresting display. Phil will help you choose and will send you home with a few cooking tips. You'll be back.

Castroville

Don Elkin's Central Texas Barbecue serves oak-fired, finger-linking beef and pork ribs worth the quick trip off Highway 1 to Castroville.

Holger Leue

CENTRAL TEXAS BARBECUE
10500 Merrit St.,
   Castroville, CA 95012.
831/633-2285.
Open: Tues.–Sun.
Price: Inexpensive to
   Moderate.
Cuisine: Barbecue.
Serving: L (except Tues.), D.
Reservations: For large
   parties only.

Smack dab in the center of minuscule downtown Castroville — self-proclaimed Artichoke Capital of the World — the righteously proud Central Texas Barbecue serves up the spicy, oak-fired, juicy fare that gives nightmares to vegetarians. Ribs — beef and pork — and lots of them form the backbone of this finger-lickin' cuisine. The slow-cooked beans are classics of the Heartland America genre, and the slaw and potato salads form impeccable sidekicks. There's nothing designer about this place, which is decorated lavishly with western memorabilia on

Credit Cards: AE, D, DC, MC, V.
Handicap Access: Yes.

every possible surface. Wooden picnic tables are decaled and varnished with cowboy souvenirs, and the dark wood walls are branded and hung with campfire trinkets. You order, pay and then pick up the grub when ready, adding condiments to your liking. It's a beer, beef and bread sort of place, with barbecue sauce good enough to have created at least two generations of faithful customers.

Monterey

CAFE FINA
831/372-5200.
47 Fisherman's Wharf #1,
   Monterey, CA 93940.
Open: Daily.
Price: Moderate to
   Expensive.
Cuisine: Contemporary
   Italian.
Serving: L, D.
Reservations:
   Recommended for
   dinner.
Credit Cards: AE, CB, D,
   DC, MC, V.
Handicap Access: No.

Energetic Italian spirit fills this waterfront trattoria equipped with its own wood-burning pizza oven imported from the Old Country and a full bar. Cafe Fina offers lighthearted atmosphere with zesty mesquite-grilled seafood, chicken and beef specialties. The fine pizzas come with inventive toppings and fragrant, fresh herbs, and the handmade pastas and raviolis reflect the warmth of the proprietors Dominic and Naida Mercurio, whose family portraits line the walls of this charming cafe. Don't miss the smoked salmon pizzettes with tomatoes and mozzarella and a goat cheese and black olive ravioli in cream sauce. Very cozy, terrific flavors and lots of fun.

El Palomar in Monterey focuses on seafood specialties and authentic Mexican dishes like chicken mole, chile rellenos and pozole.

Paul Schraub

EL PALOMAR
831/372-1032.
24 Abrego St., Monterey,
   CA 93940.

El Palomar is one of the most authentic Mexican seafood restaurants that you'll find this side of the border. Focusing on seafood specialties gener-

Open: Daily.
Price: Moderate.
Cuisine: Mexican.
Serving: L, D, Sun Br.
Reservations:
  Recommended for
  weekends.
Credit Cards: AE, DC, MC,
  V.
Handicap Access:
  Downstairs only.

ously packed full of prawns, calamari, crab, octopus, oysters or fish, it also offers a variety of chicken, beef, pork and vegetarian options. You'll find authentic Mexican dishes, such as chicken mole, chile rellenos and pozole, and several tasty combination platters, as well. The freshly made tortillas and tortilla chips are warm and hearty, and the salsa is positively divine. With a full bar, El Palomar boasts more tequilas than most gringos know exist, as well as six Mexican/Spanish beers, domestic and other imports and a modest wine selection featuring many wines from local vineyards. The service is polite, friendly and unobtrusive. The spacious, tiered floors and tastefully decorated atmosphere invite lounging in the comfortable chairs inside, as does the outside patio area, with heat lamps and a central fire pit to ward off the chill when the fog blows in. Located on Abrego St., El Palomar is within walking distance of many area hotels and lodges, and it's close to downtown Monterey's lively Alvarado St., where the locals like to barhop.

JUGEM
831/373-6463.
409 Alvarado St., Monterey,
  CA 93940.
Open: Daily.
Price: Moderate to
  Expensive.
Cuisine: Contemporary
  Japanese.
Serving: L (except
  Sat.–Sun.), D.
Reservations:
  Recommended on
  weekends.
Credit Cards: AE, MC, V.
Handicap Access: Yes.

We always feel like we're out of town, in the chic heart of Tokyo perhaps, when visiting this contemporary sushi haven in the animated center of Monterey's Alvarado St. The distinct urban style is rarely seen in small coastal towns, though it works, posing a playful contrast. Our sushi-snob friends from L.A. prefer Jugem for its wide selection of sushi and sake, and for those requiring even more exotic fare, there are several daily specials. Freshness is essential for good sushi, and Jugem does not compromise. In addition, there's a full range of reliable Japanese standards, such as tempura, teriyaki and udon noodle dishes. Start off with the edamame (steamed green soybeans) appetizer or the nasu (eggplant with sweet sauce).

LALLAPALOOZA
831/645-9036.
474 Alvarado St., Monterey,
  CA 93940.
Open: Daily.
Price: Moderate to
  Expensive.
Cuisine: American.
Serving: D.

Touted as a "Big American Menu & Martini Bar," the idea here is that you may eat or drink in either the restaurant or the bar, which flow together in a continuous lively scene. The sleek, modern design is tempered by country tables and a bit of outdoor cafe seating on spirited Alvarado St., Monterey's nightlife center. The menu recalls a time when dishes had fewer ingredients, with names most people at least recognize. Choose

Reservations:
  Recommended for large
  parties only.
Credit Cards: AE, D, MC,
  V.
Handicap Access: Yes.

among classic sandwiches, chile and meat loaf, as well as jambalaya, world championship smoked ribs, 10–24-ounce steaks and a slew of requisite pasta entrées — all in giant portions. The crowd tends toward twenty- and thirty-somethings, though families are encouraged. Contrary to the classic food menu, the bar menu is more daring, with contemporary cocktails and fourteen martini selections.

MONTEREY'S FISH HOUSE
831/373-4647.
2114 Del Monte Ave.,
  Monterey, CA 93940.
Open: Daily.
Price: Moderate.
Cuisine: Seafood.
Serving: L Mon.–Fri., D.
Reservations:
  Recommended.
Credit Cards: AE, MC, V.
Handicap Access: Yes.

A bit off the beaten path for most visitors, Monterey's Fish House is worth the five-minute drive from downtown Monterey to dine at one of the most popular local restaurants. A converted house and a staff of family and friends make for one of the most enjoyable dining experiences anywhere. The seafood is fantastically fresh, and the homemade pasta seems supernatural. Many specials are offered in appetizer or entrée portions, and you can ask for any dish to be sized accordingly. Highlights include any of the barbecued fish, the squid pasta, the Sicilian holiday pasta (described as cioppino over pasta) and, when available, the barbecued oyster appetizer and the Monterey prawns. If the Sicilian calamari is available, do not miss it. The place is always packed, and for good reason, so make a reservation.

MONTRIO
831/648-8880.
414 Calle Principal,
  Monterey, CA 93940.
Open: Daily.
Price: Moderate.
Cuisine: Modern
  Euro-American Bistro.
Serving: L Mon.–Sat., D.
Reservations:
  Recommended.
Credit Cards: AE, D, MC,
  V.
Handicap Access: Yes.

M ontrio is a classic city restaurant — sleek, modern, multitextured with an airy, high-tech feel — fueled by lively, full bars on both upper and lower levels and a friendly, energetic staff. Like the ambiance, chef Tony Baker's food is interesting and eclectic, a cross of European bistro and modern American. The menu is vegetarian friendly. The terrine of eggplant, roasted peppers and goat cheese is a great starter. Other winners include braised veal cheeks and the oven-roasted portabello mushroom with crispy polenta. Portions are large, and lunch, at under $10, is a deal. The wine list is strong on alternative and rare wines. (If you're really into wine, ask to see the Back Room List). No wonder Montrio took "Best New Restaurant of 1995," honors from *Esquire* magazine.

PARADISO TRATTORIA
831/375-4155.
654 Cannery Row,
  Monterey, CA 93940.
Open: Daily.
Price: Moderate to
  Expensive.
Cuisine: Italian.
Serving: L, D.
Reservations:
  Recommended.
Credit Cards: AE, D, DC,
  MC, V.
Handicap Access: Yes.

There's an unmistakable air of magic filling this sleek oceanfront trattoria, especially for those lucky enough to get a table overlooking the cresting waves as they lap Monterey's beautiful coast. Appetizers include an impressive assortment of grilled vegetables, as well as standard seafood favorites accented with distinctive Italian twists. Paradiso presents deliciously delicate, California-style, wood-fired pizzas and a sumptuous, warm spinach salad. The modern trattoria features endless dishes from the grill and a wide array of pasta specialties. The service seems to get more and more friendly with each item ordered. But whatever you order, make sure that you leave room for Paradiso's notoriously decadent desserts.

STOKES ADOBE
831/373-1110.
500 Hartnell, Monterey, CA
  93940.
Open: Daily.
Price: Moderate.
Cuisine: Northern
  Mediterranean.
Serving: L, D.
Reservations:
  Recommended.
Credit Cards: AE, DC, MC,
  V.
Handicap Access: Yes.

Stokes Adobe, as its name suggests, is housed in one of the more imposing examples of historical Monterey architecture, an adobe built in 1833 that was originally the home of Dr. James Stokes. It has housed a number of successful restaurants over the years, and its newest incarnation proves worthy of the space. Stokes Adobe is more than a quaint piece of tradition with some tasteful, modern embellishments, and it manages to be elegant without being the slightest bit stuffy. The eclectic country European menu is ambitious, and the well-composed dishes do not disappoint. The chef's platter of assorted small bites will launch your evening most impressively, followed by reputation-building entrées like the grilled, lavender-infused pork chop served with bread pudding and pear chutney and the rustic pata tubes with homemade fennel sausage and fresh manila clams.

Pacific Grove

THE FISHWIFE
831/375-7107.
1996 Sunset Dr., Pacific
  Grove, CA 93950.
Open: Daily.
Price: Moderate to
  Expensive.
Cuisine: Seafood.
Serving: L, D.

A supportive environment for fish fanatics, The Fishwife has two highly successful restaurants, though the Pacific Grove location offers a peek of the ocean and is recommended for visitors. Offering fresh seafood at fair prices, chef Julio Ramirez integrates flavors from his Latin American homeland into his exclusively seafood platters, sandwiches, pastas and salads. Entrées come with

Reservations:
  Recommended.
Credit Cards: AE, D, MC, V.
Handicap Access: Yes.

black beans, rice and steamed vegetables, plus your choice of a dozen piquant Fishwife sauces, such as cilantro-garlic and mango-avocado salsa. Loyal regulars favor the best freshwater tilapia in town, grilled snapper Cancún, the spicy cioppino and the seafood wrap with shrimp, crab and scallops. Try the air fries for a delicious fat-free accompaniment and the raspberry iced tea for cool refreshment at this award-winning establishment.

OLD BATH HOUSE
831/375-5195.
620 Ocean View Blvd.,
  Pacific Grove, CA 93950.
Open: Daily.
Price: Moderate.
Cuisine: Continental.
Serving: D.
Reservations: Highly
  recommended.
Credit Cards: AE, D, DC,
  MC, V.
Handicap Access: No.

Many restaurants with built-in views simply ride the coattails, but not the Old Bath House. Enviably located at Lover's Point, overlooking Monterey Bay, this restored Victorian delivers top-notch Continental cuisine with a modern twist. The dining room is small (sixty-five seats) and very narrow, but the surroundings more than compensate. The waitstaff is confident and gracious, and the food speaks for itself. Try the grilled swordfish filet over tomato sauce, apple-smoked bacon, green olives and arugula or the lavender-thyme pork chop. The food-friendly wine list is complemented by sixteen selections by the glass. The four-course, early dining menu is a gourmet bargain.

PEPPER'S
831/373-6892.
170 Forest Ave., Pacific
  Grove, CA 93950.
Open: Wed.–Mon.
Price: Moderate to
  Expensive.
Cuisine: Mexican.
Serving: L (except Sun.), D.
Reservations:
  Recommended.
Credit Cards: AE, D, DC,
  MC, V.
Handicap Access: Yes.

Pepper's seems to possess a magic formula for consistently producing fresh, delicious Mexican food, racking up more awards than we'll bother to list. Incorporating some South American flavors, plenty of local seafood and a few creative twists on traditional south-of-the-border cooking, the place seems immune to dining trends that many popular restaurants depend on. The casual dining room, blond wood furniture, cheerful art and well-worn wood floors could have been designed decades ago or yesterday. Exceedingly popular, plan on a wait at peak times. The seafood taco platter is incomparable, and the fajitas are excellent, though it's safe to order whatever interests you. Don't get your heart set on margaritas. Pepper's serves only wine and beer, but has a good selection of both.

RED HOUSE CAFE
831/643-1060.
662 Lighthouse Ave.,
  Pacific Grove, CA 93950.

Yes, it's a red house that functioned as a home from 1890-1996. On a nice day (in Pacific Grove, fog is nice), the old Victorian porch is a

Open: Tues.–Sun.
Price: Inexpensive.
Cuisine: Sandwiches and
  salads.
Serving: B, L.
Reservations: No.
Credit Cards: No.
Handicap Access: Limited.

VITO'S
831/375-3070.
1180 Forest Ave., Pacific
  Grove, CA 93950.
Open: Daily.
Price: Inexpensive.
Cuisine: Authentic Sicilian.
Serving: D.
Reservations:
  Recommended for
  weekends.
Credit Cards: AE, D, DC,
  MC, V.
Handicap Access: Yes.

Pebble Beach

BAY CLUB
831/647-7433.
Inn at Spanish Bay, 2700 17
  Mile Dr., Pebble Beach,
  CA 93953.
Open: Daily.
Price: Moderate to
  Expensive.
Cuisine: Northern Italian.
Serving: D.
Reservations:
  Recommended.
Credit Cards: AE, D, DC,
  MC, V.
Handicap Access: Yes.

CLUB XIX
831/625-8519.
Lodge at Pebble Beach,

pleasing place to sit. The informal approach — order at the counter and the food is served at your table — has made the Red House a favorite lunch spot. Though sandwiches sustain the menu, you'll find ordinary classics transformed into extraordinary creations, with the tomato-mozzarella and the grilled eggplant attracting the most votes. Each day the chef roasts turkey, chicken, pork and roast beef and concocts three salads, one soup and a special.

Despite the nondescript strip mall setting, this small, seventeen-table establishment packs in a loyal following who have crowned Vito's as *the* place for reasonably priced, authentic Sicilian food. The white table-clothed dining room is dominated by a wall mural of a typical Sicilian fishing village. But all eyes are on the generously portioned food, such as the fettuccine alla puttanesca (a zesty dish of black olives, capers, chopped tomatoes and anchovies) or the rich pollo Marsala (chicken with mushrooms in Marsala sauce). The wine list is not very exciting, and the service, though friendly, is only average. Still, this is a good place if you're on a budget.

Intimate and romantic, this club within the plush resort and golf complex on 17 Mile Dr. specializes in modern Italian cuisine. Chef Drew Previti, a student of Michelin Three-Star chef Gualtiero Marchesi, has crafted a stylish a la carte menu. The light, yet intensely flavored soups, risottos and pasta dishes are superb. Main courses, such as veal Milanese with broccoli rabe and tomatoes or fennel-seared tuna with spinach and balsamic vinegar, are beautifully presented and backed by an award-winning wine list. Desserts, such as ricotta-candied citron tart, are original and unique. In all, the dining here is as lovely as the surroundings. The Bay also has a private dining room for large parties.

Adjacent to one of the world's most fabled sites — the eighteenth green of the Pebble Beach golf links — Club XIX takes its name from the age-

17 Mile Dr., Pebble Beach,
  CA 93953.
Open: Daily.
Price: Expensive.
Cuisine: Contemporary
  Continental.
Serving: L, D.
Reservations:
  Recommended for
  dinner.
Credit Cards: AE, DC, MC,
  V.
Handicap Access: Yes.

old tease about what comes after the eighteenth hole. The answer: An unabashedly chic, airy dining room counterpointed by flawless service, stylish fabrics, fine china and crystal stemware. The outside patio, flanked by two fireplaces, provides maximum views and is best at lunch. The health-conscious cuisine of chef Lisa Magadini never fails to please. Signature dishes include handmade orecchiette pasta with a wild mushroom sauce and fresh thyme. In addition two prix fixe menus, one of which is vegetarian, are offered daily. The full bar offers a host of luxury liqueurs to conclude the meal or complement dessert.

**ROY'S AT PEBBLE
  BEACH**
831/647-7423.
2700 17 Mile Dr., Pebble
  Beach, CA 93953.
Open: Daily.
Price: Expensive.
Cuisine: Euro-Asian.
Serving: B, L, D.
Reservations:
  Recommended on
  weekends.
Credit Cards: AE, MC, V.
Handicap Access: Yes.

Everything at Roy's is on a grand scale — the dramatic Pebble Beach location, the spacious, modern dining room, the sumptuous Euro-Asian fare. This is a place to indulge yourself, the kind of restaurant that can follow a superb day without risk of anticlimax. The bi-Continental approach to cooking is well illustrated in the signature blackened ahi tuna, enhanced with both soy-mustard and beurre blanc sauces. Other popular dishes are the Szechuan charred short ribs and the ravioli with sun-dried tomatoes, garlic and ricotta cheese, but I find myself repeatedly ordering the lemongrass-crusted swordfish with a basil-curry sauce, one of the best dishes at any restaurant. Arrive a half hour before sunset to hear a bagpipe player who makes music outdoors in full Scottish regalia, with the Pacific waves keeping time in the background. Whether breezy or blustery, the outdoor patio and the music are sublime.

STILLWATER CAFE
831/625-8524.
Lodge at Pebble Beach, 17
  Mile Dr., Pebble Beach,
  CA 93953.
Open: Daily.
Price: Expensive.
Cuisine: California, with
  seafood emphasis.
Serving: B, L, D, Sun Br.
Reservations:
  Recommended.
Credit Cards: AE, MC, V.
Handicap Access: Yes.

Inside the luxuriant Lodge at Pebble Beach and overlooking the famed eighteenth hole of the Pebble Beach Golf Course, the Stillwater Cafe is striking and trendy. The artistic accents, from lamps to paintings to the stunning aqua-colored glass bar, are a rainbow of color that dazzles. The menu relies on seafood, with a few items for those preferring a more earthy focal point. A fresh, raw start is suggested with in-season oysters on the half shell (we like the sweet kumomoto best). The abalone on angel hair pasta, in appetizer or entrée portion, is delicious, and the steamed calamari is a pleasant change from the more common fried version. While the menu offers plenty of high points, some dishes attempt too much in their desire to please, obscuring, rather than enhancing, the primary flavors.

Carmel

CAFFE NAPOLI
831/625-4033.
Ocean Ave., Carmel, CA 93921.
Open: Daily.
Price: Inexpensive to Moderate.
Cuisine: Southern Italian.
Serving: L, D.
Reservations: Recommended for dinner.
Credit Cards: MC, V.
Handicap Access: Yes.

This is the real Napolitana thing, with someone in the kitchen who obviously loves food and loves cooking. The menu, grounded in the fundamentals of garlic, basil, olives and artichokes, is strong on seafood, hearty pasta dishes, southern Italian-style risotto, pizza and lightened with a selection of seven salads. With the authenticity comes some Old Country clichés that have gone out of California restaurant vogue: checkered tablecloths, garlic braids, flags and maps from the mother country. But there's nothing passé about the award-winning wine list and the very trendy line out the door as visitors join regulars waiting for one of the few coveted tables. Popular demand led to the opening of Little Napoli around the corner, with the same prices and menu.

CASANOVA
831/625-0501.
5th Ave. bet. Mission & San Carlos Sts., Carmel, CA 93921.
Open: Daily.
Price: Moderate to Expensive.
Cuisine: Country French/Italian.
Serving: L, D, Sun. Br.
Reservations: Recommended for dinner.
Credit Cards: MC, V.
Handicap Access: Yes.

Ambiance abounds in this former residence turned French Provençal dining room, consistently ranked as Carmel's most romantic restaurant. Even when the fog is in, the al fresco fountain patio is inviting, thanks to conveniently placed space heaters. Though portions are not large and the food is expensive, you get what you pay for: attentive service, classic country European fare with strong French and Italian overtones, a posh wine list. Specialties include herb-encrusted roasted rack of lamb with onion marmalade and an unforgettable paella Catalana. Lunch features similarly hearty fare, such as spaghettini "Mimmo di Capri" with beef tips, fresh tomatoes, olive oil and herb sauce. Desserts, temptingly displayed, are made on premise (the fruit tarts are standouts).

CREME CARMEL
831/624-0444.
8th Ave. & San Carlos St., Carmel, CA 93921.
Open: Daily.

Tucked into the back of a courtyard, behind an eyewear store and a household appliance repair shop, is one of Carmel's best-known secrets, Creme Carmel. The dining room is small and

Price: Expensive.
Cuisine: French/California.
Serving: D.
Reservations:
  Recommended.
Credit Cards: AE, CB, D,
  DC, MC, V.
Handicap Access: Yes.

charming. The white-clothed tables are close together, complemented by soft music and subdued lighting. Oversized wine bottles line a narrow island that runs down the center of the dining room. The friendly waitstaff, well-versed sommelier and the seasonal French-California menu add a casual accent to the atmosphere. Starters include Pacific oysters on the half shell with mignonette sauce, smoked salmon and potato pancakes with crème fraîche and Sonoma foie gras with caramelized onions and caviar with port sauce. Entrées include Pacific salmon with chervil broth and fennel ratatouille and sliced breast of duck served with green peppercorn-Madeira sauce. The menu draws widely on locally grown and harvested produce. Desserts are rich without being heavy, and the wine list is exceptional for such a small restaurant. The entire mood is unpretentious, an approach that plays well, making for a relaxing dining experience popular among locals.

FLYING FISH GRILL
831/625-1962.
Carmel Plaza, Carmel, CA
  93921.
Open: Daily in summer;
  closed Tues. in winter.
Price: Moderate.
Cuisine: Asian via
  California Seafood.
Serving: D.
Reservations:
  Recommended for
  weekends.
Credit Cards: AE, D, DC,
  MC, V.
Handicap Access: No.

While many modern restaurants strive to create a high level of bustle and therefore a presumably comfortable habitat for fast-laners, Flying Fish offers a rarefied serenity. Warm redwood booths provide a sense of privacy, and the service is reliable and friendly. The creative fusion of Japanese-filtered-through-California cuisine is a rich cultural blend, harmonizing lively Asian flavors with homegrown culinary complements. A perfect example is the signature almond sea bass, encrusted in chopped almonds, grilled and served with mashed potatoes. The chef's flair for the unusual is evident in the parchment-wrapped salmon with black beans and several seafood clay pots, cooked at your table, in broth with vegetables and savory dipping sauces. The straightforward, rare peppered ahi is always recommended, and the visually oriented will appreciate the characteristic Asian flourishes of color and line.

GRASINGS
831/624-6562.
6th Ave. & Mission St.,
  Carmel, CA 93921.
Open: Daily.
Price: Moderate.
Cuisine: Coastal
  California/French.
Serving: L, D.
Reservations:
  Recommended

Nestled between a boutique and a terrace courtyard, this quaint little restaurant may be difficult to spot from the street, but that's what makes it one of Carmel's best-kept secrets. The mood is unpretentious and casual, a popular setting among locals. The dining room is small and airy with soft lighting and white linen tablecloths. With creative control over the menu, owner and chef Kurt Grasings offers an eclectic selection of tasty seafood

Credit Cards: AE, MC, V.
Handicap Access: Yes.

and hearty pasta dishes. While French-trained, chef Grasings instills his dishes with a subtle California coastal accent. Interesting starters include fried calamari with leek rings and spicy dipping sauce, scallops with leeks and onions in a white wine butter sauce or a salmon salad with warm, roasted potatoes and spinach. Dinner features herb-crusted sea bass with lentils, bacon and roasted garlic, paella with mussels, clams and shrimp orzo pasta and spicy sausage or medallions of pork with shiitake mushroom, bacon, peas and polenta. The creations are unusual, but earnestly prepared and outstanding in their own right. In contrast to the unique dinner combinations, the desserts are elementary, but satisfying. The warm brownie with vanilla ice cream and fudge sauce is always a sure winner.

THE GRILL ON OCEAN AVENUE
831/624-2569.
Ocean Ave. bet. Dolores & Lincoln Aves., Carmel, Ca 93921.
Open: Daily.
Price: Moderate to Expensive.
Cuisine: Gourmet Grill.
Serving: L, D.
Reservations: Recommended in summer.
Credit Cards: AE, D, DC, MC, V.
Handicap Access: Yes.

Casual elegance is the name of the game at the modern-yet-cozy Grill on Ocean Ave. Bridging the gap between European presentation and Asian spice, the restaurant's creative culinary minds pay about as much attention to gastronomical aesthetics as they do taste. A medley of appetizers is almost as strong and tempting as the main courses themselves — steamed clams bathed in Chardonnay, garlic and herb broth or seared ahi crusted in sesame seeds and paired with a garlic black bean vinaigrette and seaweed. The restaurant's oak wood fired grill gives birth to such wonders as a Cajun walnut-crusted, pan-roasted Chilean sea bass in mango puree or an exquisitely delicate free-range chicken with a light mustard and rosemary cream sauce. And the desserts — this isn't typical tiramisu and ice cream territory. Pair a delicate summer fruit compote with a warming Irish coffee and you have a slice of culinary heaven.

KINCAID'S BISTRO
831/624-9626.
217 Crossroads Blvd., Carmel, CA 93921.
Open: Daily.
Price: Inexpensive.
Cuisine: Classic French.
Serving: L Mon.-Fri., D.
Reservations: Recommended but not required.
Credit Cards: AE, D, DC, MC, V.
Handicap Access: Yes.

Chef/owner Robert Kincaid made his mark in 1979 by founding the Fresh Cream restaurant (then on Cannery Row). After a ten-year absence, he returned to open Kincaid's Bistro in 1995. The accolades began as soon as the doors opened. The balancing act of presenting serious food and impeccable service in a thoroughly disarming environment is masterfully accomplished. The wood-beamed ceiling, russet-colored walls, arched doorways and oversized fireplaces create a perfect setting for classic French cuisine, which includes cassoulet a la Robert, pan-seared filet of salmon and grilled Holland Dover sole. Lunch features a less interesting, but bargain-priced, prix fixe menu, including dessert. The memory of it all will linger long after your meal.

A view toward Point Lobos at dusk is one of the nonculinary pleasures of Clint Eastwood's Mission Ranch restaurant.

Buz Bezore

MISSION RANCH
831/625-9040.
26270 Dolores Ave.,
    Carmel, CA 93921.
Open: Daily.
Price: Expensive.
Cuisine: California Ranch.
Serving: L Sat., D, Sun. Br.
Reservations:
    Recommended.
Credit Cards: MC, V.
Handicap Access: Yes.

In 1986, actor/director Clint Eastwood purchased and extensively remodeled this twenty-two-acre inn overlooking Carmel Bay. The California Ranch heritage is captured in both the decor and the menu of the restaurant. You'll find standards like baby back ribs, filet mignon and roast prime rib, but there's also a surprising amount of fresh fish. Everything is well prepared and full portioned, and the homemade desserts shine. The nightly piano bar livens the house, and the outdoor terrace is a great place to enjoy views, food and music during the Sunday Jazz Brunch Buffet, which features live acts, such as local recording artist Gennady Loktionov. There's a lot to like here, even if you don't see Clint.

PACIFIC'S EDGE
831/624-3801.
Highlands Inn, Hwy. 1,
    Carmel, CA 93921.

You couldn't ask for more: the refined luxury of a world-class hotel, spectacular coastal views *and* a superior restaurant. The Pacific's Edge features regional California cuisine, with an emphasis

Open: Daily.
Price: Expensive.
Cuisine: New
    American/Central Coast
    California.
Serving: L, D, Sun. Br.
Reservations:
    Recommended.
Credit Cards: AE, CB, D,
    DC, MC, V.
Handicap Access: Yes.

on organic local foods, backed by impeccable service and a 1,000-bottle wine list. Menu highlights include roasted dayboat sea scallops and pancetta-wrapped loin of venison. In addition, each week executive chef Cal Stamenov and cellar master Mark Jensen create a four-course, prix fixe dinner menu that can be ordered with selected wines by the glass. In February, gourmands can take in the Masters of Food & Wine, which draws an international roster of celebrity chefs and vintners for a diverse, week-long program that includes gourmet meals, wine seminars and cooking classes. If the award-winning food weren't ample excuse for a special dinner, the view from the windows is breathtaking.

RIO GRILL
831/625-5436.
Hwy. 1 at Rio Rd., Carmel,
    CA 93921.
Open: Daily.
Price: Moderate.
Cuisine: American
    Southwest/California.
Serving: L, D, Sun. Br.
Reservations:
    Recommended.
Credit Cards: AE, D, MC,
    V.
Handicap Access: Yes.

This is *the* place for beautiful people — at the bar, behind the bar, even on the walls (the bar walls feature full-color caricatures of celebrities and friends). That's why the Rio constantly wins the "Best Place to Meet People" accolade. The restaurant wins on other points too: excellent, friendly service and delicious New American food that mixes exotic (mustard-marinated rabbit with a balsamic vinegar-rum reduction sauce) with casual (the best eggplant sandwich around). The daily blackboard specials are where the culinary action is. There are unique wines by the glass and a list chock-full of topflight California wines. The high-energy dining rooms emulate an open-air Santa Fe look — lots of stylish art work, live cacti and kid-friendly butcher paper tablecloths with crayons. Book a table here in advance or expect a long wait at the door.

SANS SOUCI
831/624-6220.
Lincoln St. bet. 5th & 6th
    Aves., Carmel, CA 93921.
Open: Daily, except Wed.
Price: Expensive.
Cuisine: French/California.
Serving: D.
Reservations:
    Recommended.
Credit Cards: AE, MC, V.
Handicap Access: Limited.

Tucked inside a small, picturesque courtyard, Sans Souci has been in continuous operation since 1948. The name (French for "without a care") says it all. The elegant dining room is warmed by a fireplace, chandeliers, fresh roses and candles. Owner John Jay Williams is on hand virtually every night to greet patrons. Meanwhile, chef Aaron Welsh delights the palate with French-California Fusion cuisine. Examples include lobster and artichoke fricassee, freshwater striped bass and braised rabbit strudel. The homemade desserts are light and satisfying. A significant highlight here is a wine list packed with hard-to-get vintages from boutique wineries.

TERRACE GRILL
831/624-4010.
La Playa Hotel, Camino
  Real & 8th Ave., Carmel,
  CA 93921.
Open: Daily.
Price: Moderate.
Cuisine: Mediterranean/
  American Southwest.
Serving: B, L, D, Sun. Br.
Reservations:
  Recommended.
Credit Cards: AE, MC, V.
Handicap Access: Yes.

The neighborhood location is a little out of the way, but the Terrace Grill, located inside the La Playa Hotel, one of Carmel's oldest, is worth the trip. The dining room has a casual ambiance, complemented by colorful gardens and a peek at the ocean from the al fresco terrace. The menu, whether breakfast, lunch or dinner, is an unusually successful marriage of California, Asian, Southwest and Mediterranean cuisine. Highlights include homemade artichoke ravioli and tantalizing coconut-sesame shrimp served with wahani and arborio rice. The best part is that prices are very reasonable for the quality and the quantity offered. Another plus is the locally oriented wine list. Desserts, while homemade, don't always live up to their billing.

ZIG ZAG
831/622-9949.
Mission St. & 5th Ave.,
  Carmel, CA 93921.
Open: Daily.
Price: Moderate.
Cuisine: Seasonal
  American.
Serving: L, D.
Reservations: Strongly
  recommended.
Credit Cards: AE, MC, V.
Handicap Access: Yes.

This lighthearted addition to the Carmel dining scene is brought to you by the makers of the esteemed Sierra Mar Restaurant at the Post Ranch Inn in Big Sur. In a small space of only a dozen or so tables, Zig Zag orchestrates a distinctive styling and audacious art, and most commendably, these people recognize that the new wave of diners wants serious cooking combined with informality. Zig Zag indulges those of us who are food samplers, forever in search of new culinary ideas, by designing a menu of small dishes, termed platillos, sized somewhere between appetizers and entrées (for the more steadfast among you, there are always specials in larger entrée portions). The "Seasonal American" menu reflects an innovative California tradition with Asian and European influences and promises more than an evocative motif: Zig Zag backs up its imagination with real talent. The ahi tuna, a small miracle, and the vegetable salad, much more interesting than it sounds, are memorable. The wine list offers variety, some rare and unusual wines and an emphasis on local bottlings.

Carmel Valley

**THE COVEY AT QUAIL
  LODGE**
831/624-1582.

The dining jewel in the resort crown that is Quail Lodge, The Covey consistently covers itself with award glory for food, service, setting

Superb Continental dining served in Carmel Valley's elegant, award-winning Quail Lodge Resort has made The Covey a favorite site for celebrity guests.

Quail Lodge Resort, 8205
  Valley Greens Dr.,
  Carmel Valley, CA 93924.
Open: Daily.
Price: Expensive.
Cuisine:
  European/California.
Serving: D.
Reservations: Required.
Credit Cards: AE, CB, DC,
  MC, V.
Handicap Access: Yes.

and wine list. Overlooking one of Carmel Valley property's many lakes and lawns, the restaurant gives new meaning to the words "fabulous" and "expensive." Those who don't mind being treated like royalty can join celebrity residents of this exclusive area at sumptuously set tables, where brilliant creations long on updated classics are all heightened by fresh herbs grown in the dining room's gardens. Outstanding duck, lamb and veal dishes are not to be missed, the shrimp and scallop quenelle is featherlight, and the desserts are extravagantly satisfying. This place is elegant, catering to a very worldly set, and diners not dressed for the occasion will tend to feel out of place. But for a true taste of the luxurious, it's that very special spot.

SOLE MIO
831/659-9119.
3 Delfino Pl., Carmel
  Valley, CA 93924.
Open: Tues.–Sun.
Price: Inexpensive to
  Moderate.
Cuisine: Italian Islands.

S ole Mio transports diners to the sunny isle of Capri, the homeland of chef/proprietors Sol and Domenico Vastarella. The rustic interior is accented by antiques, candlelight and lyrical Italian music. The old-world charm carries over into the friendly, efficient service, reasonable prices and a menu based entirely on family

Serving: L, D.
Reservations:
Recommended.
Credit Cards: AE, MC, V.
Handicap Access: Yes.

recipes. The emphasis is on pasta (the fettuccine Alfredo is exceptional) and meat-based dishes such as osso buco (slow-cooked lamb shanks) and saltimbocca (free-range veal). The compact wine list has impressive breadth. And desserts, though limited, include essential standards like tiramisu. A great place for those who enjoy leisurely meals.

WHITE OAK GRILL
831/659-1525.
9 Carmel Valley Rd.,
   Carmel Valley, CA 93924.
Open: Thurs.–Mon.
Price: Moderate.
Cuisine: California/French.
Serving: L, D.
Reservations:
   Recommended.
Credit Cards: AE, D, MC, V.
Handicap Access: Yes.

It would be incorrect to say that the White Oak Grill is "worth the drive" when half of the thrill is the trip into Carmel Valley, twelve miles inland. The recent restoration of what was originally an old milk house, built in the 1890s for a dairy, takes advantage of both the old and the new. It's country all right, but sophisticated country. A limited but fine menu expresses the chef/owner's "California interpretation of Country French cuisine" and translates as flavorful, with sauces based on vegetable stocks rather than cream or butter, in the true Provençal style. Local harvests of both seafood and produce and the owner's knowledge of complementary food and wine pairings make for a most pleasurable meal. In season, al fresco seating is available under live oaks.

Big Sur

NEPENTHE
831/667-2345.
Hwy. 1, 30 miles south of
   Carmel, Big Sur, CA
   93920.
Open: Daily.
Price: Moderate.
Cuisine: Tapas/Regional
   American.
Serving: L, D, Br.
   (everyday).
Reservations: For large
   parties only.
Credit Cards: AE, MC, V.
Handicap Access: Yes.

A legendary bohemian pit stop since the day that it opened in 1949, Nepenthe has always been a gathering spot for leading literary lights seeking escape from the urban jungle. Henry Miller was a regular denizen, and Orson Welles purchased a cabin on the property for his bride, Rita Hayworth. A central fireplace and lots of rustic woodwork add to the charm of this terraced establishment hugging the rocky coastline. The new Kiva Restaurant serves a daily brunch and offers a tapas menu until dusk on its outdoor deck. The view from the terrace provides an unsurpassed glimpse of the wild beauty of this magic spot. Sooner or later everyone makes the pilgrimage here, sometimes for an evening cocktail (the Bloody Marys have few rivals), sometimes for the fine salads and exceptional burgers, but always for the view and the unique moody Central Coast atmosphere. The charming Phoenix Shop arts and crafts emporium adjoining the restaurant allows purchases of lasting souvenirs. Don't forget to bring your camera.

VENTANA RESTAURANT
831/667-2331.
Hwy. 1, 28 miles south of Carmel, Big Sur, CA 93920.
Open: Daily.
Price: Expensive.
Cuisine: California/ Mediterranean.
Serving: L, D.
Reservations: Required for dinner.
Credit Cards: AE, D, DC, MC, V.
Handicap Access: Yes.

Here in the heart of Big Sur is arguably the most beautiful setting for an inn and restaurant in the world. Perched one thousand feet above the Pacific Ocean, framed by the Santa Lucia mountain range, Ventana seems hoisted atop the world. On a clear day, the view alone is worth the drive. The restaurant, like the inn, is rustic, discreet and sophisticated. Both lunch and dinner menus play off the Central Coast "Riviera" setting and sport a classical French-California theme. Appetizers include herb soufflé with smoked salmon and goat cheese in puff pastry. Entrées like the pan-seared, potato-wrapped salmon and oak-grilled squab are complemented by an award-winning wine list and a knowledgeable staff. An in-house bakery produces a wide array of desserts, breads and pastries. The tab is rich, but so is the experience.

FOOD PURVEYORS

BAKERIES

The Central Coast taste for superior breads and pastries has prompted a delicious groundswell of exceptional bakeries. Most serve excellent coffees and provide table seating, and all serve as fashionable meeting spots for movers, shakers and artsy types.

Fifi's Cafe & French Bakery (831/372-5325; 1188 Forest Ave., Pacific Grove) Fifi's is the crème de la crème of Monterey area bakeries, famed for napoleons, cheesecakes, petit fours and berry delights to take out or to consume with espresso on the premises.

Old West Cinnamon Rolls (805/773-1428; 861 Dolliver St., Pismo Beach) The name says it all at this exhibition bakery that whips up monster cinnamon rolls, old-fashioned doughnuts, cookies, breads and rolls.

Wishart Bakery (831/624-3870; Ocean Ave., Carmel) Downtown Carmel's pastry heaven offers up fresh and heavenly muffins, scones and pastries (like a wonderful cherry-filled) that, when paired with a cup of the house coffee, is a breakfast made in heaven.

COFFEEHOUSES

L ike all artistically fertile places on the globe, the Central Coast cultivates its cafe society in coffeehouses so numerous that they're practically underfoot.

Caravali Coffees (831/655-5633; 510 Lighthouse Ave., Pacific Grove) This popular java joint specializes in house-roasted cappuccinos, dark French roasts and special blends.

FARMERS' MARKETS

T he weekly tradition of cruising the freshest locally grown produce, displayed in colorful booths by the growers themselves, has become a fixture of Central Coast life. It's a chance to meet the growers and to select their freshly harvested, certified organic fruits, nuts, vegetables and honey, plus fresh seafood, eggs, honey, cheeses and flowers in an open-air market setting.

Monterey Certified Farmers' Market (916/654-0824; Fremont St. off Aguajito Rd., Monterey Peninsula College, Monterey; Thurs. 2:30 p.m.–6:30 p.m.) This market draws purveyors from the boutique, organic produce fields of Carmel.

Old Monterey Farmers' Market (831/655-8070; Alvarado St. bet. Pearl St. & Del Monte Ave., Monterey; Tues. 4:00 pm.–7:00 p.m.) Features scores of grower's displays, plus live music and finger food booths.

ICE CREAM

T he universal favorite dessert meets its match in a bevy of Central Coast creameries.

Carmel Beach Cafe (831/625-3122; Ocean Ave. bet. Mission & San Carlos Sts., Carmel) This cafe serves sinfully delicious frozen yogurts and luscious Italian ice creams in a charming cafe.

Pieces of Heaven (831/625-3368; 3686 The Barnyard, Carmel) This shop offers samples of world-famous Ben & Jerry's ice-cream flavors like Cherry Garcia.

MICROBREWERIES

I n the 1980s, the repeal of a prohibition against selling and making beers on the same location prompted an explosion of microbreweries all over the Central Coast, where freshly made and boldly flavored handmade brews are on tap at on-site pubs. These beers bear absolutely no relation to those light beers advertised on TV. Tours are usually available, and, in many cases, glass walls allow a full view of the "exhibition brewing."

Monterey Brewing Company (831/375-3634; 638 Wave St., Monterey) This is a popular brewpub close to Cannery Row that cooks up huge vats of pale, amber and dark stout to the delight of local fans, who also explore unusual specialty brews like passion fruit and apricot.

CULTURE

The cultural tone of the Monterey Bay and Big Sur coast was set long ago by spectacular natural beauty and a welcoming climate, factors that have beckoned to and informed the creativity of writers, mavericks and artistic free-thinkers of every stripe for over 200 years. The inspiring and uncrowded landscape not only provided sanctuary for artists and, more recently, internationally acclaimed arts events, but it also shaped and freed the uncluttered, often radical directions that creative life would take here.

If there is a single dominant theme, it is eclecticism. The same coastal splendor that inspired the pens of Robert Louis Stevenson, Robinson Jeffers, John Steinbeck, Jack Kerouac and Henry Miller now hosts the music masters of the world at the annual Monterey Jazz Festival. In a part of the country where filmmaking is literally part of the scenery, the cinematic *nouvelle vague* plays nightly at handsomely restored Deco movie palaces. Contemporary artisans push the edges of handmade forms within the shadow of a Franciscan mission.

Continually reinventing its architectural environment in response to the natural rhythms of seismic temblors, this portion of the Central Coast takes visible pride in preserving the landmarks of its colorful history. Scarcely a town in the region is without tile-roofed homage to its Spanish ancestry. Victorian cottages from the boom years of the American Yankee settlement are carefully maintained as living — and lived in — postcards from the past. Here the historic co-exists comfortably with culture's latest wave.

ARCHITECTURE

The natural terrain and texture of this region is still punctuated with the earliest imports of Spanish settlers and the work of their native acolytes. The tone of thick adobe walls, sunny courtyards and renaissance Spain's Moorish arches was set by the series of sturdy missions created by Franciscan padres in the late-eighteenth century. Dotting the Central Coast, these landmarks of the first immigrant invasion of California still dominate the psychic landscape of the region, flavoring architectural thinking for generations since. Some of the jewels in this chain of Spanish influence remain, many restored over the centuries as centerpieces in Central Coast communities, most notably in Carmel.

After the missions were secularized following Mexico's divorce from Spain, their stylistic influence spilled over into adobe ranch houses and town homes, which today still exist in handsome profusion, especially in the heart of Old Monterey. When Mexico lost its claim to California and American entrepreneurs enthusiastically made their move, clapboard homes, New England-style churches and white picket fences began fleshing out the spine of Monterey Bay's Spanish outposts.

At several moments in the life of this region, the Spanish influence ascended into the baroque, leaving two lavish examples to be savored today. One is the Royal Presidio Chapel in Monterey — a gem of Spanish colonial baroque architecture, the ornate stone facade of the Royal Presidio Chapel was created in 1794 by master designers from Mexico City after the original wood and adobe structure, founded in 1770 by mission founder Junipero Serra, was destroyed. With its lyrical bell tower, original eighteenth-century statues and stations of the cross, this living legacy of the original Spanish capital in the New World remains one of the important windows on the founding spirit of the Central Coast.

CINEMA

Crossroads Cinema (831/624-8682; Crosswoods Mall, Carmel) This quaint, two-screen movie house screens first-run flicks.

Dream Theater (831/372-1494; 301 Prescott Ave., Monterey) Decorated like the Victorian parlor of your favorite aunt, this local institution offers the tops in contemporary art films (viewed from close-to-the-floor recliner seats, no less) and boasts real, hot-buttered popcorn.

Galaxy 6 (831/655-4619; 280 Del Monte Center, Carmel) As close to a Hollywood multiplex as Carmel gets, the Galaxy shows the newest movies in THX on six screens.

Golden Bough (831/372-4555; Monte Verde & 8th Ave., Carmel) Quaint neighborhood theater books first-run fare.

Lighthouse Cinema (831/372-7300; 525 Lighthouse Ave., Pacific Grove) First-run screenings in a neighborhood, movieland ambiance are the specialty of this main street theater.

State Cinemas (831/372-4555; 417 Alvarado St., Monterey) Lamentably, this 1928 beauty was cleaved into a triplex and shows only Hollywood's latest.

GARDENS

Carmel Valley Begonia Gardens (831/624-7231; 9220 Carmel Valley Rd., Carmel) This lavish nursery specializes in flowering plants, Mediterranean perennials and, of course, richly hued begonias. The extensive growing beds and nursery are available for public tour. Open daily, 8:30 a.m.–5:00 p.m.

La Playa Hotel Gardens (831/624-6476; 8th Ave. & El Camino Real, Carmel) The gardens of this graceful Mediterranean-style hotel are lavishly maintained with formal plantings of Icelandic poppies, tulips, primroses and hyacinths, as well as enough attractively grouped beds of perennial plantings to make a visit here a fragrant experience year-around.

HISTORIC PLACES

CALIFORNIA'S FIRST THEATRE
831/375-4916.
Scott & Pacific Sts.,
  Monterey, CA 92940.
Open: Call for hours.
Admission: $2 adults; $1.50 youth; $1 children.

Ironically enough, this first showcase for theatrical culture in California started life as a saloon for salty sailors in 1844. It fell victim to the emerging American population's need for civilized respectability, and, eventually, the dining room was enlarged and whale oil lamps were improvised as footlights. In the fall of 1847, the theatre marked its debut with a rousing melodrama, *Putnam, or the Iron Son of '76*. Five brave women joined the opening night audience, whose members paid a whopping $5 to watch the show. After a period of decline, the old adobe was restored again in 1937 and still enjoys a prosperous theatrical life as a venue for nineteenth-century melodramas.

CANNERY ROW
No telephone.
Off Foam St., Monterey, CA 92940.
Open: Continuously.
Admission: Free.

John Steinbeck romanticized the people of his *Cannery Row* — the madams, grocers, fisherfolk, cannery workers and bohemians — colorful characters long departed. What remain are "the quality of light, the tone, the habit, the dream" of this once-thriving amalgam of canneries, which today still sports plenty of waterfront atmosphere. Souvenir shops, boutiques, galleries and other regional attractions now fill the looming cannery buildings, whose pilings reach into the very tide pools of the Monterey Bay.

CASA DEL ORO
831/649-3364.
Corner of Scott & Oliver Sts., Monterey, CA 93940.

The adobe gained its Spanish name "house of gold" from the prevailing rumor that minors stashed gleanings from their Gold Rush escapades in the resident safe. Originally built to service American sailors, the casa thrived as a general store during the Gold Rush boom of 1849. Still preserving its mercantile atmosphere, it is colorfully stocked with nineteenth-century dry goods, bolts of cloth and tableware and burlap sacks filled with grains, beans and coffee.

CASA SOBERANES
831/649-2895.
336 Pacific St., Monterey, CA 93940.
Open: Daily.
Admission: $5 adults; $3 youth; $2 children.

Built during the 1840s by Custom House Warden Don José Rafael Estrada and later sold to Don Feliciano Soberanes, this lovely, tile-roofed colonial adobe was Europeanized with a Mediterranean - style balcony. The interior, including what has long been thought to be the prettiest adobe salon in Monterey, is attractively decorated with period New England furniture and Mexican folk art.

COLTON HALL & OLD JAIL
831/646-5640.
522 Pacific St., Monterey, CA 93940.
Open: Daily, 10:00 a.m.–5:00 p.m.
Admission: Free.

Designed as a town hall by Yankee alcade (mayor) Walter Colton in 1847-1849, this important historic landmark was quarried of local stone and housed the first Constitutional Convention of the State of California during the autumn of 1849. Over the years, it served as a school, county seat, municipal court and police headquarters and was handsomely restored in time to celebrate the Centennial of 1949. The tables and benches of the upstairs assembly hall are arranged as they were when the forty-eight delegates from around the new state gathered to design the emerging government. The original designs for the grizzly bear, which still adorns the state flag, are displayed here. At the next-door jail, desperadoes ruminating on a few final hours on earth carved their names into the walls, providing macabre entertainment for modern-day visitors.

COOPER-MOLERA ADOBE
831/649-7109.
508 Munras Ave. Monterey, CA 93940.
Open: Daily tours, 2:00 p.m., 3:00 p.m., 4:00 p.m., except Mon., Wed.
Admission: $5 adults; $3 youth; $2 children.

One of the largest extant adobes in the state, this structure was built in 1826 by English sea captain John Rogers Cooper, who converted to Catholicism and became a Mexican citizen in order to marry the renowned Californio beauty Encarnación Vallejo, sister of General Mariano Vallejo. A successful businessman, Cooper added onto the original single-story adobe as his fortune from hides, tallow and sea otter pelts grew. Tours place the visitor dramatically in touch with affluent life in the early colonial period.

CUSTOM HOUSE
831/649-2909.
1 Custom House Plaza, Monterey, CA 93940.
Open: Daily, 10:00 a.m.–5:00 p.m.
Admission: $2 adults; $1.50 youth; $1 children.

The oldest public building in California, this 1814 adobe and tile structure flew the flags of Spain, Mexico and the U.S. during its tenure as the most important port of entry into Alta California. At this site, custom taxes were levied on all trading ships during the Spanish rule, taxes that helped finance government expenses for the entire region.

Fandangos were danced here to celebrate the arrival of foreign trading vessels, many laden with finery like Chinese silks. Under the direction of wealthy Yankee Thomas Larkin, the facility was enlarged and renovated in 1841. Later, in 1846, Commander Sloat proclaimed the takeover of California by the U.S. by raising the Stars and Stripes over what was perceived then as a symbol of foreign domination. Today, this state historical monument is packed with reminders of Monterey's former shipping glory, including harpoons, vintage portraits and brocade garments worn by the wealthy Californios.

LARKIN HOUSE
831/649-2904.
510 Calle Principal,
   Monterey, CA 93940.
Open: Daily tours, 10:00
   a.m., 11:00 a.m., 12:00
   noon, except Tues.,
   Thurs.
Admission: $2 adults; $1.50
   youth; $1 children.

In creating what was to be the first two-story adobe in the Spanish capital in 1835, leading merchant Thomas Larkin invented the graceful Monterey style of Mexican adobe architecture. The encircling, second-story verandah and low-hipped roofs that characterize this house were Larkin's own design and represent a fusion of the Spanish-style adobe with New England innovations, like the extensive use of glass in windows and the symmetrical floor plan. Today, the house is beautifully restored and decorated with period antiques, including many of Larkin's own belongings and furniture.

MONTEREY PRESIDIO
831/242-5000.
Pacific St. north of Scott St.,
   Monterey, CA 93940.
Open: Daily, 24 hours.
Admission: Free.

Founded on June 3, 1770, when Gaspar de Portola claimed Monterey for the King of Spain, the second military fort in Alta California first took shape as a structure of huts and crude barricades. At the turn of the eighteenth century, the presidio was moved to its present site overlooking the majestic port immortalized by Richard Henry Dana in *Two Years Before the Mast*. First the Mexican government (1822), then the Americans (1846) erected blockhouses and gun sites, spots now commemorated with appropriate plaques. The Sloat Monument commemorates the first raising of the American flag over Monterey by U.S. naval commodore John Drake Sloat. Today, this oldest military reservation in the U.S. is one of the largest Army posts in the country and the site of the Defense Language Institute (831/647-5000). Historic markers dot the reservation, indicating Native American ceremonial rocks and the first landfalls of Sebastian Vizcaino (1602) and Father Junipero Serra (1770). The view overlooking Monterey Bay is daunting.

**OLD WHALING
   STATION**
831/375-5356.
391 Decatur St. at Heritage
   Harbor, Monterey, CA
   93940.

When adventurous Scotsman David White built this adobe residence in 1847, the walkway leading up to the house was paved with whale vertebrae. This calcified evidence of the sheer numbers of whales being dispatched from this busy

Open: Gardens open daily,
dawn to dusk.
Admission: Free.

Monterey Bay location was apt, since, upon White's departure, the house was taken over by the Old Monterey Whaling Co. as headquarters for the lucrative, and messy, processing of whale oil. Restored in 1980, the Old Whaling Station shares its gardens with what is thought to be the first brick building constructed in California.

PACIFIC HOUSE
831/649-2907.
Junc. Alvarado St., Calle
   Principal & Scott St.,
   Monterey, CA 93940.
Open: Daily, 10:00
   a.m.–5:00 p.m.
Admission: $5 adults; $3
   youth; $2 children.

Originally a hotel built in 1835 by Scotsman James McKinley, the adobe structure is today a museum documenting Monterey's historic Native American, Spanish and Mexican periods. After its disreputable origins as a sailor's saloon and lodgings, it enjoyed a brief reincarnation as a Presbyterian rectory and Salvation Army head-quarters. It was restored in the 1920s. The spacious two-story adobe is filled with graphic exhibits illustrating adobe brick making and historic metal-work from old Monterey homes. In the back, at the site of a former bullfighting ring, sits a patio with a fountain, shade-giving magnolia trees and colorful plantings, designed in the late 1920s to recreate the atmosphere of the old Spanish capitol.

STEVENSON HOUSE
831/649-2905.
530 Houston St., Monterey,
   CA 93940.
Open: Daily tours, 10:00
   a.m., 11:00 a.m., 12:00
   noon, except Mon., Wed.
Admission: $5 adults; $3
   youth; $2 children.

A highlight of Old Monterey's many attractions is this two-story adobe built in the late 1830s as a private residence with upstairs rooms rented out to boarders. One of the most famous guests of what was called The French Hotel in 1879 was Robert Louis Stevenson. In his late twenties and not yet the celebrated author that he would become, Stevenson took rooms here to be near his paramour, Fanny Van de Grift Osbourne, an American divorcée with two young children. Stevenson enjoyed his Monterey idyll for four months, during which he wrote an account of 1879 Monterey in *The Old Pacific Capital*, later drawing on the rugged coastal scenery for his celebrated *Treasure Island*. The house is fur-nished, in true literary shrine fashion, with Stevenson's books, furniture and memorabilia, including several portraits of the author. His bed and writing desk are displayed in the Robert Louis Stevenson Room of this beautifully restored monument.

TOR HOUSE
831/624-1813.
26304 Ocean View Ave.,
   Carmel, CA 93921.

As ruggedly romantic as the poet's words, this charismatic stone house and tower was built by Robinson Jeffers, who first came to Carmel with

Open: Fri.–Sat., 10:00 a.m.–3:00 p.m. by reservation. Admission: $6.

his wife, Una, in 1914. With its commanding view of the rocky coastline and stone Hawk Tower, which the poet built for his wife, the house is a haunting, Gothic presence in its quiet residential setting. Its stalwart rock walls were raised with Jeffers' own hands and contain stones gathered from the four corners of the globe, including one from the Great Wall of China, some from England, lava from Hawaii, even a porthole from the ship that took Napoleon to exile on Elba. Lovely gardens may be toured, as well as the burnished redwood interior filled with antique Oriental rugs. Truly the retreat of an artistic, maverick spirit. For reservations, contact: Robinson Jeffers Tor House Foundation, P.O. Box 2713, Carmel, CA 93921 (831/624-1813).

HISTORIC WALKING TOURS

Monterey's Path of History In the heart of Old Monterey, clustered near Fisherman's Wharf, a score of fine nineteenth-century casas, adobes and public buildings still exist as beautifully restored landmarks to this city's rich historic past. A walking tour around this **Path of History** provides an in-depth encounter with the abundant Spanish, Californio and Early American period. Administered by the **Monterey State Historic Park** (831/649-7118; 525 Polk St., Monterey, CA 93940), a two-day $5 admission pass ($3 youth; $2 children) gains access to over twenty sites. Maps and guided tour details are available at **Pacific House, Colton Hall** and the **Cooper-Molera Adobe.**

Pacific Grove Victorian House Tour Founded in the late 1870s as a Methodist summer retreat, Pacific Grove quickly blossomed with stately Victorian mansions (many now open to the public as bed and breakfast establishments), Ornate Gothic, turreted Queen Anne and even a few turreted English castle styles dominate. Some of the loveliest of these are located along Ocean View Blvd. and Lighthouse Ave., including the **Green Gables Guest House,** the **Gosby House Inn,** the **Hart Mansion,** the **Trimmer Home** and the **Sea Star.** Each year, usually in Oct., a **Victorian House Tour** (831/373-3304) gives visitors access to some of the finest of these pre-turn-of-the-century architectural beauties.

KIDS' STUFF

Dennis the Menace Playground (831/646-3866; Camino El Estero Park, Monterey) Designed by cartoonist Hank Ketcham, who created that little cartoon and movie personality, Dennis the Menace, this is a fun spot for romping on slides, futuristic jungle gyms and a steam locomotive, or for just soaking up the peaceful beauty of El Estero Lake.

Dennis the Menace Playground in Monterey, a popular family recreation spot located by El Estero Lake, was designed by cartoonist Hank Ketcham, who created that rascal, Dennis the Menace.

Shmuel Thaler

Monterey Bay Aquarium (831/648-4888; 886 Cannery Row , Monterey) With over 6,500 aquatic creatures and 100 exhibits, this multilevel facility is the big fish in the international aquarium pond. New and unusual exhibits abound, but children tend to fall in love with the Touch Tide Pool, where they can run their hands along the living surfaces of starfish, anemones and sleek bat rays. Another favorite is the Sea Otter exhibit, a two-story marine kingdom that opens onto the open air and coastal rocks, enabling a view of these playful swimmers in and out of the water. The Portola Cafe, which offers a creative cafe menu, is open for snacks and lunches daily, 10:00 a.m.–5:00 p.m.

LIGHTHOUSES

Necessity and technology conspired in the erection of these brilliant beacons during the nineteenth century, sending out their luminous message of jagged perils lurking in the fog. Armed with the high candlepower of the French Fresnel lens, which ingeniously utilized over 1,000 pieces of cut glass to magnify its light, the slender lighthouses and their stalwart attendants kept faith with mariners until the coming of automation and the computer. Always a picturesque sight, a few of these curved towers continue to shed light along

The oldest continuously operating lighthouse on the West Coast, the Point Pinos Lighthouse was built in 1855.

Shmuel Thaler

the rockiest edges of the Central California coast. The **Point Pinos Lighthouse** (Asilomar Ave. off Ocean View Blvd., Pacific Grove) was built in 1855, the oldest continuously operating lighthouse on the West Coast. It is furnished with Victorian antiques and helpful explanations of its automated workings. Open weekends for self-guided tours, 1:00 p.m.–4:00 p.m.

MISSIONS

MISSION SAN ANTONIO
831/385-4478.
Mission Rd. off Jolon Rd., Monterey, CA 93940.
Open: Daily, 10:00 a.m.–4:30 p.m.
Admission: Donations.

Nestled in the Santa Lucia Mountains, this third mission in the chain was founded in 1771, and the present church was begun in 1810. With its arched walkways and adjoining compound buildings recently restored, the isolated setting and full restoration-in-progress of the entire complex lend this lovely Franciscan outpost a haunting, frozen-in-time appearance.

MISSION SAN CARLOS BORROMEO DEL RIO CARMELO
831/624-3600.
3080 Rio Rd. & Hwy. 1, Carmel, CA 93921.
Open: Mon.–Sat., 9:30 a.m.–4:15 p.m.; Sun. 10:30 a.m.–4:15 p.m.
Admission: Donations.

Though founded by Father Junipero Serra in 1771, this second mission in the wide-ranging Franciscan enterprise was moved to its present location and completed with sandstone blocks quarried from the Santa Lucia Mountains by Serra's successor Lasuén in 1797. In its prime, the compound on the banks of the Carmel River furnished the former Spanish capital of Monterey with the bounty from its orchards, fields and sta-

The early mission days of Central California still linger in the serene walkways of Mission San Carlos Borromeo del Rio Carmelo.

Shmuel Thaler

bles and was the official headquarters of the Franciscan missionary effort in Alta California. Buried within this mission he loved so well, Father Serra is now entombed in a splendid bronze sarcophagus near the sanctuary, where he awaits the canonization for which his faithful are currently petitioning. Two other great California Franciscans, Serra's able protégé Francisco Fermin Lasuén and expedition diarist Crespi, are buried here as well. The handsome mission interior boasts a vaulted, ribbed ceiling, baroque alter and beautifully restored, hand-carved doorway lintels. Its oval-domed tower retraces Spanish architecture's debt to the conquering Moors, as does the sanctuary's star window. The adjoining museum displays the silver religious pieces that Serra brought from Mexico and contains California's first library, as well as a restored kitchen and the cell where Serra lived and corresponded with his far-flung brethren. Planted with vintage olive and pepper trees, the garden and cemetery contain the graves of over 3,000 native inhabitants, plus members of Monterey's pioneer families.

MISSION SAN JUAN BAUTISTA
831/623-4528.
2nd & Mariposa Sts., San Juan Bautista, CA 95045.
Open: Daily, 9:30 a.m.–4:30 p.m.
Admission: Donations.

Founded in 1797, Mission San Juan Bautista basilica, located ten miles inland from Monterey, is the largest in the California mission family. The forty-foot polychromed chapel walls were originally painted in 1818 by Bostonian Thomas Doak, a deserter from the ship *Albatross*. Today, the mission's large plaza skirts the entire 184-foot length of the graceful arched portico, whose thick walls keep the dark mission interior, as well as its restored dormitories and workrooms, cool in the blazing heat of summer. The lofty beams of the chapel interior are crowned by an ornate baroque alter. Behind the mission, olive and cypress trees encircle the small

Mission San Juan Bautista thrives in its historic Old West setting.

Shmuel Thaler

Native American burial ground, the view from which is a dramatic panorama of the San Andreas Fault, zigzagging through Hollister in the distance. The atmosphere makes this a remarkable window into the early days of Spanish occupation. Each summer the Cabrillo Music Festival of Santa Cruz fills the plaza and the acoustically perfect mission interior with the sounds of the living present. The innovative Hispanic performance troupe El Teatro Campesino makes its home base in this bastion of early California heritage. And it should not be forgotten that during a visit to San Juan Bautista that a movie star of major proportions is always in your midst — the mission's adjoining bell tower (now closed to the public) figured prominently in the climactic conclusion of Alfred Hitchcock's *Vertigo*.

MUSEUMS

HENRY MILLER MEMORIAL LIBRARY
831/667-2574.
Hwy. 1, Big Sur, CA 93920.
Open: Tues.–Sat., 11:00 a.m.–5:00 p.m.; closed Mon.

Built in 1981 as a land trust and ode to the late Henry Miller, the Big Sur memorial library houses an extensive collection of rare and well-known works in the town that Miller fell in love with when he was a struggling writer. It is also a community resource center and a meeting place for local artists and poets, and it plays host to art exhibits, concerts and poetry readings. The library also boasts acres of picturesque land, plus ocean views.

LA MIRADA
831/372-3689.
720 Via Mirada, Old Monterey, CA 93940.

This 1849 adobe, an extension of the Monterey Peninsula Museum of Art, displays artwork and antiques of several historical periods. A new 10,000-

Open: Thurs.–Sat., 11:00 a.m.–5:00 p.m.; Sun., 12:00 noon–4:00 p.m. Admission: $3.

square-foot addition houses the Armin Hansen Collection of California and a separate Asian art gallery.

MONTEREY MARITIME MUSEUM AND HISTORY CENTER
831/373-2469.
5 Custom House Plaza, Monterey, CA 93940.
Open: Daily, 10:00 a.m.–5:00 p.m.
Admission: $5 adults; $4 seniors; $3 youth; $2 children.

Housed in the 18,000-square-foot Stanton Center on the historic waterfront, this brainchild of the Monterey History and Art Association fills two levels and seven exhibition areas with history from the Ohlone peoples and Spanish explorers to dramatic displays of Monterey's fishing and sailing heyday. Maritime history, from a five-ton Fresnel lighthouse lens to Portuguese navigation logs and charts are on view in this exciting new museum.

MONTEREY PENINSULA MUSEUM OF ART
831/372-7591.
559 Pacific St., Old Monterey, CA 93940.
Open: Wed.–Sat., 11:00 a.m.–5:00 p.m.; Sun., 1:00 p.m.–4:00 p.m.
Admission: $3 adults; $1.50 students.

A charming fine arts museum, specializing in American and Asian artworks, photography, graphics and international folk and ethnic arts and crafts.

PACIFIC GROVE MUSEUM OF NATURAL HISTORY
831/648-3116.
165 Forest Ave., Pacific Grove, CA 93950.
Open: Tues.–Sun., 10:00 a.m.–5:00 p.m.
Admission: Free.

The front lawn offers a life-sized gray whale sculpture, and the interior is filled with displays of Californiana, from minerals and seashells to hundreds of taxidermy specimens of indigenous wildlife. The popular migrating monarch butterflies boast their own exhibit and colorful video, while rare local flora bloom in the small native plant garden just outside. A small gift store offers tempting posters, books, T-shirts and other educational souvenirs.

WHALER'S CABIN MUSEUM, POINT LOBOS
831/624-4909.
Hwy. 1, south of Carmel, Carmel, CA 93921.
Open: Daily, 11:00 a.m.–3:00 p.m.
Admission: Free.

Attracted to the huge pods of California gray whales that migrated between Arctic waters and Baja California spawning grounds, whalers began plying Pacific waters in the very early 1800s. By the mid-1840s, the Central Coast had profitable whaling stations at Moss Landing, Davenport and San Simeon. A circa 1851 cabin, built by Chinese fishing families overlooking Point Lobos' Whaler's Cove, has been carefully preserved as a museum and recalls the whaling heyday in photographs, harpoons and sailing implements and other memorabilia of the Portuguese whalers who frequented the cove in the 1860s. This tiny, weathered cabin, whose floor joists are supported by six whale vertebrae, overlooks one of the most idyllic coves on the West Coast and is one of the oldest buildings of Chinese origin remaining in the Monterey Bay area.

Monterey Bay Aquarium

Since its opening in 1984, this astonishing facility has been visited by countless avid aquarium devotees, who consider it one of the wonders of the modern world. Central Coast visitors shouldn't even consider passing it up: The aquarium truly lives up to its international reputation. Built on the edge of the enormous Monterey Bay National Marine Sanctuary, whose underwater valley dwarfs the Grand Canyon, the aquarium is state-of-the-art in every respect. Home to more than 6,500 marine creatures, it houses living exhibits illustrating the Monterey Bay's many underwater habitats. Velvety leopard sharks cruise with schools of silvery sardines in the aquarium's vast three-story kelp forests, which tower up to the sunlight filtering through 300,000-gallon exhibition tanks. Playful sea otters soar acrobatically through the waters of their special area, a re-creation of the bay floor that opens out onto the sunny rocks above. The arrangement allows viewers to watch the sea otters cavorting underwater as well as on the surface. The soft bat rays and fascinating starfish of the Touch Tide Pool are irresistible to adults and children. Special exhibits show off the frontiers of marine science, creatively wedded with arresting, interpretive display design. The tastefully stocked gift store is itself worth leisurely exploration. (831/648-4888; 886 Cannery Row at Foam St., Monterey.) Open daily, 10:00 a.m.–6:00 p.m.; in summer 9:30 a.m.–6:00 p.m.; advance tickets ($14.95 adults; $11.95 seniors and students; $6.95 ages 3-12 and disabled) can be ordered by calling 800/756-3737.

Visitors from the world over flock to the awe-inspiring marine displays at the Monterey Bay Aquarium.

Shmuel Thaler

MUSIC

Camerata Singers (831/484-1217; Carmel Mission Basilica, Mission San Antonio, Mission Rd., Monterey) The soaring, seamless voices of this world-class vocal ensemble are shown off to full advantage each winter due to the acoustics of Old California's mission settings.

Carmel Bach Festival (831/624-2046; Sunset Cultural Center, Carmel Mission Basilica, Carmel) The best of Johann Sebastian Bach and plenty of his baroque colleagues pours forth in this splendid, celebrated three-week (Jul.–Aug.) annual love affair with great music that draws devotees from around the Central Coast. Passionate performances, concerts, recitals, lectures, opera, symposia, receptions and a children's concert fill the bill — all top quality and enthusiastically attended.

Carmel Music Society (831/625-9938; Sunset Cultural Center, Carmel) After seven decades, this musical institution is still going strong during its fall-spring season, offering distinctive solo recitals for voice (by reigning divas like Frederica Von Stade), piano, flute and violin. The society also stages annual vocal and instrumental competitions and international touring ensembles.

Chamber Music Society (831/625-2212; Sunset Cultural Center, Carmel) Long the performance venue of choice for generations of Carmel culturati, the society regularly hosts visitors like the Los Angeles Piano Quartet and the Arden Piano Trio, as well California's leading string quartet ensembles, as part of this exciting six-concert series each winter and spring.

Dixieland Monterey (831/443-5260; 177 Webster St., Monterey) Two dozen of the top Dixieland band interpreters strut their stuff for three, high-stepping days every Mar. in cabaret locations throughout Fisherman's Wharf and downtown Monterey.

Keyboard Artist Series (831/624-7971; Sunset Cultural Center, Carmel) A distinctive winter-spring season of hands-on music that brings the finest new and legendary interpreters of keyboard classics to this music-loving community.

Monterey Bay Blues Festival (831/394-2652; Monterey County Fairgrounds, Monterey) Rapidly establishing a red-hot reputation, this sizzling music fest brings blues greats together for two days every Jun. for performances and jamming. New discoveries share the stage with heavyweights like B.B. King, the Neville Brothers and Etta James. In Jun., call for schedule.

Monterey County Symphony (800/624-8511; Sunset Cultural Center, Carmel) Internationally acclaimed guest artists join the resident professional symphony orchestra for an annual Oct.–May series of concerts from classical and modern repertoires.

Monterey Jazz Festival (831/373-3366; Monterey County Fairgrounds, Monterey) The oldest jazz festival in the U.S. features living legends and youthful contenders. For three days in Sept., jazz sessions on multiple stages, in a "nightclub" hot spot and in an outdoor performance arena, make the granddaddy of West Coast music fests a perennial "with it" winner. This legendary jazz venue has featured Dizzie Gillespie, Ray Charles, Tito Puente, Joe Williams, Ella Fitzgerald and Wynton Marsalis. A world-famous event with a capital W, all proceeds go to educate the budding jazz musicians of Monterey county.

NIGHTLIFE

Blue Finn Cafe & Billiards (831/375-7000; 685 Cannery Row, Monterey) Live music on the weekends, pool tables, full bar, drink specials on most nights, food and a view of Monterey Bay.

Cibo (831/649-8151; 301 Alvarado St., Monterey) Lots of festive international jazz pairs well with the casually elegant menu of Italian pastas. Also known for mixing a martini that 007 himself would fawn over.

Doc's Nightclub (831/649-4241; 95 Prescott Ave., Monterey) The area's top spot for live music, specializing in a sizzling program of rock 'n' roll and blues in an intimate setting.

Hog's Breath Inn (831/625-1044; San Carlos St. bet. 5th & 6th Aves., Carmel) Yes, this *is* the place run by Dirty Harry himself, but don't expect to see Clint Eastwood playing barkeep at this restaurant/bar. Though it, like the rest of Carmel, has no live music, it does sport outdoor seating, strong drinks and an Eastwood-specific, high-plains omelette.

Knuckles Historical Sports Bar (831/372-7171; Hyatt Regency Lobby, #1 Old Golf Course Rd., Monterey) Thirteen TV monitors and two satellite dishes feed all of the top international sporting matches into this major sports bar, which also features plenty of hefty finger food.

McGarrett's (831/646-9244; Alvarado St. & Del Monte Ave., Monterey) Dancing to a live DJ, spinning hits from the 1970s, modern rock, techno and house.

The Mucky Duck (831/655-3031; 479 Alvarado St., Monterey) An authentic British Pub, billed as the local's local, with a heated patio and a DJ on weekends.

Peter B's (831/649-4511, ext. 138; 2 Portola Plaza, Monterey) A taste of a traditional brewpub, Peter B's comes complete with sports telecasts, open-mike nights, beer-soaking victuals and live music on Thurs. nights, when locals with stars in their eyes take the stage.

Planet Gemini (831/373-1449; 625 Cannery Row, Third Flr., Monterey) Rock, country, salsa and comedy seven nights a week. Long on dancing (especially line dancing), short on laughs.

Portofino Presents (831/373-7379; 620 Lighthouse Ave., Pacific Grove) Folk, ethnic and contemporary acoustic musical stylings in a bohemian coffeehouse setting.

Tinnery at the Beach (831/646-1040; 631 Ocean View Blvd., Pacific Grove) A late-night bar menu keeps company with live jazz and classic piano bar music.

Whitey's Place (831/646-8383; 125 Ocean View Blvd., Pacific Grove) A bar in the classically rustic sense of the word, Whitey's Place is where you'll sidle up to the bar with a boilermaker, then cut a rug to the strains of live rock 'n' roll and blues on Thurs.-Sat.

THEATER

Carl Cherry Center for the Arts (831/624-7491; Guadalupe & 4th Ave., Carmel) A staple in the lives of Carmel culture hounds, the center plays host to myriad writers, art workshops, plays and dance performances. A very classy establishment.

Carmel Shakespeare Festival (831/622-0100; Outdoor Forest Theatre, Santa Rita & Mountain View Sts., Carmel) For six weeks beginning in Sept., two productions of Shakespearean classics run in repertory in the oldest outdoor amphitheater in the West, built in 1910 by Carmel's bohemian founders.

Children's Experimental Theatre (831/624-1531; Indoor Forest Theatre, Carmel) Live repertory of drama and comedy, ranging from exuberant Greek Classics to contemporary repertoire.

Gold Coast Theater Company (831/375-4916; Jack Swan's Theatre/ California's First Theatre, Scott & Pacific Sts., Monterey) The troupe stages authentic nineteenth-century melodramas in this classic theater year-round.

Golden Bough Playhouse (831/622-0100; Monte Verde & 8th Ave., Carmel) Home to the Pacific Repertory Theatre, a company that stages various productions of classic and original plays each year.

Monterey Bay Theatrefest (831/622-0100; Custom House Plaza, Monterey) In Jun., this free outdoor theater fills Monterey's waterfront with lively thespian action, from the sublime to the delightfully comic.

Staff Players Repertory Company (831/624-1531; Indoor Forest Theatre, Carmel) An offshoot of the Children's Experimental Theatre, the staff players perform classical theatre for adult audiences. During its Oct.-May season, the company produces five major shows.

Sunset Cultural Center (831/624-8511; 8th Ave. & San Carlos St., Carmel) The cultural heart and longtime gathering spot for the intensely arts-minded, local citizenry, the center houses a wide array of events year-round, including the Carmel Bach Festival, the Monterey County Symphony and Performance Carmel.

SEASONAL EVENTS

January

AT&T Pebble Beach National Pro-Am (800/541-9091; Pebble Beach).
Ben Hogan Pebble Beach Invitational (831/484-2151; Pebble Beach).

Each January, the AT&T Pebble Beach National Pro-Am presents world-class golf and gives the public an opportunity to be entertained by celebrity participants like comedian Bill Murray.

Shmuel Thaler

Living History Day (831/623-4881; Monterey).
Whalefest (831/644-7588; Monterey).

February

Carnival Monterey (831/373-3250; Monterey).
John Steinbeck Birthday Party (831/372-8512; Monterey).
Taste of Pacific Grove (831/646-6549; Pacific Grove).

March

California Chocolate Abalone Dive (831/375-1933; Monterey).
Colton Hall Birthday Party (831/375-9944; Old Monterey).
Dixieland Monterey (831/443-5260; Monterey).

April
Big Sur International Marathon (831/625-6226; Carmel).
Good Old Days Celebration (831/373-3304; Pacific Grove).
Wildflower Show (831/648-3116; Pacific Grove).

May

American Indian and World Cultures Festival (831/623-2379; San Juan Bautista).
Squid Festival (831/649-6544; Monterey).
Tor House Garden Party (831/624-1813; Carmel).
Wildflower Festival (831/373-0629; Monterey).

June

Bonsai Show (831/624-6280; Monterey).
Día de San Juan (831/623-2454; San Juan Bautista).
Mission San Antonio Fiesta (831/385-4478; Jolon).
Monterey Bay Blues Festival (831/649-6544; Monterey).
Monterey Bay Theatrefest (831/622-0100; Monterey).
Summer Art Festival (831/659-5099; Carmel).

July

Big Little Backyard Fourth of July Party (831/646-3866; Old Monterey).
Carmel Bach Festival (831/624-2046; Carmel).

August

Carmel Shakespeare Festival (831/622-0100; Carmel).
Carmel Valley Fiesta (831/659-2038; Carmel Valley).
Concours d'Elegance (831/659-0663; Pebble Beach).
County Fair (831/372-5863; Monterey).
Scottish Festival & Highland Games (831/375-8608; Monterey).
Steinbeck Festival (831/753-6411; Salinas).
Winemaker's Celebration (831/375-9400; Monterey).
YWCA Women's Walk-Run (831/649-0834; Pacific Grove).

September

Artichoke Festival (831/633-2465; Castroville).
Coastweeks (800/262-7848; Monterey).
Fiesta de San Carlos Borromeo (831/624-1271; Carmel).
Greek Festival 831/424-4434; Monterey).
Monterey Jazz Festival (831/373-3366; Monterey).
NCGA Public Links Championship (831/625-4653; Pebble Beach).
Old Monterey Santa Rosalia Festival (831/649-6544; Old Monterey).

October

Butterfly Parade (831/646-6520; Pacific Grove).
California Constitution Day (831/646-5640; Monterey).
Jewish Food Festival (831/624-2015; Carmel).
Oktoberfest (831/624-1813; Carmel).

<u>November</u>

Christmas Street Fair (805/772-4467; Morro Bay).
Holiday Arts and Crafts Fair (831/646-3866; Monterey).
Robert Louis Stevenson's Un-Birthday (831/649-7118; Monterey).

<u>December</u>

American Indian Invitational Art Market (831/648-3116; Pacific Grove).
Christmas in the Adobes (831/649-7111; Monterey).
Christmas Tree Lighting (831/646-3866; Monterey).
First Night Monterey (831/373-4778; Monterey).
Holiday Arts & Crafts Fair (831/646-3866; Monterey).
La Posada and Piñata Party (831/646-3866; Old Monterey).

RECREATION

BEACHES

Asilomar State Beach (Pico Ave. & Sunset Dr., Pacific Grove) A lavish expanse of world-class tide pools, rocky shoreline and sandy dunes makes this a destination for aficionados of serious beachfront play. Divers frequent the area searching for prized abalone, and neon-hued ice plant colonies hug the edge of the sand. Swimming is unwise due to rocks and hazardous riptides. The beach adjoins the Asilomar Conference Grounds. Parking is available along the roadway, and rest rooms are available. No entrance fee.

Carmel City Beach (Ocean Ave., Carmel) Soft white sand extends beyond a border of deep green cypress trees, offering picnic and campfire possibilities, volleyball and wheelchair-accessible rest rooms. A multitude of stairways provide beach access to this gorgeous location, predictably crowded on weekends. *Warning:* Dangerous surf/swimming conditions. No entrance fee.

Carmel River State Beach (Scenic Rd. at Carmelo St., Carmel) A favorite with divers and those who enjoy the sights and sounds of resident lagoon waterfowl, this 100-acre sandy beach fronts a teeming marsh, near the site where Spanish explorers first made landfall. The southernmost tip, known as Monastery Beach, is accessible from Hwy. 1. Prime day recreation. Parking and rest rooms. No entrance fee.

Fanshell Beach (Signal Hill Rd. at 17 Mile Dr., Pebble Beach) In the heart of scenic 17 Mile Dr., this white sand cove offers choice locations for enjoying the antics of resident sea otters, as well as fishing, picnicking and, for the hardy, swimming. Parking is available. No entrance fee.

Garrapapa State Park (Hwy. 1, 2 miles south of Malpaso Creek, Big Sur) A soaring landscape of steep cliffs, accessible along a panoramic trail, overlooks rich tide pools below and a breathtaking view. Excellent whale watching abounds in this favorite playground for sea otters, who are so captivating that you'll be tempted to get up close and personal, but leave these furry creatures in peace. Roadside parking and chemical toilets. No entrance fee.

Jade Cove (Hwy. 1, 12 miles south of Lucia) Named for the preponderance of soft green nephrite jade once found here (and enthusiastically collected by generations past), this rocky cove is today a favorite diving area, but still perfect for wandering and for sifting through the smooth pebbles in hopes of discovering some special memento. Reached by a steep trail. No facilities. No entrance fee.

Kirk Creek Beach (Hwy.1, 4 miles south of Lucia) The bluffs above the point where Kirk Creek joins the ocean afford a spectacular view. Overlooking the sandy beach are thirty-three campsites, from which a steep trail leads down to the water. Parking and rest rooms. Free for day-use, though there is a fee for camping.

Macabee Beach (Cannery Row bet. McClellan & Prescott Aves., Monterey) Wedged between restaurants, this favorite diving spot is graced by a small stretch of sand. Tourist information, outdoor shower and parking are available. No entrance fee.

Marina State Beach (Reservation Rd., Marina [Monterey county]) Voluptuous dunes skirt this 170-acre site, whose 2,000-foot-long boardwalk leads to the water. While surf conditions make for unsafe swimming, the beach offers fine fishing and a launch site for hang gliding. Wheelchair access, parking lots, rest rooms and ranger's headquarters. No entrance fee.

Monterey State Beach (Sand Dunes Dr., Monterey) A lovely stretch of dunes and a bracing view of the entire Monterey Bay highlight this sandy beach. Parking and rest rooms. No entrance fee.

Moss Landing State Beach (Hwy. 1, north of Moss Landing Harbor) Located near the extensive wetlands of Elkhorn Slough, this fifty-five-acre beach is an ideal spot for bird-watching. Picnicking, surfing, clamming, horseback riding and windsurfing are also specialties of this stretch of beach and sand dunes. No entrance fee.

Pfeiffer Beach (Hwy. 1, end of Sycamore Canyon Rd., Big Sur) A trail leads from the parking lot through cypress groves to the sandy beach encircled by monumental cliffs and sea caves. Natural rock arches channel the waves into spectacular displays of wild spray and spume. At the beach, Sycamore Creek spills into a hidden lagoon, a gorgeous sanctuary for exploring, though the surf is hazardous and gusty winds require warm clothing for all-day outings. Parking and rest rooms. No entrance fee.

Point Lobos State Reserve (west of Hwy. 1 at Carmel Highlands) Easily the crown jewel of the Monterey coastline beauty — widely considered one of the most spectacular coastal sanctuaries in the country — this 2,500-acre preserve shelters ancient cypress groves, rugged cliffs, swirling tide pools and bottle green water, lapping crystalline cove beaches. Exquisite China Beach offers sheltered swimming. Well-marked trails thread the meadows, bluffs and shoreline, presenting stunning views of sea lion and waterfowl habitats. A small museum is located in a vintage Whaler's Cabin, and diving is available by permit. Ample parking and rest rooms. Entrance fee.

Salinas River State Beach (Hwy. 1 at Potrero Rd., Moss Landing) One-stop shopping for fishing, clamming, hiking and prime bird-watching at the Salinas River Wildlife Area, just south of the beach. Accessible along a boardwalk leading through substantial dunes. Parking and rest rooms. No entrance fee.

Sand Dollar Beach (Hwy. 1, 11 miles south of Lucia) Lush fields and cypress groves frame this favorite picnic spot, with trails leading to a half-moon-shaped beach. Hang gliders love this spot and provide plenty of aerodynamic visuals. Parking and rest rooms. No entrance fee.

Willow Creek Beach (Hwy. 1, 14 miles south of Lucia) An excellent picnic spot affording views of former coastline now eroded into stately offshore rock formations. Enthusiasts still comb for bits of jade where Willow Creek meets the sea. Parking and rest rooms. No entrance fee.

The long stretch of sand and soft dunes of Zmudowski State Beach, just north of Moss Landing, offer myriad opportunities for beach-combing and bird-watching.

Zmudowski State Beach (Hwy. 1, 1 mile north of Moss Landing) A boardwalk leads through the dunes to a prime surfing and clamming beach bordered by verdant farms. Snowy plovers and their wildfowl colleagues nest in the serpentine estuary. A rich marriage of saltwater and freshwater, lined with cattails. Parking and rest rooms. No entrance fee.

BICYCLING

BICYCLE RENTALS

Adventures by the Sea Inc. (831/372-1807; 299 Cannery Row, Monterey).
Bay Bike Rentals (831/646-9090; 640 Wave St., Monterey).
Bay Bike Rentals (831/625-2453; Lincoln St. bet. 5th & 6th Aves., Carmel).
Carmel Bicycle (831/625-2211; 7150 Carmel Valley Rd., Carmel).

TOP RIDES

Berwick Park A leisurely path runs through a narrow, grassy park.
Carmel Valley Road An easy countryside ride for beginners.
Locke Paddon Park Bike path runs along the perimeter of this wetland area.
Perkins Park Paths meander through this park that overlooks Monterey Bay.
Roberts Lake Bike path runs parallel to the shoreline between Roberts Ave.
  and Pacific Grove.

The rugged coastline and inviting tide pools along Monterey's 17 Mile Drive attract cyclists and nature lovers year-round.

Shmuel Thaler

17 Mile Drive A scenic, flat course that runs along the coast through pine
  forests and Monterey cypress groves, as well as past some of the most ritzy
  domiciles on the planet.
Spanish Bay Recreational Trail Cycle through a Monterey pine forest along a
  bike path that runs from Sunset Dr. to Asilomar Blvd.

BIRD-WATCHING

Andrew Molera State Park (Hwy. 1, north end of Old Coast Rd., Big Sur) A
  lively bird sanctuary is contained at the lagoon where the Big Sur River
  flows to the ocean. Grebes and wood ducks sail the surface of this small preserve, as do geese, scoters and coots. The beach here is especially popular
  with sea otters enamored of shellfish lodged in the huge kelp beds.

Carmel River State Beach (Scenic Rd. at Carmelo St., Carmel) A lovely, protected marsh filled with winged charmers like kingfishers and hawks, pelicans and cormorants. Busy sandpipers scurry about, and herons and egrets seem to meditate among the smooth-sailing ducks and geese. There is much to delight the novice as well as experienced bird-watchers.

Crespi Pond (Ocean View & Asilomar Blvds., Pacific Grove) A freshwater pond situated near the pounding surf of Point Pinos boasts a population of resident ducks and coots, as well as the spectacle of brown pelicans, shearwater gulls and cormorants diving dramatically offshore.

One of the richest bird habitats in the United States, the shallow waters of bays and beach areas in the Elkhorn Slough are home to hundreds of species of waterfowl, such as the snowy egret.

Hillary Schalit

Elkhorn Slough (Hwy. 1 at Moss Landing) Nirvana for bird-watchers, this intertidal reserve contains 1,400 acres of wetland, marsh and dunes, all of it home to hundreds of species of wildlife, including rare California brown pelicans and California clapper rails, plus the occasional peregrine falcon and golden eagle. The abundance of birds is almost excessive, as thousands of shorebirds feed together in great agitated flocks, especially the hyperactive sandpipers, killdeers, curlews, willets and sanderlings. Here resident gulls (Western, California and Heermann's) noisily cohabitate with placid mallards and pintail ducks. In the lagoons, observe California murres, grebes, scoters and coots. Cameras and binoculars are a must. (831/728-5939; Elkhorn Slough Foundation, 1700 Elkhorn Rd., Watsonville, CA 95076.)

Lake San Antonio (San Antonio Rd. off Interlake Rd., Monterey county) A sixteen-mile-long lake recreation site tucked into the Coast Ranges, this popular boating and fishing site offers outstanding bird-watching. In the winter, the attraction is over fifty American bald eagles, who overwinter here from Nov.–Mar., feasting on the lake's fish and waterfowl population. Pontoon boat tours take visitors close to the nesting and fishing sites of these awesome raptors, whose specialty prey is trout and whose wingspan exceeds eight feet.

Point Lobos State Park (Hwy. 1, 3 miles south of Carmel) Among the many wonders of this spectacularly beautiful wilderness preserve is an abundance of birdlife (more than 250 species), including those in rocky outcroppings and on islands studded with nesting sites of Brandt's cormorant. Blue herons and white egrets are especially fond of the marshy meadows.

Salinas River Wildlife Area (Potrero Rd. west of Hwy. 1, Moss Landing) Over 250 acres of shoreline boasts sheltered dunes liberally laced with wildflowers, and just south of the beach, the 500-acre Salinas River National Wildlife Refuge is home to sandpipers, herons, egrets, brown pelicans and snowy plovers. Diving into the surf for fish, frantically pacing along the tide line, birds fill every possible niche of this fertile wildlife preserve.

Los Padres National Forest

Straddling the coast and mountains of the Central Coast from Big Sur to Santa Barbara, this mighty and diverse swath of protected natural splendor encompasses close to two-million acres of rocky shoreline, steep canyons, redwood forests and dense chaparral rising from sea level up to 6,000-foot peaks. Major rivers originate in the forest's interior, cutting a swath through rich wildlife habitats on the way to the Pacific Ocean. Paradise for backcountry hikers, Los Padres offers 1,700 miles of trails, over 260 trail camps and eighty-eight campgrounds with 1,000 sites. Purists find the wilderness potential of this preserve a refreshing alternative to commercially developed tourist destinations. Reservations are not accepted for campsites, which are limited to fourteen-day stays (805/683-6711; www.fs.fed.us Web site; 42 Aero Camino St., Goleta, CA 93016). For information about availability, road conditions and permits for backcountry treks, call 805/245-3449.

BOATING

CANOEING & KAYAKING

Adventures By the Sea (831/372-1807; 831/372-4103 Fax; 299 Cannery Row, Monterey, CA 93940) Classes, instruction, rentals, sales and tours by Monterey Bay Aquarium personnel.

Monterey Bay Kayaks (800/649-5357 CA; 831/373-5357; 693 Del Monte Ave., Monterey, CA 93940) One-stop shopping for still water and ocean kayaking, from equipment and rentals to classes and tours of Monterey Bay, Carmel Bay, Elkhorn Slough and Big Sur.

Kayaking has become the fastest growing sports activity around Monterey Bay.

Robert Scheer

CHARTERS & CRUISES

Twin Otters Diving Charters (831/656-9194; Fisherman's Wharf #2, Monterey, CA 93940) Takes up to twenty people for sight-seeing and fifteen people for scuba diving. Will match two or three interested singles with an already-booked group outing. Cruise wanders the coast as far south as Pt. Lobos, and sojourners can expect to see porpoises, whales, otters, harbor seals, sea lions and plenty of stimulating coastal scenery.

FISHING

FISHING & HUNTING REGULATIONS

California Department of Fish & Game (916-227-2244; 3211 S St., Sacramento, CA 95816) Information, licenses and tags.

CHARTERS

Chris' Fishing Trips (831/375-5951; 48 Fisherman's Wharf #1, Monterey, CA 93940) Deep-sea fishing and boats are chartered by appointment.

Monterey Sports Fishing (831/372-2203; 96 Fisherman's Wharf, Monterey, CA 93940) Half- and full-day fishing charters. Salmon and albacore party trips are available in season. Bottom fish trips for ling cod and others. Bait is provided, and licenses, tackle, rod rentals, fish cleaning and freezing services are available.

Randy's Fishing Trips (831/372-7440; 66 Fisherman's Wharf #1, Monterey, CA 93940) Deep-sea fishing trips for salmon and albacore. Bait is provided, and tackle is for rent. Licenses, sack lunches and fish cleaning are available.

Sam's Fishing Fleet (831/372-0577; Fisherman's Wharf #1, Monterey, CA 93940) There is one sixty-five-foot and three fifty-five-foot boats for deep-sea fishing. Rod rentals are available.

Tom's Sportfishing (831/633-2564; Sandholt Rd., Moss Landing, CA 95039) Private charters, open parties, nature trips, whale-watching and bay cruises are available.

RENTALS, BAIT, TACKLE

Moss Landing State Beach (831/384-7695; Moss Landing) Very good surf fishing area.

Municipal Wharf #2 (831/646-3866; Figueroa St., Monterey) Every shore-hugging fish imaginable is waiting to be lured your way.

GOLF

Baynet & Blackhorse Golf Courses (831/899-2351; McClure Way, Seaside) Service personnel and guests; 36 holes, (Bayonet) 6,577 yards, par 72, rated 72.1; (Black Horse) 6,040 yards, par 72, rated 68.4. Cart rental.

Carmel Valley Ranch Golf Course (831/626-2510; 1 Old Ranch Rd., Carmel) Public, members and guests; 18 holes, 6,055 yards, par 70, rated 67.8. Cart rental, pro shop, restaurant, bar.

Cypress Point Golf Club (831/624-2223; 17 Mile Dr., Pebble Beach) Members and guests; 6,332 yards, par 72, rated 72.3. Cart rental.

Laguna Seca Golf Course (831/373-3701; 10520 York Rd., Monterey) Public; 18 holes, 5,711 yards, par 71, rated 68.5.

Links at Spanish Bay (800/654-9300; 831/647-7495; 2700 17 Mile Dr., Pebble Beach) Public and members; 18 holes, 6,078 yards, par 72, rated 72.1. Cart rental, pro shop, restaurant, bar.

Monterey Peninsula Country Club (831/373-1556; 3000 Club Rd., Pebble Beach) Members and guests; 36 holes, (Dunes) 6,161 yards, 72 par, rated 69.4; (Shore) 6,173 yards, par 71, rated 69.7. Cart rental, pro shop, restaurant, bar.

Monterey Pines Golf Course (831/656-2167; Mark Thomas Dr. & Garden Rd., Monterey) Service personnel and guests; 18 holes, 5,574 yards, par 69, rated 67.4. Cart rental.

Old Del Monte Golf Course (408/373-2700; 1300 Sylvan Rd., Monterey) Public and guests; 18 holes, 6,007 yards, par 72, rated 69.5. Cart rental, pro shop, restaurant, bar.

Pacific Grove Municipal Golf Links (831/648-3177; 77 Asilomar Blvd., Pacific Grove) Public; 18 holes, 5,547 yards, par 70, rated 66.3. Lessons, pro shop, lockers, practice range.

Pebble Beach Golf Links (831/624-6611; 17 Mile Dr., Pebble Beach) Public and guests; 18 holes, 6,345 yards, par 72, rated 72.7. Cart rental, pro shop, restaurant, bar.

Peter Hays Golf Course (831/625-8518; 17 Mile Dr., Pebble Beach) Public; 9 holes, 785 yards, par 785, unrated.

Poppy Hills Golf Course (831/625-2035; 3200 Lopez Rd., Pebble Beach) Public, members and guests; 18 holes, 6,219 yards, par 72, rated 71.7. Cart rental, pro shop, restaurant, bar.

Quail Lodge Golf Club (831/624-2770; 8000 Valley Green Dr., Carmel) Members and guests; 18 holes, 6,141 yards, par 71, rated 70.2. Cart rental, pro shop, restaurant, bar.

At the celebrated Pebble Beach Golf Links, the only distractions to the game are the outstanding views.

Shmuel Thaler

Rancho Cañada Golf Club (831/624-0111; Carmel Valley Rd., Carmel) Public; 36 holes, (east) 5,822 yards, par 71, rated 67.3; (west) 6,071 yards, par 72, rated 69.6. Cart rental.

Spyglass Hill Golf Course (800/654-9300; 831/625-8563; Stevenson Dr. & Spy Glass Hill, Pebble Beach) Members and guests; 18 holes, 6,346 yards, par 72, rated 73. Cart rental, pro shop, restaurant, bar.

HIKING

Asilomar State Beach (Sunset Dr., Pacific Grove) The action here centers around a challenging stretch of rocky shore offering breathtaking views of boiling white water tides and wild crashing surf that punctuate the impossibly turquoise Monterey Bay waters. A sandy beach wanders into soft, pillowy dunes filled with native plants and waterfowl habitats. The renowned tide pools fanning out from the bluffs can occupy days of absorbing exploration. Ample parking and rest rooms provide hiking base camp amenities.

Garrapata State Park (Hwy. 1, 2 miles south of Malpaso Creek, Big Sur) Hiking the cove and bluffs at this coastal gateway to Big Sur rewards the naturalist with spectacular views of the coast from the top of a 1.2-mile trail. The trails also provide prime sea otter watching, since this stretch is part of the lengthy Sea Otter Game Refuge, extending offshore down to the San Luis Obispo county line. Explore the tide pools filled with exquisite miniature shellfish and crustacea. For more information, call 831/667-2315.

Julie Pfeiffer Burns State Park (Hwy. 1, 11 miles south of Big Sur State Park, Big Sur) Sprawling from the edge of the ocean up through forested ridges filled with creeks and waterfalls, this 2,000-acre preserve contains abundant hiking trails. Especially worthwhile are paths leading to splendid ocean view overlooks at McWay Waterfall, which spills fifty feet into the sea. Magnificent sea caves and sharp rock crags rim the soft sand at many of the park's beaches, including Partington Cove, accessible by a trail that cuts across a wooden footbridge and through a 200-foot-long tunnel carved into the cliffs at Partington Creek. The park closes at sunset and charges a day-use fee.

Mission Trail Park (Mountain View St. & Crespi Ave., Carmel) Redwood groves and wildflower meadows fill this verdant area, laced with miles of trails eventually converging at the Carmel Mission. Deer safely graze in this stretch, little-known to outsiders but much-loved by local hikers. Ocean vistas can take your breath away.

Pfeiffer Beach Trail (Sycamore Canyon Rd. at Hwy. 1, just south of Big Sur State Park entrance) Once you reach the Forest Service parking area, follow the sandy trail to the small lagoon formed where Sycamore Creek meets the beach. This is an absolutely stunning coastal seascape festooned with caves, tortured rock formations and swirling water. Not for swimming and usually pretty windy, it's well worth the effort to get there. Scenes from the 1960s Liz Taylor/Richard Burton film, *The Sandpiper,* were filmed at this location.

Point Lobos (Hwy. 1 at Riley Ranch Rd., Carmel) Treat yourself to an all-day excursion exploring this incredible 2,500-acre preserve, encompassing pristine coves set with jewellike beaches, jagged rock outcroppings, ancient cypress groves, myriad tide pools, marshlands and isolated meadows. The diversity of landscape is staggering (especially bountiful are spring wildflower displays when meadows are carpeted with iris and lilac), and well-marked trails loop in and around all of the most beautiful stretches, liberally dotted with hundreds of species of native plants, birds and other wildlife. Walking is effort-

The diversity of Point Lobos' 2,500 acres is staggering — pristine coves, ancient cypress groves, numerous tide pools and secluded meadows bountiful with wildflowers.

Shmuel Thaler

less, even along the steeply curving **Cypress Grove Trail,** in surroundings this magnificent. **Bird Island Trail** skirts close to a mile of densely packed brush overlooking exquisite China Cove and Gibson Beach, as well as the cormorant-encrusted Bird Island just offshore. The area deserves multiple visits, especially to the interpretive historic displays at the nineteenth-century **Whaler's Cabin Museum.** There is an admission fee and ample parking throughout the preserve. For information and brochures, call 831/624-4909.

Salinas River State Beach (Hwy. 1 at Potrero Rd., Moss Landing) Dunes caress the wealth of estuary wildlife at this 250-acre haven for clamming and hiking, especially along the steep dune trails. The beach adjoins the Salinas River Wildlife Area, which offers abundant bird-watching opportunities.

Shoreline Park (Ocean View Blvd. bet. Point Cabrillo & Lover's Point, Pacific Grove) Stretching along the rocky cliffs and sheltered sandy coves that boast magnificent views of Monterey Bay, the park's paths wind steeply down to tiny beaches, where hazardous surf (not to mention chilly water) precludes swimming. A paved pedestrian trail threads the length of the park along a railroad right-of-way, interconnecting a series of scenic park settings with plenty of benches for gawking at the incredible seascape. Street parking, no facilities.

Spanish Bay Pedestrian Trail (Spanish Bay Rd. at 17 Mile Dr., Pebble Beach) The Monterey pine forests of this world-renowned stretch of cliffs, tide pools and pounding surf are accessible via many pedestrian and cycling paths looping from Sunset Dr. at 17 Mile Dr. **The Shoreline Trail** can be accessed by strolling through the Spanish Bay Hotel toward the dunes. A mile-long stretch of path fans around Point Joe and leads to cozy pocket beaches and prime bird-watching areas at Seal Rock and Bird Rock.

Ventana Wilderness (Hwy. 1 at Big Sur Coast) Much of the Big Sur Coast and Santa Lucia Mountains lie within this 150,000-acre preserve, itself embraced by the two-million-acre Los Padres National Forest. The forest encompasses over 1,700 miles of hiking trails, of which the finest are contained within the very rugged and isolated Ventana Wilderness, a magnificently wild terrain of forests and coastal canyons. The **Bottchers Gap/Devils Peak Trail** leads four steep miles into the deep forest up to stunning views high above the ocean. For multiday backpacking excursions, the forty-mile-long **Pine Ridge Trail** begins on the coast, threads the Big Sur River and ends up at China Camp. Between May-Oct., campfire permits are required for backpacking excursions (831/385-5434). Trails lead into the wilderness area, and maps, permits and information are available at Palo Colorado Rd. off Hwy. 1, 10 miles south of Carmel.

HORSEBACK RIDING

Cypress Stables (831/372-0511; 550 Aguajito Rd., Carmel, CA 93923).
Nasom Ranches (831/625-8664; P.O. Box 2336, Carmel Valley, CA 93924).

NATURE PRESERVES & PARKS

Elkhorn Slough National Estuarine Research Reserve (831/728-2822; 1700 Elkhorn Rd. near Dolan Rd., Moss Landing) Five miles of trails thread this enchanting 1,400-acre reserve, which includes one of the country's largest salt marshes, as well as nutrient-rich tidal flats supporting countless marine communities. Formed by the confluence of the freshwater Salinas River and saltwater tides, this briny cradle of life is home to more than 250 wildlife species, including golden eagles, herons, egrets, clapper rails and endangered California brown pelicans. Bring binoculars! The dunes surrounding this fragile ecosystem explode with wildflowers in the spring and, within the watery estuary fingers, spawn astonishing quantities of fish, shrimp and oysters. Weekend guided walks occur at 10:00 a.m. and 1:00 p.m., and a visitors' center (open Wed.–Sun., 9:00 a.m.–5:00 p.m.) provides exhibits, maps and brochures.

Point Lobos State Reserve (831/624-4909; Hwy. 1 at Riley Ranch Rd., Carmel) Even in a region famous for sheer breathtaking visuals, Point Lobos is memorable. Widely considered the most beautiful spot on the Central Coast, its 1,225 seafront acres (plus 1,300 more acquired in mid-1993) comprise a glorious marriage of rocky headlands, exquisite cove beaches, transparent waters and fairyland forests of pine and moss-festooned cypress. On misty mornings, its magic is total. On sunny days, every hue of the deep green meadows, turquoise water and ivory beaches is intensified. Trails — many sparkling with crushed abalone shell — lead to panoramic points, each more awesome than the last, through meadows crowned with wild irises, orchids, lilacs and lupines in the spring. Where marshes meet tide pools and beaches, blue heron stalk, and Bird Rock shimmers black with huge nesting cormorants. Its hidden cove beaches and mysterious sea caves are said to have inspired Robert Louis Stevenson's *Treasure Island*. If — heaven forbid! — one could only visit a single spot on the Central Coast, this should be it.

Sea Otters

Once hunted to the edge of extinction for its thick, lustrous fur, the playful southern sea otter now thrives, hunts and swims the Central Coast between Santa Cruz and San Luis Obispo. Humans are easily charmed by these creatures, with whiskered faces and bodies extending up to 4-feet long. Especially prolific in the kelp beds along Monterey Bay, the intelligent otter is enamored of shellfish, for which it dives with admirable speed and skill, consuming them by lying on its back and hammering open the shells using rocks. Sea otters forage continuously for the enormous quantity of food (two tons a year) needed to maintain its body temperature in cold waters. Protected by state and federal law, otters can be spotted by watching for seagulls who dive for the portions of shellfish discarded by the furry mammal.

Sea otters consume an enormous quantity of food in order to maintain their body temperatures and playful activities in cold waters.

SURFING

Lover's Point (Ocean View Blvd., Pacific Grove) Reef break, lefts off a small point; easy to ride, only breaks on a big swell, intermediate to advanced; really rocky spot.

Marina State Beach (Reservation Rd., Marina [Monterey county]) Sand bottom, lefts and rights; advanced; really bad rips.

Moss Landing State Beach (Hwy. 1, north of Moss Landing Harbor) Sand bottom, lefts and rights; breaks like Hawaii Pipeline, swells come from the deep and hit the reef and jack straight up, always bigger than it looks, intermediate to advanced only; has rips and shifty peaks, respect its raw power.

Salinas River State Beach (Hwy. 1 at Potrero Rd., Moss Landing) Reef bottom, lefts and rights; intermediate to advanced, sharky, rips, lots of debris floating around.

Sand City Beach (Sand City) Sand bottom, lefts and rights; beginner to intermediate; can get small rips.

Zmudowski State Beach (Hwy. 1, 1 mile north of Moss Landing) Sand bottom, lefts and rights; intermediate to advanced; can get rips.

TENNIS

PRIVATE

Carmel Valley Racquet and Health Club (831/624-2737; 27300 Rancho San Carlos Rd., Carmel).

Mission Tennis Ranch (831/624-9536; 26260 Dolores Ave., Carmel).

PUBLIC

Bay Club at Inn at Spanish Bay (805/647-7500; 2700 17 Mile Dr., Pebble Beach).

Carmel Valley Racquet Club (831/624-2737; 200 Clocktower Pl., Carmel).
Mission Tennis Ranch (831/624-4335; 26260 Dolores Ave., Carmel).
Monterey Tennis Center (831/372-0172; 401 Pearl St., Monterey).

Whale of a Time

The California gray whale roams the waters of the Pacific coast, migrating annually from Canada down to warm water calving areas in Mexico. During the early winter months, these magnificent creatures can be easily viewed from vantage points all along the Central Coast, spouting water high into the air and thrashing their enormous tails. At **Montaña de Oro State Park** near San Luis Obispo, whales can be observed from the cliffs during their annual migration. Other well-known spots for viewing the leviathans are **Año Nuevo State Reserve, Greyhound Rock** and **Davenport Landing** from bluffs overlooking the sea in the northern Central Coast and **San Simeon Landing** and **Moonstone Beach** near Cambria in the south. In the Big Sur area, the rocky tip of **Soberanes Point** in Pfeiffer Big Sur State Park is a favorite whale-watching area, as is **Garrapata State Park** and **Point Lobos State Reserve**. A pair of binoculars and patience are all that's required. And the sight of these enormous creatures cruising the coast in pods of up to twenty individuals is truly awesome. The **Whale Center** (650/441-1106) offers tours of great viewing spots, while the **Oceanic Society** (415/441-1104; Bldg. E, Fort Mason, San Francisco, CA 94123) and the **American Cetacean Society** (831/646-8743; P.O. Box HE, Pacific Grove, CA 93950) will provide detailed information and tips, if contacted by telephone or mail.

SHOPPING

The past, the present and a plethora of cultural styles form the backdrop for the area's inviting network of shopping districts. From Spanish-style arcades to boutiques housed in Victorian gingerbread homes, the shopping is vigorous and plentiful. Antiques and collectibles from all over the world, housed in old barns, canneries and sleek adobe shops, repeat the pattern of trade in an era where most goods were brought in from "back East" or "around the Horn."

ANTIQUES & COLLECTIBLES

Alicia's Antiques (831/372-1423; 835 Cannery Row, Monterey) Run by a former pal of John Steinbeck's, this time warp shop is a bastion of ambiance-bathed antiques and jewelry, each one bearing a story that the proprietress will be happy to share.

Carmel Valley Antiques & Collectibles (831/624-3414; Valley Hills Shopping Center, Carmel Valley) The focus is on vintage quilts, glassware, antique furniture, jewelry and accessories, plus oodles more to make your past perfect mouth water.

Moss Landing Antique & Trading Co. (831/633-3988; Moss Landing Rd., Moss Landing) One of the best of a plethora of fine and funky antique stores lining the pier of this fishing village. Strong on nineteenth-century estate collections.

Trotter's Antiques (831/373-3505; 301-303 Forest Ave., Pacific Grove) Discerning collection of fine, rare and invariably exquisite antique furniture and appointments from the eighteenth and nineteenth centuries.

The Tuck Box (831/624-6365; Dolores Ave. bet. Ocean & 7th Aves., Carmel) Famous since 1925 as an utterly quaint tearoom, this slice of fairy-tale charm also sells petite and precious porcelain gifts, cookbooks, teapots and preserves. A local landmark.

ARTS & CRAFTS

Carmel Art Association (831/624-6176; Dolores Ave. bet. 5th & 6th Aves., Carmel) Since the 1930s, this respected gallery has showcased the oil paintings, graphics, sculpture and watercolors of the best California artists.

Coast Galleries (831/624-2002; across from The Lodge on 17 Mile Dr., Pebble Beach) A glorious mixed bag of Old Masters and contemporary regional artworks. Of special interest are the collections of original watercolors and prints by former Big Sur resident and literary giant Henry Miller. (Another location is on Hwy. 1; 831/667-2301).

Conway of Asia (831/624-3643; Ocean & 7th Aves., Carmel) Fabulous art treasures from Tibet and lands to the east fill this fabulous gallery, including Himalayan altars, ancient Buddhas, silks, brocades, icons and a sensual array of Oriental rugs.

Gallery Sur (831/626-2615; 6th & Dolores Aves., Carmel) A new photographic gallery in this hotbed of gallery action showcases breathtaking seascapes of the Central Coast by top local photographers.

Photography West Gallery (831/625-1587; Dolores Ave. bet. Ocean & 7th Aves., Carmel) The heavyweights of Carmel's internationally recognized photographic community — Ansel Adams, Edward Weston, Imogene Cunningham and others — are represented here.

Sun Country (831/625-5907; in the Doud Craft Studios, Ocean Ave. & San Carlos St., Carmel) Irresistible handcrafted delicacies like handmade glass marbles, jewelry boxes of exotic and domestic woods and a significant collection of American kaleidoscopes whose spectacular one-of-a-kind effects will produce the "Oh Wow!" effect in even the most jaded connoisseur.

Village Artistry (831/624-7628; Dolores Ave. bet. Ocean & 7th Aves., Carmel) Bold and colorful contemporary blown glass, handwrought jewelry, fanciful furniture and exquisite ceramics jam this bastion of fine local arts and crafts.

Weston Gallery (831/624-4453; 6th Ave. near Lincoln Ave., Carmel) Named for Carmel's famous native son, photographer Edward Weston, the gallery features exceptional nineteenth- and twentieth-century photographs, including the work of another local legend, Ansel Adams. (Another location is at Dolores Ave. near 7th Ave., Carmel).

BOOKS

The Book Tree (831/373-0228; 118 Webster St., Monterey) Specializing in foreign language books, women's studies classics and children's literature, this shop also boasts plenty of best-sellers.

Bookworks (831/372-2242; 667 Lighthouse Ave., Pacific Grove) An in-house coffeehouse serves espresso, croissants and light sandwiches to denizens who comb the endless shelves for regional authors, every newspaper under the sun, foreign language classics and books for children.

Old Monterey Book Co. (831/372-3111; 136 Bonifacio Pl., Monterey) Those on the look out for that rare, unusual and out-of-print classic will revel in the discerning possibilities tucked away in this popular shop.

Thunderbird Bookshop (831/624-4995; The Barnyard, Hwy. 1 & Carmel Valley Rd., Carmel) This landmark bookstore is packed with a stellar collection of current and classic works and offers an adjoining restaurant for lingering long over your latest purchase.

CLOTHING

American Tin Cannery Factory Outlets (831/372-1442; 125 Ocean View Blvd., Pacific Grove) Just around the corner from the Monterey Bay Aquarium is this shop-till-you-drop island of factory outlets — Carole Little, Geoffrey Beene, Royal Doulton, Mattel, Van Heusen, Maidenform — and restaurants housed inside one of the area's historic canneries.

Buff Lagrange (408/625-6506; Lincoln & Ocean Aves., Carmel) Exceptional European clothing in sensuous fabrics, wonderful cuts and the latest designs.

Girl By Girl (831/626-3368; Mission St. & 7th Ave., Carmel) Featuring the trendiest of the trends by only the most *chichi* designers, this store (self-billed as selling gourmet women's clothing) features dresses, bags, shirts, skirts and more by BCBG, Cynthia Rowley, Nicole Miller and others.

Reincarnation Antique Clothing (831/649-0689; 214 17th St., Pacific Grove) Carrying on the timeless California tradition of vintage fashion, this charming store invokes high-fashion nostalgia with its amazing selection of earlier epoch clothing, jewelry, hats and irresistible accessories.

R.K. Shugart (831/624-7748; Dolores Ave. bet. 7th & 9th Aves., Carmel) Top-quality and deluxe designer women's wear, from exciting contemporary sportswear to elegant and sexy evening wear.

Shopping Complexes

Central Coast villages, towns and cities invariably offer fine shopping districts, clustered tightly around central downtown art, theater and civic bastions. Monterey's historic **Cannery Row** is a veritable gauntlet of shopping pleasures, lined and festooned with antique stores, wineshops, T-shirt and upscale clothing boutiques and everything in between.

Those devoted to the huge, generic mall concept will also find ample opportunities to flex their credit cards in huge, brand-name department stores. But dotting this region are also several tastefully organized centers boasting fine and innovative shops that offer the best in regional consumerism. **Carmel Crossroads,** on Hwy. 1 just south of Carmel, is one especially inviting conglomeration of upscale bistros, culinary boutiques and exceptional clothing emporia, all served up and sculpted in a western ranch club mood.

Monterey's historic Cannery Row is a shopper's paradise, lined with a delightful array of shops.

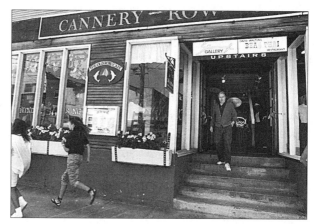

Shmuel Thaler

JEWELRY

Fourtané Estate Jewelers (831/624-4684; Ocean Ave. at Lincoln Ave., Carmel) Elegant jewelry, watches and objet d'art from the nineteenth and twentieth centuries make this splendid treasure trove of vintage estate luxuries a must-visit.

Jewel Boutique (831/625-1016; The Barnyard, Carmel Valley Rd., Carmel) Custom-designed and imported jewelry shares this shop with fabulous antique and estate items.

Mark Areias Jewelers (831/624-5621; 5th Ave. & San Carlos St., Carmel) This authorized Cartier dealer stocks bedazzling baubles, both contemporary and antique. (Another location is at #31 Dear Park Center, Aptos; 831/688-2799).

Silver Feather Trading Company (831/624-3622; Carmel Plaza, Carmel) A cache of turquoise and silver fuels the visual appeal of this well-stocked dealer in authentic Native American jewelry and artwork.

SPECIALTY

Carmel Candy & Confection Company (831/625-3559; Ocean & Junipero Aves., Carmel) The candy store sells something for all species of the sweet tooth. From imported taffies to the most sinful dark chocolates to the hard candy that you ate when you were a tyke, this confection company has it all.

The Cheese Shop (831/625-2272; Carmel Plaza, Carmel) Undecided about which Italian varietal will match perfectly with an aged cheese? The Cheese Shop is one-stop shopping for wines that range from cheap and tasty to expensive and delicious. The friendly and knowledgeable staff also offers tastings of all the cheeses in the house.

Golf Arts & Imports (831/625-4488; 6th & Dolores Aves., Carmel) Golf widows and linksmen alike will be fascinated by this whimsical conglomeration of golf art, reproductions and historical originals. Oodles of golf antiques and paraphernalia like Scottish tartan club covers and golf logo silk ties from Italy are among the treasures.

Mediterranean Market (831/624-2022; Ocean Ave. & Mission St., Carmel) Olive oils, condiments, breads, imported cheeses and meats, plus a huge selection of domestic and international wines round out this tasty shop o' specialty foods.

Owl's Nest (831/624-5509; San Carlos St. & 7th Ave., Carmel) This shop recaptures the past with a fascinating selection of artist-made dolls, provocative Teddy bears and other stuffed animals.

SPORTS

On the Beach Surf Shop (831/624-7282; Ocean Ave. & Mission St., Carmel) Be a surfer . . . or just dress like one. Everything that you will need is for sale, from surfboards and wet suits to in-line skates, skateboards and boogieboards. All this shop lacks is immediate proximity to great surfing. (Another location is at 693 Lighthouse Ave., Monterey; 831/646-WAVE).

The Treadmill (831/624-4112; 149 The Crossroads, Carmel) If the shoe fits, especially if it's designed for action, it's bound to be part of this major selection of top brands and styles for running, walking, tennis and aerobics. Active wear and fitness accessories for men and women also can be had. Similar gear for youngsters is available a few doors down at Treadmill Jr. sports boutique for kids (831/624-2210; 116 The Crossroads, Carmel).

CHAPTER FIVE
Gold Coasting
SAN LUIS OBISPO &
THE SANTA YNEZ VALLEY

San Luis Obispo Chamber of Commerce

The charming mission and college town of San Luis Obispo is a gateway to many recreational destinations.

Missionaries, winemakers, ranchers, movie stars — all have found slices of paradise in this geographically diverse chunk of the Central Coast that encompasses oak-studded hillsides and coastal canyons just a few miles inland from the Pacific Ocean.

San Luis Obispo, a post-hippie-era, college town retreat, founded by busy Franciscan Junipero Serra, still boasts its mission in the heart of lands owned by Chumash descendants. Prime cattle country, the lands around San Luis Obispo supplied the leather needs of the early Spanish settlers, just as they are ranched for beef today. California State Polytechnic College (affectionately known as Cal Poly) dominates the intellectual landscape of this small, off-the-beaten-track community. Down the coast, a series of lovely beach towns is crowned by the sand dunes of Pismo Beach. A string of ancient volcanoes have left their dark basalt cinder cones to punctuate the undulating hills, known for

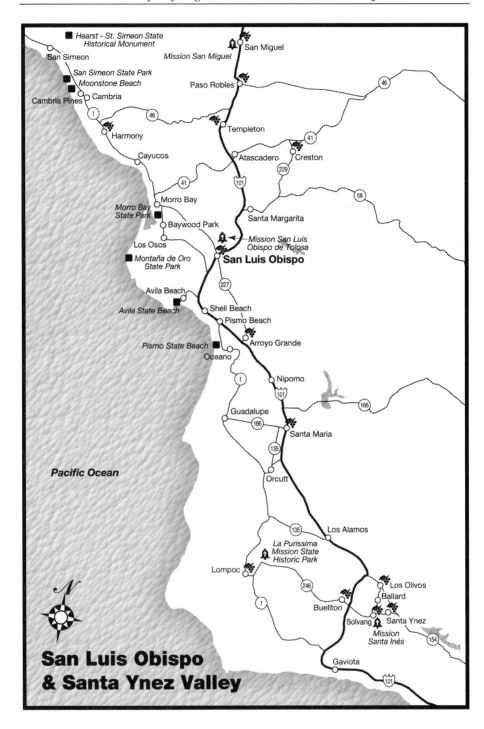

Hearst - St. Simeon State Historical Monument

San Simeon

San Miguel

Mission San Miguel

San Simeon State Park
Moonstone Beach

Paso Robles

Cambria Pines   Cambria

46

1   46

Harmony

Templeton

41

Cayucos

Atascadero   Creston

229

101

41   Morro Bay

58

Morro Bay State Park

Santa Margarita

Baywood Park

Mission San Luis Obispo de Tolosa

Los Osos

San Luis Obispo

Montaña de Oro State Park

227

Avila Beach

Shell Beach

Avila State Beach

Pismo Beach

Pismo State Beach

Arroyo Grande

Oceano

1

Nipomo

101

Guadalupe

166

166

Santa Maria

135

Pacific Ocean

Orcutt

135   Los Alamos

La Purissima Mission State Historic Park

Lompoc

246   Los Olivos

Ballard

1   Buellton

Solvang   Santa Ynez

Mission Santa Inés

154

San Luis Obispo & Santa Ynez Valley

Gaviota

101

their electric green in the winter and their explosion into riots of wildflowers each spring.

South of San Luis Obispo, the mighty coast ranges turn to velvet as the Santa Lucia Mountains form the soft folds of the Santa Ynez Valley. Superbly situated to take full advantage of long sunny days and fog-cooled evenings, this Eden, located a mere ten miles from the coast, is home to award-winning wineries. The area has also established a reputation among equestrians and has attracted landed gentry on the merits of its excellent climate and hidden-away sense of isolation. Here the ranches of the famed and mighty — entertainer Michael Jackson, cowboy idol Fess Parker, former President Ronald Reagan — sprawl over incomparable acreage, lush with oak forests and rich in ocean views. Driving, bicycling and hiking are all great ways to experience this area — the region lends itself to easy-access exploration. Small communities like Los Olivos oblige with secluded restaurants (movie stars have sought refuge here for years) prime bed and breakfasts, vintage motels and stellar arts and crafts galleries.

LODGING

Where the emphasis is on beach-oriented action, well appointed and conveniently located motels, ranging from oceanfront to awesomely uncategorizeable, are the dominant form of lodging. Visitors will also encounter a healthy selection of cozy B&Bs, some ensconced in creatively renovated nineteenth-century hotels, offering romance, seaside gardens and rooms with a view. Here are the idiosyncratic stops that make this area such a great escape. Many of the loveliest Victorian manors of Cambria, San Luis Obispo and the Santa Ynez Valley have been cozily transformed into inviting bed and breakfast lodgings for the comfort of the weary traveler.

Credit Cards

AE – American Express	DC – Diner's Club
CB – Carte Blanche	MC – MasterCard
D – Discover Card	V – Visa

SAN LUIS OBISPO COAST

Cambria

BEACH HOUSE BED & BREAKFAST INN
Innkeepers: Joan Apathy, Penny Hitch & Kernn MacKinnon.

Looking for all the world like a quintessential Central Coast private beach house, this comfortable wood and glass oceanfront home consists of seven rooms of varying sizes, all with private

805/927-3136;
805/927-9850 Fax.
6360 Moonstone Beach Dr.,
Cambria, CA 93428.
Price: $125–$155, includes
breakfast.
Credit Cards: MC, V.
Children: Two people per
room limit.
Smoking: Not in rooms.
Handicap Access: No.

baths and cable TVs. Two rooms come with fireplaces, and one lofty, second-floor room provides a king-sized bed and a private deck that opens onto the stunning seascape vistas of Moonstone Beach. Refreshments, including wines and cheeses, are offered at sunset, and morning is the best time to explore the grassy bluffs networked with inviting walking trails, which overlook the tide pools and surf just outside the front door. A full breakfast is offered each morning at the Beach House's restaurant down the street. The sunsets are beautiful, and Hearst Castle is fifteen minutes up Hwy. 1.

BLUE WHALE INN
Innkeepers: Bob & Karleen
Hathcock.
805/927-4647.
6736 Moonstone Beach Dr.,
Cambria , CA 93428.
Price: $160–$210.
Credit Cards: MC, V.
Children: Allowed with
limits.
Smoking: Not in rooms.
Handicap Access: No.

Each of this B&B's six spacious rooms is decorated with soft pastel upholstery, plump comforters, canopy swags, comfortable couches, charming wallpaper, vaulted ceilings and airy skylighting. A long, dressing room area counter is appointed with beautifully packaged amenities, and there's an in-room refrigerator, a fireplace, a separate bathroom, with a view of the rolling hills behind the shoreline, and cable TV tucked away in a colorful armoire. You can hear the soothing waves all night long; you could live forever in these rooms. But most guests enjoy taking in the sunset while sipping complimentary wine or gazing through the telescope in the main lounge at whales and waterfowl cruising the coast. An inviting gift shop stocked with fine local crafts and beachy souvenirs is located just off the picture window-lined dining room, where full breakfasts usually involve terrific coffee, fresh juices and fruits, cereals and yogurt, as well as gingerbread pancakes with lemony syrup fresh from the adjoining kitchen. Regular visitors to the inn like to take a bracing walk along the hiking trails lacing the bluffs over spectacular Moonstone Beach, which is across the lane from the inn. This is one of the best overnights this area has to offer.

FOGCATCHER INN
Innkeeper: Brenda Devine.
800/425-4121; 805/927-
1400; 805/927-0204 Fax.
6400 Moonstone Beach Dr.,
Cambria, CA 93428.
Price: $105–$160, includes
breakfast.
Credit Cards: AE, D, DC,
MC, V.

Conjuring scenes from a Bronte novel, this contemporary neo-English inn with multipaned windows, thatched roof and subtle half-timbering offers gracious overnight accommodations a few steps from the melodic surf and endless tide pools of Moonstone Beach. Set on bluffs crisscrossed with hiking trails, the inn offers such luxuries as a heated pool and a hot tub, as well as sixty guest rooms stocked with refrigerators, fireplaces, micro-

Children: Allowed with limits.
Smoking: Yes.
Handicap Access: Yes.

waves, coffeemakers, TVs and honor bars. There's even a bridal suite — remember, this *is* honeymoon country. In the main gathering room, a complimentary breakfast of muffins, coffee, cereals, fresh fruit and juices tunes up guests for a day of beachcombing, antiquing in Cambria village or touring the eye-popping sights of San Simeon.

J. PATRICK HOUSE
Innkeepers: Barbara & Mel Schwimmer.
800/341-5258: 805/927-3812: 805/927-6759 Fax; jph@jpatrickhouse.com E-mail; www.jpatrick house.com Web site.
2990 Burton Dr., Cambria, CA 93428.
Price: $100–$120, includes breakfast.
Credit Cards: AE, D, MC, V.
Children: Limited.
Smoking: No.
Handicap Access: No.

A cozy, two-story log house, situated in the pines overlooking Cambria's east village, fronts an old-fashioned arbor leading to the eight guest rooms — seven with wood-burning fireplaces and all with private baths. The Early American decor of the main house is echoed in the attractive rooms, which are liberally adorned with floral wallpaper and wicker furniture. Afternoon wine and cheese are offered in front of the sitting room fireplace, and the sunny dining room serves up a full breakfast each morning highlighted by freshly ground coffee, fruits, juices, muffins and homemade cinnamon rolls. Personalized service and friendly atmosphere come with the attractive turf.

OLALLIEBERRY INN
Innkeepers: Carol Ann & Peter Irsfeld.
888/927-3222; 805/927-3222; 805/927-0202 Fax; OlallieberryInn@thegrid. net E-mail; www.olallie berry.com Web site.
2476 Main St., Cambria, CA 93428.
Price: $90–$175, includes breakfast.
Credit Cards: MC, V.
Children: Not appropriate.
Smoking: Not in rooms.
Handicap Access: Yes.

A period-decorated 1873 Greek Revival home provides nine inviting rooms, six with fireplaces and each with private bath, updated for contemporary convenience at no sacrifice of yesteryear ambiance. The main parlor is the setting for evening wine tastings with appetizers, and more than one libation has been enjoyed at the wooded glade and creek bordered by the inn's back lawn. Each guest room is uniquely decorated, with Victorian antiques accentuating the graceful high ceilings. A full breakfast greets guests in the morning, and the turn-of-the-century cottages, shops and galleries of downtown Cambria are a pleasant stroll away.

Morro Bay

INN AT MORRO BAY
Innkeeper: Robert Kemper.
800/321-9566; 805/772-5651; 805/772-4779 Fax.
60 State Park Rd., Morro Bay, CA 93442.

O verlooking the glittering expanse of Morro Bay and its dramatic Morro Rock (and just a thirty-minute drive from Hearst Castle), this full-service facility offers inviting accommodations. Swim in the expansive pool, sip local wines while

Price: $70–$255.
Credit Cards: AE, CB, D, DC, MC, V.
Children: Yes.
Smoking: Yes.
Handicap Access: Yes.

enjoying the breathtaking view or enjoy breakfast in your own brass bed. Rooms, many with fireplaces, offer full amenities, and the inn's restaurant serves up fine seafood and California cuisine, featuring the area's renowned fresh produce. The beaches, trees and estuary of Morro State Park, as well as the rare waterfowl of the Blue Heron Rookery, are right outside your window.

San Luis Obispo

The Apple Farm Inn in San Luis Obispo is located next to an old mill house and working farm.

APPLE FARM INN
Innkeepers: Bob & Katy Davis.
800/255-2040 CA; 805/544-2040; 805/546-9495 Fax.
2015 Monterey St., San Luis Obispo, CA 93401.
Price: $109–$239.
Credit Cards: AE, MC, V.
Children: Yes.
Smoking: Yes.
Handicap Access: Yes.

Even an overworked word like "charming" finds new currency in reference to this Victorian inn, which is a veritable country village of cozy overnight rooms threaded in and around an old mill house. Four-poster beds, flowered wallpaper, ruffled linens, overstuffed couches and deep tubs add romance to the very contemporary amenities like a heated swimming pool and a Jacuzzi. Each room boasts its own fireplace, and morning brings coffee or tea to your room (the inn's fine restaurant serves a full range of culinary classics). Splendid views of the surrounding hills and the huge waterwheel turns hypnotically on its nineteenth-century foundations.

GARDEN STREET INN
Innkeepers: Dan & Kathy
 Smith.
805/545-9802;
 805/545-9403 Fax.
1212 Garden St., San Luis
 Obispo, CA 93401.
Price: $90–$160, includes
 breakfast.
Credit Cards: AE, MC, V.
Children: Over 15 only.
Smoking: Outside decks
 only.
Handicap Access: One
 suite.

The high ceilings, grand staircase and jewellike, stained-glass trimmings of this Italianate 1887 Italianate/Queen Anne have been lovingly restored to the heyday atmosphere of this frontier town. Tastefully decorated with antiques and artistic family memorabilia, the inn offers nine rooms and four suites, each with private bath. Romantics will love the six rooms with fireplaces and whirlpool tubs, as well as the evening wine and cheese selection. There's a well-stocked library for the enjoyment of guests, and a full homemade breakfast is served amidst the original stained-glass splendor of the house's Morning Room.

MADONNA INN
Innkeeper: Alex Madonna.
800/543-9666; 805/543-
 3000; 805/543-1800 Fax.
100 Madonna Rd., San Luis
 Obispo, CA 93401.
Price: $97–$198.
Credit Cards: MC, V.
Children: Yes.
Smoking: No.
Handicap Access: No.

There's simply nothing like the Madonna Inn, an only-in-California poem to fantasy and excess in ubiquitous stonework and shocking pink, where each room is decorated like a B-movie set. No one ever forgets an overnight in the cavelike Flintstones Suite with its rock waterfall shower or the men's room with its own waterfall urinal — straight from central casting. A no-holds-barred "motel," this epic of red velvet and chandelier overkill (matched by an architectural hodgepodge of an exterior) is wonderful fun for those who really want an experience that they can write home about. Expect to be amazed by the eccentric decor of every one of the 110 rooms and suites, all with cable TVs. The bar looks like an old-fashioned carousel, and the amazing restaurant (yes, you have seen it in many Hollywood movies) serves up serious homemade fare and gargantuan barbecued steaks. There are oodles of souvenir, gift, clothing and coffee shops. You may not be planning a second honeymoon, but you'll wind up having one anyway given the fantasy sensory bombardment.

Pismo Beach

SANDCASTLE INN
Innkeeper: Jim Trent.
800/822-6606; 805/773-
 2422; 805/773-0771 Fax.
100 Stimson Ave., Pismo
 Beach, CA 93449.
Price: $75–$225, includes
 breakfast.
Credit Cards: AE, CB, D,
 DC, MC, V.

Attractions of this very contemporary, Mediterranean seaside retreat include plump couches and chairs, huge beds with soothing floral prints and a plethora of ocean views available from the patios, decks and picture windows. Fifty-nine overnight rooms, including suites with fireplaces, offer complete comfort and views of the picturesque fishing pier and oceanfront. Each room

Children: Yes.
Smoking: Yes.
Handicap Access: Yes.

has its own TV/VCR, refrigerator and coffeemaker. A complimentary Continental breakfast greets guests in the morning, and the best place to enjoy breakfast is just after you've exited the swirling Jacuzzi on the glass-enclosed deck.

SANTA YNEZ VALLEY

Los Olivos

The Los Olivos Grand Hotel combines turn-of-the-century ambiance with twentieth-century comforts.

Kim Reierson

**LOS OLIVOS GRAND
  HOTEL**
Innkeeper: Ken Mortensen.
800/446-2455; 805/688-
  7788; 805/688-1942 Fax.
P.O. Box 526, 2860 Grand
  Ave., Los Olivos, CA
  93441.
Price: $175–$340, includes
  breakfast.
Credit Cards: AE, D, DC,
  MC, V.
Children: Yes.
Smoking: No.
Handicap Access: Yes.

Situated in the gemlike western village of Los Olivos, this luxury hideaway combines turn-of-the-century atmosphere with thoroughly twentieth-century comforts. A terrific base from which to explore the scenic wineries of the Santa Ynez Valley, the elegant hotel boasts twenty-one spacious overnight rooms, plus public rooms, an award-winning restaurant, a swimming pool and a Jacuzzi. Each room has been tastefully decorated in period style with armoires, brass beds, floral comforters and antique chandeliers. Every room also boasts a fireplace, TV, wet bar and refrigerator. Guests can relax poolside or can stroll the hotel's arbors and gardens after both the complementary full breakfast or afternoon wine and appetizers. Bicycles are available for touring tiny Los Olivos, its art galleries and wine-tasting rooms.

Ballard

The modern Ballard Inn in the Santa Ynez Valley wine country recreates the 1800s with its charming verandah and antique-filled rooms.

Buz Bezore

BALLARD INN
Innkeeper: Kelly Robinson.
800/638-2466;
  805/688-7770.
2436 Baseline Ave., Ballard,
  CA 93463.
Price: $160–$195, includes
  breakfast.
Credit Cards: AE, MC, V.
Children: Allowed with
  limits.
Smoking: Outside only.
Handicap Access: Yes.

Fronted by one of tiny Ballard's two or three streets, this contemporary inn looks like it stepped out of the late-nineteenth century with wraparound verandah, polished wood dining room and antique-filled overnight rooms. Each room holds its own special charm, built around Old West themes and featuring fine craft work, brass and wicker beds and magnificent comforters, quilts and upholsteries, plus Victorian armoires and commodes transformed into sinks. Seven of the fifteen rooms have wood-burning fireplaces, and each has a full private bath. The welcoming parlor lays out an amazing afternoon appetizer display, which can include smoked trout, cheeses, pickled asparagus and crackers, along with excellent vintages of Santa Ynez wineries. The inn's friendly staff serves up a glorious full breakfast of pancakes or poached eggs and thick slabs of country bacon, and a Continental buffet is also laid on a carved sideboard. After breakfast, a tour of this captivating wine country is in order via the Ballard's complimentary mountain bikes. The Ballard also is home to Cafe Chardonnay, with Doyenne Kelly Robinson and her staff earning a Four Diamond AAA award for five consecutive years. They also are highly knowledgeable about the local microwineries and will guide you to memorable tastings.

Solvang

ALISAL GUEST RANCH
Innkeeper: David
Lautensack.
800/4-ALISAL; 805/688-
6411; 805/688-2510 Fax;
info@alisal.com E-mail;
www.alisal.com Web
site.
1054 Alisal Rd., Solvang,
CA 93463.
Price: $335–$415, includes
breakfast and dinner.
Credit Cards: AE, MC, V.
Children: Yes.
Smoking: Yes.
Handicap Access: Yes.

Part guest ranch, part golf resort and all western hospitality, this legendary facility opened its 10,000 acres of working ranch to guests in 1946. Some visitors never leave the sprawling swimming pool, the tennis courts or the two golf courses, with PGA professionals on staff. Others fish for catfish, bluegill and largemouth bass or sail on the ranch's 100-acre lake. But most come to strip away the cares of civilization and to ride the miles of unparalleled equestrian trails winding through magnificent hills and sycamore groves. Leaving at dawn, wranglers lead guests into the beautiful country where a campfire breakfast of ham, eggs and pancakes awaits. But it's not all rustic. After cocktails at the Oak Room Lounge, guests can enjoy California cuisine in the Old West ambiance of the dining room. Overnight rooms all boast fireplaces and cozy decor. A two-night minimum is required, and during midweek and most weekends, all golf, tennis and horseback riding are free as part of the package deal. The ranch also offers year-round activities for children, including riding lessons, a petting zoo and an arts and crafts program. This is a very special getaway for those who like to "rough it" in style.

DINING

In addition to sparkling fresh seafood harvested each day from teeming Pacific waters, this area headlines its long-standing tradition for serious Western dining, involving aromatic oak pit grills, steaks slathered in barbecue sauce, even buffalo burgers. The exceptional produce from surrounding small farms is legendary, even in a state graced with a year-round growing season. The following San Luis Obispo and Santa Ynez Valley eateries provide some of the top gastronomic occasions to experience the best this stretch of the coast has to offer.

Dining Price Code

The price range below includes the cost of a single dinner that includes an appetizer, entrée, dessert and coffee. Cocktails, wine, beer, tax or gratuities are not included. *Note:* Smoking is not allowed in any restaurant or eatery in the state of California.

Inexpensive	Up to $10
Moderate	$10–$25
Expensive	$25–$40
Very Expensive	$40 or more

Credit Cards

AE – American Express	DC – Diner's Club
CB – Carte Blanche	MC – MasterCard
D – Discover Card	V – Visa

SAN LUIS OBISPO COAST

Cambria

BRAMBLES
805/927-4716.
4005 Burton Dr., Cambria, CA 93428.
Open: Daily.
Price: Moderate to Expensive.
Cuisine: Continental.
Serving: D, Sun. Br.
Reservations: Recommended.
Credit Cards: AE, CB, D, DC, MC, V.
Handicap Access: Yes.

Long one Cambria's top dinner houses, Brambles occupies an English-style home built in 1874. Over the years, numerous additions have turned the building into charming dining rooms surrounded by a thicket of garden. While prime rib with Yorkshire pudding is a house signature, the salmon broiled over the oak wood pit is exceptional, as are all of the fresh, Continental seafood dishes. Stellar steaks come sizzling from the oak wood pit, and a selection of attractive chicken and pasta specialties rounds out the menu. Greek and Caesar salads are created from the fresh bounty of small Central Coast market gardens. Sampling regional wines that are difficult to come by outside the area is made effortless by the restaurant's extensive wine list, winner of a *Wine Spectator* Award for Excellence.

IAN'S
805/927-8649.
2150 Center St., Cambria, CA 93428.
Open: Daily.
Price: Moderate to Expensive.
Cuisine: California.
Serving: D.
Reservations: Recommended.
Credit Cards: AE, MC, V.
Handicap Access: Yes.

A sleek, very contemporary dining room adorned with sophisticated wall sconces, upholstered banquettes and bold original artwork, Ian's creates some of the finest California cuisine in the area. Fresh local produce from area farms and gardens collaborate in an array of arresting appetizers, such as the duck quesadilla studded with pumpkin seeds and golden raisins and topped with salsa fresca, avocados, tomatoes and cilantro. Also wonderful is warm, grilled asparagus on baby greens with goat cheese and toasted pine nuts. The restaurant does a remarkable roast chicken with creamy garlic mashed pota-toes. Duck, rabbit and lamb appear in exciting guises on this menu, as do sen-suous Central Coast abalone and exquisite prawn presentations. The service is excellent, the ambiance sophisticated yet casual and the wine list excels in Central Coast vintages.

LINN'S MAIN BIN
805/927-0371.
2485 Village Ln., Cambria,
    CA 93428.
Open: Daily.
Price: Moderate.
Cuisine: Country
    American.
Serving: B, L, D, Sun. Br.
Reservations: No.
Credit Cards: AE, D, MC, V.
Handicap Access: Yes.

A Cambria original, located on picturesque Old West Main St., Linn's is partly a huge cafe, like an American country tearoom and half gourmet gift shop and bakery. The area's largest regional wine list complements a homemade menu, strong on homemade soups, signature pot pies and imagi-native sandwiches, all fueled by the fresh produce from Linn's own farms.

ROBIN'S
805/927-5007.
4095 Burton Dr., Cambria,
    CA 93428.
Open: Daily.
Price: Inexpensive to
    Moderate.
Cuisine: Eclectic Ethnic.
Serving: L, D.
Reservations:
    Recommended on
    summer weekends.
Credit Cards: MC, V.
Handicap Access: Limited.

T ucked into a 1930s Spanish-style house set with antique oak tables and ethnic crafts on the walls, Robin's is a thoroughly charming, eclectic dining experience. The emphasis on delicious, nat-ural ingredients — the menu contains a wealth of vegetarian dishes — has been sifted through ethnic cuisines ranging from the Far East to Latin America. The result is a menu, with exciting spices and sea-sonings. Magnificent produce, packed with just-picked flavor, powers inventive salads mated with curries, toasted nuts and glorious dressings, and the curried chicken salad sandwich served on a crois-sant with lettuce, tomatoes, cucumbers and toasted almonds is divine. Thai stir-fried beef explodes with the flavor of mint, ginger, garlic, chiles and peanuts, and all of the black bean and pasta dishes are imaginative. And nobody gets past the counter of lavish desserts, of which French apple pie, tiramisu and frangipane tart with wine-poached pears are only a few temptations. The finest from small local wineries is available by the glass or by the split, making for an excellent tasting opportunity. The patio seating, surrounded by a lush arbor, is very appealing.

SOW'S EAR CAFE
805/927-4865.
2248 Main St., Cambria, CA
    93428.
Open: Daily.
Price: Moderate.
Cuisine: American.

L ocally grown herbs and vegetables pack vibrant flavor into each dish graciously served and skillfully presented in this fine country cafe. The entrées run the gamut of country American favorites, all given a uniquely Central Coast spin. Shellfish linguine with Greek olives, fennel, feta

Serving: D.
Reservations:
  Recommended.
Credit Cards: MC, V.
Handicap Access: Limited.

cheese and tomatoes is a popular item, as are the chicken and dumplings and grill-roasted chicken breast with fresh rosemary. A lovely appetizer salad of fresh spinach is topped with sesame-crusted chicken, oranges, almonds and honey-lime dressing. The heartland attitude is continued by desserts like warm blueberry bread pudding with brandy hard sauce and milk chocolate cheesecake with hazelnut crust. The freshly baked bread is wonderful, and the mood is unpretentiously friendly.

Harmony

OLD HARMONY PASTA FACTORY
805/927-5882.
2 Old Creamery Rd. & Hwy. 1, Harmony, CA 93435.
Open: Daily.
Price: Moderate.
Cuisine: Italian.
Serving: L, D, Sun. Br.
Reservations:
  Recommended on weekends.
Credit Cards: AE, MC, V.
Handicap Access: Yes.

A stone's throw from the coast, the tiny village of Harmony is devoted lock, stock and barrel to a community of thriving arts studios housed in renovated farm buildings. In what was once the butter-cooling room of an old creamery, the Old Harmony Pasta Factory presents imaginative Italian cookery in the mellowest possible setting. Fetchingly decorated with lush plants and encircled by tiny gardens setting off the weathered wood buildings, this skylighted restaurant whips up a dreamy orange cream linguine and tiny pizzas, as well as classics like scampi, pork tenderloin Marsala, chicken Alfredo and a myriad of other pastas. The garden patio, with its relaxing view of the splendid coastal foothills, is the place to take meals. Sunday brunches include favorites like eggs Benedict and omelettes packed with garden fresh produce and herbs.

Morro Bay

DORN'S ORIGINAL BREAKERS CAFE
805/772-4415.
801 Market St., Morro Bay, CA 93442.
Open: Daily.
Price: Moderate.
Cuisine: Country American.
Serving: B, L, D.
Reservations:
  Recommended on weekends.
Credit Cards: MC, V.
Handicap Access: Yes.

An old World War I vintage real estate office was converted in the early 1940s to the Breakers Cafe. A success since the day it opened, Dorn's specializes in seafood served in the perfect inspirational setting, overlooking the dramatic, ancient volcanic plug of Morro Rock and the Morro Bay harbor. Breakfasts are served until 2:00 p.m. daily, offering a huge choice of pancakes, egg dishes and French toast creations. Many in the know come for the classic Boston clam chowder and highly prized Morro Bay abalone. Freshly made pastas are also quite good.

**PARADISE
  RESTAURANT**
805/772-5651.
Inn at Morro Bay, 19
  Country Club Dr., Morro
  Bay, CA 93442.
Open: Daily.
Price: Expensive.
Cuisine: Continental.
Serving: B, L, D, Sun. Br.
Reservations:
  Recommended.
Credit Cards: AE, CB, D,
  DC, MC, V.
Handicap Access: Yes.

Housed in a popular, coastal overnight lodge, Paradise showcases fine California cuisine, often with a French accent, and grand views of the ocean at Morro Bay State Park. The elegant and comfortable dining room excels in sophisticated dinners, where appetizers can include zucchini blossoms stuffed with chicken truffle mousse and balsamic butter or country pâtés and salads of seasonal greens. Local king salmon is poached with fresh sorrel sauce, and roast duckling arrives napped with blueberry cream sauce. A grilled halibut served with tomato-basil fettuccine, lemon olive oil and ginger is especially memorable. Classic breakfasts and lunches feature seafoods, and pastas are also served.

San Luis Obispo

APPLE FARM
805/544-6100.
2015 Monterey St., San Luis
  Obispo, CA 93401.
Open: Daily.
Price: Moderate.
Cuisine: American.
Serving: B, L, D.
Reservations:
  Recommended.
Credit Cards: AE, D, MC,
  V.
Handicap Access: Yes.

Housed in a fascinating, well-decorated B&B complex, complete with gardens, orchards and working waterwheel, this welcoming country-style restaurant specializes in generous portions of down-home foods with all of the trimmings. Grilled fish specials of Louisiana catfish, halibut and New Zealand orange roughy come, as do all dinners, with homemade soup or salad, hot corn bread, vegetable and choice of potatoes. Turkey pot pie, barbecued baby back ribs, even homemade meat loaf will please those looking for hearty, old-fashioned comfort foods. Apple desserts are the house signature.

GARDENS OF AVILA
805/595-7365.
1215 Avila Beach Dr., San
  Luis Obispo, CA 93401.
Open: Daily.
Price: Moderate to
  Expensive.
Cuisine: California Cuisine.
Serving: L (except Sun.), D,
  Sun. Br.
Reservations:
  Recommended.
Credit Cards: AE, D, MC,
  V.
Handicap Access: Yes.

From the windows and terraces of this attractive contemporary restaurant, housed in a popular inn, diners can feast on the view of oak groves and secluded mineral water tubs dotting the hillside. Another sort of feast awaits inside, thanks to a sensitively designed menu, showcasing local produce, seafoods and grilled meats. Appetizers like Mediterranean crab cakes served with ricotta penne or a Jamaican jerk vegetable quesadilla show off the kitchen's passion for multicultural flavorings. Roasted tri-tip and grilled chicken sandwiches are on the lunch menu, while dinner sports tiger prawns, blackened snapper with fried soft-shell crayfish and duck confit calzone, with local wines on the wine list. The ambiance is relaxed and the harbors of Avila Beach are just down the road.

RHYTHM CAFE
805/541-4048.
1040 Broad St., San Luis
  Obispo, CA 93401.
Open: Daily.
Price: Inexpensive to
  Moderate.
Cuisine: California Fusion.
Serving: B (Sat.), L, D, Sun.
  Br.
Reservations: No.
Credit Cards: Cash or
  checks only.
Handicap Access: Yes.

Overlooking the landscaped terracing and native plantings along the sleepy San Luis Creek, on whose banks Father Junipero Serra established the area's wealthiest mission in the late-eighteenth century, the attractive little bistro affords a mesmerizing view of the ducks and waterfowl in this peaceful oasis. An exciting menu concentrates on fresh produce and California attitudes, with dashes of Asian, Mediterranean and East Indian stylings. Grilled oysters on the half shell are presented with mignonette and fiery wasabe soy sauce, and a Greek salad comes sided with grilled lamb on skewers. Entrées include a baked whole trout with polenta, sautéed leeks and pancetta and seared sea scallops with orange-ginger butter and crispy udon noodles. This is a nice place for light meals of soup, salad and freshly made sourdough before crossing the creek and taking in the historic mission sights.

Avila Beach

OLD CUSTOM HOUSE
805/595-7555.
324 Front St., Avila Beach,
  CA 93424.
Open: Daily.
Price: Moderate.
Cuisine: Seafood.
Serving: B, L, D.
Reservations: No.
Credit Cards: AE, D, MC,
  V.
Handicap Access: Yes.

In 1927, when San Luis Obispo Bay was once an official U.S. Port of Entry, this simple and charming structure was built to house the business of customs. Today, it serves as a waterfront restaurant, specializing in the fresh seafoods harvested along the Central Coast. The outdoor patio dining is very popular, affording soothing views of gardens and fish ponds and warding off marine fog with strategically placed heaters. An oak pit barbecue turns out beef and pork classics, and the casual breakfasts offer eggs cooked every way imaginable.

Pismo Beach

**GIUSEPPE'S CUCINA
ITALIANA**
805/773-2870.
891 Price St., Pismo Beach,
  CA 93449.

A favorite with locals for more than ten years, Giuseppe's in downtown Pismo Beach presents a staggering selection of Southern Italian fare amid a crowded yet crisp atmosphere. In addition to a spectrum of pasta offerings, Giuseppe's also

Open: Daily.
Price: Moderate.
Cuisine: Southern Italian.
Serving: D, L (Mon.–Fri.).
Reservations: No.
Credit Cards: AE, D, MC, V.
Handicap Access: Yes.

features fourteen seafood, chicken and meat specialties. The restaurant is especially noted for its robust flavors and generous servings, and all entrées include soup or salad. While the wine list isn't particularly inspired, it offers enough choices to accommodate any dish. A take-out pizza and pasta menu is also available for those who prefer a sunset dinner at the beach four blocks down.

Nipomo

JOCKO'S
805/929-3686.
Tefft St. & Thomas Rd., Nipomo, CA 93444.
Open: Daily.
Price: Inexpensive to Moderate.
Cuisine: Oak Pit Barbecue.
Serving: B, L, D.
Reservations: Required on weekend nights and Sun.
Credit Cards: MC, V.
Handicap Access: Limited.

Seemingly in the middle of a very beautiful nowhere, Jocko's is legendary throughout the Central Coast for having world-class beef. The interior decor — rife with paper place mats, hanging plants and cattle brands burned into the woodwork — seems never to have left the 1950s (when Jocko's was founded). Even the separate bar, well worn by regulars, seems from another time. But the steaks are the true holy grail: massive Spencer steaks, thick, tender and loaded with the sort of flavor that invokes nostalgia, start at around $7. And that includes serious french fries, homemade tomato salsa and pots of succulent pinquito beans. Conceivably the finest steak house in the country, Jocko's regularly converts even the most die-hard vegetarian.

SANTA YNEZ VALLEY

Santa Maria

CHEF RICK'S ULTIMATELY FINE FOODS
805/937-9512.
4869 S. Bradley Rd., Santa Maria, CA 93454.
Open: Mon.–Sat.
Price: Moderate to Expensive.
Cuisine: Southern Eclectic.
Serving: L, D.
Reservations: Recommended Wed.-Sat.
Credit Cards: AE, MC, V.
Handicap Access: Yes.

Don't let the strip mall setting fool you: Chef Rick's serves up flavors that rival any on the Central Coast. Just ask the local wineries, who frequently employ the restaurant's catering service to accentuate their wines and enchant their guests. Owner Rick Manson orchestrates a daring menu that spans virtually every mood and texture. The New Mexican grilled garlic chicken is especially savory, as is the Louisiana spicy sautéed corn-crusted striped sea bass. On the appetizer front, the coconut-beer shrimp is a local classic, and the Louisiana-blackened halibut salad in red wine-mustard vinaigrette is an entire meal. Paired with an exciting selection of local wines, Chef Rick's dishes yield an extravaganza for the senses.

VINTNERS BAR & GRILL
805/928-8000.
3455 Skyway Dr. (Santa Maria Airport Hilton), Santa Maria, CA 93454.
Open: Daily.
Price: Moderate to Expensive.
Cuisine: Eclectic.
Serving: B, L, D.
Reservations: Recommended for dinner.
Credit Cards: AE, D, MC, V.
Handicap Access: Yes.

The Vintners Bar & Grill is a sensualist's dream, integrating old-style ambiance with contemporary cuisine. Pick any of the more than 100 selections of Central Coast labels on the wine list and simply divide the low bottle price by four. Select a cigar off the menu and enjoy it in the "wildlife outdoor sanctuary." A wraparound bar, hardwoods galore and broad windows aside the airport runway consummate the lavish yet casual atmosphere. While its menu tackles everything from polenta Tuscany to charbroiled filet mignon, Vintners Bar & Grill is especially successful with seafood dishes, which range from broiled albacore served on a Tuscan salad to a seafood en brodo, featuring mussels, clams, shrimp and fresh catch in a white wine sauce. Meanwhile, a knockout espresso chocolate torte awaits.

Los Olivos

MATTEI'S TAVERN
805/688-4820.
Hwy. 154, Los Olivos, CA 93441.
Open: Daily.
Price: Moderate to Expensive.
Cuisine: American Regional.
Serving: L (Sat.–Sun., Fri. in summer), D.
Reservations: Recommended.
Credit Cards: MC, V.
Handicap Access: Yes.

Dripping vintage western ambiance, this gracious roadhouse built in 1886 once was a stagecoach overnight stop. Its long front verandah drips wisteria, the huge bar, fireplace and fir floors are originals and the wicker sunroom and brick patio provide lovely dining surrounded by gardens and a magnificent bower of antique yellow roses. Still a lure for locals and visitors alike (who come for the tavern action as much as the fine regional dining), Mattei's has seen its share of film world celebrities, especially during its days as an overnight hideaway. Mickey Rooney and Ava Gardner were married here, and John Barrymore rented one of the estate cottages each summer during his heyday. Today, fine al fresco lunches are a top draw, especially the charbroiled burger with world-class french fries or the homemade chicken pot pie. Fine contemporary salads, fresh seafoods and appropriately Western-style steaks flesh out the bill of fare. The hot apple crisp with vanilla ice cream is the stuff that diets are destroyed for. Set in the middle of Santa Ynez Valley wine country, the tavern boasts a fine listing of locally made vintages, and the service is warm and attentive.

Ballard

BALLARD STORE
805/688-5319.
2449 Baseline, Ballard, CA
  93463.
Open: Wed.-Sun.
Price: Moderate to
  Expensive.
Cuisine: American French.
Serving: D, Sun. Br.
Reservations:
  Recommended on
  weekends.
Credit Cards: AE, D, DC,
  MC, V.
Handicap Access: Yes.

A conspicuous landmark in this minuscule, wine country hamlet is the Ballard Store, a 1930s grocery, filled with rural ambiance and the sweet smells of freshly baked bread. The restaurant is something of a religious shrine to locals who treat out-of-town guests visiting the Santa Ynez viticultural region to its heavenly fare. The eclectic menu offers an early bistro supper featuring fresh presentations from local farms and gardens, a prix fixe dinner menu and a la carte selections. Among seafood options, the cioppino has won many converts, and the duck and beef entrées have a delicious French accent. The Champagne Sunday Brunch is bountiful and wildly popular.

FOOD PURVEYORS

BAKERIES

Old West Cinnamon Rolls (805/773-1428; 861 Dolliver St., Pismo Beach) The name says it all — an exhibition bakery that whips up monster cinnamon rolls, old-fashioned doughnuts, cookies, breads and rolls.

COFFEEHOUSES

L ike all artistically fertile places on the globe, the Central Coast cultivates its cafe society in coffeehouses so numerous that they're practically underfoot.

Side Street Cafe (805/688-8455; 2375 Alamo Pintado, Los Olivos) This cafe provides a laid-back forum for lovers of movies, live music and fine coffee and tea, especially in the lovely back garden shaded by rose arbors and magnificent locust trees.

FARMERS' MARKETS

Cambria Certified Farmers' Market (805/927-4715; Cambria Dr. & Main St., Cambria; Fri., 2:30 p.m.–5:30 p.m.) This farmers' market presents the best-looking and -tasting produce that the coast can generate.

Every Thursday evening, a block of downtown San Luis Obispo overflows with a spectacular display of fresh produce, flowers, oak wood barbecues and street musicians, all part of the acclaimed Certified Farmers' Market.

Jay Swanson

San Luis Obispo Certified Farmers' Market (805/544-9570; Higuera & Chorro Sts., San Luis Obispo; Thurs., 6:30 p.m.–9:00 p.m.) This market fills this block of downtown San Luis Obispo with one of the most spectacular street markets on the Central Coast, featuring street musicians and jugglers, oak wood barbecues stocked with grilling meats and, of course, the legendary fresh produce, flowers, nuts, honey, eggs and herbs of this hothouse growing area highlights the action. Everybody in town shows up.

MICROBREWERIES

SLO Brewing Company (805/543-1843; 1119 Garden St., San Luis Obispo) This old-fashioned exhibition brewery is graced with a classic pool hall straight out of *The Hustler* and creates fine brews like Brickhouse Pale, Garden Alley Amber and Cole Porter, plus seasonal specialties.

CULTURE

ARCHITECTURE

The main streets of San Luis Obispo bristle with whole blocks of beautifully maintained, nineteenth-century stores, banks, workshops and warehouses. Up the hill from the Spanish land grant of San Simeon, San Francisco architect Julia Morgan gave tangible form to the overripe fantasies of pioneer son William Randolph Hearst in a Spanish baroque castle, which still astonishes

One of the many restored Victorian residences updates the past on San Luis Obispo's Buchon Street.

visitors to this incomparable setting between the Santa Lucia Mountains and the Pacific Ocean.

CINEMA

San Luis Obispo's Edward's Fremont cinema showcases first-run, contemporary cinema in a 1930s Deco movie palace.

Jay Swanson

Edward's Fremont (805/541-2141; 1025 Monterey St., San Luis Obispo) Another beauty from a bygone era, carved up to fit the small screen needs of the shrinking modern world. Thirties Deco outside, first-run four-plex inside.

Palm Theatre (805/541-5161; 817 Palm St., San Luis Obispo) A longtime favorite with the college crowd and local buffs, this thinking person's movie palace specializes in first-run art films.

GARDENS

Hearst Castle Gardens (800/444-7275; Hwy. 1, San Simeon) To surround his 130-room hilltop castle, media baron William Randolph Hearst envisioned gardens on a wildly opulent scale. A twenty-man crew headed by Nigel Keep hauled acres of soil up the hillside to create a series of terraces that were then planted with over 100,000 trees, thousands of rose bushes and acres of Hearst's favorite flower, the camellia. More than a half-million flowers were propagated in the castle's greenhouses to stock the grounds, which include a once glorious, mile-long pergola. Magnificent sculpture pieces also adorn the grounds. Tour IV of the many Hearst Castle-guided visits is largely devoted to the gardens. Open daily, 8:30 a.m.–3:00 p.m.

Mission Plaza (805/543-6850; Chorro & Monterey Sts., San Luis Obispo) At the site of the Mission San Luis Obispo, founded in 1772, visitors may enjoy the sunny cloistered garden where early Franciscan fathers meditated. In front of the Mission, a terraced plaza offers soul-soothing landscaping and plantings that wind down to and along the banks of the peaceful San Luis Creek. Open daily, dawn to dusk.

HISTORIC PLACES

AH LOUIS STORE
805/543-4332.
800 Palm St., San Luis Obispo, CA 93401.
Open: Mon.–Sat., 10:00 a.m.–5:00 p.m.
Admission: Free.

Resolutely bound to its nineteenth-century origins, this brickwork monument to its 1874 builder, an enterprising Cantonese immigrant named Ah Louis, still stands on the corner of the former Chinese district of downtown San Luis Obispo, dispensing an eclectic inventory of Asian goods along with architectural ambiance. The store was just a small corner of the enterprising Ah Louis' empire. Coming to California to find gold in the 1850s, he ended up working to create county roads, establishing the area's first brickworks and launching a seed business and half a dozen farms before he was finished.

HEARST CASTLE
Hwy. 1, San Simeon, CA 93452.
Open: Daily, 8:00 a.m.–4:00 p.m.

The site of America's only genuine castle by the sea, overlooking the Pacific Ocean north of Cambria, was the setting of family camping trips when future media magnate and political star

Admission: $14 adults; $7 children ages 6-12; tickets must be reserved by calling MISTIX (619/452-1950 or 800/444-7276); daily tours, starting at 8:20 a.m., except Thanksgiving, Christmas, New Year's Day.

maker William Randolph Hearst was a boy. In 1919, Hearst hatched his grandiose scheme of transforming a magical spot on his father's quarter-of-a-million-acres of ranch land into a showpiece of architecture and international artworks. Plundering the treasure houses of Europe, Hearst dismantled entire medieval chapels, Renaissance villas and Greco-Roman temples, hauling back the priceless artifacts to decorate the interior of the 100-room Casa Grande (a Spanish Baroque theme park designed by San Francisco architect Julia Morgan) and a spate of palatial guest houses for his celebrity friends.

Shmuel Thaler

Splendid Greco-Roman pools are among the architectual treasures of the Hearst Castle in San Simeon.

Byzantine tile work now gleams from the lofty towers and spectacular indoor swimming pool. A library that Hearst built for his personal study contains over 5,000 volumes in one of the world's finest rare book collections and one of the greatest caches of Greek vases. Surrounding this part sublime, part outrageous monument to consumption was once the world's largest private zoo, and zebras, Barbary sheep, Himalayan goats and deer still remain to delight contemporary visitors.

During the 1920s to 1940s, the world's rich and famous came and stayed at Hearst Castle for opulent weekends of grand partying. Guests included Winston Churchill, Charlie Chaplin, Gary Cooper, Ben Hecht, Groucho Marx, Douglas Fairbanks, Joan Crawford, Charles and Ann Morrow Lindbergh, Louella Parsons, Cary Grant and, of course, Hearst mistress Marian Davies, whose relationship with the eccentric millionaire was immortalized in Orson Welles' *Citizen Kane.*

Still a bastion of sensory overload — many of the art treasures that Hearst feverishly collected sit unpacked in the castle's basement stronghold — San Simeon is one of the top visitor attractions in the country. The castle may be visited only on guided tours, and given the sheer scale of the monument, it takes four tours to encompass all of the sites. Tour I is designed for first-time visitors and includes the gardens, one of the Mediterranean guest houses, the ground floor of the main house and the outdoor Roman pool. Tour II moves through the upper floors of the main house, including Hearst's private suites, libraries, guest room, kitchen and both pools. Tour III sweeps through the thirty-six bedrooms of the guest wing, as well as the pools and gardens. Tour IV, offered only in the summer, wanders along the perimeter grounds, gardens, wine cellar and ground floor of the largest guest house. All of the tours involve climbing many stairs, and special arrangements for visitors in wheelchairs may be made by calling 805/927-2020.

OLD GRIST MILL
805/688-4815.
1760 Mission Dr., Solvang, CA 93463.
Open: Can be viewed from the road.
Admission: Free.

Designed and built by reformed pirate Joseph Chapman in 1820, this New England-style mill ground grains once harvested at Mission Santa Inés. Its workings provide a glimpse of the earliest American presence in this area. While the privately owned complex is not open to the public, the fascinating millworks are on full display from the road.

HISTORIC WALKING TOURS

San Luis Obispo Heritage Walks The seven-square-block heart of downtown San Luis Obispo serves up a great walking tour through the eclectic architectural and historic past of the mission town. A free **Heritage Walks** brochure, available at the Chamber of Commerce (805/781-2777; 1039 Chorro St., San Luis Obispo, CA 93401) will get you started. In addition to the **Ah Louis Store** and the splendid **Mission San Luis Obispo de Tolosa,** a stop should be made at the **Dallidet Adobe** (1185 Pacific St.), built in the 1850s by Frenchman Pierce Hyppolite Dallidet, one of the area's pioneer viticulturists. Among the stately Victorian mansions of the area, must-visits include the 1875 **Jack House** (546 Marsh St.) and the grand 1895 **Erickson Home** (687 Islay St.). The ornate brick and terra-cotta facade of the circa 1893 **J.P. Andrews Bank Building** (Osos & Monterey Sts.) furnishes a prime example

The stylish brick and terra-cotta facade of the 1893 J.P. Andrews Bank Building is one of the historic sights available on the self-guided Heritage Walks of downtown San Luis Obispo.

Jay Swanson

of nineteenth-century, mercantile prosperity. Several fine adobes furnish windows on the town's Mexican era, most notably the **Murray Adobe** (747 Monterey St.) and the **Sauer-Adams Adobe** (964 Chorro St.), built in 1830.

KIDS' STUFF

San Luis Obispo Children's Museum (805/544-5437; 1010 Nipomo St., San Luis Obispo) A museum facility entirely devoted to exhibits of interest to youngsters, involving lots of fun and educational and touching exhibits. Lots to do here: Slip down dinosaur slides, explore the engines of a fire station, design homes, serve lunch at a diner, play with computers and watch each other on closed-circuit TV monitors. Check out the beehive and ant farm — they aren't hands-on, but maybe that's just as well.

LIGHTHOUSES

Necessity and technology conspired in the erection of these brilliant beacons, clinging to the rockiest edges of the Central California coast during the nineteenth century, warning of all of jagged perils lurking in the fog. Armed with the high candlepower of the French Fresnel lens, which ingeniously utilized over 1,000 pieces of cut glass to magnify its light, the slender lighthouses and their stalwart attendants kept faith with mariners until the coming of automation and the computer. Always an inspiring sight, a few of these curved towers continue to shed light along the Central Coast. **Piedras Blancos Lighthouse** (Hwy. 1, 5 miles north of San Simeon), located on white guano-encrusted rocks, was named by Portuguese explorer Juan Rodriquez Cabrillo in 1542. A lookout was built in 1864 during the heyday of the whaling era, and in

1875, the first brick and steel lighthouse was completed. The glass prisms of its French Fresnel lens were illuminated by a vapor lamp that consumed up to five tons of kerosene annually. Visible for up to twenty-five miles, the original lamp was automated in 1949, and today, sheds its light out to sea every fifteen seconds. Since the National Fish and Wildlife Service moved into the white beacon in the 1970s, it's been closed for public tour. Nonetheless, it forms a true monument to countless dangerous voyages on the high seas in the last century.

MISSIONS

LA PURISIMA MISSION STATE HISTORIC PARK
805/733-3713.
2295 Purisima Rd., Lompoc, CA 93436.
Open: Daily, except Thanksgiving, Christmas, New Year's Day.
Admission: Donations.

Founded in 1787 as the eleventh of California's Franciscan missions, Mission La Purísima Concepción was once a huge ranch and farming complex situated near a thriving Chumash village called Alsacupi. After a devastating earthquake in 1812 shook the adobe walls to ruins, the mission was moved, reconstructed and eventually, fell back into decay. While original walls remain, an extraordinary restoration was begun nearby that today is a living museum — the only recreation of an entire mission structure: its corrals, workshops, storerooms, padre's apartments and aqueduct system. So seamless is the restoration that visitors to the 900-acre grounds can sample a bit of mission life on tours of the gardens, tannery, reservoir, soap factory, residences, workrooms and main church.

Handsomely restored, the eighteenth-century Mission San Luis Obispo de Tolosa ministers to a vibrant, present-day congregation.

Jay Swanson

MISSION SAN LUIS OBISPO DE TOLOSA
805/543-6850.

The fifth in the series of missions founded by Franciscan Padre Serra and specifically named for Saint Louis, bishop of Toulouse, France, this

Monterey & Chorro Sts., San Luis Obispo, CA 93401.
Open: Daily, 9:00 a.m.–4:00 p.m.
Admission: $1.

settlement was one of the wealthiest of the missions. A large population of Native American converts helped tend the mission's extensive holdings of cattle, sheep, horses and fertile land on the banks of San Luis Obispo Creek. A serious restoration, which uncovered hand-hewn beams, began in the 1930s. Still a thriving parish church, the mission is crowned by a graceful bell tower and cool cloister gardens. A very fine museum provides glimpses of early mission life and the daily work habits of the resident fathers and neophytes.

MISSION SAN MIGUEL ARCÁNGEL
805/467-3256.
Mission St. east of Hwy. 101, San Luis Obispo, CA 93401.
Open: Daily, 9:30 a.m.–4:30 p.m.
Admission: Donations.

Still in use today by robed Franciscan friars, Mission San Miguel Arcángel was founded in 1797 by Padre Lausán to bridge the gap between Missions San Luis Obispo and San Antonio de Padua. Sixteenth in the mission chain, its prime location on the Salinas River allowed it to thrive as both an agricultural center and ranch. Destroyed by fire and earthquake and suffering the indignities of service as a saloon, dance hall and warehouse, the mission was returned to the Franciscans in the late 1920s and restored. Its beautiful interior was rebuilt along authentic guidelines. The gardens frame a graceful Moorish fountain, and a self-guided tour of the grounds, cemetery and church begins at the small gift shop.

MISSION SANTA INÉS
805/688-4815.
1760 Mission Dr., Solvang, CA 93463.
Open: Mon.–Sat., 9:30 a.m.–5:30 p.m.; Sun., 12:00 noon–5:00 p.m.
Admission: Donations.

Founded in 1804, the original, simply rendered mission chapel was replaced after a mighty 1812 earthquake. A brick and adobe structure, the new mission boasted tile roof and floors (said to be the first ever used in mission construction). The red-tiled motif would become the dominant feature of what we now consider the Spanish Mission style. After the inevitable decline that afflicted missions after secularization, the building was restored in the twentieth century and is now famed for its extensive gardens, lovely bell tower campanile, native-crafted frescoes and hand-carved door. This mission features a fascinating museum, showcasing rare artifacts from the Franciscan colonization.

MUSEUMS

CAL POLY UNIVERSITY NATURAL HISTORY MUSEUM

Biology professors and students maintain this small collection of mounted specimens and photographs of regional wildlife, including revolv-

805/756-2788.
Cal Poly Univ., Science
  Bldg., Rm. 285, San Luis
  Obispo, CA 93401.
Open: Weekdays, 8:00
  a.m.–5:00 p.m.
Admission: Free.

ing exhibits of current research activities. The space in which the exhibits appear is intended primarily as a study space for students.

**ELVERHOY DANISH
  HERITAGE MUSEUM**
805/686-1211.
1524 Elverhoy Way,
  Solvang, CA 93463.
Open: Wed.–Sun., 1:00
  p.m.–4:00 p.m.
Admission: Free.

Built in the style of an eighteenth-century Danish farmhouse, this spacious private home/museum recounts the dream of a little Denmark in the New World that Solvang founders brought to this lush dairy country. Filled with authentic Danish arts and crafts, furniture and tools, the museum documents the immigrant experience in the Central Coast.

**HANS CHRISTIAN
  ANDERSEN MUSEUM**
805/688-2052.
1680 Mission Dr., Solvang,
  CA 93463.
Open: Sun.–Thurs., 9:30
  a.m.–6:00 p.m.; Fri., Sat.,
  9:30 a.m.– 8:00 p.m.
Admission: Free.

Lovingly devoted to the author of the beloved children's fairy tales, this small museum is filled with exhibits recounting Anderson's life and boasts original letters, photographs and Andersen artwork and book illustrations.

**MORRO BAY MUSEUM
  OF NATURAL
  HISTORY**
805/772-2694.
State Park Rd. at White's
  Point, Morro Bay, CA
  93442.
Open: Daily, 10:00
  a.m.–5:00 p.m.
Admission: Donations.

Commanding a stunning panoramic view of the bay estuary and stately Morro Rock, the museum offers informative dioramas and interpretive displays of local flora, fauna, geology and the history of the Native Americans who once called this area home. A trail leads from the museum to the top of White's Point, passing indigenous sites along the way.

**SAN LUIS OBISPO
  HISTORICAL
  MUSEUM**
805/543-0638.
696 Monterey St., San Luis
  Obispo, CA 93401.
Open: Wed.–Sun., 10:00
  a.m.–4:00 p.m.
Admission: Free.

Housed in a graceful Richardsonian Romanesque mansion made of local granite and sandstone, designed by prolific California architect William Weeks, the museum's exhibits present a colorful overview of the history of the county, from Chumash days through the mission and rancho periods to the present day. A complete Victorian parlor invites a glimpse into the nineteenth-century, American frontier days. There are also many hands-on displays designed for youngsters.

Housed in a handsome, nineteenth-century structure, the San Luis Obispo Historical Museum chronicles the area's colorful past.

Jay Swanson

SANTA YNEZ VALLEY HISTORIC SOCIETY MUSEUM
805/688-7889.
3596 Sagunto St., Santa Ynez, CA 93460.
Open: Fri.–Sun., 1:00 p.m.–4:00 p.m.
Admission: Free.

One room of this tiny but fascinating museum is devoted to Native Americans, focusing especially on Chumash culture and artifacts. Other displays show daily life in the nineteenth century. Next door a carriage house shows off a varied collection of stagecoaches, wagons, carriages and buggies that once transported people, their mail and their belongings up and down the Central Coast.

MUSIC

Basin Street Regulars (800/443-7778; 805/773-4382; Veteran's Hall, 780 Bello St., Pismo Beach) Hot Dixieland jazz by guest bands and able jam session musicians shake the rafters of this hall all afternoon on the last Sun. of each month.
California State Old Time Fiddlers Association (800/443-7778; 805/773-4382; Moose Lodge, 180 Main St., Pismo Beach) Music the way that they used to make it during the rip-roaring Sat. night barn dances of the last century sets toes a tappin' on the first and third Sun. of each month.
San Luis Obispo County Symphony (805/543-3533; 1160 Marsh St., San Luis Obispo) This resident orchestra enlists the talents of top area soloists and guest virtuosos in presenting its fall-spring season of classic repertoire symphonies and concertos.

NIGHTLIFE

Chili Peppers (805/547-1163; 1009 Monterey St., San Luis Obispo) Dancing takes center stage on salsa nights, and live blues and rock bands regularly swing through this bar/restaurant.

Graduate (The) (805/541-0969; www.graduaterestaurants.com Web site; 990 Industrial Way, San Luis Obispo) The main action is country and western, including entire evenings devoted to western dance, plus some live rock 'n' roll.

Harry's (805/773-1010; Cypress & Pomeroy Sts., Pismo Beach) Dancing to one of the area's top country and country-rock bands every single night.

Mother's Tavern (805/541-8733; 725 Higuera St., San Luis Obispo) Local and out-of-town bands specialize in good ol' rock 'n' roll and blues, plus dance nights.

Mr. Rick's (805/595-9500; 480 Front St., Avila Beach) This beachfront bar and nightclub features rock 'n' roll, reggae or blues on most nights of the week.

Old Camozzi's Saloon (805/927-8941; 2262 Main St., Cambria) Live music, local color and plenty of watering hole ambiance housed within an authentic nineteenth-century saloon.

Old Cayucos Tavern (805/995-3209; 130 N. Ocean, Cayucos) Rock 'n' roll live, plus karaoke weekly.

Rose and Crown (805/541-1911; 1000 Higuera St., San Luis Obispo) Live bands play a bit of jazz and rock on the weekends at this English-style pub that offers traditional darts, as well as not-so-traditional dancing.

SLO Brewing Company (805/543-1843; 1119 Garden St., San Luis Obispo) Rock, reggae and the funky local stuff, plus great brews.

Sweet Springs Saloon (805/528-3764; 990 L.O.V.R., Los Osos) Satellite TVs, pool tables and shuffleboard make this a prime gaming spot, but it's also the heart of rock 'n' roll, with live music on the weekends.

Tortilla Flats (805/544-7575; 1051 Nipomo St., San Luis Obispo) It's mad, passionate dancing to creative DJ music every night of the week.

THEATER

Cal Poly Theatre (805/541-5369; Cal Poly Univ., San Luis Obispo) Pacific Repertory Opera performances are among the many theatre offerings presented on the stage of the California State Polytechnic University campus throughout the fall–spring academic year.

Solvang Theater Under The Stars (800/549-PCPA; Solvang Festival Theater, Second St., Solvang; also in the Marian Theatre, Santa Maria) Nightly, except Mon., all summer long, the outdoor theater rings with myriad theatrical treasures, ranging from heavyweight classics and Shakespearean gems to contemporary and comic capers performed by the repertory company of the Pacific Conservatory of the Performing Arts. Tickets cost $11–$19.

SEASONAL EVENTS

January

Mozart's Birthday Party (805/543-4580; San Luis Obispo).
Polar Bear Dip (800/563-1878; Cayucos).

February

Chili Cook-Off (805/927-3624; Cambria).
Mardi Gras Jazz Festival (805/773-4382; Pismo Beach).
Mumbo Gumbo Mardi Gras (805/634-1414; San Luis Obispo).
Oyster Festival (805/995-1200; Cayucos).
Pro Surfing Tour (805/773-4382; Pismo Beach).
Real Men Cook Food Fair (805/688-6144; Solvang).
Sea Fare & Wine List Review (805/773-4382; Pismo Beach).
Storytelling Festival (805/688-6144; Solvang).

March

Celebration of Zinfandel (805/238-0506; Paso Robles).
Century Bike Ride (805/943-9440; Santa Maria).
Paderewski Festival (805/238-0506; Paso Robles).
Rib Cook-Off (805/541-0286; San Luis Obispo).
San Luis Obispo Rib Cook-Off (805/541-0286; San Luis Obispo).
Taste of Solvang (805/688-6144; Solvang).

April

Easter Bonnet Parade (805/772-4467; Morro Bay).
Hans Christian Anderson Fairy Tales Festival (805/688-3317; Solvang).
Italian Street Painting Festival (805/544-9251; San Luis Obispo).
Petal and Palettes Art and Flower Show (805/927-3624; Cambria).
Seafood Festival (805/563-1878; Cayucos).
Strawberry Festival (805/473-2250; Arroyo Grande).
Vintner's Festival (805/688-0881; Solvang).

May

Antique Fair (805/773-4382; Pismo Beach).
Antique Gas Engine Show (805/995-1200; Cayucos).

Antique Show (805/927-3862; Cambria).
Art in the Park (805/772-2504; Morro Bay).
Cinco de Mayo Festivities (805/541-8000; San Luis Obispo).
Festival of Beers (805/544-2266; Avila Beach).
Great Western Bicycle Rally (805/238-0506; Paso Robles).
La Fiesta de San Luis Obispo (805/543-1710; San Luis Obispo).
Los Rancheros Visadores (805/688-3317; Solvang).
Petal and Palettes Art and Flower Show (805/927-3624; Cambria).
Roll Out the Barrels Wine Festival (805/541-5868; San Luis Obispo).
Wildflower Festival (805/238-0506; Paso Robles).

June

Afternoon of Epicurean Delight (805/543-1323; San Luis Obispo).
Beach Fest (805/773-4382; Pismo Beach).
Chili Cook-Off (805/927-3163; Cambria).
Gem and Mineral Show (805/995-1200; Cayucos).
Mission Antonio Fiesta (805/385-4478; Jolon).
Scandinavian Midsummer Festival (805/688-6144; Solvang).

July

Art in the Park (805/772-4467; Morro Bay).
Central Coast Renaissance Faire (805/474-9571; San Luis Obispo).
Fireworks off the Pier (805/995-1200; Cayucos).
Fourth of July Beach Fireworks (805/773-4382; Pismo Beach).
Fourth of July Parade (805/543-1323; San Luis Obispo).
Fourth of July Parade and Fireworks (805/927-3624; Cambria).
Heritage Day at the Dallidet (805/781-2777; San Luis Obispo).
Japanese Friendship Festival (805/543-1323; San Luis Obispo).
Midsummer Street Fair (805/772-4467; Morro Bay).
Mozart Festival (805/781-3008; San Luis Obispo).
Portuguese Celebration (805/563-1878; Cayucos).
Renaissance Faire (805/474-9571; San Luis Obispo).

August

Festival of the Bears (805/528-4884; Los Osos).
Mid-State Fair (805/239-0655; Paso Robles).
Mission Santa Inés Fiesta (805/688-4815; Solvang).
Pine Dorado Festival (805/927-3624; Cambria).
Portuguese Festival and Parade (805/773-4382; Pismo Beach).

September

Antique Show (805/995-1200; Cayucos).
Danish Days (805/688-3317; Solvang).
Harvest Festival (805/489-9091; Arroyo Grande).
Mission San Miguel Fiesta (805/238-0506; San Miguel).
Wine Festival (805/541-1721; San Luis Obispo).
Woodcarvers' Show (805/927-4710; Cambria).

October

Art Association Home Tour (805/927-8190; Cambria).
Celebration of Harvest (805/688-6144; Solvang).
Clam Festival (805/773-4382; Pismo Beach).
Colony Days Celebration (805/466-2044; Atascadero).
Day in the Country (805/688-6144; Los Olivos).
Harbor Festival (805/772-1155; Morro Bay).
Jubilee-by-the-Sea Jazz Festival (805/773-4382; Pismo Beach).
Morro Bay Harbor Festival (805/772-1155; Morro Bay).
October Festival (805/929-1583; Nipomo).
Oktoberfest (805/528-4884; Baywood Park).
Pioneer Day (805/238-0506; Paso Robles).
Pumpkins on the Pier (805/773-4382; Pismo Beach).
Valley Harvest Arts Festival (805/736-6565; Lompoc).

November

Christmas Street Fair (805/772-4467; Morro Bay).
Craft Fair (805/461-4000; Atascadero).
Dixieland Jazz Festival (805/688-8000; Solvang).
Harvest Celebration (805/541-5868; San Luis Obispo).
International Film Festival (805/546-3456; San Luis Obispo).
Santa's House (805/544-4355; San Luis Obispo).
Tree Lighting (805/461-5000; Atascadero; 805/773-4382; Pismo Beach).

December

Christmas at the Castle (805/927-2093; San Simeon).
Christmas Festival (805/927-3624; Cambria).
Christmas in the Plaza (805/781-2777; San Luis Obispo).
Christmas Parade (805/528-4848; Los Osos; 805/541-8000; San Luis Obispo).
Deck the Tree Ceremony (805/995-1200; Cayucos).
Lighted Boat Parade (805/772-4467; Morro Bay).
Winterfest Celebration (805/468-6765; Solvang).

RECREATION

BEACHES

The public fishing pier at Avila State Beach is the background for endless games of seaside Frisbee at San Luis Obispo Bay.

Jay Swanson

Avila State Beach (Front St. bet. Harford Dr. & San Rafael St., Avila Beach) Tucked next to a tiny sailing village, this beach claims the public fishing pier and boasts playground equipment, outdoor showers, rest rooms and a view of the gracefully curving San Luis Obispo Bay. In the spring and summer, lifeguards are on duty. Parking is ample. No entrance fee.

Baywood Park Beach (west of Pasadena Dr., bet. Santa Ysabel Ave. & Baywood Way, Baywood Park) The mudflats of Morro Bay are accessible at low tide from this small sandy beach, which is set with picnic tables and benches. Plenty of parking. No entrance fee.

Cayucos Beach (Pacific Ave., bet. 1st & 22nd Sts., Cayucos) Clearly marked, public access stairways lead down to the beach through residential property. Parking, but no facilities. No entrance fee.

Cayucos State Beach (west of N. Ocean Dr., Cayucos) A beachfront pier attracts fishing aficionados to this local recreation spot, where barbecue and picnicking facilities abound. The pier, which is prettily lit at night, is wheelchair accessible. Parking and rest rooms. No entrance fee.

Leffingwell Landing (Hwy. 1 & Moonstone Beach Dr., Cambria) Beautifully maintained hiking trails wander the sagebrush and lupine-filled bluffs and cypress groves above the swirling tide pools and brown sandy beach below. Excellent whale and sea otter watching from benches placed at vista points. Boat ramp, parking, rest rooms and picnic areas. No entrance fee.

Moonstone Beach (Moonstone Dr., Cambria) Prime beachcombing for gnarled driftwood and for the occasional moonstone agate is available along this sheltered stretch that adjoins San Simeon State Beach. Tide pools protect a wealth of starfish and anemones. Hiking trails lace the formidable bluffs lining the water's edge. Parking, no facilities. No entrance fee.

Beachcombers on the wide sand flats of Morro Strand near San Luis Obispo enjoy the amenities of the Central Coast, fascinating tide pools and shorebirds, intriguing driftwood and a balmy, year-round climate.

Jay Swanson

Morro Strand State Beach (Studio Dr. bet. 24th St. & Cody Ave., Cayucos [North]; Hwy. 1 bet. Yerba Buena Ave. & Atascadero Rd., Morro Bay [South]) The northern stretch of the beach is accessible by numerous stairways and walkways leading from streets intersecting Studio Dr. A paved parking lot at the end of 24th St. offers rest rooms and picnic tables. The southern section of the beach (formerly Atascadero State Beach) offers almost two miles of sand and dunes, studded with ice plants in a splendid setting for contemplating the volcanic crags of Morro Rock. There are 100 campsites at the end of Yerba Buena Dr. Parking, rest rooms, showers. Fee for camping but none for day use.

Ocean City Park Beach (Ocean Blvd. bet. Vista Del Mar & Capistrano Aves., Pismo Beach) Stairways leading down to the sand also give visitors access to the many tide pools along this stretch. Benches and picnic tables perch on a grassy park overlooking the ocean. Parking, no facilities. No entrance fee.

Pismo State Beach (from Wilmar Ave. at Pismo Beach) Twenty miles of coast are embraced by this beach area, from the sandy beaches, checkered with volleyball courts, just north of the Pismo Beach Pier down to the 4,000 acres of sweeping Nipomo Dunes, which once starred as the Sahara Desert in Cecil B. DeMille's celluloid epic, *The Ten Commandments*. Campgrounds, eucalyptus groves, dune buggy playgrounds and marshlands dot this coastal recreation mecca. Parking, rest rooms and ample opportunities for seafood dining. Entrance fees for campgrounds.

Port San Luis Beach (end of Harford Dr., Avila Beach) A seawall protects the sandy beachfront, accessed by two stairways that adjoin a 1,300-foot pier built for boat launch and hoist facilities. Parking and rest rooms. Fee for boat launch and storage.

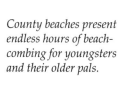

County beaches present endless hours of beachcombing for youngsters and their older pals.

Dan Coyro

Ragged Point Beach (Hwy. 1, 15 miles north of San Simeon) Sweeping vistas of Big Sur are available from the bluff top overlook of this rocky spit of coastline. Near a grassy picnic area with tables, a steep trail leads down to the tiny beach and past a waterfall that's quite lovely after winter rains. Parking and rest rooms. No entrance fee.

Santa Rosa Creek Beach (Hwy. 1, south end of Moonstone Beach Dr., Cambria) A parking lot provides access to both the Santa Rose Creek marshlands and the rugged tide pools of the rocky coastline. Benches invite lingering and picnicking. No facilities, no entrance fee.

Shamel County Park (Windsor Blvd. & Nottingham Dr., Cambria) In this park, which fronts a popular beach, outdoor recreational possibilities include a playground, a sports field and a swimming pool. Parking and rest rooms. No entrance fee.

Sherwood Drive Beach (Sherwood Dr. bet. Wedgewood & Lampton Sts., Cambria Pines Manor) Another good way to descend the wildflower-covered bluffs down to the sand and rocks is via paths along Sherwood Dr. Parking is no problem, though facilities are nil. No entrance fee.

Beachcombing Tips

All-day beach foraging and wandering can yield countless simple treasures and, at areas where creeks meet the coastline, plentiful driftwood curiosities. Tide pool areas are often surrounded by beautiful rocks and glass fragments, smoothed and rounded by the elements. The trick is to come early in the day when tiny sand dollars, the odd weathered bottle and even round, bottle-glass floats are washed up on the shores. Mornings after storms yield the most interesting sea-tossed objects and driftwood by the ton. Bring a day pack or canvas bag for collecting and during foggy mornings and evenings, a warm sweater to provide the comfort necessary for a long day's beachcombing.

William R. Hearst Memorial State Beach (Hwy. 1 on San Simeon Rd., San Simeon) One of the many prime natural playgrounds left to the state of California by the eclectic tycoon is this outstanding fishing and swimming area, nestled in the protective beauty of San Simeon Point. A 1,000-foot fishing pier, well stocked with fishing equipment and boat rentals, sits to the west of the main parking area. A eucalyptus grove and grassy expanse near the park's entrance suggest fine picnicking possibilities. Parking and rest rooms. Entrance fee.

BICYCLING

BICYCLE RENTALS

Beach Cycle Rentals (805/773-5518; 150 Hinds Ave., Pismo Beach).
Beach Cycle Rentals II (805/773-5318; 519 Cypress St., Pismo Beach).

TOP RIDES

Atascadero Recreation Trail This trail begins at the intersection of Modoc Rd. & Encore Dr. and ends at Goleta Beach.
Los Osos Valley Road A popular twelve-mile scenic course through the Los Osos Valley. Sights include pastureland, hills and volcanic cones.
Montaña de Oro Over fifty miles of trails are laid out through this 7,000-acre area.
Moonstone Beach One of the most beautiful stretches of coastline in California, through which bike paths skirt the shoreline on one side, and wild, open fields backed by volcanic plugs and gentle rolling hills adorn the other.

BIRD-WATCHING

Montaña de Oro State Park (2 miles south of Los Osos via Los Osos Valley/Pecho Rd.) A profusion of native and migrating birds find their way to the sheltered coves and windswept bluffs of this sprawling 8,400-acre preserve. Enormous albatross and pelicans soar above the cliffs, which in the summer become the nesting site for the elusive pigeon guillemot and black oystercatcher. It's a never-ending canvas of diverse, winged wildlife in a setting of splendid isolation.
Morro Bay State Park (Hwy. 1, Morro Bay) Within this confluence of nutrient-rich mudflats and bay, the 576-foot-high volcanic plug Morro Rock soars like a miniature Gibralta, with its steep slopes an ecological preserve for the endangered peregrine falcon. Nesting falcons are protected here, and the rock is closed to entrance. Binoculars are important for those intent upon catching a glimpse of the spectacular raptor. In the winter and fall, thousands of other migrating birds join the falcons and can be viewed from the broad beach as they feed on the clams, oysters and shrimp that burrow into

the rich ooze of the tidal mud. A stopping point on the Pacific Migratory Flyway, the bay and beach attract over 250 species of native and migrating birds. Tucked into the bay estuary is a dense stand of eucalyptus trees that forms the largest great blue heron rookery between San Francisco and the Mexican border. From Jan. until midsummer, the enormous birds will mate, build nests, lay eggs and nudge their fledglings into flying shape in this rookery. Docents at the State Park's Museum of Natural History provide guided walks during the nesting season (805/772-2694).

Nipomo Dunes Preserve (end of Main St., Guadalupe) Encompassing magnificent dunes, including the largest on the West Coast, this rare habitat shelters myriad bird species, including endangered species, such as the California least tern. In the fall, look for cinnamon teals, black brants, ruddy ducks and mallards.

Pismo State Beach (Hwy. 1, Pismo Beach) Six miles of spectacular beach encompass the Pismo Dunes Preserve, home to myriad shorebirds, especially sandpipers and sanderlings. The waves literally come to life when tens of thousands of sooty shearwaters congregate to fish for tiny anchovies, and California brown pelicans provide amazing feats of daredevil diving.

BOATING

CANOEING & KAYAKING

Central Coast Kayaks (805/773-3500; 1879 Shell Beach Rd., Shell Beach, CA 93449) Instruction, tours, lessons, sales and rentals.

Good Clean Fun Surf & Sport (805/995-1993; 136 S. Ocean Front, Cayucos, CA 93430) Instructional tours, lessons, sales and rentals. Private charters, group rates and school outings.

Kayaks of Morro Bay (805/772-1119, 699 Embarcadero; Morro Bay, CA 93442) Provides guided outings and instruction in sea kayaking. No experience needed. Call for reservations, weekends only.

CHARTERS & CRUISES

Central Coast Cruises (805/772-4776; 501 Embarcadero, Morro Bay, CA, 93442) Ocean and nature cruises, private parties and weddings, with special event catering.

Kanu2U/ Subsea Tours (805/772-8085; 699 Embarcadero, Morro Bay, CA 93442) Outrigger canoes, and occasionally their semisubmersible ship, are available for summertime tours.

FISHING

FISHING & HUNTING REGULATIONS

California Department of Fish & Game (916-227-2244; 3211 S St., Sacramento, CA 95816) Information, licenses and tags.

CHARTERS

Virg's Landing at Morro Bay (805/772-1222; 1215 Embarcadero, Morro Bay, CA 93442) Half-day, full-day and twilight day trips for halibut and albacore. Local trips for rockfish and other bottom species. Two-day trips are available for ling cod. Tackle rentals.

Virg's Landing at San Simeon (805/927-4676; Old Hwy. 1, San Simeon, CA 93452) Located in William Randolph Hearst State Beach. Half-day, all-day and twilight trips are available for bottom fish. Good local ling cod fishing. Bait, tackle and charters are available, plus rod and reel rentals, licenses.

RENTALS, BAIT, TACKLE

Avila State Beach (along Front St. in Avila Beach) Jan.-Oct. are the best months for surf fishing from the pier or beach. Attractions are walleye and barred surf perch, jack smelt, kelp greeling, silver perch and starry flounder.

Leffingwell Landing (Moonstone Beach Dr., San Simeon) Surf fishing nirvana. Picnic area and barbecue facilities are a plus.

Montaña de Oro State Park (805/528-0513; Pecho Rd., Los Osos) Surf fishing and clamming abound. Picnic areas and rest rooms are available.

Sportfishing is one of the big attractions of the long beachfront that stretches from Cambria to San Luis Obispo.

Jay Swanson

Morro Bay Sandspit (Morro Bay) Surf and rock fishing for perch, jack smelt, kelp greeling, mackerel, steelhead, halibut and flounder attracts serious and amateur anglers.

Pismo State Beach (805/489-2684; on the beach from Pismo Beach south to Oceano) Surf fishing for walleye and barred surf perch, jack smelt, kelp greeling, silver perch and starry flounder.

Pismo State Beach Pier (805/489-2684; Winds Ave., Pismo Beach) Fishing is free, and no license is required. Facilities at the pier are lit at night. Red snapper, ling and rock cod, perch, bluegill, sand dab, sea bass, jack smelt, walleye and barred surf perch beckon.

Port San Luis Pier (San Luis Obispo) Fishing is free, and no license is required. Catches include red snapper, perch, bluegill, sand dab, sea bass, jack smelt, walleye, barred surf perch and ling and rock cod.

GOLF

The rich and famous and not-so-famous are welcome to enjoy Central Coast panoramas on the links at the Alisal Guest Ranch in Solvang.

Alisal Guest Ranch (805/688-4215; 1054 Alisal Rd., Solvang) Members and guests; 18 holes, 6,100 yards, par 72, rated 68.5. Cart rental, pro shop, restaurant, bar, dress code.

Avila Beach Resort Golf Course (805-595-2307; 2 miles west of Hwy. 101 off Avila Dr., San Luis Obispo) Public; 18 holes, 6,048 yards, par 71, rated 60. Cart and club rental, pro shop, restaurant, cocktail lounge and lessons.

Black Lake Golf Resort (805/481-4204; 1490 Golf Course Ln., Nipomo) Public; 18 holes, 6,068 yards, par 72, rated 68.8. Cart and club rental, pro shop, restaurant, clubhouse, coffee shop and snack bar.

Laguna Lake Municipal Golf Course (805/781-7309; 11175 Los Osos Valley Rd., San Luis Obispo) Public; 9 holes, 1,306 yards, par 30, unrated. Cart and club rental, pro shop, lessons and snack bar.

La Purisima Golf Course (805/735-8395; 3455 State Hwy. 246, Lompoc) Public; 18 holes, 6,657 yards, par 72, rated 72.8. Cart rental, pro shop, restaurant, lessons, individual and group reservations.

Morro Bay Golf Club (805/772-4560 for tee times; 805/772-4341 for pro shop) State Park Rd., Morro Bay) Public; 18 holes; 6,113 yards, par 71, rated 69.1. Cart and club rental, pro shop, lessons, snack bar.

Pismo State Beach Golf Course (805/481-5215; 9 LeSage Dr., Grover City)

Public; 9 holes, 2,795 yards, par 54 for 18, unrated. Cart and club rental, pro shop, restaurant, clubhouse, locker room and snack bar.

San Luis Golf & Country Club (805/543-4035; 255 Country Club Dr., San Luis Obispo) Members and guests; 18 holes, 6,390 yards, par 72, rated 70. Cart and club rental, restaurant/bar and lessons.

Sea Pines Golf Course (805/528-1788; 250 Howard St., Los Osos) Public; 9 holes, 2,728 yards, par 56 for 18, unrated. Cart and club rental, pro shop, restaurant.

Village Country Club (805/733-3537; 4300 Clubhouse Rd., Lompoc) Members and guests; 18 holes, 6,269 yards, par 72, rated 69.6. Cart rental.

Zaca Creek Golf Course (805/688-2575; 223 Shadow Mountain Dr., Buellton) Public; 9 holes, 3,088 yards, par 58 for 18, rated 50. Pro shop.

HIKING

Leffingwell Landing Bluffs (Moonstone Beach Dr. at Hwy. 1, just north of Cambria) A stretch of windswept bluffs dotted with cypress groves, coastal lupines and dense grasses is laced with well-maintained hiking trails, some leading down to tide pools and cove beaches where moonstone agates may be found, others to benches set at seascape vista points. Prime sea otter viewing. Parking and rest rooms.

Los Osos Oaks State Park (Los Osos Valley Rd. at Palomino Dr., Los Osos) The rare sight of gnarled, primeval coast live oak is yours for the hiking of two well-marked miles of trails in this beautiful preserve. Vistas of the enchanting Los Osos Valley, punctuated by distinctive volcanic plugs (the so-called Seven Sisters, of which Morro Rock is the most famous, but by no means the most interesting) are available from the trail. Hikers must honor trail markings along this complex and sensitive ecosystem.

Montaña de Oro State Park, near Los Osos, offers sheltered cove beaches, wildflower bluffs and over fifty miles of hiking and riding trails within its 8,400 acres.

Jay Swanson

Montaña de Oro State Park (end of Pecho Rd., Los Osos) This is a wild expanse of fields, canyons, bluffs and cove beaches formerly part of the sprawling Spooner Ranch. Over fifty miles of hiking and equestrian trails are contained within these 8,400 acres bordering three miles of coastline. The 1.5-mile **Hazard Canyon Trail** winds through enchanted forests and shaded slopes, with several trails descending from bluff tops down to the beach and others piercing the heart of vast eucalyptus groves, one of the state's favored winter nesting spots for the monarch butterfly. The **Montaña de Oro Bluffs Trail** skirts Spooner's Cove where seals lounge near coastal tide pools, offering springtime glimpses of the golden poppies and the wild mustard that lends luster to the park's name. Parking and rest rooms.

Morro Bay Sandspit Trail (Morro Bay at Estero Bay) A five-mile trail excursion along the sandspit, dividing the two bays, offers a chance to wander through sand dunes and to explore shell mounds left by the Chumash ancestors.

Pismo Dunes Preserve (Arroyo Grande Creek off Hwy. 1, Pismo Beach) Protected from vehicle traffic, mountainous sand dunes form a mysterious landscape from the ocean to a mile inland, extending southward for a mile and a half from Arroyo Grande Creek. For obvious reasons, hikers have long been obsessed with this area.

Pismo State Beach (Pismo Beach) A twenty-mile-long stretch of coastline offers maximum hiking and beach recreation opportunities. Sand dunes, eucalyptus groves and waterfowl viewing are among the sights available to walkers. An especially appealing hiking loop circumnavigates Oceano Lagoon where it meets the beach, offering saltwater and freshwater wildlife observation, notably the endangered California brown pelican and the California least tern. At Oso Flaco Lake, south of Oceano, take the four-mile-long **Nipomo Dunes Trail** and delve into a sea of dune-hugging wildflowers (asters, daisies, coreopsis and vibrant magenta sand verbena) and acres of wheat-colored dunes.

Point Conception Trail (Jalama County Park off Hwy. 1, 20 miles southwest of Lompoc) Follow public access to the tip of the coast where the continent abruptly shifts eastward, intersects private ranch lands and crosses marvelous sand dunes. Isolated cove beaches attract the sun worshipper, while surfers, surf anglers and independent hikers favor the splendid isolation. The twelve-mile, round-trip trail allows views of offshore rocks that form favorite lounging beds of seals, and the lighthouse (visitors are not allowed) adds to the scenic visuals.

Point Sal Trail (Brown & Point Sal Rds. just west of Guadalupe) The dirt and tarmac of Point Sal Rd. leads to this steep point, where trails gain access to tiny sandy beaches below. Extremely rugged and very much off the beaten path, the main trail weaves a dizzying course between high, sheer cliffs and the wildlife-filled tide pools and beaches below. There are terrific whale-watching opportunities at the end of the trail, where the Santa Maria River spills into the sea. In general, this one's for experienced hikers with nerves of steel.

San Simeon State Beach (Hwy. 1 & San Simeon Creek, San Simeon) Hiking trails abound along this popular beach campground bordered by San Simeon and Santa Rosa Creeks. Nestled at the foot of the Santa Lucia Mountains, the landscape is isolated and popular with campers.

Santa Rosa Creek Bluffs (Hwy. 1, at the south end of Moonstone Beach Dr., Cambria) Bold bluffs, overlooking prime tide pools and brown sand beaches near the charming marshlands of Santa Rosa Creek, are filled with excellent hiking trails that are reached from a convenient parking area.

HORSEBACK RIDING

Horseback riders find the foothills and canyons of the Santa Ynez Valley filled with miles of scenic equestrian trails.

Circle Bar B Stables (805/968-3901; 1800 Refugio Rd., Goleta, CA 93117).

El Capitan Equestrian Center (805/685-2741; 10920 Calle Real, Goleta, CA 93117).

Holder Park Equestrian Center (805/929-4447; Holder Park Ln., Nipomo, CA 93444).

Livery Stables Inc. (805/489-8100; 1207 Silver Spur Pl., Oceano, CA 93445).

Raintree Ranch Equestrian Center (805/967-6995; 6040 La Goleta Rd., Goleta, CA 93117).

Trail Horse Rentals (805/238-5483; Paso Robles).

NATURE PRESERVES & PARKS

Montaña de Oro State Park (805/528-0513; 2 miles south of Los Osos via Los Osos Valley/Pecho Rd, Los Osos) 8,000 unspoiled acres of rugged cliffs, deeply forested canyons, tide pools and hidden cove beaches provide spectacular vantage points for wildlife observation. Playful sea otters and migrating California gray whales are the headliners here, as are the sweeping hilltop bluffs filled with California poppies, coreopsis and lupine. In the winter, monarch butterflies congregate in the extensive eucalyptus forests. Splendid views up and down the coast for 100 miles are available from the park's highest point, 1,300-foot Valencia Peak. Superb hiking, horseback riding and camping far from the madding crowd.

Morro Bay State Park (805/772-2560; east of Embarcadero via State Park Rd., Morro Bay) A profusion of wildlife is protected within the embrace of this 2,000-acre preserve, famed for the expansive mudflats that attract shorebirds by the tens of thousands. Eucalyptus groves, housing the largest blue heron rookery between San Francisco and Mexico, fill with nests of the elegant, four-foot-tall bird beginning in late Jan. The park also includes the Morro Estuary Natural Preserve, home to ancient, moss-draped pygmy oaks and myriad marsh birds, including the Audubon warbler. The Park's Museum of Natural History (805/772-2694) provides guided walks of the area.

Tide Pooling

On the southern coast, **Asilomar State Beach** showcases outstanding tide pools, laced with intricate seaweed beds that extend out into the crashing surf of this world-famous, rocky coastline. **Point Lobos State Reserve** is another treasure trove of rewarding tide pools hugging soft sand pocket beaches. Further south, guided tide pool exploring is provided by the **Morro Bay State Park Museum of Natural History** (805/772-2694). Also, the rocky stretches between **San Simeon** and **Piedras Blancas** yield up especially rewarding pockets easily accessible to the inquiring beachcomber.

Tide pools, filled with the delicately balanced ecology of tiny marine creatures, abound along the rocky stretches of the Central Coast, like this rich expanse near Cayucos.

Jay Swanson

SURFING

Hazard Canyon (end of Pecho Rd., Los Osos) Reef break, lefts and rights; for experienced surfers only; can get rips, cold water, sharks, jagged reef. Only for diehards, it's called Hazard for a reason and help is a long way away.

Morro Rock Harbor Entrance (Morro Rock Harbor, Morro Bay) Small sandbar on the inside of the break walls, all lefts; needs powerful swell but can be super clean, rarely gets above three feet. Paddling across the entrance can be hazardous — during tide change, the small opening in the entrance turns into a river.

Morro Rock Jetty (Hwy. 1 bet. Yerba Buena Ave., & Atascadero Rd., Morro Bay) Sand bottom, beach break, lefts and rights; fun beach peaks break all year, smaller surf is clean, larger swells get big and hairy. Beginner to advanced. *Note:* warm water emitted from nearby PG&E plant.

Pismo Beach Pier Northside breaks all year during any swell, making it and its sandy bottom popular with local and visiting surfers, regardless of skill level.

Jay Swanson

Pismo Beach Pier Northside (Wilmar Ave at Pismo Beach, Pismo Beach) Sand bottom, lefts and rights; fun spot, breaks all year during any swell, larger swells are too consistent and lined up to make it worth the paddle. Beginner to advanced, depending on swell size.

TENNIS

PRIVATE

Avila Bay Club (805/595-7600; P.O. Box 2149, Avila Beach).
San Luis Obispo Golf & Country Club (805/544-9880; 255 Country Club Dr., San Luis Obispo).

PUBLIC

Arroyo Grande High School (805/473-4205; 495 Valley Rd., Arroyo Grande).
Cuesta College (805/544-3211; Rte. 1, San Luis Obispo).
Elm Street Park (805/473-5478; Elm & Ash Sts., Arroyo Grande).
Monte Young Park (South St. & Napa Ave., Morro Bay).

Pismo Beach Municipal Courts (805/773-4656; Wadsworth Ave. & Bello St., Pismo Beach).

Sinsheimer Park (805/781-7300; Southwood Dr., San Luis Obispo).

South Bay Community Park (805/528-3325; Los Osos Valley Rd. & Palisades Ave., Los Osos).

SHOPPING

The hunting in San Luis Obispo and the Santa Ynez Valley is still good for memorabilia from the Central Coast's Wild West days or for the delicate china and glassware that formed small islands of European culture in rough whaling or ranching communities. Few can resist the charms of the region's many rustic old towns and restored civic centers from bygone eras, all filled with delightful arrays of small shops, galleries and cafes. Visitors can spend days combing tiny antique stalls lining the piers of a fishing village and then find themselves faced with the most sophisticated designer possibilities just around the corner.

ANTIQUES & COLLECTIBLES

Antique Center (805/541-4040; 6 Higuera St., San Luis Obispo) Thirteen dealers have joined forces to offer an array of Early American and country furniture, glassware, lighting and singular antique jewelry.

The Glass Basket (805/772-4569; 245 Morro Bay Blvd., Morro Bay) The specialty of the house is a glittering display of highly collectible American cut glass and pastel-hued, Depression glass tableware. There's also lots more in the way of antique and collectible must-have items.

Lynda Flynn's (805/544-3255; 950 Chorro Blvd., San Luis Obispo) A charming shop in an historic area, offering decorator objets d'art, plus oodles of antique and collectible paraphernalia to spark the whim of the true yesteryear aficionado.

Solvang Antique Center (805/968-2322; 486 First St., Solvang) Housed in the historic, half-timbered Old Mill Shoppes building in the middle of this Danish theme park village, the center offers an array of fine antiques, silver, cut glass, estate jewelry and American oak from over fifty collections.

ARTS & CRAFTS

Bali Isle Imports (805/544-7662; 1038 Chorro St., San Luis Obispo) A tropical treasure trove of vibrant hand-screened batik textiles, masks, carved wood and exotic jewelry from Bali crams this distinctive import palace.

Cody Gallery (805/688-5083; 2366 Alamo Pintado Ave., Los Olivos) Opulent

Hand-carved masks from Indonesia are among the folk crafts found at Bali Isle Imports in San Luis Obispo.

Paul Schraub

oils and bronze sculptures highlight regional themes in this gallery smack in the middle of the Santa Ynez wine country.

Damaka (805/544-5450; 733 Higuera St., San Luis Obispo) An exciting and different assortment of sassy imports, from textiles and jewelry to woodwork and ceramics, tilt heavily to Mexican and Latin American origins. Some space is reserved for California contemporary items.

Gallery Los Olivos (805/688-7517; 2920 Grand Ave., Los Olivos) Sunny showrooms filled with revolving collections of regional and California-theme artworks, plus ongoing exhibits of local works by Santa Ynez Artist Guild members.

Hands Gallery (805/543-1921; 672 Higuera St., San Luis Obispo) Glazed and wildly innovative ceramic ware and sculpture forms the core of this progressive gallery, which also carries playful wood and metal designs by local artisans.

Harmony Pottery Works (805/927-4293; Old Hwy. 1, Harmony) One-stop shopping is here for the collector of top-quality, handcrafted ceramic and stoneware pottery. This spacious showroom offers a wide range of styles and glazes in ware created by top local ceramists.

Phoenix Studios (805/927-4248; Old Hwy. 1, Harmony) Museum-quality art glass is blown and sold on site. The gallery next door showcases the best work of area glass artisans.

Santa Barbara Ceramic Design Studio Outlet Store (805/686-5770; 1645

Copenhagen Dr., Solvang) Art Deco designs dance across the rich array of ceramic clocks, frames, tiles and vases created by this renowned group of Central Coast artisans. Retail outlets include the Smithsonian and Horchow catalogs, but here you can visit and purchase at significant savings.

Seekers Collection & Gallery (805/927-4352; 4090 Burton Dr., Cambria) A breathtaking selection of handblown, museum-quality glass jewelry, sculpture and furniture from 200 of the country's top art glass designers make this store's two floors of shimmering finery a feast for the senses. Possibly the best of its kind in the entire state. (Another location is at 801-B Main St., Cambria; 805/927-8777.)

Simpson-Heller Gallery (805/927-1800; 2289 Main St., Cambria) A fine collection of regional paintings, sculpture and multimedia works distinguishes this airy, inviting gallery in the middle of the ultracharming nineteenth-century village.

CLOTHING

Ambiance (805/541-0988; 714 Higuera St., San Luis Obispo) Locally designed and made contemporary clothing for women in natural fabrics and soft earth tones make this an environmentally sensitive fashion destination.

Ann's (805/543-8250; 895 Monterey St., San Luis Obispo) High-quality contemporary women's apparel looks especially inviting displayed inside one of the area's classiest nineteenth-century downtown buildings.

Decades (805/546-0901; 685 Higuera St., San Luis Obispo) Racks and racks of top-condition, vintage clothing and flashy accessories distinguish this shop, which also specializes in camp collectibles of all kinds from the 1940s to 1960s.

London Fog Factory Stores (805/773-5755; Pismo Coast Shopping Plaza, Pismo Beach) This Central Coast outlet offers vast selections of their fabled rainwear and outerwear, plus timelessly styled slacks, sport shirts, sweaters and stormy weather accessories, all at substantial savings.

JEWELRY

Andrews Jewelers (805/543-4543; 720 Higuera, San Luis Obispo) A bedazzling array of custom contemporary designs, showcasing fine diamond, gold and set gemstone work, is available at this friendly boutique.

Casa de Oro/Sheila Hollingshead Jewelry (805/927-5444; 4090 Burton Dr., Cambria) Innovative jewelry designs are featured in this very contemporary, jewelry-as-wearable-art emporium.

The Gold Concept (805/544-1088; 740 Higuera St., San Luis Obispo) Here you'll find contemporary jewelry designs, bold gold work and unusual gem selections.

SPECIALTY

Central Coast Wine Room (805/927-7337; 10 Old Creamery Rd., Harmony) A wine lover's paradise, this retail tasting room offers samples of the best varietals in the area.

Country Classics (805/549-0844; 849 Monterey St., San Luis Obispo) While a huge selection of tasteful, country-themed gifts, Victorian and French country home furnishings and scented soap and folk art provides the content here, the real gem is the old country store itself — the historic Sinsheimer Brothers building, a trip to the past with hardwood floors and lofty twenty-foot ceilings.

Farmers' Market (805/544-9570; Higuera St. bet. Osos & Nipomo Sts., San Luis Obispo) Not exactly a store, this weekly street fair offers some of the finest in local fruits and veggies, plus fresh flowers, seasonal goodies and more.

Farm Supply Company (805/543-3751; 675 Tank Farm Rd., San Luis Obispo) This farm supply depot, which caters to the needs of real area ranchers, brims with all of those Western accoutrements for riding the range, while mending fences — overalls, saddle blankets, feed troughs and grooming supplies. A surefire thrill for city slickers.

Games People Play (805/541-GAME; 1119 Chorro St., San Luis Obispo) A fascinating, family-friendly haven of gamesmanship, filled with new and vintage comic books, plus board and role-playing games of astonishing variety.

Jedlicka's (805/688-2626; 2883 Grand Ave., Los Olivos) Preparing you to saddle up and ride off into the sunset, this ultimate Western store outfits real ranchers (and those who just want to look like John Wayne) in Tony Lama boots and Stetson hats. There are acres of silver belt buckles, saddles, bridles and bits. It even smells like the Old West.

Southern Port Traders (805/7721649; 801 Embarcadero, Morro Bay) An eclectic array of clothing, crafts, jewelry and, oddly enough, percussion instruments.

SPORTS

Central Coast Surfboards (805/541-1129; 736 Higuera St., San Luis Obispo) Boards for all sports — surfboards, sailboards, skateboards, boogieboards — abound in this well-stocked water sport center.

Mountain Air Sports (805/543-1676; 667 Marsh St., San Luis Obispo) No matter what sport that you've a hankering for, this sports store has the gear. Carries some of the best brands in camping, backpacking and climbing gear.

CHAPTER SIX
Grape Expectations
WINERIES

Wines of California . . . inimitable fragrance and soft fire . . . and the wine of bottled poetry.

Robert Louis Stevenson, *The Wrong Box*, 1889

Central Coast winemaking offers vintages drawn from many of the world's greatest wine grapes grown in California, with a twist by innovative vintners.

Mya Kramer

Blessed by the need for sacramental wines used in celebrating the Catholic Mass, wine production arrived in California with the Franciscan missionaries in the late-eighteenth century. After experiments with native grapes proved unacceptable, European vinifera vines were imported for cultivation. By the 1850s, under the influence of European viticultural entrepreneurs, California winemaking had expanded up and down the state and fueled by the welcoming climate, became a thriving industry during the last half of the nineteenth century.

Though new-world winemaking managed to survive a phylloxera infestation in the 1880s and the loss of vast cellars in the infamous earthquake of 1906, Prohibition dealt a near fatal blow to the industry. Pummeled but not beaten, California winemaking had to rebuild and reinvent itself following the Repeal Act of 1933.

Recognizing that the Central Coast region boasted growing conditions similar to those of the great European viticultural centers of the Rhine, Bordeaux and Burgundy, experts from the University of California at Davis began rediscovering areas ripe for vineyard planting. Many of these pockets were located along the eastern slopes of the Coast Ranges in the Santa Cruz, Monterey and San Luis Obispo areas and in the Santa Ynez Valley behind Santa Barbara. Grape-growing microclimates flourish throughout the region's mountains and sunny coastal slopes, with each unique collaboration of soil and climate (called *terroir* by the French) and varietal, creating intriguing variations in the final product. Thanks to mild temperatures, fog-cooled evenings and a long, dry growing season, Central Coast wines are celebrated for their intensity of flavor, length of life and elegance of structure. The region has come to be noted for its award-winning Chardonnays, Sauvignon Blancs, Cabernet Sauvignons, Merlots and Syrahs.

The most recent renaissance of wine-growing interest rode on the tails of the 1960s trend away from mega-agriculture. Even though well over three-quarters of the wine made in the United States is produced in California (the best-known from Napa and Sonoma), increasingly, some of the most intriguing California wines are flowing from small wineries along the Central Coast. Thanks to the compactness of these facilities — most are so small that their wines rarely leave their respective areas — winemakers here are famed for their abilities to grow grapes and create wines by hand.

In the resulting boom of microwineries in the 1970s, the Central Coast of California came into its own, claiming the attention of both the region's population and international aficionados.

PROMINENT VARIETALS

Through trial and error, some European vinifera grape varieties have been found to prosper when catalyzed by Central Coast soils and climate. Producing the most celebrated regional wines are the Chardonnay and Cabernet Sauvignon grapes. Chardonnay is the great white wine of French Burgundy, a dry, buttery, applelike wine, whose depth and fruit are heightened by oak aging. Cabernet Sauvignon, the grape behind the celebrated red wine of Bordeaux, is full-bodied, fragrant, often with tones of cherry and bell pepper, and is far and away the top red varietal produced in California.

In addition to the two aforementioned and extensively planted grapes, other varietals have met with acclaim. One of the earliest planted in California, Zinfandel is a vigorous red grape that produces a bold wine with berrylike aroma. Pinot Noir, the temperamental "holy grail" of Burgundian red wine grapes, is finding its way to some fine wines of dry and elegant structure. The spicy Alsatian Gewürztraminer is another popular California white varietal, as is the fruity, faintly grassy Sauvignon Blanc, long used to create the white wines of Bordeaux and the Loire. Rhône varietals, such as Syrah and Petite Sirah, are on the ascendance in the Central Coast, their velvety and complex wines gaining increasing attention.

Essential Wine-Tasting Protocol

There is nothing pretentious about wine tasting on the Central Coast, an activity enthusiastically pursued by weekend visitors to the area's many small tasting rooms. Tasting room staff are happy to guide the novice through winemaking techniques and tips for maximizing appreciation of the wines being poured. Like all collaborations of nature and art, wine should be enjoyed by all of the senses.

Before tasting, pause to notice the color and clarity of the wine. Hold the glass up to the light to admire its full luster and, ideally, clarity. Rotate the wine gently in the glass and then smell deeply, noticing the bouquet that often will be reminiscent of a wide range of fruits, flowers and earthiness. Now you're ready to take a small sip. Trill it against the roof of the mouth (this may take practice) to help make maximum palate contact. Here's where the wine shows off its range of sweetness, tartness, body and, when swallowed, its finish.

Clearing the palate with water or bread is crucial for sampling successive wines. And those strategically placed buckets are there for a reason. Spitting out excess wine will insure that both you and your palate stay intact during multiple tastings. If you plan to make an afternoon of it, it's a wise idea to designate a driver who sips nothing stronger than juice or mineral water during a series of winery visits.

SANTA CRUZ MOUNTAINS WINE AREA

As with so many features of the Central Coast landscape, winemaking began in Santa Cruz with the coming of the Franciscan fathers in the late-nineteenth century. When the Mission Santa Cruz was founded, the missionaries quickly planted river benchlands below the church with the sweet Spanish grape required for wines used in the Catholic Mass. After the missions were secularized and European settlers came to seek post-Gold Rush fortunes in lumber, shipping and agriculture, the European vinifera grapes were planted in fog-cooled pockets of the mountains.

Commercial winemaking in the area began in 1863 with the first plantings of grapes by brothers George and John Jarvis in the Vine Hill district near the 2,000-foot summit of the Santa Cruz Mountains. By 1870, over 300 acres of the mountains had been dedicated to wine grapes, and there were over a dozen winemakers in business in Santa Cruz county by 1875. The new fad for wine-growing mushroomed too quickly, and a glut of grapes caused the fledgling industry to fall during a worldwide depression in the late 1870s.

Still, optimists pressed onward, and by the late 1880s, three respected vintners — Santa Cruz Mountain Wine Company, Mare Vista and the Ben Lomond Wine Company — were sending wines to competitions around the country and the world. But natural disasters, another depression, a world war and finally Prohibition eventually smothered the young industry. Grape stakes disappeared into the weeds until the most recent revival of winemaking interest in the 1960s.

Intent upon mining the rural splendor of the redwoods and the seaside, refugees from urban areas and Cold War-era Silicon Valley decided that doing their own thing would include winemaking. The region has long attracted mavericks, from 1940s forefathers Chaffee Hall and Martin Ray (early believers in the power of the modern premium wine industry) to "Rhône ranger" Randall Grahm in the mid-1980s.

Since the 1970s, Santa Cruz Mountain wines have gained in finesse and renown, fueled by a boom of over two dozen almost exclusively family-run microwineries that have sprung up to capture the unique terroir of the stony mountain soil and the dry, fog-cooled growing season. Latter-day pioneers like David Bruce, Ken Burnap, Dexter Ahlgren and Robert Roudon were joined in the 1980s by a host of young entrepreneurs increasingly intent upon developing tiny, far-flung vineyards in this area's diverse landscape. Exceptional Chardonnays, Gewürztraminers, Rieslings and Cabernets are already emerging from this young aggregation, demonstrating the regional characteristics of elegance and long-lived structure.

Valerie and Dexter Ahlgren have placed their critically acclaimed Ahlgren Vineyard at the forefront of California's challenge to French Cabernets and Chardonnays.

Robert Scheer

AHLGREN VINEYARD
Winemaker: Dexter Ahlgren.

Bonded in 1976, Ahlgren Vineyard is a highly respected operation run by Dexter and Valerie

831/338-6071; www.virtual vineyard.com Web site. P.O. Box 909, Boulder Creek, CA 95006. Tours: Sat., 12:00 noon–4:00 p.m. Tastings: Sat., 12:00 noon–4:00 p.m. Specialties: Chardonnay, Cabernet Sauvignon, Semillon, Zinfandel.

Ahlgren. Ahlgren turns out some of the most famous Cabernet Sauvignons and Semillons in California. Sixteen consecutive vintages of Ahlgren Chardonnay from Monterey's Ventana Vineyard have taken countless awards for their rich, clean bouquet and flavors. Renowned wine critic Robert Parker considers Ahlgren's Cabernets "usually among the best wines of the vintage." The approach here is strictly handmade, and the low volume of production makes these wines coveted by serious collectors. The winery facility, tucked beneath the family's private home, is located in a mountain setting surrounded by forests and offers views of the redwood-draped canyons from the resident picnic tables.

The tasting room at Bargetto Winery, the Santa Cruz area's oldest winery, hosts guests from all over the world.

Covello & Covello

BARGETTO WINERY
Winemaker: Paul Wolford.
831/475-2258;
831/475-2664 Fax.
3535 N. Main St., Soquel, CA 95073.
Tours: Mon.–Fri. by appointment.
Tastings: Mon.–Sat., 9:00 a.m.–5:00 p.m.; Sun., 11:00 a.m.–5:00 p.m.
Specialties: Cabernet Sauvignon, Chardonnay, Gewürztraminer, Pinot Noir.

Soquel is home to the Santa Cruz Mountains' oldest winery, Bargetto, whose spacious brick tasting room on Main St. is packed with history, extending to pre-Prohibition days when the enterprising Bargetto brothers kept frontier restaurants well stocked with sturdy Italian red wines. Today, a third generation is in charge of the large facility, which offers tours of its vast cellars. Visitors also can enjoy exhibits of artwork in the winery's gallery and sip and picnic at an outdoor courtyard overlooking Soquel Creek. Producing over 30,000 cases annually, Bargetto is far and away the largest winery in the area, enjoying a renaissance of excellence with their Chardonnay and Cabernet Sauvignon. Don't leave without sampling the winery's distinctive mead (a honey-fermented drink) and the fruit wines, including olallieberry, raspberry and apricot, distributed under the Chaucer's label. A well-stocked gift store provides packaged samplers of top vintages, wine paraphernalia and souvenir items. Bargetto's fine wines are also available for tasting and sales at its tasting room on Monterey's Cannery Row.

The Rhône Ranger of Bonny Doon Vineyard, maverick winemaker Randall Grahm, helped put Santa Cruz area wines on the map.

Jock McDonald

BONNY DOON VINEYARD
Winemaker: Randall Grahm.
831/425-4518; 831/425-3528 Fax; wwwbonny doonvineyard.com Web site.
10 Pine Flat Rd., Santa Cruz, CA 95061.
Tours: By appointment.
Tastings: Daily, 11:00 a.m.–5:00 p.m.
Specialties: French Rhône varietals, Italian varietals, dessert wines.

The unmistakable sense of adventure and maverick instincts of internationally acclaimed winemaker Randall Grahm are apparent everywhere at this rustic mountaintop winery appointed with state-of-the-art equipment. The vineyards are planted with Grenache, Mouvèrdre, Syrah, Marsanne and Roussane, an indication of Grahm's early interest in the Rhône region of France. Innovation yields collector's item Rhône-style red wines, velvety dessert wines, award-winning Chardonnays and Italian varietal white wines, as well as the occasional bracing eau de vie and distilled brandy. Darling of the international media, Grahm, dubbed "America's most avant-garde winemaker" by *Connoisseur* magazine, produces vintage after astonishing vintage of distinctive wines, highlighted by clever labels that play on old-world classics, such as Cigare Volant and Clos de Gilroy. Shaded picnic tables are situated just up the hill from the tasting room, which also stocks a T-shirt collection showcasing Grahm's celebrated campy wine label designs. They've recently opened a new tasting room in Paso Robles.

BYINGTON WINERY & VINEYARD
Winemaker: Greg Bruni.
831/354-1111;
831/354-2782 Fax.
28150 Bear Creek Rd., Los Gatos, CA 95030.
Tours: By appointment for 8 or more.
Tastings: Daily, 11:00 a.m.–5:00 p.m.
Specialties: Chardonnay, Pinot Noir, Cabernet Sauvignon.

Superbly situated on a hilltop with a stunning view of the Monterey Bay, this recent addition to the area's fine wineries offers tasting, picnicking and special event ambiance at a sprawling Italianate château, crowning the slopes of vineyards. Easily the area's most imposing winery facility, this tile-roofed mansion boasts a high-ceilinged tasting room overlooking barbecue pits available for impromptu afternoon grills. Gift items are long on wine logo specialties. Complex Chardonnays are among the highlights of steel magnate Bill Byington's cellars, and a visit provides an in-depth encounter with the sheer beauty of this redwood mountain kingdom overlooking the sea.

DAVID BRUCE WINERY
Winemaker: David Bruce.
831/354-4214;
831/395-5478 Fax.
21439 Bear Creek Rd., Los Gatos, CA 95030.
Tours: No.
Tastings: Daily, 12:00 noon–5:00 p.m.
Specialties: Pinot Noir, Chardonnay, Petite Sirah, Cabernet Sauvignon.

Physician David Bruce enjoys courting controversy with his pioneer experiments in White Zinfandel, Late-Harvest vintages and Rhône-style reds. In the vanguard of the Central Coast's current, premium winemaking boom, the winery was begun in 1964 and has captured a lion's share of awards over the past decade for its Burgundian-style Chardonnays and Pinot Noirs. The large facility (30,000 cases annually) sits amid a scenic, twenty-five-acre estate vineyard near the summit of the Santa Cruz Mountains. While the tasting facility is bare bones — the raison d'être is the impressive array of wines, notably an Estate Pinot Noir — the view of the steeply terraced vineyards and the Monterey Bay beyond is bewitching, offering picnic possibilities.

DEVLIN WINE CELLARS
Winemaker: Chuck Devlin.
831/476-7288;
831/479-9043 Fax.
P.O. Box 728, 3801 Park Ave., Soquel, CA 95073.
Tours: No.
Tastings: Weekends, 12:00 noon–5:00 p.m.
Specialties: Chardonnay, Merlot.

A small thirty-acre winery located at the end of a country road, Devlin is run by Chuck and Cheryl Devlin and their young son Thomas, whose artwork has graced labels of vintages past. Critically acclaimed for a succession of Chardonnays, Merlots and Cabernets, the winery excels in its emphasis upon premium wines, all affordably priced. The estate overlooks redwood forests and the Monterey Bay and is a favorite spot for picnics and private parties. Launched in the late 1970s, Devlin's vintages have taken many awards at the most presti-

Chuck and Cheryl Devlin of Devlin Wine Cellars help fuel the youthful infusion of Santa Cruz area winemaking talent.

Robert Scheer

gious state competitions and even accompanied President Reagan on a tour of China during the mid-1980s.

Hallcrest Vineyards' winemaker John Schumacher uses a "wine thief" to extract a sample of red wine for a blend tasting.

Robert Scheer

HALLCREST VINEYARDS
Winemaker: John Schumacher.
800/491-9463 CA; 831/335-4441; 831/335-4450 Fax.
379 Felton Empire Rd., Felton, CA 95018.
Tours: By appointment.
Tastings: Daily, 11:00 a.m.–5:30 p.m.

One of the most atmospheric wineries of the area, Hallcrest enjoys a hallowed reputation. Begun in the 1940s by post-Prohibition, premium winemaking pioneer Chaffee Hall, the winery created legendary Cabernet Sauvignon and Riesling from its estate vines, many of which survive today. After a brief incarnation as Felton-Empire Vineyards, the compound reverted to the Hallcrest name under the recent proprietorship of U.C. Davis-trained wine-

Specialties: Chardonnay, Riesling, Zinfandel, organic wines.

maker John Schumacher, who carries on the tradition of exquisite White Rieslings produced from those fabled estate grapes. Handmade, full-bodied Zinfandels and crisp, buttery Chardonnays also are specialties of this small wine facility. Recently, the winery has begun bottling a line of certified organic, sulfite-free wines under the Organic Wine Works label. The wooden cottage tasting room, picnic lawns and cellars overlooking the Henry Cowell redwoods form the backdrop for a superb day of wine tasting. Hallcrest's star-studded, outdoor musical concert series regularly brings some of the top names in jazz, blues and acoustic groups to the terraced lawns and gnarled oaks nestling at the foot of the vineyards.

Mirassou's enologist Sean Lin hand-riddles individual bottles of sparkling wine, just one step in the labor-intensive "méthode champenoise" process.

MIRASSOU CHAMPAGNE CELLARS
Champagnemaker: Sean Lin.
831/395-3790.
300 College Ave., Los Gatos, CA 95032.
Tours: Daily, 1:30 p.m., 3:30 p.m.
Tastings: Daily, 12:00 noon–5:00 p.m.
Specialties: Sparkling wines.

The Mirassou family has been producing wine in the Santa Clara Valley for over 100 years. Recently, the winery purchased the cellars and compound of the old Sacred Heart Novitiate Winery, which combined the making of sacramental and secular wines since 1888. Grapes from Mirassou's vast vineyard holdings are turned into fine sparkling wines (Blanc de Blancs and Blanc de Noirs) using the labor-intensive méthode champenoise process. The facility forms the heart of in-depth tours and tastings, while the terraced dining area is the site of exceptional wine dinners and holiday functions.

OBESTER WINERY
Winemakers: Paul & Sandy Obester.
650/726-9463;
650/726-7074 Fax.

From this small, ranch-style winery situated at the foot of the mountains in the seaside town of Half Moon Bay, winemaker Paul Obester produces exceptional varietals. The handsome tasting room

12341 San Mateo Rd. (Hwy. 92), Half Moon Bay, CA 94019.
Tours: No.
Tastings: Daily, 10:00 a.m.–5:00 p.m.
Specialties: Chardonnay, Sauvignon Blanc, Zinfandel, Sangiovese.

has long been a fixture of any day trip to this charming village, where Paul and Sandy Obester create delightfully floral Gewürztraminers and toasty Chardonnays, in addition to a long list of elegantly structured Sauvignon Blancs. Most of the label's product can be sampled at the tasting room, which also offers specialty food items, Obester's line of mustards and dressings and wine-related books.

ROUDON-SMITH VINEYARDS
Winemaker: Bob Roudon.
831/438-1244; 831/438-5123 Fax.
2364 Bean Creek Rd., Scotts Valley, CA 95066.
Tours: By appointment.
Tastings: Sat., 11:00 a.m.–4:00 p.m.; Sun., by appointment.
Specialties: Cabernet Sauvignon, Chardonnay, Gewürztraminer, Petite Sirah, Pinot Noir, Zinfandel claret.

One of the earliest pioneers of the handmade wine boom of the 1970s, Roudon-Smith was founded in 1972 by two couples seeking escape from the high-tech industry of Silicon Valley. While a new vineyard of Chardonnay grapes matured on a sunny canyon slope where the Roudon and Smith families settled, the small winery began producing long-lived varietals from selected local vineyards by traditional methods. Wines designed to be partnered with fine food are the specialties of this award-winning house, best exemplified by a full-bodied Zinfandel, elegantly structured Estate Chardonnay and Santa Cruz Mountain Pinot Noir. Keeping production down to around 10,000 cases a year, Texan Bob Roudon likes to "stand back and let the grapes do the work," a technique that has produced vintages packed with true varietal characteristics.

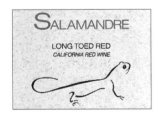

SALAMANDRE WINE CELLARS
Winemaker: Wells Shoemaker.
831/685-0321; 831/685-1860 Fax.
108 Don Carlos Dr., Aptos, CA 95003.
Tours: By mailing list invitation.
Tastings: By mailing list invitation.

The quirky label, named for a rare amphibian found only in a small sector of the Santa Cruz Mountains, tells a lot about the inventive approach of winemaker Shoemaker to his microyield of Burgundian-style Chardonnays. Always experimenting, the winemaker continues to charm and to surprise with distinctive vintages of whatever grapes currently capture his fancy. Always intriguing, Shoemaker delights in innovative combinations, such as a blend of intensely floral White

Specialties: Chardonnay, Gewürztraminer, Merlot.

Riesling and Muscat Canelli, which he called White Dove. Every inch of this minuscule operation is covered by hand, from selective picking of grapes from the Santa Cruz Mountains and Arroyo Seco region of Monterey county to the crushing, bottling and lugging of boxes. Salamandre wines may be found in restaurants and wine stores throughout Santa Cruz county, and the label, graced with the embossed emblem of the long-toed salamander, is a regional keepsake.

SANTA CRUZ MOUNTAIN VINEYARD
Winemaker: Ken Burnap.
831/426-6209.
2300 Jarvis Rd., Santa Cruz, CA 95065.
Tours: By appointment.
Tastings: By appointment.
Specialties: Cabernet Sauvignon, Merlot, Pinot Noir.

Winemaker Ken Burnap is widely regarded as one of the prime movers of the recent boom in small, premium wineries. In 1974, he purchased fourteen acres, covered with Pinot Noir grapes, in the Santa Cruz Mountains. The site, originally planted by John Jarvis in 1863, is one of the oldest vineyards in the Santa Cruz Mountains. The spot was graced with all of the growing conditions that the exacting winemaker required, from the southern exposure, hillside terrain to well-drained, rather poor soil that could encourage deep roots and intensity of flavor. Vines are hand-tended and hand-harvested, and the labor-intensive production techniques reach fruition in powerful, big-shouldered red wines. The Merlots are pure velvet, and the Pinot Noirs are memorable. Visitors should make time for an appointment at this highly regarded winery — an hour spent with Burnap provides a crash course in local winemaking.

SOQUEL VINEYARD
Winemakers: Peter Bargetto, Paul Bargetto & Jon Morgan.
831/462-9045;
831/429-8680; www.all-n-all.com Web site.
7880 Glen Haven Rd., Soquel, CA 95073.
Tours: By appointment.
Tastings: Sat., 10:30 a.m.–3:30 p.m.; Sun.–Fri., by appointment.
Specialties: Cabernet Sauvignon, Chardonnay, Pinot Noir, Merlot.

One of the area's newest wineries, this tiny facility can easily be toured in a few minutes, but the excellent tasting opportunities demand a lengthier stay. The focus here is on small quantities of handmade wines showcasing the intensely flavored grapes of the region. Still in its infancy, this vibrant young enterprise has already attracted much attention in regional and national competitions — the Cabernets and Chardonnays are justly acclaimed, but the Pinot Noir is especially appealing.

STORRS WINERY
Winemakers: Stephen & Pamela Storrs.

A husband-and-wife winemaking team of the first order, Pamela and Steve Storrs are both U.C., Davis oenology graduates and have already

U.C., Davis-trained winemakers Steve and Pam Storrs special-ize in a line of Chardonnays created exclusively with grapes from the Santa Cruz Mountains.

Paul Schraub

831/458-5030; 831/458-0464 Fax; www.wine access.com Web site. Old Sash Mill #35, 303 Potrero St., Santa Cruz, CA 95060.
Tours: By appointment.
Tastings: Fri.–Mon., 12:00 noon–5:00 p.m.; daily, 12:00 noon–5:00 p.m. (except Wed.) in summer.
Specialties: Chardonnay, Merlot, Riesling, Zinfandel.

endowed this tiny facility with glory at statewide competitions. The emphasis is upon a series of Chardonnays created exclusively with grapes from the Santa Cruz Mountains. And, given the widely diverse topography of selected vineyards, the results are as distinct as they are distinctive. The small tasting room regularly attracts inquiring wine buffs, and the winemakers are always available to explain, discuss and compare notes. The winery, housed behind the sleek tasting area, is essentially a glorified warehouse where all of the sorcery of winemaking, from blending to cellaring, is on view. Don't miss the complex, toasty Chardonnay from Gaspar Vineyard, the crisp Vanamanutagi Vineyards Chardonnay and the supple Merlots.

Vintners' Passport Weekends

Four Saturdays a year, the two dozen wineries of the Santa Cruz Mountains collaborate on an "open house" that stretches from the summit of the redwood mountains to hilltops overlooking the ocean in south Santa Cruz county. Many of the tiniest facilities, rarely open to the public, have an opportunity to show off their finest. The weekends allow visitors a chance to meet the winemakers, tour cellars and sample wines unavailable anywhere else. For dates and locations, contact Santa Cruz Mountains Winegrowers Association (831/479-9463; P.O. Box 3000, Santa Cruz, CA 95063).

OTHER SANTA CRUZ MOUNTAINS WINE AREA WINERIES

Aptos Vineyard (831/688-3856; 831/662-9102; 7278 Mesa Dr., Aptos, CA 95003) Extremely small bottlings of Pinot Noir, grown on Judge John Marlo's small estate, are evocative of the fabled vintages of Burgundy. Regularly honored at California's top competitions, these Pinots are so rare that they seldom find their way any further than the cellars of local admirers. But they're well worth looking for when you're in the area. No tours or tastings are available.

Crescini Wines (831/462-1466; P.O. Box 216, Soquel, CA 95073) Premium Cabernet Franc and Cabernet Sauvignon are the specialty of this tiny, family-operated winery located in the redwoods of the Soquel Valley. Headed by winemaker Richard Crescini, it produces just under 1,000 cases annually. No tours, but tastings are available by appointment.

Equinox (831/338-2646; 831/338-8307; 290 Igo Way, Boulder Creek, CA 95006) Barry Jackson produces a méthode champenoise sparkling wine that is both rounded and austerely dry. Plenty of long-lived microbubbles fill this pleasing sparkler, whose flinty bouquet offers a clean, crisp finish. No tours, but tastings are available at select public functions.

Jory Winery (831/356-2228; P.O. Box 1496, Los Gatos, CA 95031) Winemaker Stillman Brown creates distinctive Chardonnay, Merlot and Pinot Noir vintages. No tours, but tastings are available at select public functions.

Kathryn Kennedy Winery (831/867-4170; 831/867-9463; www.kathrynkennedy winery.com Web site; 13180 Pierce Rd., Saratoga, CA 95070) This microwinery, headed by winemaker Marty Mathis, specializes in the creation of 100 percent Estate Cabernet Sauvignon. He also makes Lateral, a blend of Cabernet Franc and Merlot. No tours or tastings are available.

McHenry Vineyard (530/756-3202; (Bonny Doon); Mailing address: 330 Eleventh St., Davis, CA 95616) A small, redwood-encircled winery in the Bonny Doon mountaintop area, this facility turns out lustrous Pinot Noirs at the hand of U.C., Davis anthropologist/winemaker Henry McHenry from estate grapes planted on four acres, located five miles from the ocean. Nov. tours are for those on the mailing list, but no tastings.

Mount Eden Vineyards (831/867-5832; 831/867-4329 Fax; 22020 Mt. Eden Rd., Saratoga, CA 95070) Founded by post-Prohibition maverick Martin Ray, this small mountaintop facility draws on vineyards planted by Ray in the 1940s, as well as newer vines from which winemaker Jeffrey Patterson creates Cabernet Sauvignon, Chardonnay and Pinot Noir. Tours are available by appointment.

Nicasio Vineyards (831/423-1073; 483 Nicasio Way, Soquel, CA 95073) Small quantities of Cabernet Sauvignon, Chardonnay, Riesling and Zinfandel, handmade from carefully selected vineyards, come from this small facility, founded in 1950 by Hewlett-Packard engineer Dan Wheeler and one of the first of the new generation of post-Prohibition wineries. Wines are aged naturally in an enormous sandstone cave hollowed out of the nearby hillside, and the results have won admirers and awards for decades. Tours and tastings are available by appointment.

P and M Staiger (831/338-4346; 1300 Hopkins Gulch Rd., Boulder Creek, CA 95006) Winemaker Paul Staiger specializes in a Cabernet Sauvignon/Merlot blend and Chardonnay. Tours and tastings are available by appointment.

River Run Vintners (831/726-3112; 65 Rogge Ln., Watsonville, CA 95076) A family-run winery tucked into the coast ranges behind Santa Cruz, winemaker J.P. Pawloski's small facility produces a wide range of fine wines, most notably its bold, much-honored Zinfandels and Syrahs. This is a fine introduction to the regional style of bold varietals. Tours and tastings are available by appointment.

Silver Mountain Vineyards (831/353-2278; 831/353-1898; silvermt@ihot;

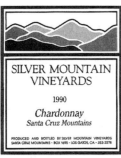

www.webwinery.com Web site; P.O. Box 3636, Santa Cruz, CA 95063) Shaken but not defeated by the 1989 earthquake, Jerold O'Brien's small winery turns out stylish Chardonnay from its estate vineyard, located at the summit of the Santa Cruz Mountains in an area planted by early viticulturists. Other offerings are Montag (a Bordeaux blend), Pinot Noir and Zinfandel. Tours and tastings are available by appointment, except on Passport Weekends and Vintners' Festival.

Troquato Vineyards (831/866-6700; 1791 Pollard Rd., Los Gatos, CA 95032) Winemaker Angelo Troquato specializes in Estate-Bottled Cabernet Sauvignon and Merlot, as well as Chardonnay and Zinfandel. No tours or tastings are available.

Trout Gulch Vineyards (831/688-4380; 3875 Trout Gulch Rd., Aptos, CA 95003) Winemaker Bernie Turgeon (a founder of J. Lohr Winery) and Paul Wofford specialize in Chardonnay and Pinot Noir. No tours or tastings are available.

Zayante Vineyards (831/335-7992; 831/335-5770; 420 Old Mount Rd., Felton,

CA 95018) Winemaker Greg Nolten spent several decades in the winemaking business before beginning his own efforts in earnest in 1988. Currently expanding vineyards at an historic, old hilltop ranch where the winery is housed, Nolten creates just under 1,000 cases annually entirely by hand. The first estate Chardonnay, a complex, full-flavored beauty, was released in 1992, but is available only at the winery. Also, quite special is a spicy Syrah, with Cabernet Sauvignon and Zinfandel filling out Zayante's dance card. Tours are available by appointment. An anniversary celebration is held on the third weekend in May.

MONTEREY WINE AREA

While grapes were planted as early as 1791 by Franciscan fathers at Mission Soledad in the Salinas Valley, on the leeward side of Monterey's coastal mountain range, this fertile, agricultural paradise wasn't fully recognized as a potential vineyard region until the 1960s, when vintners began utilizing the underground resources of the Salinas River for irrigation. Growers who solved the apparent climactic drawbacks of the dry, breezy valley by planting vines parallel to the prevailing winds now supply vast quantities of grapes for huge operations like Mirassou, Almaden, Paul Masson and Wente Brothers.

Given the coolness of this growing area, whose temperatures are the lowest in the Central Coast region (thanks to Salinas Valley breezes and the proximity to ocean fogs), Monterey grapes luxuriate in a lengthy ripening process. The leading white grapes — Chardonnay, Sauvignon Blanc and Gewürztraminer — respond especially well to these conditions with pronounced intensity and length of vintage life. Though a relative newcomer to the California winemaking scene, Monterey is earning increasing respect for its grapes and locally produced wines.

CHALONE VINEYARD
Winemaker: Dan Karlson.
831/678-1717.
Hwy. 146 & Stonewall
  Canyon Rd., Soledad, CA
  93960.
Tours: Weekdays, by
  appointment; weekends,
  11:00 a.m.–4:00 p.m.
Tastings: Weekdays, by
  appointment; weekends,
  11:00 a.m.–4:00 p.m.
Specialties: Chardonnay,
  Chenin Blanc, Pinot
  Blanc, Pinot Noir.

World famous for its lusty and elegant Chardonnays and Pinot Noirs, Chalone cultivates its 100-plus acres of grapes at a 2,000-foot elevation on the east face of the Coast Range. Founded in 1969 by influential winemaker Richard Graff, one of the vigorous pacesetters of recent California winemaking, Chalone was an early leader in coaxing Burgundian-style wines out of the coastal climate. Today, the winery is part of an empire that includes Edna Valley Vineyard, Carmenet and Acacia wineries. Graff's never-ending quest for the great California Pinot Noir continues to be well received, and Chalone's Chardonnays are regarded among the top made in the country. Tours of the vineyards and facilities put wine buffs in touch with some of the finest wines and most knowledgeable winemakers in the country.

**CHÂTEAU JULIEN
  WINERY**
Winemaker: William
  Anderson.
831/624-2600;
  831/624-6138 Fax.

Founded in 1982 by Robert and Patricia Brower, this award-winning winery provides tastings of its splendid Chardonnays and Cabernet Sauvignons at a glittering French-style country château, complete with turrets, copper flashing, stained-glass

8940 Carmel Valley Rd.,
Carmel, CA 93923.
Tours: By appointment.
Tastings: Weekdays, 8:30
a.m.–5:00 p.m.;
weekends, 11:00
a.m.–5:00 p.m.
Specialties: Cabernet
Sauvignon, Chardonnay,
Merlot.

appointments and antique furnishings. Set in the heart of the affluent, Old Spanish California ambiance of Carmel Valley, the winery is famous for full-bodied, accessible vintages of complex, spicy Chardonnays and satiny Merlots. The varietals — all made from Monterey county grapes — also include a delightful blend of Semillon and Sauvignon Blanc, called Meritage White. Look for the 1989 Cabernet Sauvignon that took a double gold in the 1993 San Francisco Fair National Wine Competition. Wine-related gifts are available for those who crave special souvenirs in addition to the wonderful wines.

CLONINGER CELLARS
Winemakers: Dave Paige &
John Estell.
831/758-1686;
831/758-9769 Fax.
1645 River Rd., Gonzales,
CA 93926.
Tours: By appointment.
Tastings: Mon.-Fri., 11:00
a.m.–4:00 p.m. ; Sat.,
Sun., 11:00 a.m.–5:00 p.m.
Specialties: Cabernet
Sauvignon, Chardonnay,
Pinot Noir.

A new, small winery formed from the partnership of four long-standing Salinas Valley winemaking families, Cloninger Cellars has already won acclaim for its first release, a 1988 full-bodied, creamy Chardonnay. The first appearance of this wine was in a very limited, 1,000-case release. The intention is ultimately to increase the vineyard size from its current ten acres to 200-plus acres, with a production focus on Cabernet Sauvignon and Pinot Noir, in addition to the award-winning Chardonnay.

DURNEY VINEYARD
Winemaker: Miguel
Martin.
831/659-6220.
Center St., Carmel Valley,
CA 93924.
Tours: No.
Tastings: Mon.–Fri., 10:00
a.m.–4:00 p.m.;
weekends, 11:00
a.m.–5:00 p.m.
Specialties: Cabernet
Sauvignon, Chardonnay,
Chenin Blanc, Pinot Noir.

In a beautiful side pocket of the Santa Lucia Mountains, over eighty acres of estate vines planted over the past twenty-five years are fed by underground springs and grown without the use of herbicides or pesticides at this 1,200-foot elevation winery. The first vineyard and winery in Carmel Valley, the estate was conceived by William and Dorothy Durney in the mid-1960s, and the original acreage was appropriately named Rancho del Sueno, meaning "dream ranch." The Spanish-style chapel, built as the cornerstone of the wine estate in 1973, serves as the Durney logo. All of the award-winning wines are created from the fruit of estate vineyards, over half of which are of planted to the superior Cabernet Sauvignon grape. While the winery is quite remote, Durney's excellent varietals are well showcased at area restaurants and wine stores.

HAHN ESTATES
Winemaker: Art Nathan.
831/678-2622;
831/678-2005 Fax.
37700 Foothill Rd., Soledad,
CA 93960.
Tours: Daily, 11:00
a.m.–4:00 p.m.
Tastings: Daily, 11:00
a.m.–4:00 p.m.
Specialties: Cabernet
Sauvignon, Chardonnay,
Merlot, Cabernet Franc,
Viognier.

The long-standing interest of the Hahn family in California winemaking recently resulted in the establishment of this estate, whose premium wines are fed by five vineyards located in Monterey county on the west side of the Salinas Valley. Nicky Hahn first encountered the ideal grape-growing climate of Monterey in 1980 and was one of the original partners in Smith & Hook Winery, with 1991 marking the introduction of wines bearing the Hahn Estates logo. This label's top wines include Cabernet Sauvignon, Merlot and Chardonnay. Great picnic spots overlooking Salinas Valley make a visit to this vineyard a special occasion.

JEKEL VINEYARDS
Winemaker: Joel Burnstein.
831/674-5522; 831/674-
3769 Fax.
40155 Walnut Ave.,
Greenfield CA 93927.
Tours: By appointment.
Tastings: Daily, 11:00
a.m.–4:00 p.m.
Specialties: Cabernet Franc,
Cabernet Sauvignon,
Chardonnay,
Johannisberg Riesling,
Late-Harvest
Johannisberg Riesling,
Pinot Noir.

In less than twenty years, an original planting of 140 acres of vineyards east of the Coast Range has resulted in an established winery producing upward of 80,000 cases of fine wines each year. The superb Chardonnays and Cabernet Sauvignons are the stuff of local legends. A red barn houses the main facility, and the tasting room, with its arbor draped with wisteria is a classic portrait of a Coastal California winery encircled by vineyards. Jekel bottles Cabernet Franc (long the favored blending grape of Bordeaux-style Cabernet Sauvignons) as its own varietal with big berry- and pepper-laden results. The extensive grounds, tasting and sales rooms are open to wanderers and picnickers, the tasting room atmosphere is friendly and helpful and the sampling pours are generous.

JOULLIAN VINEYARDS
Winemaker: Ridge Watson.
831/659-2800; 831/659-
2802.
20300 Cachagua Rd.,
Carmel Valley, CA 93924.
Tours: By appointment.
Tastings: By appointment.
Specialties: Cabernet
Sauvignon, Chardonnay,
Sauvignon Blanc.

The Joullian and Sias families, who first created the winery, selected Carmel Valley as their estate vineyard because of the area's reputation for producing rich, intensely flavored grapes. In 1981, the group was joined by winemaker Ridge Watson, who brought international experience in France and Australia to the emerging winery. In 1983, 655 acres of 1,400-feet-elevation benchlands were purchased, followed by another forty acres of rocky Arroyo Seco loam. Over three-quarters of the vineyard is devoted to the noble varietals of Bordeaux, resulting in an array of complex Cabernets, Merlots and Sauvignon Blancs.

Robert Scheer

Estate-grown grapes from southern Monterey county have helped Lockwood winemaker Larry Gomez develop a reputation for creating bold, award-winning wines.

LOCKWOOD VINEYARD
Winemaker: Larry Gomez.
800/753-1424; 831/753-
1424; 831/753-1238 Fax.
P.O. Box 1997, Salinas, CA
93902.
Tours: By appointment.
Tastings: No.
Specialties: Cabernet
Sauvignon, Chardonnay,
Merlot, Pinot Blanc.

In only a decade, this winery, with its estate-grown grapes, has established a reputation for turning out bold, much-honored vintages. The unconventional approach to marketing here involves sales strictly through mail order. Lockwood wines, produced on 1,650 acres of vineyards, have taken many top awards since the first 1989 vintage. The rich, rounded 1990 Cabernet Sauvignon was judged Best of the Region in the 1992 California State Fair competition, and the 1991 Lockwood Vineyard, Monterey White Riesling took a gold medal.

MONTEREY VINEYARD
Winemaker: Ken Greene.
831/675-4000;
831/675-4060.
800 South Alta St.,
Gonzales, CA 93926.
Tours: Please call for
information.
Tastings: Please call for
information.
Specialties: Cabernet
Sauvignon, Chardonnay,
Merlot, Pinot Noir,
Sauvignon Blanc.

Owned by the giant Seagrams Company, this high-profile winery established in 1976 produces sturdy varietals and blends on its 1,100 acres in the southern Salinas Valley. This is a large, half-million-case-per-annum operation, with a lavishly appointed Spanish-style tasting center that boasts an exhibition gallery and landscaped picnic area. The grounds feel like a park, replete with ponds, geese and picnic tables on the lawn. The tour provides a close look at high-production, winemaking techniques. The specialties of the house, including red and white blends and a range of Chardonnays, Pinot Noirs and Cabernets, are all astonishingly affordable.

MORGAN WINERY
Winemaker: Dean DeKorth.
831/751-7777.

Morgan Chardonnays consistently win awards for this small winery located in the heart of John Steinbeck country. Established by Dan and

590 Brunken Ave., Salinas, CA 93901.
Tours: By appointment.
Tastings: By appointment.
Specialties: Chardonnay, Pinot Noir, Zinfandel, Sauvignon Blanc.

Donna Lee in 1982, Morgan currently produces 20,000 cases annually of Sauvignon Blanc, Pinot Noir, Zinfandel and Chardonnay, which is considered among the finest in the state, utilizing time-honored methods of barrel fermentation, contact on lees and aging in a variety of French oak barrels. The results are as dramatic as the fog-drenched, marine-influenced microclimate that generates a rare intensity of flavor and distinct varietal characteristics.

SMITH AND HOOK WINERY & VINEYARD
Winemaker: Art Nathan.
831/678-2132;
831/678-2005 Fax.
37700 Foothill Rd, Soledad, CA 93960.
Tours: No.
Tastings: Daily, 11:00 a.m.–4:00 p.m.
Specialties: Chardonnay, Cabernet Franc, Masterpiece, Cabernet Sauvignon, Merlot, Viognier.

A charming estate in a classic rancho setting, this respected winery produces fine red wines from Monterey area grapes. Especially fine tasting is found in the luscious, peppery red wines, Cabernet Sauvignon and Cabernet Franc, coaxed to glory by the warm Santa Lucia Highlands. The drive to the winery is a treat, and the picnic area boasts a spectacular view across the broad Salinas Valley. The tasting room is available for weddings, picnics and conferences.

VENTANA VINEYARDS
Winemaker: Doug Meador.
800/237-8846; 831/372-7415; 831/655-1855.
2999 Monterey-Salinas Hwy. 68, Monterey, CA 93940.
Tours: No.
Tastings: Daily, 11:00 a.m.–5:00 p.m.
Specialties: Cabernet Sauvignon, Gold-Stripe Chardonnay, Magnus, Riesling, Sauvignon Blanc, Merlot, Syrah.

Doug and LuAnn Meador are the owners of this vine-covered winery, housed on one of the most award-winning vineyards in the country. Grapes flourish in the 400-acre vineyard planted in gravely soil on the arid banks of the Arroyo Seco River. Meador is widely regarded as one of the top growers in California, and his wines are excellent, notably the fruity Sauvignon Blanc and peppery Cabernet Sauvignon. The charming, stonework tasting headquarters and the grounds provide a taste of Coastal California rustic elegance.

Monterey County Vintner and Grower Association

If you would like to receive a colorful, fact-filled brochure on the Monterey wine area, contact this group. This is definitely an organization that has a handle on how to disseminate information on its wines (831/375-9400; 831/375-1116 Fax; P.O. Box 1793, Monterey, CA 93942; Attention: Amanda Robinson).

OTHER MONTEREY WINE AREA WINERIES

Bernardus Winery (831/659-4300; 831/626-9313 Fax; 21810 Parrot Ranch Rd., Carmel Valley, CA 93924) Tucked into the rolling ranch lands of Carmel Valley, this very new and very small operation directs its attention to the reds and whites of France's fabled Bordeaux region. Winemaker Don Blackburn produces especially notable Marinus (Cabernet/Merlot blend), Chardonnay, Sauvignon Blanc and Pinot Noir from its estate Jamesburg vineyards. Tours and tastings are available by appointment.

Calera Wine Company (831/637-9170; 11300 Cienega Rd., Hollister, CA 95023) Winemaker Belinda Gould specializes in Chardonnay, Pinot Noir and Viognier. Tours and tastings are available by appointment.

Canandaigua Riverland Vineyards (831/675-2481; 800 S. Alta St., Gonzales, CA 93926) Winemaker Ed Filice heads the project to revitalize the famed Masson name and to elevate it to rarer critical climes. Success at that mission appears to be within sight. Blanc de Noirs sparkling wine, Cabernet Sauvignon, Chardonnay and Merlot are good values and quite tasty. Tours and tastings are available by appointment.

Cienega Valley Winery & Vineyards (831/636-9143; 9970 Cienga Rd., Hollister, CA 95023) Neophyte winemaker Pat DeRose of this small mom-and-pop label entered the fray with his first crush Cabernet Franc and Zinfandel in the fall of 1993. Pinot St. George is a vineyard favorite. Tours and tastings are available by appointment.

Cygnet Cellars (831/637-7559; 831/638-0376 Fax; P.O. Box 1956, Hollister, CA 95023) Winemaker Jim Johnson favors hearty, full-bodied Carigne, Petite Sirah and Zinfandel bottlings. No tours or tastings are available.

Georis Winery (831/659-1050; 4 Pilot Rd., Carmel Valley, CA 93924) Winemaker Walter Geris, who owns Carmel's renowned Casanova Restaurant (justly praised both for its food and its wine list), makes Merlot and Cabernet Sauvignon. All of the Merlots are prizewinners, and releases average around 500 cases. If you can find a bottle at a Monterey Peninsula restaurant or wineshop, snap it up. Tours are available by appointment, but tastings are offered daily.

Limestone Winery (831/637-6443; 1781 Limekiln Rd., Hollister, CA 95023) Winemaker Gabriel Heredia produces Pinot St. George, Orange Muscat and Zinfandel. Tours and tastings are available by appointment.

Paraiso Springs Vineyards (831/678-0300; 831/678-2584 Fax; 38060 Paraiso Springs Rd., Soledad, CA 93960) From 400 acres of premium grapes first planted in 1973, this small winery produced its first vintage of Chardonnay in 1987. Since then, distinctive Pinot Blanc, Pinot Noir and Johannisberg Riesling bottlings have followed from winemaker Phillip Zorn. The facility is located in the Spanish California setting of the Santa Lucia Highlands. Tours are available by appointment, but tastings are offered weekdays, 12:00 noon-4:00 p.m.; weekends, 11:00 a.m.–5:00 p.m.

Robert Talbott Vineyards (831/675-3000; 831/675-3120 Fax; P.O. Box 776, Gonzales, CA 93926) Winemaker Sam Balderas specializes in high-quality, lovely crafted Chardonnays and Pinot Noirs. No tours or tastings are available.

A Taste of Monterey

This second-floor mecca of wine nostalgia is housed in an old cannery building overlooking the blue waters of the Monterey Bay. Wines may be purchased by the glass, and a major array of souvenir gifts and specialty foods may be purchased in the giftware area. The visitors' center is filled with photographs, wine paraphernalia and memorabilia of over thirty local Monterey county wineries. A wide range of vintages is available for sampling and, of course, purchasing (831/646-5446; 700 Cannery Row, Monterey, CA 93940).

SAN LUIS OBISPO WINE AREA

The history of winemaking in San Luis Obispo county begins in 1797 at Mission San Miguel Arcángel, where Franciscan missionaries produced their customary sacramental wines from adjacent vineyards. After the Gold Rush, the region became increasingly populated by European settlers who brought French and Italian varietals to their expansive farmlands. One early winery, established by Andrew York in 1882, is still in operation as York Mountain Winery outside Templeton.

San Luis Obispo county's modern winemaking era dates back to the 1960s when, as in Monterey county, the region was targeted by U.C., Davis researchers as prime winegrowing terrain. The county subsequently developed two distinct viticultural areas approximately thirty miles apart. To the north, the Paso Robles wine country enjoys hot summer afternoons and cool nights, a climate that is particularly conducive to Bordeaux and Rhône varietals, as well as Zinfandel. Down towering Cuesta Grade and into the southern end of the county, Edna and Arroyo Grande Valleys feature a largely marine-influenced atmosphere where Burgundian varietals reign.

Over the past twenty years, San Luis Obispo county has enjoyed tremendous progress in its cellars and its vineyards, yielding a selection of regional wines whose trademarks are poise and elegance. In addition, nature has placed the county's vibrant winegrowing communities in countryside so lovely, so exquisitely Central Coast, that just following the winding lanes from winery to winery is an intoxicating experience.

ADELAIDA CELLARS
Winemaker: John Munch.
805/239-8980;
805/239-4671 Fax.

Emphasizing natural winemaking techniques, Adelaida adheres to the philosophy that exquisite wines are made not in the cellar but in the vineyard. Founded in 1981, Adelaida coaxes

5805 Adelaida Rd., Paso
Robles, CA 93446.
Tours: By appointment.
Tastings: Daily, 11:00
a.m.–5:00 p.m.
Specialties: Cabernet
Sauvignon, Pinot Noir,
Zinfandel, Chardonnay.

intense varietal character from its grapes by pruning for low yields on its seventy-five-acre vineyard. The wines are fermented with native yeasts, and sulfite additions are kept to a minimum. Adelaida's Chardonnays are 100-percent barrel fermented, and the reds spend the latter half of their fermentation cycle in the barrel, an unorthodox winemaking approach that yields wines of unique and exceptional character. The winery and tasting room are set on ranch lands, ranging well above 2,300 feet.

ARCIERO WINERY
Winemaker: Steve Felten.
805/239-2562;
805/239-2317 Fax.
5625 E. Hwy. 46, Paso
Robles, CA 93446.
Tours: Daily, 10:00
a.m.–5:00 p.m.; summer
weekends, 10:00
a.m.–6:00 p.m.
Tastings: Daily, 10:00
a.m.–5:00 p.m.; summer
weekends, 10:00
a.m.–6:00 p.m.
Specialties: Cabernet
Sauvignon, Chardonnay,
Chenin Blanc, Muscat
Canelli, Nebbiolo, Petite
Sirah, Sangiovese,
Zinfandel.

A Mediterranean-style, red tile-roofed winery and tasting complex is highlighted by a visitor center, lavish landscaping and a beautiful picnic area — the perfect spot to begin a self-guided tour of how the fine house wines are created. The upscale facility boasts luxurious appointments, including chandeliers and a fireplace, and supports some fine winemaking, evidenced in a memorable selection of Cabernets, Chardonnays and Petite Sirahs. Visitors can also taste wines from Arciero's new sister label Eos. The gift store is well stocked with wine-related goodies and gourmet deli items. The fortunes amassed by brothers Frank and Phil Arciero extend to professional racing and to an exhibit of famous race cars.

CASTORO CELLARS
Winemaker: Niels Udsen.
805/238-0725; 805/238-
2602 Fax.
1315 N. Bethel Rd.,
Templeton, CA 93465.
Tours: By appointment.
Tastings: Daily, 11:00
a.m.–5:30 p.m.
Specialties: Cabernet
Sauvignon, Merlot,
Chardonnay, Gamay,
Muscat Canelli, Pinot
Noir, Zinfandel,
Zinfandel port.

L ovely views from the vineyards and an antique-filled tasting room are among the pleasures of a visit to these cellars. Gourmet and wine-related gift items are available, as well as samples of the award-winning Cabernet Sauvignons, considered among the most consistent and well priced of all California Cabs. Like many market savvy and contemporary, Central Coast winemakers, Niels Udsen is among a handful of California winemakers who are adding delightful experiments in unfermented grape juice to his bottling line. The results so far have yielded an especially refreshing, nonalcoholic Zinfandel elixir that is blissful on a warm day. Far from a mere gimmick, nonalcoholic grape juices, created with all the care given to premium wines, stand to be highly competitive in a market fond of its bottled waters and designer soft drinks. The winery comes equipped with a prime picnic spot that offers views of the pastoral charms of the Templeton area.

CLAIBORNE & CHURCHILL VINTNERS
Winemaker: Clay Thompson.
805/544-4066;
805/544-7012.
2649 Carpenter Canyon Rd., San Luis Obispo, CA 93401.
Tours: Daily, 11:00 a.m.–5:00 p.m.
Tastings: Daily, 11:00 a.m.–5:00 p.m.
Specialties: Alsatian Gewürztraminer and Riesling, Muscat Canelli, Chardonnay, Pinot Noir.

Founded in 1983, Claiborne & Churchill remains ahead of its time in the production of Alsatian-style Gewürtraminers and Rieslings, proving that these varietals, when vinified to dryness, can be just as elegant and food-friendly as any other California white wine. A former professor of languages at the Univ. of Michigan, winemaker Clay Thompson recently moved his winery operations to a new facility on the rural perimeter of Edna Valley. A testament to environmental architecture, the winery employs energy-efficient straw bales in its walls, obviating any need for air-conditioning or refrigeration. A small bar in a corner of the cellar hosts friendly tastings, and impromptu tours are given upon request.

EBERLE WINERY
Winemaker: Gary Eberle.
805/238-9607;
805/237-0344 Fax.
E. Hwy. 46 (3.5 miles from Paso Robles), Paso Robles, CA 93447.
Tours: By appointment.
Tastings: Daily, 10:00 a.m.–5:00 p.m.; in summer, 10:00 a.m.–6:00 p.m.
Specialties: Cabernet Sauvignon, Chardonnay, Muscat Canelli, Syrah.

Eberle is a prime destination for discovering the regional flavor of the estate's Cabernets, Chardonnays and Muscat Canelli. Gary Eberle became professionally acquainted with winemaking while studying at U.C., Davis. His Chardonnays warmly glow with butter and spice, and his Zinfandels are powered by bold varietal characteristics. But he's also been known to have some fun with two-fisted blends like the popular "Eye of the Swine." The winery is situated with a view of the estate vineyards, and the cellar floor can be viewed from the elegant tasting room adjoining the winery. The patio is the perfect place to enjoy monthly, gourmet winemaker dinners, accessible by advance reservations.

EDNA VALLEY VINEYARD
Winemaker: Clay Brock.
805/544-5855;
805/544-7292.
2585 Biddle Ranch Rd., San Luis Obispo, CA 93401.
Tours: By appointment.
Tastings: Daily, 10:00 a.m.–5:00 p.m.

A member of the internationally renowned Chalone Wine Group, this midsized winery is best known for using classic Burgundian winemaking techniques to craft elegant Chardonnays and Pinot Noirs from the valley's famed Paragon Vineyard. Winemaker Clay Brock, formerly with Santa Maria Valley's Byron Winery, also masterminds a spectrum of limited-production wines,

Specialties: Chardonnay, Pinot Noir, sparkling wine.

including Pinot Blanc, Viognier and Syrah. The winery's new hospitality center features a retail marketplace, lush landscaping and a panoramic view of Edna Valley. Monthly special events and concerts are another winery trademark. Picnickers are encouraged to explore the tasting room's gourmet offerings and to enjoy them amid one of the valley's finest settings.

HARMONY CELLARS
Winemaker: Chuck Mulligan.
800/432-9239; 805/927-1625; 805/927-0256.
3255 Harmony Valley Rd., Harmony, CA 93435.
Tours: Daily, 10:00 a.m.–5:00 p.m.; in summer, 10:00 a.m.–5:30 p.m.
Tastings: Daily, 10:00 a.m.–5:00 p.m.; in summer, 10:00 a.m.–5:30 p.m.
Specialties: Cabernet Sauvignon, Chardonnay, Johannisberg Riesling, Pinot Noir, Zinfandel, Zinjoli.

Located near the charming artisan village of Harmony near scenic Hwy. 1, Harmony Cellars features a comfortable tasting room and a solid selection of classic varietals. Harmony Cellars is also known for some playful wines, including a light Beaujolais-style Zinfandel called Zinjoli, as well as two Christmas-themed wines: Santa's Reserve and Christmas Blush. Scenically wedged between the ocean and the rolling foothills of the Santa Lucia Mountains, the winery provides idyllic picnicking conditions.

The picnic area at Justin Winery hugs the productive vineyards.

JUSTIN WINERY
Winemaker: Steve Glossner.
805/237-4150;
805/238-7382 Fax.
11680 Chimney Rock Rd., Paso Robles, CA 93446.

An essential destination for red wine enthusiasts, Justin Winery specializes in Bordeaux and Italian varietals grown at a seventy-five-acre estate vineyard in the Paso Robles countryside. Justin's Bordeaux-style flagship blend, Isosceles, is

Tours: No.
Tastings: Weekdays, 11:00
a.m.–4:00 p.m.;
weekends, 10:00
a.m.–5:00 p.m.
Specialties: Cabernet
Sauvignon, Cabernet
Franc, Merlot, Meritage,
Nebbiolo, Sangiovese,
Shiraz, Orange Muscat,
Chardonnay.

MASTANTUONO WINERY
Winemaker: Pasquale
Mastantuono.
805/238-0676;
805/238-9257 Fax.
2720 Oak View Rd.,
Templeton, CA 93465.
Tours: No.
Tastings: Daily, 10:00
a.m.–5:00 p.m.; in
summer, 10:00 a.m.–6:00
p.m.
Specialties: Cabernet
Sauvignon, Chardonnay,
Muscat Canelli,
Zinfandel.

MERIDIAN VINEYARDS
Winemaker: Chuck
Ortman.
805/237-6000;
805/239-5715 Fax.
7000 E. Hwy. 46, Paso
Robles, CA 93446.
Tours: By appointment.
Tastings: Daily, 10:00
a.m.–5:00 p.m.
Specialties: Cabernet Blanc,
Cabernet Sauvignon,
Chardonnay, Pinot Noir,
Syrah, Zinfandel.

PEACHY CANYON WINERY
Winemaker: Tom
Westberg.
805/237-1577;
805/237-2248 Fax.
1480 N. Bethel Rd,
Templeton, CA 93446.

one of the Central Coast's benchmark "Meritage" wines. Cozy tastings are conducted over a glasstop table amid English-style gardens. Top chefs from around the U.S. host Justin's monthly Guest Chef Dinners. The estate also features a three-room B&B and a full-time chef for those seeking an ideal "wine country" getaway.

The tasting room, busily appointed in Italian hunting lodge fashion, presents a dazzling array of interesting varietals. Winemaker Pasquale Mastantuono concentrates on dry-farmed grapes, which produce lusty Zinfandels and rich, rounded Cabernets. The castlelike winery building overlooks stands of majestic oaks, and picnickers in the winery's charming gazebo are often serenaded by live music during warm weather. There is a well-stocked gift store, and deli items are available for sale to take outside into the attractive garden area.

Thanks to savvy marketing and a superior, moderately priced product, Meridian has established itself as a leader in the market for Central Coast wines. Meridian's Chardonnay is highly drinkable, both crisp and creamy, and is fast becoming one of the most popular, affordable Chardonnays in the state. The Pinot Noir is supple and rounded, and the Syrah launches a rewarding assault on the palate. The award-winning wines are created from Santa Barbara county and Edna Valley grapes.

A must-stop for Zinfandel lovers, Peachy Canyon features a new, environmentally friendly, straw-bale facility and a tasting room converted from a one-room schoolhouse built in 1886. The winery was established by former school teachers Doug and Nancy Beckett in 1988 and now farms more than forty vineyard acres. Peachy Canyon

Tours: No.
Tastings: Daily, 11:00
a.m.–5:00 p.m.
Specialties: Zinfandel,
Cabernet Sauvignon,
Merlot, Meritage,
Chardonnay.

**SAUCELITO CANYON
VINEYARD**
Winemaker: Bill
Greenough.
805/489-8762;
805/543-2111 Fax.
1600 Saucelito Creek Rd.,
Arroyo Grande, CA
93420.
Tours: No.
Tastings: Daily, 10:30
a.m.–4:30 p.m. at the
Talley Vineyards tasting
room.; closed Tues.,
Wed., Oct.-May.
Specialties: Zinfandel,
Cabernet Sauvignon.

**SILVER CANYON
WINERY**
Winemaker: Greg Propper.
805/238-9392;
805/238-3975.
11240 Chimney Rock Rd.,
Paso Robles, CA 93446.
Tours: No.
Tastings: Daily, 10:00
a.m.–5:00 p.m.
Specialties: Cabernet
Sauvignon, Merlot,
Cabernet Franc, Late-
Harvest Cabernet Franc,
Chardonnay.

TALLEY VINEYARDS
Winemaker: Steve
Rasmussen.
805/489-0446;
805/489-0996 Fax.
3031 Lopez Dr., Arroyo
Grande, CA 93420.
Tours: No.

Zinfandels are known for their luscious textures and full-blown flavors, and vineyard-designated Zinfandel from the famed Dusi ranch is also one of the region's finest. Peachy Canyon's Merlot is another example of the winery's commitment to excellence. Production remains at about 10,000 cases.

Anchored to a ten-acre, dry-farmed vineyard in the remote hinterlands of Arroyo Grande Valley, Saucelito Canyon produces one of California's finest Zinfandels. Homesteaded in the 1870s and resurrected a century later by Bill Greenough, the estate yields wines noted for their sensuous textures, layered flavors and elegant composition. An adherent to the no-nonsense school of winemaking, Greenough leaves the talking to his vineyard, and the vineyard speaks volumes. Saucelito Canyon and its Zinfandels exemplify the traditional estate-wine model as refracted through California's new-world personality.

Producing estate wines in the classic Bordeaux tradition, Silver Canyon produces 4,000 cases annually from its 100-acre vineyard in the Santa Lucia range west of Paso Robles. The vineyard's unfertilized volcanic and limestone soils maintain an excellent natural mineral content, adding dimension and personality to Silver Canyon's age worthy red wines. The winery's Chardonnay is also loaded with character, while its Late-Harvest Cabernet Franc puts a unique twist on that varietal. The tasting room, located in a farmhouse built in the 1860s, overlooks the estate lake and vineyard. An adjacent gallery features vineyard artwork by artist and winery owner Gary Conway.

The Talleys, longtime local farmers, have struck Burgundian gold with the world-class Pinot Noirs and Chardonnays that are produced at their winery in Arroyo Grande Valley. Three estate vineyards, two in Arroyo Grande Valley and one in nearby Edna Valley, yield vineyard-designated wines known for their complexity and elegance.

Tastings at Arroyo Grande's Talley Vineyards are provided in a charming, two-story adobe built in 1863.

Tastings: Daily, 10:30
   a.m.–4:30 p.m.; closed
   Tues., Wed., Oct.–May.
Specialties: Pinot Noir,
   Chardonnay, Sauvignon
   Blanc, White Riesling.

Talley's Pinot Noirs are among the finest produced in California, while its Chardonnays and Rieslings boast captivating varietal intensity. Tastings are provided in an 1863 two-story adobe, surrounded by a broad lawn and flower gardens that accentuate the estate's old-world atmosphere. Be sure to visit the white gazebo — a favorite stop for picnickers.

TOBIN JAMES CELLARS
805/239-2204;
   805/239-4471 Fax.
8950 E. Union Rd., Paso
   Robles, CA 93446.
Tours: No.
Tastings: Daily, 10:00
   a.m.–6:00 p.m.
Specialties: Zinfandel,
   Cabernet Sauvignon,
   Cabernet Franc, Merlot,
   Syrah, Chardonnay,
   Sauvignon Blanc, Late-
   Harvest Zinfandel.

Under the quirky guidance of renegade owner and winemaker Tobin James, this small-production facility provides one of California's most engaging winery destinations. Loaded with Wild West nuances and anchored by a 100-year-old hardwood bar, the tasting room features gunslinger movie cutouts, a mock jail for entertaining children and an ever-present Australian Shepherd named Cisco. The wines are equally unique, boasting alluring, full-blown flavors and fanciful names, such as Ballistic Zinfandel, Bull's-Eye Syrah, Morningstar Cabernet Sauvignon and Pandemonium Sauvignon Blanc.

WILD HORSE WINERY &
   VINEYARD
Winemaker: Ken Volk.
805/434-2541;
   805/434-3516 Fax.
1437 Wild Horse Winery
   Court, Templeton, CA
   93465.
Tours: By appointment.

Wild Horse does a fine job of maximizing the regional potential of bold red varietals and crisp, fruity Chardonnays. Its outstanding white wines include a spicy Gewürztraminer, and the Pinot Noirs are regularly anointed at the heavyweight California State Fair annual competitions. At its welcoming tasting room, these wines, as well

WILD HORSE™

1989
CABERNET SAUVIGNON
PASO ROBLES

Tastings: Daily, 11:00
a.m.–5:00 p.m.
Specialties: Cabernet Franc,
Merlot, Zinfandel, Pinot
Noir, Chardonnay,
Gewürztraminer,
Malvasia Bianca, Pinot
Blanc.

as rare specialties available only at the winery, including Dolcetto, Negrette and Trousseau, are displayed for the enjoyment of visiting tasters. Tricia Volk, winemaker Ken's able business cohort and wife, is the author of a book of recipes geared to specific offerings of Central Coast wineries.

WINDEMERE WINERY
Winemaker: Cathy
MacGregor.
805/542-0133.
3482 Sacramento Dr., Ste. E,
San Luis Obispo, CA
93401.
Tours: Thurs.–Sun., 11:00
a.m.–4:00 p.m.
Tastings: Thurs.–Sun., 11:00
a.m.–4:00 p.m.
Specialties: Zinfandel,
Pinot Noir, Cabernet
Sauvignon, Chardonnay.

After earning a masters degree in enology at U.C., Davis and working at wineries on the North Coast, free-spirited Cathy MacGregor returned to her roots and established her own winery, Windemere, in San Luis Obispo. The daughter of another local vineyard owner Andy MacGregor, whose coveted grapes appear in vineyard-designated wines across California, she produces bold, ripe Chardonnays loaded with tropical fruit flavors. A Zinfandel sourced from Paso Robles' famed Dusi Vineyard is another favorite from Windemere. Located in a small industrial unit on the outskirts of San Luis Obispo, Windemere features tastings in the midst of its busy cellar.

**YORK MOUNTAIN
WINERY**
Winemaker: Steve
Goldman.
805/238-3925;
805/238-0428.
7505 York Mountain Rd.,
Templeton, CA 93465.
Tours: No.
Tastings: Daily, 10:00
a.m.–5:00 p.m.

Having withstood the ravages of time, including Prohibition, this winery is over 100 years old. On its vineyard-encrusted mountaintop, the venerable winery offers antique appointments and a tasting room with a sturdy stone fireplace. All wines can be tasted for a nominal fee, and the gift area stocks plenty of wine books, wine paraphernalia and gourmet food items. Since it is the oldest surviving winery in this stretch of the Central

Specialties: Cabernet Sauvignon, Chardonnay, Sauvignon Blanc, Merlot, Pinot Noir, Zinfandel, sherry.

Coast, it's the obvious excuse to while away a pleasant afternoon in the foothills of the Santa Lucia Mountains.

International Wine Center

Located a few steps from the windswept bluffs of Cambria's Moonstone Beach, the Center is nestled amidst the spectacular plantings of Moonstone Gardens. Not only beautiful, this international wine-shopping spot also is an education, with a staff of knowledgeable wine raconteurs who'll guide you through top regional wines, as well as a spate of world-class and offbeat vintages from the rest of California and the world beyond. Proprietor Calvin Wilkes even stocks a world-class selection of rare teas and boutique beers. Over 200 wines are poured for tasting each year. All of your questions about wine protocol, growing techniques and tasting etiquette will be answered. Bottle and case prices offer tempting bargains. Open daily, 11:00 a.m.–5:00 p.m., a tasting fee of $1 per person is charged (800/733-1648; 805/927-1697; Moonstone Gardens, Hwy. 1, Cambria, CA 93428).

Wine entrepreneur Wilkes recently opened a tasting annex, cleverly called 927-WINE, and during a daily tasting of nine international and California wines, a hefty selection of imported cheeses is served along with several fresh breads (805/927-WINE; 788 Main St., Cambria, CA 93428).

The Crushed Grape Wine Center

Gifts of gourmet foods and wines from the San Luis Obispo area, as well as around the world, are available at this bonanza for bon vivants. The wine bar is really the heart of the action, pouring an eclectic assortment of California vintages with the accent on the Central Coast. Bottled wine selection and gourmet gift baskets make delicious souvenirs of the region (805/544-4449; Madonna Rd. at Hwy. 101, San Luis Obispo, CA 93401).

Linn's at the Granary Wine Center

Local winemakers without their own tasting rooms pool their resources at this centrally located fruit and vegetable stand/meeting place, recently expanded into an elegant wine tasting room, gourmet food store, bakery and gift shop. A lengthy and ever-changing tasting list allows visitors to sample from over eighty award-winning wines of local, family-owned wineries too small to boast their own tasting rooms. A $3 tasting fee includes a souvenir wineglass. Each month a "Meet the Winemaker" series brings one of the top alchemists of local winemaking to Linn's for talks, tastings and oenological enlightenment (805/237-4001; 12th St. & Riverside Ave., Paso Robles, CA 93446).

OTHER SAN LUIS OBISPO WINE AREA WINERIES

Alban Vineyards (805/546-0305; 8575 Orcutt Rd., Arroyo Grande, CA 93420) A pioneer in California's increasing embrace of Rhône varietals, John Alban makes handcrafted wines from Viognier, Roussanne, Syrah and Grenache. The winery is proving that Edna Valley, long known for its success with Burgundian varietals, is also prime terrain for so-called "Rhône Rangers." Tours and tastings are available by appointment.

Corbett Canyon Vineyards (805/544-5800; 805/544-7205 Fax; 2195 Corbett Canyon Rd., Arroyo Grande, CA 93420) Located about eight miles southeast of San Luis Obispo, this expansive, Spanish-style winery produces value-oriented Cabernet Sauvignon, Chardonnay, Merlot, Pinot Noir and Sauvignon Blanc. No tours or tastings are available.

Creston Vineyards (805/434-1399; 805/434-2426 Fax; Hwy. 101 & Vineyard Dr., Templeton, CA 93465) A fine vineyard and winery headed by winemaker Tim Spear coaxes definitive regional characteristics out of Cabernet Sauvignon, Chardonnay, Merlot, Pinot Noir, Sauvignon Blanc, Semillon and Zinfandel vintages. Special tasting-room-only bottlings are also produced. Tours are available by appointment, but tastings are available daily, 10:00 a.m.–5:00 p.m.

Dark Star Cellars (805/237-2389; 2985 Anderson Rd., Paso Robles, CA 93446) This small, family winery concentrates on small lots of Merlot and Cabernet Sauvignon made from local vineyards. A Bordeaux-style blend called "Ricordati" is also produced. Tastings are available on weekends and holidays, 11:00 a.m.–5:00 p.m.

Fratelli Perata Winery (805/238-2809; 1595 Arbor Rd., Paso Robles, CA 93446) This is a family-owned and -operated winery, specializing in bold red wines made from grapes produced by beautiful hillside vineyards. Recently, brothers Joe and winemaker Gene have added a promising Nebbiolo varietal to their Cabernet Sauvignon, Chardonnay, Merlot, Sangiovese and Zinfandel vintages. Tours and tastings are available by appointment.

Grey Wolf Cellars (805/237-0771; 805/237-9866 Fax; 2174 W. Hwy. 46, Paso Robles, CA 93446) Showcased in a sixty-year-old farmhouse, Grey Wolf's wines emphasize small lots of premium Zinfandel, Cabernet Sauvignon, Chardonnay, Fumé Blanc and Muscat Canelli. Tastings are available daily, 11:00 a.m.–5:30 p.m.

Laetitia Vineyard and Winery (805/481-1772; 453 Deutz Dr., Arroyo Grande, CA 93420) Established in 1995 on the site of the former Maison Deutz sparkling wine facility, Laetitia specializes in Pinot Blanc, Chardonnay and Pinot Noir crafted by French winemaker Christian Roguenaut. Tastings are available daily, 11:00 a.m.–5:00 p.m.

Martin Brothers Winery (805/238-2520; 805/238-6041 Fax; E. Hwy. 46 at Buena Vista, Paso Robles, CA 93446) Italian varietals are the specialty of winemaker Dominic Martin, who offers the fun of sampling a wide range of distinctive wines, including Aleatico, Cabernet Etrusco, Chardonnay in Botti, Grappa de Nebbiolo, Nebbiolo Vecchio, Vin Santo, Zinfandel Primitivo and the new sparkling Moscato Allegro. Seasonal concerts are presented in the winery amphitheater in the spring and summer. Tastings are available Sun.–Thurs., 11:00 a.m.–5:00 p.m.; Fri., Sat., 11:00 a.m.–6:00 p.m.

Midnight Cellars (805/239-8904; 805/237-0383 Fax; 2925 Anderson Rd., Paso Robles, CA 93446) This new, family-owned winery focuses on premium Cabernet Sauvignon, Merlot, Zinfandel and Chardonnay. Winemaker Rich Hartenberger uses grapes solely from the Paso Robles area, and a recently planted twenty-acre estate vineyard will soon enhance the winery's production. Tastings are available daily, 10:00 a.m.–5:30 p.m.

Mission View Estate Vineyard & Winery (805/467-3104; 805/467-3104 Fax; Hwy. 101 at Wellsona Rd., San Miguel, CA 93451) Located just east of historic Mission San Miguel, the winery's extensive vineyards generate especially fine Cabernets and Zinfandels. Chardonnay, Muscat Canelli and Sauvignon Blanc also delight visitors in a tasting room awash with traditional Spanish tile work and beamed ceilings. Picnicking on the redwood deck offers a view of the vineyards and the Mission beyond. Tastings are available daily, 10:00 a.m.–5:00 p.m.

Norman Vineyards (805/237-0138; 7450 Vineyard Dr., Paso Robles, CA 93446) This small winery specializes in estate-grown Zinfandel, Pinot Noir, Cabernet Sauvignon and Chardonnay. Tastings are available on weekends and holidays, 11:00 a.m.–5:30 p.m.

Pesenti Winery (805/434-1030; 2900 Vineyard Dr., Templeton, CA 93465) The oldest, originally family-owned winery in the Paso Robles area, Pesenti was established in 1934 on vineyards planted in 1923. The wine-lined tasting room boasts a staggering list of varietals for sampling. Tastings are available daily, 9:00 a.m.–5:30 p.m.

Poalillo Wineyards (805/238-0600; 1888 Willow Creek Rd., Paso Robles, CA 93446) Located on the west side of Paso Robles, Poalillo produces premium, estate-grown Zinfandels, Cabernet Sauvignons and Chardonnays with an emphasis on fruit intensity. Tours and tastings are available by appointment.

Sylvester Winery (805/227-4000; 805/227-6128 Fax; 5115 Buena Vista Dr., Paso Robles, CA 93446) Specializing in Zinfandel, Cabernet Sauvignon, Sangiovese and Chardonnay, Sylvester features a spacious tasting room, a small delicatessen and vintage train cars. Founded in 1995, the winery produces 25,000 cases from 200 estate vineyard acres. Tastings are available daily, 11:00 a.m.–5:00 p.m.

Treana Winery (805/238-6979; 805/238-4063 Fax; 2175 Arbor Rd., Paso Robles, CA 93446) The charming Tuscan atmosphere of this small, family-run winery showcases estate-grown Cabernet Sauvignons and Zinfandels made by winemaker Chris Phelps. Winemaker Austin Hope oversees the production of Treana's white wines, which include Chardonnay, Muscat Canelli, Rosato and a Rhône-style blend. Tastings are available daily, 10:00 a.m.–5:00 p.m.

Twin Hills Ranch Winery (805/238-9148; 2025 Nacimiento Lake Dr., Paso Robles, CA 93446) Gardens with a shaded picnic area and a visually arresting country French-style, half-timbered tasting room crown this family-owned estate, encircled by almond trees and vineyards. In addition to Zinfandel, Cabernet Sauvignon and Chardonnay, the winery also features a critically acclaimed California Dry Sherry made in the traditional Spanish solera method. Tastings are available on weekdays, 12:00 noon–4:00 p.m.; on weekends, 11:00 a.m.–5:00 p.m.

SANTA YNEZ VALLEY WINE AREA

As with the other major winemaking districts of the Central Coast, the Franciscan mission fathers got the ball rolling back in 1782, planting the first vineyards in Santa Barbara and then up into the Santa Ynez Mountains. Soon, 6,000 gallons of wine a year were being made, thanks to the labors of Chumash converts, who crushed the grapes by footwork and fermented the juices in tar-coated cowhides.

Clearly the state of the art has evolved and has captured the fancy of California wine aficionados, who are looking for new, distinctive and top-of-the-line Central Coast wines, with the lush valleys and canyons of the Santa Ynez Mountains offering a wide range of possibilities. Over 11,000 acres are planted to grapes, with new vineyards springing up daily. Unique to this versatile winemaking area is the transverse range of these coastal mountains. Reflecting the sharp inward angle of the west coast, the mountains run east-west, a feature that allows the inland flow of cooling fog and ocean breezes. The slow ripening of grapes grown under this coastal influence makes for intense development of varietal characteristics.

The inland valleys offer a warmer, drier microclimate, which results in a range of characteristics that emulate conditions in Bordeaux and the Rhône. Since Santa Ynez Valley area wineries aggressively embrace the grapes of France's Rhône district, this is the place to look for especially fine Syrahs, Petite Sirahs and Viogniers, in addition to exemplary Sauvignon Blancs, Chardonnays and Pinot Noirs. A few innovators, including Hollywood legend Fess Parker, have turned the ranch lands of the Santa Ynez Valley into country winery getaways.

Los Olivos Tasting Room & Wineshop

This is a user-friendly, wine-tasting depot that provides a tasting tour of some of the Santa Ynez Valley area's finest wineries — wineries too small to provide their own tasting facilities. For $3, you can sample six to eight pours of outstanding area vintages from tiny facilities like Claiborne & Churchill, Ojai, Qupé and Au Bon Climat. The man behind the bar, Chris Benzinger, will fill your ear with delicious, behind-the-scenes tidbits about styles, awards, winemaking personalities and tasting tips. This establishment, smack in the middle of the two streets that make up the village of Los Olivos, is a required pit stop for all buffs intent upon sampling the unique charms of Santa Ynez Valley winemaking. Open daily, 11:00 a.m.–6:00 p.m. (805/688-7406; P.O. Box 640, 2905 Grand Ave., Los Olivos, CA 93441).

BRANDER VINEYARD
Winemaker: Fred Brander.
805/688-2455.
P.O. Box 92, Hwy. 154 at
   Roblar, Los Olivos, CA
   93441.
Tours: By appointment.
Tastings: Daily, 10:00
   a.m.–5:00 p.m.
Specialties: Bouchet,
   Sauvignon Blanc.

Overlooking the ranch lands of former President Ronald Reagan and superstar Michael Jackson, this pink faux château winery and tasting facility serves up its fine wines with one of the most alluring views of the Santa Ynez Valley. Tasting room manager Lovette Twobirds, a sharp-minded, charismatic melding of Cherokee and Irish roots, is a crash course in appreciation of area wines ("Trilling is a peek into the future," she rhapsodizes). Under her guidance, you'll be enthralled by the fruity, butterscotchy Chardonnays and crisp, complex Bordeaux-style Sauvignon Blancs. A very special blend of Cabernet Franc, Cabernet Sauvignon and Merlot called Tête de Cuvée Bouchet sings of blackberries, cassis and spice. Stock up here or sign up for the mailing list.

BYRON VINEYARD & WINERY
Winemaker: Byron "Ken"
   Brown.
805/937-7288;
   805/937-1246 Fax.
5230 Tepusquet Rd., Santa
   Maria, CA 93454.
Tours: By appointment.
Tastings: Daily, 10:00
   a.m.–4:00 p.m.
Specialties: Chardonnay,
   Pinot Blanc, Pinot Noir,
   Sauvignon Blanc, Pinot
   Gris.

The road to this well-respected, ten-year-old winery is one of the most splendid country lanes in this stretch of the Coast Range. The picnic area on the steep slope of Tepusquet Creek is the site of many special wine and food events. The Spanish-inspired, barnlike tasting room provides samples of the winery's award-winning products, highlighted by crisp and distinctive white wines. The excellent Byron Chardonnays, adorned with glory at major national competitions, invariably find themselves paired with innovative California cuisine in the south Central Coast's best restaurants. If you're tempted to do some purchasing while you're at the tasting room, don't hesitate to follow that impulse.

FESS PARKER WINERY
Winemaker: Eli Parker.
805/688-1545.
P.O. Box 908, 6200 Foxen
   Canyon Rd., Los Olivos,
   CA 93441.
Tours: Daily, 11:00 a.m.,
   1:00 p.m., 3:00 p.m.
Tastings: Daily, 10:00
   a.m.–5:00 p.m.; $3 fee
   includes free logo glass.
Specialties: Chardonnay,
   Johannisberg Riesling,
   Merlot, Muscat Canelli,
   Pinot Noir, Syrah.

Though his son Eli manages the large, attractive winery, headquartered in a building of native stone and roofed in copper, the chance to catch a glimpse of the gracefully aging Western movie hero is part of the deal. The setting is classic California rolling ranch land. The winery is equipped for a myriad of public tastings, concerts, conferences and food events, and 1992 marked the first harvest of grapes grown on the 715-acre ranch. Already, the winery's Pinot Noir and Chardonnay are being marketed across the country and, of course, at Disneyland.

Alison Green of Santa Ynez Valley's landmark Firestone Vineyard is one of California's pioneer women winemakers.

FIRESTONE VINEYARD
Winemaker: Alison Green.
805/688-3940;
    805/686-1256 Fax.
P.O. Box 244, 5017 Zaca
    Station Rd., Los Olivos,
    CA 93441.
Tours: Daily, 10:00
    a.m.–4:00 p.m., every 45
    minutes.
Tastings: Daily, 10:00
    a.m.–4:00 p.m.
Specialties: Cabernet
    Sauvignon, Chardonnay,
    Gewürztraminer, Late-
    Harvest Johannisberg
    Riesling, Merlot,
    Sauvignon Blanc,
    Riesling.

Overlooking hundreds of acres, which are planted to all of the major grape varietals of the Central Coast, this award-winning winery essentially started the recent surge of interest in the Santa Ynez Valley area as a winemaking contender. In the early 1970s, founder Brooks Firestone broke with family tradition (he is the grandson of rubber baron Harvey Firestone) and decided to make wine, not tires. While the Chardonnays are exceptional and have been served in far-flung diplomatic settings, the Rieslings set the tone, especially the unctuous Late-Harvest vintages and a new and unprecedented Dry Riesling. Winemaker Alison Green was trained in Alsace and puts a pleasingly dry spin on her much-honored Gewürztraminer. The huge, contemporary hacienda winery, well-appointed tasting and gift area and adjoining picnic patio all overlook a mosaic of vineyards lining Zaca Station Rd., one of the prettiest country lanes in California.

**FOLEY ESTATES
    VINEYARD AND
    WINERY**
Winemaker: Alan Phillips.
805/688-8554;
    805/688-9327 Fax.
1711 Alamo Pintado Rd.,
    Solvang, CA 93463.
Tours: Available if
    attendants aren't too
    busy.

Here is another one of those tiny, quintessential Santa Ynez area wineries set in oak-studded rolling hills. The picnic area is irresistible and the tasting in a cozy cottage involves a wide range of premium red and white wines. The small facility specializes in microlots of handmade wines and is known for its Cabernet Sauvignon and Sauvignon Blanc. Talented winemaker, Alan Phillips, leads the

Tastings: Daily, 10:00 a.m.–5:00 p.m.
Specialties: Cabernet Sauvignon, Chardonnay, Merlot, Pinot Noir, Sauvignon Blanc.

crew in this busy winery recently purchased by William P. Foley II and his wife Carol.

GAINEY VINEYARD
Winemaker: Kirby Anderson.
805/688-0558; 805/688-5864 Fax.
P.O. Box 910, 3950 E. Hwy. 246, Santa Ynez, CA 93460.
Tours: Daily, 11:00 a.m., 1:00 p.m., 2:00 p.m., 3:00 p.m.
Tastings: Daily, 10:00 a.m.–5:00 p.m.
Specialties: Cabernet Franc, Cabernet Sauvignon, Chardonnay, Johannisberg Riesling, Merlot, Pinot Noir, Sauvignon Blanc.

Over sixty acres of estate vines surround the red-tile roofed, Spanish-style winery complex announced by a procession of romantic pep-pertrees. This is as much a community cultural center as it is tasting facility for Gainey's highly respected vintages. Gainey consistently proves its marketing savvy and viticultural excellence by producing innovative and affordable vins ordinaire like the surprisingly sturdy Rece$$ion Red. The tasting room overlooks the vineyard-laden hills and pours a selection of wines, including award-winning Sauvignon Blanc and Chardonnay, plus the highly regarded Pinot Noir. Tours begin at a particularly instructive "Visitor's Vineyard," a demonstration planting that shows off the various cultivation techniques and the trellising required by different grapes and allows visitors a chance to sample the fruit. This popular winery also is the site for a wide range of cooking classes, art shows, concerts and wine-appreciation workshops.

LINCOURT VINEYARD
Winemaker: Alan Philips.
800/864-3443; 805/688-8381; 805/688-3764.
343 N. Refugio Rd., Santa Ynez, CA 93460.
Tours: No.
Tastings: Daily, 10:00 a.m.–5:00 p.m.
Specialties: Cabernet Sauvignon, Syrah, Chardonnay, Merlot, Pinot Noir, Sauvignon Blanc, Chenin Blanc, Trousseau Gris.

Located on historic ranch lands in the heart of present-day Chumash country, this pioneer winery draws from over 100 acres of vineyards, including those originally planted in the late 1960s, for its premium production of Cabernet Sauvignon, Chardonnay, Sauvignon Blanc and Gewürztraminer. The small, friendly tasting room is set prettily in the midst of vineyards and rolling ranch country. There's an interesting gift store, which is lined with awards and trophies, and picnics on the redwood deck afford a view of yesteryear in the West.

MOSBY WINERY
Winemaker: Bill Mosby.

Tastings, concerts on the lawn and cooking classes are among the events available at this

Visitors to Mosby Winery's rustic tasting room can enjoy elegant Chardonnays and Pinot Noirs.

Kim Reierson

805/688-2415;
  805/686-4288 Fax.
P.O. Box 1849, Hwy. 101 at
  Santa Rosa Rd., Buellton.
  CA 93427.
Tours: By appointment.
Tastings: Daily, 10:00
  a.m.–4:00 p.m.;
  weekends, 10:00
  a.m.–5:00 p.m.
Specialties: San Giovesse,
  Chardonnay, Distillato di
  Prugne Selvaggie,
  Grappa Traminer,
  Nebbiolo, Pinot Grigio,
  Zinfandel, Primitivo,
  other Italian varietals.

small, family-run winery that leans heavily toward Italian varietals and top California grape vintages. The elegant Chardonnays and Pinot Noirs set the tone, and the potent grappas attract high honors at major competitions. An old red barn houses the winery and tasting room, and there's a mid-nineteenth-century adobe on the farm property. The place is definitely rustic, though the wines are anything but.

QUPÉ WINE CELLARS
Winemaker: Bob Lindquist.
805/688-2477; 805/686-
  4470 Fax.
P.O. Box 440, Los Olivos,
  CA 93441.
Tours: No.
Tastings: No.
Specialties: Syrah,
  Chardonnay, Marsanne,
  Mourvèdre, Viognier.

The winery's unusual name is a Chumash word for "poppy," the ubiquitous golden state flower. Enjoying increasing celebrity, the wines are outstanding (notably the black raspberry-scented Syrahs from Santa Barbara's coveted Bien Nacido Vineyard) and tend to be available at fine markets, restaurants and the Los Olivos Tasting Room (see p. 258). Specializing in Chardonnay and the wines of the Rhône, winemaker Bob Lindquist creates spellbinding vintages of great depth and endless finish. This is a label to watch, and since most of the tiny output is scooped up by the finest and trendiest Central Coast and Southern California restaurants, buyers should jump at the rare opportunity to stock their cellars with this rising star of the California oenological firmament.

RANCHO SISQUOC WINERY
Winemaker: Carol Botwright & Stephan Bedford.
805/934-4332; 805/937-6601 Fax.
6600 Foxen Canyon Rd., Santa Maria, CA 93454.
Tours: No.
Tastings: Daily, 10:00 a.m.–4:00 p.m.
Specialties: Cabernet Sauvignon, Chardonnay, Johannisberg Riesling, Merlot, Sauvignon Blanc, Sylvaner.

The pastoral Sisquoc River Valley frames the large ranch on which the label's redwood and stone facility sits. Bonded in 1977, the tiny winery's entire line of acclaimed wines produced from estate grapes are available exclusively at the tasting room, which adjoins a shaded lawn, gardens and a picnic area sheltered by huge oaks. The complex Chardonnays and Sauvignon Blancs are outstanding for drinking now and for cellaring.

Richard Sanford shows off award-winning grapes at his Sanford Winery in the Santa Ynez Valley.

Roland & Karen Muschenetz

SANFORD WINERY
Winemaker: Bruno D'Alfonso.
805/688-3300; 805/688-7381 Fax.
7250 Santa Rosa Rd., Buellton, CA 93427.
Tours: No.
Tastings: Daily, 11:00 a.m.–4:00 p.m.

Oozing Old West scenery and atmosphere, this small winery founded in 1981 is tucked into the foothills of the Santa Lucia Range, west of Solvang on farmlands draped with weathered buildings. Sanford wines are respected as some of the finest to pour forth from this glamorous winemaking valley. The lush, toasty Chardonnays and soft, rich Pinot Noirs regularly show up on expert's

Specialties: Chardonnay, Pinot Noir, Pinot Noir-Vin Gris, Sauvignon Blanc.

"best of California" lists. The cozy, rustic tasting room sports a friendly potbellied stove, and picnics may be taken at tables next to a gentle creek.

Kim Reierson

Daniel Gehrs, one of the Central Coast's reigning superstar winemakers, keeps Zaca Mesa Winery's tasting room well stocked with quality vintages.

ZACA MESA WINERY
Winemaker: Dan Gehrs.
805/688-3310;
  805/688-8796.
P.O. Box 899, 6905 Foxen Canyon Rd., Los Olivos, CA 93441.
Tours: Daily, 10:00 a.m.–4:00 p.m.
Tastings: Daily, 10:00 a.m.–4:00 p.m.
Specialties: Chardonnay, Pinot Noir, Syrah.

Moving his base of operations from the Santa Cruz Mountains to the Santa Ynez Valley, talented winemaker Dan Gehrs does delightful things with Chardonnay, Syrah and a host of other Rhône grape varietals. Zaca Mesa wines are some of the best-known and best-received wines made in the area, and the rustic winery has been producing award winners since 1972. Housed in a wooden barn, the winery is among a bevy of tiny establishments dotting Foxen Canyon Rd., and a leisurely afternoon picnicking here will have you fantasizing about buying property.

Santa Barbara County Vintners' Association

For a map of this area's excellent wineries, the helpful folks at this first-class organization would be glad to send you a map if requested (805/688-0881; P.O Box WINE, Los Olivos, CA 93441).

OTHER SANTA YNEZ VALLEY WINE AREA WINERIES

Los Olivos Vintners (800/824-8584; 805/688-9665; 805/686-1690 Fax; 2923 Grand Ave., Los Olivos, CA 93441) Founded in 1981, the winery creates a wide range of fine varietals, such as Chardonnay, Cabernet Sauvignon, Riesling and

Muscat, plus a huge, olivesque Sauvignon Blanc and a prize-winning Pinot Noir. The tasting room in downtown Los Olivos offers samples daily, 11:00 a.m.–6:00 p.m., as well as sales of bottles and cases and other wine-related paraphernalia in a country store atmosphere. No tours are available.

Babcock Vineyards (805/736-1455; 805/736-3886 Fax; 5175 Hwy. 246, Lompoc, CA 93436) Winemaker Bryan Babcock creates an award-winning Gewürztraminer, as well as appealing Chardonnay, Pinot Noir, Sauvignon Blanc and Sangiovese. An attractive picnic area surrounded by vineyards is another drawing card. Tours and tastings are available Fri. and weekends, 10:30 a.m.–4:00 p.m.

Barnwood Vineyards (805/766-9199; P.O. Box 31, Hwy. 33 at Quatal Canyon Rd., Ventacopa, CA 93214) Winemaker Larry Hogan originally bottled his Cabernet Sauvignon, Chardonnay and Merlot at Austin Cellars, but all that changed with the crush of 1993. Now Barnwood has its own quarters, as well as its own vines. Tours and tastings are available by appointment.

Buttonwood Farm Winery (805/688-3032; 805/688-6168 Fax; P.O. Box 1007, 1500 Alamo Pintado Rd., Solvang, CA 93463) It's new, it's small and the fine Sauvignon Blancs and Merlots made by winemaker Mike Brown are attracting attention. The Cabernet Franc and Cabernet Sauvignon offerings also are smart. No tours, but tastings are available daily, 11:00 a.m.–5:00 p.m.

Cambria Winery (805/937-1777; 805/934-3589 Fax; 5475 Chardonnay Ln., Santa Maria, CA 93454) Winemaker Dave Guffy creates 60,000 cases of Chardonnay and Pinot Noir yearly. Tours are available by appointment, but tastings are available on weekends, 10:00 a.m.–5:00 p.m.

Carrari Vineyards (805/344-4000; P.O. Box 556, 439 Waite St., Los Alamos, CA 93440) Legendary grower Joe Carrari grows grapes for the big boys, but also bottles some of his own (orchestrated by the maestro to his lusty specifications at Paul Masson). His user-friendly quaffs are headed by Carrari's blend of Cabernet Franc, Cabernet Sauvignon, Gamay, Merlot, Pinot Noir and Zinfandel. No tours or tastings are available.

Central Coast Wine Warehouse (805/928-9210; 900 E. Stowell Rd., Santa Maria, CA 93454) Winemaker Kim McPherson specializes in Chardonnay and Pinot Noir. No tours or tastings are available.

Chimère (805/922-9097; 805/922-2462 Fax; 547 W. Betteravia, Ste. D, Santa Maria, CA 93455) Gary Mosby was the original winemaker at Edna Valley and left to produce Chardonnay, Gamay, Pinot Blanc and Pinot Noir at his own independent label in 1988. His dad, William, heads Mosby Winery at Vega Vineyards. Tours and tastings are available by appointment.

Foxen Vineyard (805/937-4251; Rte. 1, Box 144-A, Foxen Canyon Rd., Santa Maria, CA 93454) Nestled among the vineyards that surround this country road, the small winery boasts winemakers Richard Doré and Bill Wathen's excellent reserve Cabernet Sauvignon, Chardonnay, Chenin Blanc, Merlot and Pinot Noir. Tours and tastings are available Fri. and weekends, 12:00 noon–4:00 p.m.

Houtz Vineyards (805/688-8664; P.O Box 897, 2670 Ontiveros Rd., Los Olivos, CA 93441) Small and rustic, the winery is housed in a California-style redwood barn smack in the middle of a fully functional farm, filled with all manner of animals. While no tours are offered, tastings of winemaker David Houtz' Cabernet Sauvignon, Chardonnay and Sauvignon Blanc, as well as picnicking near a small pond, are available weekends, 12:00 noon-4:00 p.m.

J. Kerr Wines (805/688-5337; P.O Box 7539, Santa Maria, CA 93456) Sales of the Chardonnay and Syrah vintages produced by this very small winery, led by winemaker John Kerr II, are conducted through wholesale distribution and at the Los Olivos Tasting Room (see p. 258). No tours are available.

Kalyra Wines (805/963-0858; P.O Box 865, Buellton, CA 93427) Fairly new and very small, the winery produces a few hundred cases each of Chardonnay, Merlot, port and natural German-style sparkling wine. Winemaker Michael Brown also plays around with fortified dessert wines. His handcrafted work can be found at fine wineshops in the Santa Barbara area and at the Los Olivos Tasting Room (see p. 258). No tours or tastings are available.

Respected winemaker Robert Longoria creates stunning Santa Ynez Valley wines under his Robert Longoria Wines label.

Richard Longoria Wines (805/688-0305; P.O. Box 186, Los Olivos, CA 93441) Gifted alchemist Rick Longoria has been making Pinot Noir on his own since 1982 and now is producing Cabernet Franc, Merlot, and Chardonnay. No tours are available, but samples of his labors are available at the Los Olivos Tasting Room (see p. 258).

Vita Nova (No telephone; P.O. Box 822, Los Olivos, CA 93441) Two celebrated winemakers, Jim Clendenen from Au Bon Climat and Bob Lindquist from Qupé, have joined forces to whip up some new ideas in Cabernet Franc, Cabernet Sauvignon, Merlot and Sauvignon Blanc, as well as a stunning Chardonnay. All the better for their admirers, who can stop by the Los Olivos Tasting Room (see p. 258) for some stunning samples. No tours are available.

CHAPTER SEVEN
Nuts & Bolts
INFORMATION

In any emergency, travelers seeking ambulance, fire or police services need only dial 911 on the nearest telephone, and help will be sent immediately.

Christopher Gardner

This chapter is a one-stop Central Coast survival guide. Filled with hard facts, it is compiled with both the local and the visitor in mind, providing guidance in the following areas.

AMBULANCE, FIRE, POLICE

Remember that 911 is the telephone number to call to request an ambulance or to report a fire or a situation requiring immediate police response — in short, for any and all emergency situations anywhere on the Central Coast.

AREA CODES

The area code for Santa Cruz and Monterey is 831. For San Luis Obispo county and the Santa Ynez Valley, it's 805.

BIBLIOGRAPHY

The Central Coast has long inspired storytellers, historians and novelists to put pen to paper. Bookstores in the region usually boast special sections devoted to lore, cuisine, natural history, reminiscence and fiction about this fascinating and mercurial wedge of the Golden State. Public libraries are additional fonts of literature about this land and its people, from the archival diaries of the Spanish explorers to charming tourism guides, spanning the past two centuries. Reference librarians specialize in directing newcomers to a wealth of browsing material on everything from tide pools to winemaking. Here are a few suggestions to get you started.

Books You Can Buy

AUTOBIOGRAPHY, BIOGRAPHY, REMINISCENCE

Boutelle, Sara Holmes. *Julia Morgan, Architect.* Color photos by Richard Barnes. New York: Abbeville Press, 1988. 265 pp., index, illus., photos, $55. A richly told and rewarding biography of the remarkable California architect whose elegantly rustic Arts and Crafts hand-shaped many landmarks of the northern California coast. Morgan, the first American woman admitted to the Beaux Arts enclave of Paris, is best known for surviving the wild imagination of William Randolph Hearst during the building of his San Simeon castle. A meeting with a remarkable woman.

Dunn, Geoffrey. *Santa Cruz is In the Heart.* Capitola: Capitola Book Company Publishing, 1989. 198 pp., illus., photos, $10.95. Delicious anecdotes, courageous pioneers and charismatic characters spill from these pages of crisply written memoirs by the scion of a third-generation Italian fishing family.

Gilliam, Harold and Ann. *Creating Carmel: The Enduring Vision.* Salt Lake City: Peregrine Smith Books, 1992. 234 pp., index, photos, $14.95. In-depth, play-by-play history of a mellow, exclusive arts colony on Monterey Bay from its mission origins to the bohemian boom and cultural vitality of today.

Master storyteller James D. Houston discovers the spirit of the Golden State in his literate, accessible investigation of Californians: Searching for the Golden State.

Robert Scheer

Houston, James D. *Californians: Searching for the Golden State.* Santa Cruz: Otter B Books, 1992. 288 pp., $10.95. Reminiscence, anecdote, environmental puzzling and historical detective work pour from the pages of this literary treasure hunt for the spirit of the Golden State. Accessibly shaped by a master storyteller.

Robinson, Judith. *The Hearsts: An American Dynasty.* New York: Avon Books, 1992. 420 pp., index, photos, $15. Compelling biographical portrait of a mighty family carving out and living the American Dream in bigger-than-life style. You'll meet pioneer silver miner George and his son William Randolph (whose thinly disguised excesses were brilliantly etched in *Citizen Kane*). But perhaps the most influential and interesting Hearst was WRH's mother, Phoebe, the strong-willed matriarch who left her fortune to her son and her mark on much of the Central Coast.

CULTURAL STUDIES

Clark, Donald. *Santa Cruz County Place Names.* Santa Cruz: Santa Cruz Historical Society, 1986. 552 pp., illus., maps, $23.95. Oral histories, folklore and rare archival information conspire in this fascinating encyclopedia of Santa Cruz county places and how they got their names, both official and colloquial.

_____. *Monterey County Place Names.* Carmel Valley: Kestrel Press, 1991. 661 pp., index, maps, $21.95. The tireless Librarian Emeritus of the University of California, Santa Cruz continues his exploration of the origin of official and unofficial place-names, this time ranging throughout the vast history of the territory that comprised the most important outpost of Spanish domination in Old California.

Lydon, Sandy. *Chinese Gold.* Capitola: Capitola Book Company Publishing, 1985. 550 pp., illus., photos, $24.95. An eye-opening and brilliantly researched bit of historical detective work that reveals the full flower, productivity and enterprise of Chinese immigrants throughout the Central Coast. Written with flourish and confidence, this book bursts with archival photographs and eye-witness accounts through which a slice of the past lives on vividly.

Margolin, Malcolm. *The Ohlone Way.* Illustrated by Michael Harney. Berkeley: Heyday Books, 1978. 168 pp., index, illus., $9.95. A sensitive and sympathetic glimpse inside the lives of these gentle hunter/gatherers, recounting their nomadic movements, artistic preoccupations, hunting rituals and metaphysical beliefs. It creates the lost world of an extinct cultural group that lived only 200 years away from us.

Miller, Bruce W. *Chumash.* Los Osos: Sand River Press, 1988. 135 pp., index, photos, $8.95. Knowledgeable, clearly written, historical and archaeological tome, tracing the fortunes of these early Central Coast natives. Placing the hunter/gatherer peoples in intelligible, historical context, the book includes chapters on religion, rock painting, basketry and social customs, plus illustrative photographs of native harpoons, seal effigies and basket masterpieces.

FICTION

Haslam, Gerald W., ed. *Many Californias: Literature from the Golden State.* Reno: University of Nevada Press, 1992. 250 pp., index, $14.95. Handy one-stop literary tour guide through some of the best minds that ever penned the West. A contemporary sampler filled with excerpts, poems and stories from Californians like Wallace Stegner, Maxine Hong Kingston, Joan Didion, Raymond Chandler, Toshio Mori, Jack London, Richard Henry Dana and John Muir.

Jeffers, Robinson. *Cawdor/Medea.* New York: New Directions, 1970. 191 pp., $10.95. A riveting introduction to the moody genius of a Central Coast master. Written in 1928, *Cawdor* is a stormy, narrative love poem set on the turbulent Big Sur coast. Jeffers' 1946 verse adaptation of the Greek tragedy *Medea* was created for Dame Judith Anderson.

Stegner, Wallace. *Angle of Repose.* New York: Penguin Books, 1971. 568 pp. $14.99. A Pulitzer Prize-winning exploration of the fears, failures, hopes, dreams and sheer toughness of a California pioneer family whose energies and accomplishments shaped the landscape of contemporary Central California. One of the best introductions to how the West was really won.

Steinbeck, John. *Grapes of Wrath.* New York: Penguin Books, 1939. 580 pp., $7. The Salinas-born, Nobel Prize winner crafted this American classic out of the blood, sweat and tears of Okie immigrants seeking to escape dust bowl depression in the relative paradise of Coastal California. The literary song of the dispossessed still resonates with regional power.

Stevenson, Robert Louis. *The Works of Robert Louis Stevenson.* London: Octopus Publishing Group, 1989. 687 pp., $7.98. Filled with the classic tales penned by the man who brought us *Treasure Island,* which was inspired by his long, romantic visits to the Monterey Coast.

HISTORY

Hamman, Rick. *California Central Coast Railways.* Boulder: Pruett Publishing Company, 1980. 307 pp., index, illus., photos, $45. A copiously illustrated and lovingly documented train buff's guide that tracks the expansion of the Central Coast via rail. The rich saga of the opening of commercial lines throughout the Central Coast is the story of men who demonstrated both engineering expertise and sheer courage in blasting iron highways through the coastal mountains. Terrific archival photographs enhance the exciting ride.

McPhee, John. *Assembling California.* New York: Farrar, Straus and Giroux, 1993. 303 pp., $21. Master wordsmith McPhee continues his explorations into the geologic mysteries of the New World by laying down the geology of California, layer by layer, seismic fold by tectonic plate. Told through anecdote, poetic spin, parable, wry wit and salty observation — in others words, the inimitable McPhee style — this gem traces the imaginary intersection of human and geologic time in the Golden State, from deserts to Coastal ranges, spicing up the journey with a dash of earthquake consciousness. A superb introduction to the invisible mind-set of California.

Starr, Kevin. *Americans and the California Dream: 1850-1915.* New York: Oxford University Press, 1973. 479 pp., index, photos, $15.95. Rich interweaving of the tales of Yankee speculators, explorers and politico-cultural big shots who came to find and to fabricate their version of the promised land. Contains vivid portraits of potent citizens, from Luther Burbank and Jack London to Phoebe Hearst and Isadora Duncan.

Woodbridge, Sally B. *California Architecture: Historic American Buildings Survey.* San Francisco: Chronicle Books, 1988. 270 pp., index, illus., photos, $25. A richly detailed and scholarly overview of California's architectural history — from Native American to postmodern — precedes this encyclopedia of important historic landmarks throughout the state. Structures are placed in the cultural landscape as far back as they can be traced. Believe it or not, this is a real page-turner.

NATURE GUIDES

Bakker, Elna. *An Island Called California.* Berkeley: University of California Press, 1984, 2nd ed. 455 pp., index, maps, illus., photos, $15. An eye-opening walk through the ecological niches of California, this is a vivid aid to the nonscientist in interpreting the diversity of flora and fauna. Strong sections on seashore, salt marshes and sea cliff ecology.

LeBoeuf, Burney, and Stephanie Kaza. *The Natural History of Año Nuevo.* Pacific Grove: Boxwood Press, 1981. 414 pp., index, illus., photos, $12.95. Exhaustively detailed, this is the definitive overview of a unique natural sanctuary — from the history of original whaling settlers to detailed reports on weather, tide pools, plants, currents and shore life. The authors are leading authorities on the life and times of the elephant seal and, with their astute help, these remarkable creatures loom larger in their favorite coastal habitat.

Munz, Phillip A. *Shore Wildflowers of California, Oregon and Washington.* Berkeley: University of California Press, 1973. 112 pp., index, illus., photos, $10.95. This bible of coastal flora is well illustrated, clearly written and helpfully grouped according to flower color.

Schoenherr, Allan A. *A Natural History of California.* Berkeley: University of California Press, 1992. 768 pp., $38. An overriding ecological awareness distinguishes this expansive exploration of the biological and geological diversity of California. Natural communities, their interactions and origins spring to life in a concise and highly engaging style.

PHOTOGRAPHIC STUDIES

California Coast. Photographs by Larry and Donna Ulrich; text by Sandra L. Keith. Portland: Graphic Arts Center, 1990. 160 pp., photos, $40. The entire California coast comes alive in these splendid, oversized photographic pages. A visual armchair stroll up and down the state, photographed in all weather and seasons and from breathtaking points of view. For dreaming over, before finding it a prominent resting place on the coffee table.

Crouch, Steve. *Fog and Sun, Sea and Stone: the Monterey Coast.* Portland: Graphic Arts Center Publishing Co., 1980. 157 pp., photos, $19.95. Sensitive marriage of text and images convey the natural wonders, elusive and bold, as well as man-made traces that adorn this vibrant stretch of the Central Coast.

_____. *Steinbeck Country.* Portland: Graphic Arts Center Publishing Co., 1973. 189 pp., index, photos, $28.50. Gorgeous color photos and evocative text by the talented Crouch, who has a real feel for the Central Coast ambiance mythologized by Steinbeck. Includes plenty of quotes from the Nobel Prize winner's writings.

Books You Can Borrow

Baer, Morley, et. al. *Adobes in the Sun: Portraits of a Tranquil Era.* San Francisco: Chronicle Books, 1980. 144 pp., illus., photos. Historic adobes of Monterey as captured by a Bay Area master image maker.

Gleason, Duncan and Dorothy. *Beloved Sister — The Letters of James Henry Gleason, 1841-1859: From Alta California and the Sandwich Islands.* Glendale: The Arthur H. Clark Company, 1978. 217 pp., index, illus. Letters from a globe-trotting Englishman, who became the county clerk of Monterey in 1857, tell the story of daily life, political intrigue and back-breaking travel conditions during California's Mexican colonial period.

Gudde, Erwin G. *California Place Names.* Berkeley: University of California Press, 1974. 431 pp., index. A fact-filled encyclopedia of the lore, history, color, romance and charismatic individuals whose names loom large throughout the state.

Hague, Harlan, and David J. Langum. *Thomas O. Larkin: A Life of Patriotism and Profit in Old California.* Norman and London: University of Oklahoma Press, 1990. 294 pp., index, photos. Focusing on the life and times of the wealthy Monterey merchant who helped finesse the Americanization of Spanish California, this book offers in-depth historical insights and analysis of the entrepreneurial spirit that civilized the New World's final frontier.

Hoover, Mildred Brooke, et al. *Historic Spots in California, 3rd ed.* Stanford: Stanford University Press, 1966. 597 pp., index, photos. County-by-county walking tour through the state's hotbeds of history. Exhaustively detailed entries on Central Coast landmark regions, chronicling the people, politics, settlements and battles that won the West.

Nordhoff, Charles. *California for Travelers and Settlers.* [1872] Centennial Printing, Berkeley: Ten Speed Press, 1973. 255 pp., illus. Utterly mesmerizing firsthand account of the journey west by the columnist for a popular nineteenth-century East Coast newspaper. Filled with lore and anecdotes of the day and eyewitness analysis of the then little-known natural wonders. Nordhoff's tales so extolled the balmy climate and therapeutic seaside atmosphere that they helped launch a westward migration still in progress today. Included are many charming accounts, often laced with the prevailing ignorance and racism of the day. Crucial reading for any serious student of the California Zeitgeist.

Nunis, Doyce B., Jr., ed. *The California Diary of Faxon Dean Atherton: 1836-1839.* San Francisco: California Historical Society, 1964. 235 pp., index. The man who gave his name to a suburban town nestled in the Coast Ranges speaks to us from the pages of vivid diaries kept during tempestuous ocean voyages along the California coastline from Baja California to the Oregon border and from Hawaii to Boston.

Stanger, Frank M. *South from San Francisco: San Mateo County, California, Its History and Heritage.* San Mateo County Historical Association, 1963. 208 pp., index, photos. Captivating minutiae concerning the wild-eyed dreamers and sturdy folk who logged, ranched, built and cultivated the wild coastal lands surrounding San Francisco. Liberally littered with archival photographs of the way they were.

Winslow, Jr., Carleton M., and Nickola L. Frye. *The Enchanted Hill: The Story of*

Hearst Castle at San Simeon. Millbrae: Celestial Arts, 1980. 168 pp., index, illus., photos. Lush with glossy color photos and Hearst family album snapshots, this oversized volume tracks the construction of the amazing Spanish baroque complex that housed the fantasies and celebrity guests of newspaper magnate William Randolph Hearst.

CLIMATE, WEATHER, WHAT TO WEAR

The very expression "Mediterranean climate," which most appropriately describes the prevailing meteorological ambiance of the Central Coast, conjures balmy days filled with sunshine and temperate, frost-free winters. For most of this almost 300 miles stretch of California, that image is gloriously accurate. Santa Cruz' summer days average in the mid-to-high seventies, while further south in the Santa Ynez Valley, the warmest days tend to add ten degrees to that figure. This is idyllic beach climate, with summer evenings cooling down pleasantly into the fifty-degree range.

Winters in the rainier northern stretch of the Central Coast offer days ranging from fifty degrees, hitting the seventies during the glorious "false spring" of January and February. Along this coast, summer beach weather begins sometime in March and extends through the end of October. The dry season — often without a drop of rain save for the very rare occasional shower — lasts from May through mid-November.

While the summer is by far the most popular touring season, fall and winter offer days mild enough to require only a sweater or light jacket. Free of the summer crowds, the so-called "off" season rewards the traveler with open roads and crowd-free destinations. Locals revel in the luxury of deserted beaches and unencumbered hiking through lush mountain forests. All Central Coast residents know that the most beautiful months here — especially with warm, bright sunny days and fog-free nights — are May and October.

The Central Coast boasts sunny, mild temperatures year-round, so pack for outdoor activities, but don't forget a sweater or jacket for chilly nights or foggy mornings.

Don Fukuda

A word about the famous coastal fog is in order. The moisture-laden, low-lying clouds that hug the Central Coast during summer evenings and early mornings are responsible for the area's year-round vegetation, extended growing season and mighty redwood forests. It can also come as a surprise to visitors expecting to hit the beaches on summer mornings, only to find the fog obscuring the sun. As locals are fond of telling first-time visitors, the fog inevitably "burns off" by noon, leaving the afternoon gloriously cloud-free and perfect for outdoor activities. In the summer, the fog rolls back in around sunset, so even in the warmest weather, it's important to come prepared with sweater, jacket and long pants. The Central Coast claims to have invented the "layered look" in deference to the tendency for a single day to run the gamut of weather and temperature changes.

Wherever and whenever you're traveling along the Central Coast, it's a good idea to pack comfortable walking shoes, a warm sweater or down vest and a bathing suit. Most nightspots and restaurants in this area stress casual dress, so a tie and high heels usually aren't required. Still, it's smart to pack at least one outfit that makes you feel smartly dressed for exploring some of the upscale evening destinations, especially in downtown Monterey and Carmel.

HANDICAPPED SERVICES

Progressive in more than politics and attitudes, Californians have led the way in providing access to all of the resources of this region to persons with disabilities. Government buildings of every kind — from libraries to rest rooms — have been retrofitted to accommodate that access, mandated by law to be completed in 1995. Under aggressive action on the part of the State Department of Parks and Recreation, many of the most attractive (and usually least accessible) beaches, trails, parks and forests have been equipped with facilities affording ample enjoyment to all.

Campsites at Pismo State Beach, Morro Bay State Park and Pfeiffer Big Sur State Park have been created for wheelchair access. Many beaches now boast special wheelchairs that enable beachcombing along the surf, and at Año Nuevo State Research, a portable wheelchair-friendly trail can be arranged to provide visitors a close-up look at elephant seal rookeries.

Information about lodgings, restaurants and cultural attractions, noting accommodations for persons with disabilities may be obtained by turning to specific sections of this book. City departments of Parks and Recreation, which may be reached through TDD numbers for the hearing impaired, also will provide detailed and up-to-date information on facilities in each area.

By checking county transit listings in the local telephone directory, visitors can find out about wheelchair-accessible services like **Dial-A-Ride.** Information about tours and trips specifically designed for persons with disabilities is provided by the **Center for Independent Living in Berkeley** (510/841-4776). To reserve wheelchair-accessible campsites at selected State Parks, contact the **California Department of Parks and Recreation** in Sacramento (916/445-6477).

You also might check out Erick Mitiken's *Wheelchair Rider's Guide*, which covers natural areas from Half Moon Bay down to Santa Cruz and from Big Sur to San Luis Obispo county. This free guide is available from the **California State Coastal Conservancy** (415/646-1015).

HOSPITALS & EMERGENCY MEDICAL SERVICE

A ll of the hospitals listed below have emergency rooms that remain open 24 hours a day.

Santa Cruz Coast

Dominican Hospital (831/462-7710; 1555 Soquel Ave., Santa Cruz).

Seton Medical Center Coastside (650/728-5521; 600 Marina Blvd., Moss Beach).

Watsonville Community Hospital (831/761-4741; 298 Green Valley Rd., Watsonville).

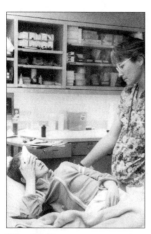

Central Coast hospitals and clinics offer some of the best emergency, short-term and sports injury medicine in the nation.

Hillary Schalit

Monterey Coast

Community Hospital of the Monterey Peninsula (831/624-4531; 23625 W. Holman Hwy., Monterey).

San Luis Obispo Coast

Arroyo Grande Community Hospital (805/489-4261; 345 S. Halcyon Rd., Arroyo Grande).
French Hospital Medical Center (805/543-5333; 1911 Johnson Ave., San Luis Obispo).
General Hospital (805/781-4800; 2180 Johnson Ave., San Luis Obispo).
Sierra Vista Regional Medical Center (805/546-7600; 1010 Murray Ave., San Luis Obispo).

Santa Ynez Valley

Lompoc District Hospital (805/735-3351; 508 E. Hickory Ave., Lompoc).
Santa Ynez Valley Cottage Hospital (805/688-6431; 700 Alamo Pintado Rd., Solvang).

REAL ESTATE

It's only natural that a visit to the Central Coast can provoke love at first sight. For some, that first crush gives way to a longing to own a luscious slice of this pie. That longing will not be satisfied cheaply, however, since the landscape here is considered some of the most desirable available anywhere. Since much of the coast is state, city and county owned, land is at a premium. Prices along the Central Coast of California, even under recession conditions, are among the highest in the country. Considering what the buyer is getting, however, price is rarely considered the main issue.

While the median price for a single-family dwelling starts at above $200,000 in the most widely sought-after areas, the Central Coast offers varied possibilities, from oceanfront property and ranches to mountain retreats and quiet neighborhood bungalows. Only those in search of subdivision property will be disappointed.

Current information on the Central Coast real estate market is readily available. Statistics and referrals are available from the **Santa Cruz Association of Realtors** (831/464-2000), **Monterey Peninsula Board of Realtors** (831/373-3002), **San Luis Obispo Association of Realtors** (805/541-2282) and **Santa Barbara Association of Realtors** (805/963-3787). These agencies will happily provide names of reputable real estate agents and brokers, most of whom are listed in the Yellow Pages of local telephone directories.

ROAD SERVICE

For members, **AAA-California State Automobile Association** maintains a toll-free, 24-hour emergency telephone number (800/400-4222), as does the **National Automobile Club** (800/622-2130).

TOURIST INFORMATION

Most cities and counties on the Central Coast have tourist-friendly visitors' bureaus eager to send potential travelers information packages on their particular area's bountiful charms. By all means contact these bureaus, who will then shower you with glossy photographs, maps and guides to selected attractions in their areas. Much of the forwarded hype should be perused with a modicum of disbelief (after all, these folks represent members eager for your disposable income). Still, enough good information, hard facts and suggestions are provided to at least provide a starting place for carving out your own itinerary.

Santa Cruz Coast

Aptos Chamber of Commerce (831/688-1467; Redwood Village #12, 9099 Soquel Dr., Aptos, CA 95003).
Capitola Chamber of Commerce (831/475-6522; 621 Capitola Ave., Capitola, CA 95010).
Half Moon Bay Coastside Chamber of Commerce (650/726-8380; P.O. Box 188, 225 S. Cabrillo, Hwy. 1, Half Moon Bay, CA 94019).
San Mateo County Convention & Visitor Bureau (800/288-4748; 650/348-7600; 111 Anza Blvd. Ste. 410, Burlingame, CA 94010).
Santa Cruz County Conference & Visitors Council (800/833-3494; 831/425-1234; 701 Front St., Santa Cruz, CA 95060).

Monterey Coast

Big Sur Chamber of Commerce (831/667-2100; P.O. Box 87, Big Sur, CA 93920).
Cannery Row Underground Information (831/372-8512; 851 Cannery Row, Monterey, CA 93940).
Carmel Business Association (800/964-7358; 831/624-2522; P.O. Box 4444, San Carlos & Seventh Sts., Carmel, CA 93921).
Monterey Peninsula Visitors & Convention Bureau (831/649-1770; P.O. Box 1770, 380 Alvarado St., Monterey, CA 93942).

Pacific Grove Chamber of Commerce (831/373-3304; P.O. Box 167, Forest & Central Aves., Pacific Grove, CA 93950).

Point Lobos Natural History Association (831/624-4909; Rte. 1, Box 62, Carmel, CA 93923).

San Luis Obispo Coast

Cambria Chamber of Commerce & Visitors Bureau (805/927-3624; 767 Main St., Cambria, CA 93428).

Cayucos Chamber of Commerce (805/995-1200; P.O. Box 141, 150 N. Ocean Ave., Cayucos, CA 93430).

Hearst Castle/San Simeon State Park (805/927-2093; 750 Hearst Castle Rd., San Simeon, CA 93452).

Los Osos/Baywood Chamber of Commerce (805/528-4884; P.O. Box 6282, 2190 Ninth St., Ste. B, Los Osos, CA 93402).

Morro Bay Chamber of Commerce (800/231-0592; 805/772-4467; 895 Napa St., Ste. A1, Morro Bay, CA 93442).

Pismo Beach Convention & Visitors Bureau (800/443-7778; 805/773-1661; 581 Dolliver St., Pismo Beach, CA 93449).

San Luis Obispo County Visitors & Conference Bureau (800/634-1414; 805/541-8000; 1041 Chorro St., Ste. E, San Luis Obispo, CA 93401).

San Simeon Chamber of Commerce Visitors Information (800/342-5613; 805/927-3500; 805/927-8358 Fax; P.O. Box 1, 9255 Hearst Dr., San Simeon, CA 93452).

Santa Ynez Valley

Buellton Chamber of Commerce (805/688-7829; P.O. Box 231, 140 W. Hwy. 246, Buellton, CA 93427).

Lompoc Valley Chamber of Commerce (805/736-4567; P.O. Box 626, Lompoc, CA 93438).

Solvang Conference & Visitors Bureau (800/468-6765; 805/688-0701, ext. 515; P.O. Box 70, Solvang, CA 93464).

Fishing & Hunting Regulations

California Department of Fish & Game (916/227-2244; 3211 S St., Sacramento, CA 95816) Information, licenses and tags.

IF TIME IS SHORT

In the three distinct geographical areas of the Central Coast, there are a few "musts." These are the accommodations, eateries, cultural attractions and wonders of nature that travelers should not miss.

SANTA CRUZ COAST

Lodging

Casablanca Inn (831/423-1570; 831/423-0235 Fax; Beach & Main Sts., Santa Cruz) Located just across the street from Santa Cruz's main beach, the colorful Boardwalk and the Cocoanut Grove Ballroom, the Casablanca Inn offers bountiful ocean views and the soothing sounds of the waves to lull guests to sleep. Essentially a small hotel ringed with attractive motel units, the multilevel, Mediterranean-style main building hangs on the hillside just above its own Casablanca Restaurant, long regarded as one of the best in town. The restaurant's extensive wine list regularly wins *Wine Spectator* awards for comprehensiveness.

Dining

Chez Renee (831/688-5566; 9051 Soquel Dr., Aptos) Considered by many among the very top dining spots of the Monterey Bay area, the intimate ambiance is personally orchestrated by Renee Chyle, who also creates some of the exquisite desserts. Though the restaurant boasts an award-winning wine list, especially strong in French and California vintages, including many from the Santa Cruz Mountains, the food is the whole point. Jack Chyle is a sorcerer with duck, which he prepares with fresh, seasonal fruit and berry sauces and splashes with a palette of wines or liqueurs. And chef Chyle's pastas, seafoods and game dishes are all sublime.

Cultural Attraction

Santa Cruz Beach Boardwalk (831/423-5590; 400 Beach St., Santa Cruz) More than twenty exciting rides, including an old-fashioned, wooden roller coaster, Giant Dipper, make this heaven for youngsters. Rides at either end of the Boardwalk, including a Ferris wheel, bumper cars, "underground" train excursions and a vintage 1911 carousel, will please the very young. Wilder rides, including the state-of-the-art, stomach-churning Typhoon, will test the endurance of teenagers and impress even the most jaded thrill seeker. And don't miss the nearby **Santa Cruz Surfing Museum** (831/429-3429; at the Lighthouse, W. Cliff Dr. near Pelton Ave., Santa Cruz), the only surfing museum in the world, with its eclectic collection of vintage longboards, videos, photographs and memorabilia, including the first wet suit.

Recreation

Big Basin State Park (14 miles north of Santa Cruz on Hwy. 9, extending to Hwy. 1, 30 miles north of Santa Cruz) Eighty miles of hiking trails on more than 18,000 acres of archetypal redwood forest stretch down to the rocky Pacific coastline. Founded in 1902, Big Basin was the first state park in the California system. Its crystal-clear streams, waterfalls, wildlife-rich meadows, fern canyons and old-growth redwoods provide some of the finest hiking on the West Coast.

MONTEREY & BIG SUR COAST

Lodging

Highlands Inn (800/682-4811 CA; 831/624-3801; 831/626-1574 Fax; Hwy. 1, Carmel) This world-class resort perched in the Carmel Highlands overlooks the spectacular coastline of Point Lobos. The rooms are equipped with huge beds, fireplaces, TVs, plush terry robes, well-stocked refrigerators and king-sized whirlpool tubs for two. Lavish landscaping hugs the network of walkways leading down to the magnificent stone lodge, headquarters for a bistro overlooking the swimming pool, cocktail lounge and the Pacific's Edge dining room with its breathtaking views of the surf and tide pool below.

Dining

Ventana Restaurant (831/667-2331; Hwy. 1, 28 miles south of Carmel, Big Sur) Perched one thousand feet above the Pacific Ocean, Ventana seems hoisted atop the world. On a clear day, the view alone is worth the drive. The restaurant, like the inn, is rustic, discreet and sophisticated. Both lunch and dinner menus play off the Central Coast "Riviera" setting and sport a classical French/California theme. Appetizers include herb soufflé with smoked salmon and goat cheese in puff pastry. Entrées like the pan-seared, potato-wrapped salmon and oak-grilled squab are complemented by an award-winning wine list and a knowledgeable staff.

Cultural Attraction

Monterey Bay Aquarium (831/648-4888; 886 Cannery Row, Monterey) Since its opening in 1984, this astonishing facility is one of the wonders of the modern world. Built on the edge of the Monterey Bay National Marine Sanctuary, whose underwater valley dwarfs the Grand Canyon, the aquarium is state-of-the-art in every respect. Home to more than 7,000 marine creatures, it houses living exhibits illustrating the Monterey Bay's many underwater habitats. Leopard sharks cruise with schools of silvery sardines in the aquarium's three-story kelp forests, which tower up to the sunlight, filtering through 300,000-gallon exhibition tanks. Playful sea otters soar acrobatically through the waters of their special area, a gorgeous re-creation of the bay floor that opens out onto the sunny rocks above. The fascinating bat rays and starfish of the Touch Tide Pool are irresistible to even adult children.

Recreation

Point Lobos (831/624-4909; Hwy. 1 at Riley Ranch Rd., Carmel) Treat yourself to an all-day excursion exploring this incredible 2,500-acre preserve, which encompasses pristine coves set with jewellike beaches, jagged rock outcroppings, ancient cypress groves, tide pools, marshlands and isolated meadows. The diversity of landscape is staggering, especially the spring wildflower displays when meadows are carpeted with iris and lilac, and well-marked trails loop in and around all of the most beautiful stretches, liberally dotted with hundreds of species of native plants, birds and other wildlife.

SAN LUIS OBISPO COAST & THE SANTA YNEZ VALLEY

Lodging

Ballard Inn (800/638-2466; 805/688-7770; 2436 Baseline Ave., Ballard) This contemporary inn looks like it stepped out of the late-nineteenth century with a wraparound verandah, polished wood dining room and antique-filled guest rooms. Each room holds its own special charm, built around Old West themes and featuring brass and wicker beds, magnificent comforters, quilts and upholsteries, plus Victorian armoires and commodes transformed into sinks. In the morning, the inn's friendly staff serves up a full breakfast, but there also is a Continental buffet laid on the carved sideboard. Having worked up an appetite, a tour of this captivating wine country is in order via the Ballard's complimentary mountain bikes. The Ballard also is home to Cafe Chardonnay.

Dining

Jocko's (805/929-3686; corner of Tefft St. & Thomas Rd., Nipomo) Jocko's is legendary throughout the Central Coast for carrying world-class beef. The interior decor — paper place mats, hanging plants and cattle brands burned into the woodwork — seems never to have left the 1950s (when Jocko's was founded). Even the separate bar, well worn by regulars, seems from another time. Conceivably the finest steak house in the country, Jocko's regularly converts even the most die-hard vegetarian. It's a couple miles from the coast, but the drive through the rolling hills of the southern Salinas Valley is worth the detour.

Cultural Attraction

Hearst Castle (805/927-2020; Hwy. 1, San Simeon) The site of America's only genuine castle by the sea overlooks the Pacific Ocean north of Cambria. In 1919, William Randolph Hearst hatched his grandiose scheme of transforming a magical spot on his father's quarter-of-a-million-acre ranch land into a showpiece of architecture and international artworks. Plundering the treasure houses of Europe, Hearst dismantled entire medieval chapels, Renaissance villas and Greco-Roman temples, bringing back the priceless artifacts to decorate the interior of the 100-room Casa Grande (a Spanish Baroque theme park designed by San Francisco architect Julia Morgan) and many palatial guest houses for his celebrity friends. San Simeon — one of the top visitor attractions in the country — may be visited only on guided tours. Given the sheer scale of the castle, it takes four tours to see all of the sites.

Recreation

Montaña de Oro State Park (end of Pecho Valley Rd., Los Osos) This park is a wild expanse of fields, canyons, bluffs and cove beaches formerly part of the sprawling Spooner Ranch. Over fifty miles of hiking and equestrian trails are contained within 8,400 acres, bordering three miles of coastline. The 1.5-mile Hazard Canyon Trail winds through forests and shaded slopes, several trails descend from bluff tops down to the beach and others pierce the heart of vast eucalyptus groves, one of the state's favored winter nesting spots for the colorful monarch butterfly. The Montaña de Oro Bluffs Trail skirts Spooner's Cove and seals lounging near coastal tide pools, offering springtime glimpses of the golden poppies and mustard that lend to the park's name.

Index

DINING BY PRICE CODE

DINING BY CUISINE

About the Authors

Paul Schraub

Buz Bezore has been raising journalistic hell on California's Central Coast for over twenty years, most recently as the editor of *Metro Santa Cruz*. Under his stewardship, the newspaper has garnered more than twenty state and national awards for writing and graphics during its short four–year history. He won top honors for lifestyle coverage in both the 1998 and 1997 California Newspaper Publishers Association's Better Newspapers Contest. A fourth-generation Californian, Bezore graduated from the University of California, Santa Cruz with a degree in film and anthropology, taught film at various schools for the Bureau of Indian Affairs, worked at a psychiatric hospital and produced a local, cable TV variety show before entering the journalistic non–mainstream. In his free time, he enjoys baseball, beer, bodysurfing, cooking transcultural meals and conversations with women. He also is soft at work on a satiric novel about the booming alternative press.

Christina Waters is a fifth-generation Californian who has written about people and places on the Central Coast for the past twenty years. The James Beard Foundation named her 1995's best newspaper wine writer and 1997's best newspaper writer on spirits. She also took top honors for food writing in 1996 and arts writing in 1997 at the Association of Alternative Newsweeklies awards ceremonies. In 1998, she won first place for criticism in the California Newspaper Publishers Association's Better Newspapers Contest. Born in Santa Cruz, Waters spent her childhood living in Europe and on the East Coast. Armed with an expanded palate and a degree in anthropology, she did her Ph.D. work at the University of California, Davis and moved back to Santa Cruz, working as a journalist for a variety of regional and national publications. In her spare time, she enjoys sampling the eclectic and award–winning wines of the Central Coast and is coaxing a novel out of her computer.